SOLDIERS TO CITIZENS

Soldiers to Citizens

*The G.I. Bill
and the Making of
the Greatest Generation*

SUZANNE METTLER

OXFORD
UNIVERSITY PRESS
2005

OXFORD

UNIVERSITY PRESS

Oxford University Press, Inc., publishes works that further
Oxford University's objective of excellence
in research, scholarship, and education.

Oxford   New York
Auckland   Cape Town   Dar es Salaam   Hong Kong   Karachi
Kuala Lumpur   Madrid   Melbourne   Mexico City   Nairobi
New Delhi   Shanghai   Taipei   Toronto

With offices in
Argentina   Austria   Brazil   Chile   Czech Republic   France   Greece
Guatemala   Hungary   Italy   Japan   Poland   Portugal   Singapore
South Korea   Switzerland   Thailand   Turkey   Ukraine   Vietnam

Published by Oxford University Press, Inc.
198 Madison Avenue, New York, New York, 10016
www.oup.com

Oxford is a registered trademark of Oxford University Press

Library of Congress Cataloging-in-Publication Data
Mettler, Suzanne.
Soldiers to citizens : the G.I. bill and the making
of the greatest generation / Suzanne Mettler.
p. cm.   Includes bibliographical references and index.
ISBN-13: 978-0-19-518097-8
ISBN-10: 0-19-518097-6
1. World War, 1939–1945—Veterans—Education—United States.
2. Retired military personnel—Employment—United States—History—20th century.
3. World War, 1939–1945—Social aspects—United States.
4. Veterans—United States—Conduct of life—History—20th century.
5. Veterans—Political activity—United States—History—20th century.
6. United States—Social conditions—1945–
I. Title.
UB357.M475 2005
305.9'0697'097309045—dc22   2005004298

1 3 5 7 9 8 6 4 2
Printed in the United States of America
on acid-free paper

To my mother, Elinor Fox Mettler,
and to the memory of my father, John J. Mettler Jr.

Fourscore and seven years ago our fathers brought forth on this continent a new nation, conceived in liberty and dedicated to the proposition that all men are created equal . . . It is for us the living . . . to be dedicated here to the unfinished work which they who fought here have thus far so nobly advanced . . . that from these honored dead we take increased devotion to that cause for which they gave the last full measure of devotion . . . that we here highly resolve that these dead shall not have died in vain, that this nation under God shall have a new birth of freedom, and that government of the people, by the people, for the people shall not perish from the earth.

—Abraham Lincoln, Gettysburg Address

Contents

Preface

L
ittle did I know when I began the research for this book that it would lead me into the scholarly adventure of a lifetime.

Broadly speaking, I am interested in how particular governing arrangements affect citizens' engagement in public life, and the implications for the vibrancy of democracy. I study American political development, investigating how public policies, once established, have influenced citizens' views about government and their participation in civic and political affairs.

In my first book, I examined this question by probing the extent to which New Deal social and labor policies reached different groups of citizens, and how their rules and procedures affected citizens' relationship to government. My ability to understand citizens' experiences was limited, though, because appropriate sources of evidence simply did not exist. The archival materials and government documents I mined told me much about how political actors and institutions responded to citizens, but little about the reverse.

For my next project, therefore, I decided that I must find a way to learn from citizens themselves about their experiences of a public program. It would make sense, I reasoned, to move somewhat forward in time, so that in addition to using traditional, existing sources, I could also learn from people who had been actual program beneficiaries. After the sweeping policy innovations of the 1930s, the G.I. Bill marked America's next creation of a major public program. To my surprise, I found that this popular law has received relatively little attention from scholars. Somewhat arbitrarily, then, I settled on the G.I. Bill as the subject of my study, and I determined to focus on the impact of its most utilized component, the education and training provisions, on World War II veterans.

Although survey research came into vogue in the 1940s, and numerous surveys were conducted of veterans and of citizens generally during that decade and in the years following, none of them combined questions about G.I. Bill usage and civic and political activity. In order to have the means to examine large patterns of program usage and its effects, I decided that I would need to survey members of the World War II generation myself. Also, to help me understand how individuals experienced the G.I. Bill's benefits and perceived its effects in their own lives, and conversely, why some individuals did not utilize the program, I would conduct a much smaller number of personal, in-depth interviews with veterans, both G.I. Bill users and nonusers.

I began to seek a systematic means of reaching members of the World War II generation who could participate in the survey. Relatives, friends, and colleagues put me in touch with their neighbors, uncles, and fathers who belonged to veterans' groups, and they in turn sent me to organizational leaders, several of whom offered me access to their groups' mailing lists. I also contacted colleges and universities, requesting names and addresses of alumni from the Class of 1949. After many months of such searching and deliberating about which groups might best help generate a representative sample of veterans, and after developing a twelve-page mail survey booklet and testing it with a focus group of veterans in Syracuse, I was ready to conduct the survey. I had become worried, though, about how well this approach would work: survey experts warned me that I would be lucky if 20 percent of the sample responded.

A lively team of graduate students aided me as we assembled the first mailing to over two thousand individuals, stuffing and stamping envelopes deep into the night for several days on end. Every survey was accompanied by a personally addressed letter requesting the recipient's participation, and I signed every one by hand in the admittedly superstitious hope that it would somehow help generate a strong response. Finally, I delivered several boxes full of envelopes to the post office, then settled down to wait.

I didn't have to wait long. Eleven days later, I found a huge stack of return envelopes waiting for me, each one containing a completed survey. As well, I began to receive phone calls from veterans who wanted to tell me firsthand what it had been like to serve in the infantry. One man, after relating stories from the front lines, said, "It's been over fifty years, and I've never told anyone this before." In subsequent days, hundreds and hundreds of return envelopes flooded in. As we opened the mountains of envelopes, we found that several respondents not only had filled out the lengthy survey, which featured over two hundred questions, but also had sent additional materials: long letters telling me more about themselves, clippings from newspapers, and even photographs. After three weeks, when the returns had dwindled, our survey team convened again, to send a new mailing to nonrespondents, a process that we repeated a third and final time another month later. Ultimately, the survey generated a stunning 74-percent response rate, and more than 10 percent of all respondents had done more than send in the survey, whether by enclosing additional materials or contacting me by phone.

In the meantime, I conducted interviews with veterans in all regions of the nation. Before each trip, I would send letters to veterans from the survey lists who lived in the vicinity of wherever I was going, letting them know that I was seeking to learn about veterans' experiences of public programs and involvement in public life after the war, and asking them if they were willing to be interviewed. In each instance, the majority replied and agreed to participate, leaving me to make choices about which offers to accept so that I would meet veterans from a variety of different communities in a given area. I found my way to their apartment buildings, retirement communities, and homes in a wide array of residential neighborhoods. Veterans and their families welcomed me warmly and graciously. Before each interview began, I did not know whether the individual had used the G.I. Bill's education or training benefits. Long before getting to the questions about the program or even military service, I asked each veteran to specify turning points—events, occurrences, or relationships that had changed the subsequent course of his or her life. Each person I interviewed thought carefully before responding. Some mentioned a person who had served as a mentor early in life, or spoke of their spouse of some fifty years; others identified military service or career opportunities. What struck me was that in response to such a personal and probing question, several also mentioned the G.I. Bill, particularly its education and training provisions. Also, though I asked only a few questions about military service, veterans often volunteered much more information about that time in their lives. They pulled out discharge papers, photographs, and Bronze Stars and other medals, and they related memories of training and wartime that they have carried with them throughout their lives. I began to realize how essential it was to understand this part of their stories, which constituted the very basis through which they had become seen as deserving of and eligible for the G.I. Bill. I had not previously had any particular interest in military service, but the more I listened to the veterans, the more respect I gained for what that had meant in their lives, the high price of citizenship they had paid, and how deeply they seemed to care about America.

And that was just the beginning. The next rounds of surveys to additional groups of veterans, in subsequent years, also produced high response rates and brought me more letters and phone calls. The interviews continued to introduce me to people whose voices now echo in my mind. Several of the subjects, sad to say, have died in the years since I first met them, and some have grown incapacitated, but others are flourishing, and they check in with me from time to time to inquire about the progress of the book and to wish me well. Compelling, too, has been the dynamic process of analyzing these rich and different kinds of evidence. The process of discovery has been facilitated by a community of scholars who have encouraged me and prodded me to delve further and to dig deeper to make sense of what I have found. All told, from start to finish, my work on this project has been a privilege and a joy.

Acknowledgments

To say that this book relied upon an army of support is hardly the exaggeration it might seem. My gratitude goes, first of all, to each of the veterans who allowed me to interview them, and the hundreds of veterans and nonveterans from the World War II generation who took the time to respond to the survey. For their willingness to put me in contact with their members, I am thankful to the associational leaders of the 87th, 89th, and 92nd Infantry Divisions of the U.S. Army; the 379th Bombardment Group and the 783rd Bomb Squadron, 465th Bomb Group of the U.S. Army Air Force; and Women in Military Service for America, Inc. Veterans Jim Amor, Albert Burke, Shelby Clark, Elmer Ebrecht, Donald Johnson, Jack Meyer, David Reeher, William Perry, and Richard Werner provided essential assistance, as did Celeste Torian. As well, officials at several institutions responded kindly to my requests and allowed me to contact their Class of 1949 alumni: Boston College, Brooklyn College, Morehouse College, Northwestern University, Pomona College, Syracuse University, University of Georgia, University of Texas, Vanderbilt University, Washington State University, and Wayne State University.

I also gathered materials for this study from a variety of other sources. Michael K. Brown at the University of California at Santa Cruz kindly shared with me critical materials that he unearthed in his own research in the National Archives. Major Darrell Driver at the U.S. Military Academy at West Point responded to my numerous questions with extraordinarily helpful replies. Joe Hovish at the American Legion National Headquarters in Indianapolis offered welcome assistance. Theda Skocpol generously shared with me her approach to classifying organizations, which made possible the analysis in Chapter 7. Joseph Thompson, Undersecretary for

Benefits, U.S. Veterans Administration, provided valuable documents. I was aided as well by the staff at the Franklin D. Roosevelt Library in Hyde Park, New York; the National Archives in both College Park, Maryland, and Washington, D.C.; and the Hoover Institution Library and Archives, Stanford University, Palo Alto, California.

By contrast to the relatively lonely work of library and archival research, a project involving surveys and interviews is a highly collaborative process. I shudder to think how I would have managed without the wisdom, patience, and generosity of Eric Welch, who advised me on survey design and administration and eased my transition into quantitative analysis. In the Maxwell School, my colleague Jeff Stonecash has been a pillar of support throughout, always willing to hear out my challenges and to offer vital advice. Rogan Kersh helped in myriad ways and offered warm friendship. Others gave encouragement and key ideas, including Kristi Andersen, Joe Cammarano, Madonna Harrington-Meyer, Peg Hermann, Patricia Ingraham, Vernon Greene, Rosemary O'Leary, Grant Reeher, Sally Selden, Tim Smeeding, and Doug Wolf. Several graduate students provided excellent research assistance: Dionne Bensonsmith, Joe Blasdel, Mark Brewer, Premek Macha, Lanethea Mathews-Gardner, Andrew Milstein, Wagaki Mwangi, Lori Beth Way, Amy Widestrom, and McGee Young. Rita Reicher and the team at Knowledge Systems and Research, Inc. performed the data entry with fine professionalism, and Collette Fay carefully transcribed the interviews and created a marvelous database.

I am enormously grateful to a wonderful community of scholars who have given me an appropriate blend of encouragement and criticism throughout this project. For pointing the way through their own scholarship, voicing incisive questions and comments, and offering warm support, I am thankful to Andrea Campbell, Jacob Hacker, Paul Pierson, Theda Skocpol, and Joe Soss. Over the years, I received helpful comments on earlier drafts of portions of the book from Nancy Burns, Michael Dawson, Patricia Graham, Ira Katznelson, Phil Klinkner, Jerome Legge, Robert Lieberman, Ann Chih Lin, Gretchen Ritter, Elaine Sharp, Margaret Weir, and participants in seminars at Harvard University, the University of Michigan, Syracuse University, the University of Wisconsin, and Yale University. Mark Brewer, Steve Teles, Rick Valelly, and an anonymous reviewer each generously took the time to read the complete manuscript and offered invaluable advice for revisions. The book also bears the influence of the marvelous group of political scientists that made up the APSA Task Force on Inequality and American Democracy, on which I had the privilege of serving. Eileen McDonagh has been a steadfast friend and mentor, for whose support I am ever grateful.

Institutional support enabled me to gain the time, resources, and assistance necessary for this project. A postdoctoral fellowship from the National Academy of Education proved vital to begin, and a grant from the Spencer Foundation permitted me to continue. In the Maxwell School at Syracuse University, the Center for Policy Research, Center for Demography and Economic of Aging, and the Dean's Office each contributed financial support at key stages. Kelley Coleman and Bethany Walawender in the Campbell Institute of Public Affairs came to my aid on several occasions, as did Jacquie Meyer and Candy Brooks in the Political Science Department, and the Maxwell ICT group.

A superb group of individuals enabled me to transform my manuscript into this book. My agent, Lisa Adams, lent expert advice and support. It has been a genuine privilege to work with Tim Bartlett, a marvelously perceptive editor with a sense of vision and an ability to push me the extra mile. My thanks, too, go to the entire team at Oxford University Press, including Kate Hamill, Helen Mules, and Sue Warga, for their expertise and care in producing the book.

Wayne Grove, the love of my life, has made it all possible and all worthwhile. Early on, he—as a good economist—played devil's advocate to my evolving research design plans; throughout the research process, he helped me weather the travails, indulged me in hundreds of conversations about my findings, offered insights from his vast wealth of knowledge, and shared in my growing excitement; and through the seemingly endless writing process, when I kept promising that the book's completion lay just around the corner, his love, companionship, and care sustained me. Our daughters, Sophie and Julia, fill our lives with joy; they have patiently lived with this project, helped keep me on task, and delighted me with their questions and recommendations. I am blessed by the steadfast support of my fabulous siblings, Patrick, Jody, Jeanne, Meg, and Sally, and each of their spouses and families, including my nephew Joseph Bosnick, a Marine, who carries on the spirit of those in this book. And while dear friends Lynn and Tim Borstelmann and Steve Meyer and Eileen Strempel might have been puzzled by my fascination with "G.I. Joe," they have filled my years of work on this project with celebration.

My parents have exemplified all that is great about the greatest generation. My father, John J. Mettler Jr., grew up on a dairy farm in upstate New York during the Depression and attended a one-room schoolhouse. He was able to go to college thanks to the public, land-grant side of Cornell University, where he enrolled in 1940 to pursue his dream of becoming a veterinarian. After the war began, he and his classmates enlisted in the

Army and completed their studies as part of the Army Specialized Training Program. From 1944 to 1947 he served in the Pacific, stationed on the islands of Guam, Saipan, Oahu, and Chichi Jima. When he returned home, he had one goal in mind, and contrary to what readers might expect, it was not using the G.I. Bill, but something even more wonderful: marrying my mother, Elinor Fox, whom he had known since childhood. She consented and left behind her budding career in New York City to move to the rural area where he had grown up and where he began his veterinary practice. Over the next decade and a half, they welcomed into the world all six of us, our birth years spanning those of the baby boom generation. We have been blessed all of our lives by their deep and steadfast love.

Besides us, they loved our community and cared deeply about public life. Each of their lives defined active citizenship. Both took turns leading the PTA, and they became devoted members of their church. My father grew involved in local politics, served on the zoning and planning boards, helped with the 4-H Club, and took part in the VFW, American Legion, and Lions Club, as well as belonging to the American Veterinary Medical Association and related professional associations. My mother steered into being the International Friendship Exchange, the local history society, a rails-to-trails association, and countless other events and activities, and she started and ran the local newspaper, making it a model of community journalism. Ever attentive to political happenings on a larger scale, both of them always cared passionately about America, felt pride in its accomplishments, and yearned for it to embody more fully its best ideals.

Both of my parents lent their support to this project from the moment I first came up with the idea. They proceeded to instruct me on such matters as draft classifications, military ranks, and myriad other topics about World War II and the years following, and they pointed me toward veterans who could help me gain access to mailing lists for the survey. My father died four years ago, and we all miss him so. How I wish he were here to see the book finished at last. My mother has continued to be an effervescent source of ideas, information, and encouragement as I have brought it to completion. This book is dedicated, with tremendous love, admiration, and gratitude, to both of them.

Syracuse, New York

Suzanne Mettler
April 2005

SOLDIERS TO CITIZENS

Introduction
Civic Generation

W hen he was young, Luke LaPorta never imagined that he would attend college, let alone obtain a doctorate. The son of an Italian immigrant, LaPorta grew up in an ethnic neighborhood in Queens, New York. During the Great Depression, his family, like many during that time, struggled to get by, needing public assistance to make ends meet. Although he had been a good student in high school, college seemed entirely out of the question. Nobody in his family or even in his neighborhood had gone: there wasn't the money for it, and it was not something that people like them could even consider. Once LaPorta finished high school, World War II had begun, so he enlisted in the Navy and served aboard a minesweeper that patrolled the Atlantic coast of the United States.

Upon his return from the war, LaPorta had an experience that would profoundly change the course of his life. He accompanied friends from the military on a campus visit to Syracuse University, though having no intention of actually going himself. "It was a lark. We were going to have a lot of fun." While there, the school official who was assisting his friends turned to LaPorta, asked him about his academic record, and then said, "Why don't you come to school here, too? You've got the G.I. Bill!" The words struck LaPorta like a revelation, and he was thrilled and overwhelmed by the idea. He returned home to tell his parents, who shared his excitement. His mother said, "Luke, you go! You can always work!" One week before he was to depart for college, LaPorta's father had an accident and became unable to work. Although LaPorta felt he should stay home and support his parents, they insisted that he seize the opportunity to pursue his education. So, he recalls, "I packed a bag—some shirts and five or six pairs of socks, and that was it. I was one of the first kids to come [to Syracuse University] on the G.I. Bill."

Over time, LaPorta would earn a bachelor's degree, a master's degree, and eventually a doctorate. His education enabled him to attain a standard of living far greater than any his parents might have hoped for. Equally important, LaPorta involved himself to an extraordinary degree in community activities and organizations. He devoted himself to establishing and coaching a vast number of youth sports teams. In 1950, he started the state's first chartered Little League in his own town; over the next decade, he helped develop more than sixty such organizations throughout the region. Time and again, he served as a delegate to Little League Congresses, the international meetings that brought together representatives of local and regional leagues, and then, for fifteen years, he served as chairman of the board of International Little League Baseball, Inc. He became a well-loved and honored member of his community for his decades of public service to young people. Reflecting back over his life, LaPorta credited the G.I. Bill with getting him started, explaining that he could not have afforded college without it, and even more fundamentally, that he had not even thought of himself as capable of pursuing higher education. "It was a hell of a gift, an opportunity, and I've never thought of it any other way," he commented. "Sometimes I wonder if I really earned what I've gotten, to be frank with you."

In recent years, popular books have celebrated the virtues of the generation of Americans who, like Luke LaPorta, were born in the early twentieth century, especially in the 1910s and the 1920s. The hallmark of this literature—exemplified by Tom Brokaw's *The Greatest Generation*, Stephen Ambrose's *Citizen Soldiers*, and Robert Putnam's *Bowling Alone: The Collapse and Revival of American Community*—is its power to evoke nostalgia and a keen sense that the United States is losing much with the passing of this generation.[1] Yet none of these books explains why those who came of age around the time of World War II exhibited throughout their lives such remarkable commitment to the principles and practices of democracy. Neither have they considered the significance of the intensive government involvement that was so commonplace in the lives of this renowned group of Americans. There is a story that remains to be told about this generation, and it is a story with profound implications for our lives today.

The "greatest generation" is composed of individuals who spent their childhoods in families struggling to survive the Great Depression, and who came of age with World War II. "They answered the call," Brokaw writes, "to help save the world from the two most powerful and ruthless military machines ever assembled, instruments of conquest in the hands of fascist maniacs."[2] They included the citizen soldiers—the ordinary citizens charged with the utmost obligation of civic duty, to defend the nation—who stormed the beaches of Normandy, who trekked through the cold European winter of 1944–45 and liberated the concentration camps, and who dug in at Guadalcanal, Iwo Jima, and Okinawa.[3] They were also the vigilant citizens who stayed behind to defend the home front and support the war effort by working in defense industries, saving scrap metal and rubber, planting Victory gardens to raise their own food, and shopping as conscientious consumers to make sure retailers honored price controls.[4]

Once victory came, the members of this generation participated as active citizens in the peace that followed. They joined civic organizations at record rates, producing what Robert Putnam depicts as a "golden age" of American civic life.[5] A wide array of organizations flourished, including fraternal associations such as the Masons, Elks, Moose, United Methodist Women, and Order of the Eastern Star; service groups including the Lions, Kiwanis, and Rotary; professional associations such as the American Chemical Society and the American Psychological Association; labor unions; and churches and church-affiliated groups.[6] These same young adults involved themselves intensely in political life through voting, party membership, working on political campaigns, and myriad other activities. Bolstered by their participation, voter turnout hit twentieth-century peaks.[7]

Through such intense activity, these Americans earned their reputation as the "civic generation."[8] Their involvement in public life epitomized cherished ideals at the heart of American democracy: widespread participation by ordinary citizens and the articulation of political voice by a broad cross section of the populace. Among towering figures of American political thought, from Thomas Jefferson to Elizabeth Cady Stanton to Martin Luther King Jr., citizens' participation has been considered essential to fulfill the promise of representative government. While popular forms of mass participation have shifted historically, both types in which the World War II generation took part—formal politics and civic associations—have long been viewed as forms of "good citizenship," means whereby ordinary citizens could be part of public life and exert their influence on it.[9] As French visitor Alexis de Tocqueville observed in the 1830s, a time when only white men were allowed to participate in formal politics, Americans "of all ages, all conditions, and all dispositions" exhibit a propensity to "constantly form associations" of all varieties: "not only commercial and industrial . . . but [also] religious, moral, serious, futile, very general and very limited, immensely large and very minute."[10] Throughout American history, these organizations served as a training ground to prepare adult citizens for participation in democratic politics. They brought citizens together and gave them opportunities to practice collective debate and decision making and to hone their organizing skills. They produced civic leaders by electing officers and committee members who served on a rotating basis, and had responsibility for running group meetings, organizing events, and representing their local chapters at state, regional, or even national meetings.[11] As well, many civic organizations actively encouraged participation in politics and educated their members on public issues. Some advocated for specific forms of legislation, and others formed the front lines of social movements, including the postwar struggle for civil rights.[12] Of course, some citizens circumvented the associational route and jumped directly into politics, whether at the local level or beyond. Through all such forms of involvement, members of the World War II generation helped fortify and invigorate the practices of self-governance.

As the twentieth century proceeded, this remarkable generation remained engaged, even when, by many indicators, democratic well-being in the United States began to show signs of distress. Beginning in the 1970s, Americans began to vote less, to trust each other less, to trust government less, and to disengage from political parties and other forms of political action. The large, federated civic organizations that had thrived at midcentury saw their membership rolls diminish.[13] Interestingly, however, not all citizens were distancing themselves from public life. In fact, members of the generation that had grown up amid the New Deal and World War II remained as involved as ever. Their parents' generation had tended to participate less in public life as they became older; many of their children and especially their grandchildren never became involved in the ways they had from quite early on in their lives. Those in the civic generation proved themselves to be steadfast citizens, keeping organizations alive and electoral turnout levels respectable rather than receding from public life with the aging process and leaving it to the next generations to carry on.[14]

In confronting the lack of civic involvement in contemporary America, we might ask ourselves what made this generation so committed to public life. Some scholars propose that the experiences of uniting for the common good during the war—both in the armed forces and on the home front—may have helped foster the lasting inclination toward civic involvement.[15] This may have been compounded, others reason, by World War II's reputation as the "good war," the most recent war in American memory that was universally understood to be necessary and just. Yet while the emphasis on war is understandable, it fails to serve as a sufficient explanation for the civic generation's high levels of involvement. Wartime brought with it as many factors that could help unravel the civic fabric as ones that could strengthen its fiber. Studies of civic involvement in the latter part of the twentieth century find that, all else equal, veterans generally have not been more active in civic affairs than nonveterans of the same age group.[16] For many, the aspects of military service that induce solidarity were likely offset by the harrowing experiences of warfare. Many veterans returned home with symptoms of an unnamed malady that only decades later became recognized as post-traumatic stress disorder. As well, after having given much of their lives for the public good already, veterans were typically anxious to pursue personal goals and to do so in a hurry. On the home front, the war and especially its aftermath brought massive dislocation of jobs and families. Patterns of relocation already under way in earlier decades hastened as families moved in vast numbers from farms to cities, from East to West, and from South to North. Newcomers did not easily become involved in their new communities, and tensions emerged between old and new populations.[17] All told, the experience of the war and its aftermath fail to explain adequately why the generation that emerged from them became so public-spirited. This book entertains an alternative explanation.

Rather than focusing exclusively on how members of the civic generation experienced war, we might turn our attention to their experiences of government. They lived through the formative years of childhood and early adulthood at precisely the time when national government was becoming more involved in citizens' lives than ever before, particularly in the realm of social provision.[18] For the first hundred years after the drafting of the Constitution, American citizens had looked primarily to their state and local governments to define the scope of their rights and responsibilities. The limits of states' governing capacity combined with the Supreme Court's insistence that states refrain from intervening in economic affairs meant that early on, states did little to ensure the economic security of individuals and families. Adults who fell upon difficult times had to rely on their extended families or church congregations; in the absence of such support, they could be relegated to the local poorhouse and lose their children to an orphanage.[19] Meanwhile, the national government involved itself primarily in activities far from most citizens' lives: facilitating internal improvements such as roads, canals, bridges, and post offices, setting subsidies and tariffs, protecting patents, and issuing a common currency.[20] After the Civil War, the national government began to affect citizens' lives more directly through pensions to veterans and their widows; by the end of the nineteenth century and the beginning of the twentieth, these pensions had become generous and expansive, reaching 18 percent of the U.S. population age sixty-five and over.[21] Still, the nascent social programs of the 1910s and 1920s, geared toward mothers and their children, were established primarily at the state and local levels.[22]

Only with the New Deal—through policies enacted as members of the civic generation climbed through the middle years of childhood and became teenagers—did national government begin to affect directly the lives of vast numbers of citizens, across all age groups. In the worst years of the Depression, millions of the unemployed found work through relief programs such as the Works Progress Administration (WPA) and Civilian Conservation Corps (CCC), and many people saw electricity come to their communities for the first time through the Tennessee Valley Authority. Families began to see their well-being enhanced by major new social programs established by the Social Security Act of 1935 (including unemployment insurance, Aid to Dependent Children, and programs for the elderly) and by labor policies (namely, the National Labor Relations Act of 1935, which sanctioned unionization, and the Fair Labor Standards Act of 1938, which mandated the minimum wage and overtime pay). Citizens witnessed national government working on their behalf, ensuring their economic security and well-being and protecting them from what President Franklin D. Roosevelt termed the "vicissitudes" of private life, the uncertainties of the marketplace, and the inability of families to care for their own amid such travails.[23]

Once they reached the age of eighteen, the vast majority of men of the civic generation—and some women as well—answered the call of duty and began their military service. Certainly in the war itself, they witnessed government assuming a powerful role. But it was after they returned home that they encountered what has become known as a landmark public policy, the G.I. Bill of Rights. Formally called the Servicemen's Readjustment Act of 1944, the law extended numerous social benefits to returning veterans of World War II. Any veteran who received a discharge status other than dishonorable after at least ninety days of service qualified for extensive unemployment benefits, low-interest guaranteed loans to buy a home, farm, or business, and financial assistance to pursue additional education or training. Until they found a job, veterans could qualify for unemployment benefits of $20 a week for up to one year; the average veteran used only 19.7 weeks' worth of the "52-20 Club," as the program was called, with only 14 percent exhausting their full entitlement. Twenty-nine percent took advantage of the loan guarantee provisions: 4.3 million purchased homes at low interest rates, and 200,000 purchased farms or businesses. The construction industry received an enormous boost: by 1955, nearly one-third of new housing starts nationwide owed their backing to the Veterans Administration.[24]

Of course, when most people think of the G.I. Bill they think of its education and training benefits, and with good reason: 51 percent of World War II veterans, a total of 7.8 million, took advantage of them. Indeed, the usage rates for those provisions far surpassed the program creators' greatest expectations. By 1947, veterans accounted for 49 percent of students enrolled in American colleges. Ten years after World War II, 2.2 million veterans had attended college under the law's provisions. And for every veteran who used the G.I. Bill to attend college, more than twice as many—a total of 5.6 million—seized the opportunity to acquire training below the college level.[25] By attending G.I. Bill–financed vocational or business schools or by utilizing the bill's subsidy of apprenticeships, on-the-job training, or on-the-farm training, they gained preparation and credentials for a wide array of occupations.

Among the beneficiaries of such programs was Sam Marchesi, who had an eighth-grade education. He had dropped out of school after his father died in order to help support his mother and eight siblings. The war began a few years later, and Marchesi enlisted in the Army. Sent to the Pacific theater, he served in Australia, China, and finally the Philippines. During the invasion of Manila, he was badly wounded in battle, earning a Purple Heart. While Marchesi recuperated, Red Cross nurses urged him to use the G.I. Bill to develop new skills for supporting himself after the war. He used the benefits both for vocational training in architectural drawing and estimating and for on-the-job training as an apprentice carpenter. It enabled him to become a successful custom builder. "I think it was a great thing that the government did, to give us this opportunity to pick up where we left off," he commented. "We had to face the world. We had to make a living. Thank God the government had the doors open for us."

The G.I. Bill granted one year of education or training to veterans who had served for at least ninety days, with an additional month of education for each additional month of service, up to a maximum of forty-eight months. All tuition and fees were covered, up to a total of $500 per year—more than any university charged at that time—and veterans received monthly subsistence payments of $75 if single, $105 with one dependent, and $120 with two or more dependents.[26] By 1955, the federal government had spent a total of $14.5 billion—$108 billion in 2002 dollars—for the education and training provisions.[27]

To appreciate the scope of the G.I. Bill's influence, we must consider that among men born in the United States in the 1920s—those of the generation in question—fully 80 percent were military veterans.[28] And unlike veterans of the Vietnam War and today's all-volunteer force, they were broadly representative of the general male population. The majority of them served in World War II, and over half of that group used the G.I. Bill's education and training provisions; those born later in the 1920s were more likely to have served in the Korean War, and 42 percent of them utilized a new and very similar version of the education and training provisions.[29] Overall, close to half the men of the civic generation took advantage of the education or training benefits of the G.I. Bill.

The central question posed by this book is how this landmark public program, one so widely experienced among men of the civic generation, might have affected beneficiaries' involvement in the practices of democratic citizenship. Answering this question is complicated by the fact that despite the G.I. Bill's popular reputation as a highly successful program, we know surprisingly little about even its first-order effects, meaning the scope of its coverage and the depth of its socioeconomic impact.[30] To be sure, the bill's higher education provisions in particular have been lauded, cited as the source of vast social change on the presumption that they expanded access to advanced education for over two million Americans.[31] But evidence for such claims has been surprisingly rare.[32] Several studies have shown that veterans enjoyed academic and occupational success after the war that surpassed that of nonveterans, but they neglected to isolate the effects of the G.I. Bill in producing such success.[33] A few scholars have evaluated selected effects of the G.I. Bill, such as educational attainment.[34] The most comprehensive of these studies found an increase in formal schooling of nearly three years among beneficiaries of the G.I. Bill's higher education provisions.[35] However, these studies are limited in their ability to explain the determinants of program usage, leaving it unclear whether the provisions were genuinely accessible to the average veteran. They also tend to overlook entirely the effectiveness of the subcollege programs, which did not extend educational attainment as it is typically measured but did enhance job skills.[36] And inquiry into the G.I. Bill's impact on subsequent participation in civic and political life—the focus of this study—has been practically nonexistent.[37] Despite the fact that historian Arthur Schlesinger Jr. singled out the bill as "the most underrated national turning point" because it "contributed enormously to the release of economic and intellectual energy that carried postwar America to the summit of the world," and management guru Peter Drucker identified it as the single factor most responsible for transforming the United States into a "knowledge society," we know little about the actual effects of this program on the individuals who benefited from it.[38]

Recently, in the absence of comprehensive empirical studies, the education and training provisions of the G.I. Bill have been targeted by scholars attacking what they consider to be wrongheaded popular "myths" of the program's inclusiveness and democratizing effects. They characterize the policy as inherently elitist and charge that it created new inequalities in American society. Some claim that the G.I. Bill merely bestowed privilege on already privileged veterans, paying the college tuition of those who could have obtained education at their own expense while doing little for veterans from less advantaged backgrounds.[39] As Lizabeth Cohen argues, "The vehicle most often credited with moving working-class Americans into the postwar middle class . . . orchestrated much less social engineering than it promised and has been given credit for."[40] Others argue that it worsened educational inequalities between black and white Americans, and between men and women.[41] These analyses, if valid, would imply that any subsequent effects on beneficiaries' participation in democracy would likely have compounded social and economic disparities with civic and political inequality. However, such claims tend to be based on sketchy evidence, typically anecdotal in nature, or drawn from case studies of selected localities or institutions.

At stake in this book, then, are the record and the reputation of one of the most sweeping programs ever enacted in the United States, with regard to its affect on beneficiaries' life opportunities and whether it made them better citizens. In order to investigate these questions, I needed to use a range of available resources and talk to some veterans myself. Government documents and archival materials illuminated the program's origins and manner of implementation, and existing surveys of veterans provided useful information about their usage of its benefits. No existing materials, however, would permit systematic comparisons of subsequent civic and political involvement of program users versus nonusers. I turned, therefore, to the veterans themselves, collecting surveys from over fifteen hundred members of the World War II generation and conducting in-depth interviews with twenty-eight veterans from all regions of the United States. (For full descriptions of data collection procedures, see Appendices A–D.) Drawing on all of these sources, I have put the G.I. Bill's education and training benefits to the test, assessing the program's effects on veterans' subsequent participation in civic and political activities.

My central finding, which this book documents and explains, is that the G.I. Bill's education and training provisions had an overwhelmingly positive effect on male veterans' civic involvement. Those veterans who utilized the provisions became more active citizens in public life in the postwar years than those who did not. Certainly it is not surprising that advanced education would facilitate civic participation; remarkably, however, the program's effects transcended the impact of education itself. Comparing two nonblack male veterans who grew up in the same

socioeconomic circumstances and who attained the same level of education, the individual who used the G.I. Bill belonged to 50 percent more
civic organizations and participated in 30 percent more political activities
and organizations than the nonrecipient.[42] Beneficiaries became more intensely involved in public life, in activities long considered to be critical to
self-governance and therefore the lifeblood of American democracy.[43]

How can we explain these positive effects of the G.I. Bill's education and training provisions on democratic participation? What was it
about this policy that made it reap consequences in the realm of civic
life? The answer lay in its fundamental inclusivity, magnanimity, and life-
transforming power among male veterans. These attributes were reflected, in part, through the value of the education and training it financed,
which were praised by veterans for their impact on their lives, and also
through the rules and procedures by which it was administered. Veterans commonly responded that the benefits of the bill were generous and
accessible and that they felt treated with respect, on terms equal to those
of other veterans, regardless of their class, race, or religious background.
Importantly, their deservingness for the generous benefits was considered to be beyond question, given that through their military service
they had put themselves in harm's way for the sake of the nation. In
turn, by experiencing treatment as "first-class" citizens in the program,
beneficiaries became more fully incorporated as members of the citizenry and thus developed a stronger predisposition to assume the roles
of active participants within it. Subsequently, in the postwar era, G.I.
Bill beneficiaries from across the spectrum of educational attainment
participated at higher levels in civic and political activities than would
otherwise have been expected.

For some, such as Luke LaPorta, such involvement took the form of
membership and leadership in mainstream civic organizations—in his
case, Little League, Babe Ruth, and numerous community sports organizations. Others mobilized to challenge the status quo. Henry Hervey,
an African American and a former Tuskegee Airman, used the G.I. Bill
to gain a bachelor's degree at Northwestern University. Afterward, however, he found the job market to be as pervaded by racial discrimination
as ever. "I went to every bank in downtown Chicago and presented my
credentials, and I got the same job offer I would have gotten if I had not
gone to college: it was either a janitor or a mailroom clerk." Following
the positive experience of the G.I. Bill and having gained the skills fostered by the education it financed, Hervey joined those who mobilized
to change the system. "By that time you learn you can fight city hall, and
you have to fight, and there are ways you can bring pressure to make

changes." Black G.I. Bill users, in fact, became a major impetus within the emergent civil rights movement.

The inclusivity of the G.I. Bill did have limits.[44] Women, who were not drafted, constituted just 2 percent of the armed forces in World War II, and though the G.I. Bill was available to female veterans, they used it at somewhat lower rates because advanced education fit less neatly with their gender roles in the postwar era than it did with men's. More important, the exclusion of the vast majority of women from the program, given that they were civilians, widened the gender divide in educational attainment. In turn, the incorporation of a generation of men into the polity exacerbated the gender gap in active citizenship, highlighting the power of government programs to stimulate the participation of some groups relative to others.

Nonetheless, just as the G.I. Bill transformed the lives of veterans who used it, they in turn helped to change America. Prior to the war, advanced education had been restricted predominantly to the privileged, especially to white, native-born, elite Protestants. The social rights offered by the G.I. Bill broadened educational opportunity to veterans who were Jewish or Catholic, African American, and immigrants as well as to those whose families had struggled in the American working class for generations. Once G.I. Bill beneficiaries became active citizens, they altered the civic landscape of the United States, helping to make the political system yet more inclusive and egalitarian during the middle decades of the twentieth century.

In suggesting that a public program enhanced participation in American democracy, this book is at odds with prevailing views about the relationship between government and civic involvement. Indeed, over the last quarter century, as citizens' activity and interest in public affairs have waned, political leaders have argued that modern government itself might deserve the blame. The "welfare state," including many of the social policies of the New Deal, has borne the brunt of such criticism on the grounds that it fosters dependency among recipients, thus undermining their sense of civic obligation, and that it substitutes for institutions of civil society, such as churches and voluntary associations, thus weakening them.[45] While such ideas had percolated in American politics since the early 1960s, it was President Ronald Reagan who lent national prominence to the new public philosophy, announcing in his first inaugural address in 1981, "Government is not the solution to our problem; government is the problem." His administration proceeded to act on such principles by cutting taxes and reducing spending on social programs, except those for the elderly.[46] Next, President George H. W. Bush suggested that government agencies emasculate the vibrancy of civil society and called instead for "a thousand points of light," voluntary efforts by Americans to care for those in need.

The demise of previously secure public programs has become, over time, more politically feasible. Some have deteriorated due to neglect, as in the case of the minimum wage, food stamps, Pell grants, and unemployment insurance, where policy makers have failed to maintain the real value of benefits harmed by inflation.[47] Other programs have faced more serious restructuring, as in the case of welfare, which was fundamentally altered under the terms of 1996 legislation signed into law by President Bill Clinton, and potentially Social Security, which President George W. Bush hopes to transform into a system that includes private, individual retirement accounts. While the events of September 11, 2001 stimulated new support for government involvement in citizens' lives for the purposes of national security, skepticism about the effectiveness of social programs persists.

Yet claims that government programs undermine good citizenship still remain unsubstantiated by solid evidence. In fact, most scholarship proceeds in a manner disconnected from public discourse about how government programs may influence civic engagement.[48] Thus, despite the growth of social spending over the twentieth century, we know little about whether core programs have fostered active involvement in public life or complacency, or whether they have promoted public-spiritedness or selfish individualism.[49]

Arguably, to the extent that government programs and regulations have become a more important part of everyday life, they may have critical effects—for good or for ill—on citizens' attitudes about government and their participation in the political system.[50] First, the sheer amount of resources distributed by government is likely to influence civic engagement.[51] Today the U.S. government spends 15.8 percent of the gross domestic product on public social expenditures, facilitating a considerable infusion into citizens' lives.[52] Whether these resources are distributed in the form of dollar payments or as goods and services such as food, education, or health care, they have implications for beneficiaries' material well-being and life opportunities, and thus in turn are likely to influence their rate of civic involvement. Greater resources—particularly advanced education—tend to lead individuals to employment and social situations in which they develop greater civic skills and social networks, thus elevating their capacity for participation in public life.[53] As well, policy resources may boost civic engagement if they increase citizens' sense that government is for and about people like them and that they have a stake in government, prompting them to mobilize politically.[54] Andrea Campbell found Social Security and Medicare to have such "resource effects" on beneficiaries' political participation, boosting involvement particularly among those with low incomes given that they are especially reliant on the program benefits.[55]

As well, public policies offer citizens routine, day-to-day encounters with government and are likely to constitute their most personal and informative experiences of government in action.[56] These seemingly mundane experiences are likely to be more instructive about citizens' relationship to government and their status within the polity than are their far less frequent visits to the voting booth, almost nonexistent encounters with elected officials, and impersonal sound bites of political advertising. Citizens attain penetrating messages from government, for example, when they fill out their tax forms every April, wait for a monthly Social Security check, apply for unemployment insurance, or consider how the perceived quality of their local public school affects the market value of their home.[57] Their perceptions of a policy's fairness, its effectiveness, and its value in their life are significant, then, because they may derive, on that basis, their view about government's general responsiveness toward people like them.[58] Joe Soss found that Social Security disability insurance, with its routinized procedures, elevates recipients' sense that government is responsive to people like them, while Aid to Families with Dependent Children, through which recipients encountered nonresponsive agencies, had the opposite effect.[59] As well, program beneficiaries may acquire a sense of their own status in the polity, of how people like them are regarded—for instance, with respect or with stigma—and the extent to which they are included among the citizenry.[60] Program messages may be diffused, of course, if benefits are designed in a way that makes government's role less visible; Jacob Hacker argues that employer-financed health and pension plans cultivate little public activism given that their design obscures the public subsidies that help finance them.[61] Ultimately, to the extent to which such "interpretive" or "cognitive" effects are conveyed by policies, they may influence citizens' psychological predisposition or inclination to civic engagement, and thus in turn affect the extent to which citizens later participate in civic and political activities.[62]

We now turn to the education and training benefits of the G.I. Bill, to explore how they transformed the soldiers of World War II into active citizens for peacetime democracy. We will probe the significance of the resources they offered—both for higher education and for subcollege training—and the scope of their coverage among veterans, in order to understand how they helped elevate civic participation. We will examine the tenor of the messages the program conveyed to veterans through its rules, procedures, and manner of implementation; how beneficiaries perceived its inclusivity and its value in their lives; and how such interpretive effects could have been transformed into consequences for civic involvement. Throughout the book, readers will find stories about and quotations from the veterans who were interviewed for the project, who come primarily but not exclusively from the same units as those surveyed; these veterans are identified by pseudonym, or, if they chose, by name.[63] The responses of the survey participants, by contrast, are typically presented as aggregate quantitative results, except in a few cases in which individual written responses from the surveys are presented anonymously.

Beyond its implications for the civic generation, the story of the G.I. Bill bears critical lessons for contemporary policy-making efforts. From the 1970s to the present, Americans have grown increasingly unequal in terms of income and wealth, producing a highly stratified society; also, by several measures, civic engagement has dwindled, particularly among less advantaged citizens. To be sure, those who have more education and income participate at much higher levels, and have greater political power, than those who have less. In this context, the example of a public program of the past that produced egalitarian consequences for both socioeconomic status and civic participation, ameliorating inequalities and fostering engagement, demands serious consideration. It is imperative to understand the means whereby the G.I. Bill had such effects so that we can ponder the implications for policy making today.

1

Creating the G.I. Bill

T he end of World War II seemed to signal to Americans at least a moment of relief from a decade and a half of struggle. After the stock market crashed in 1929, unemployment and impoverishment ravaged the nation. The despair they produced hung like a dust cloud that would not abate until, on December 7, 1941, a different crisis emerged. With the attack on Pearl Harbor, a nation long reluctant to enter the growing world war found itself undeniably catapulted into the conflict. Jobs at last became plentiful, but goods grew scarce, and all citizens were asked to do their part to sacrifice and help support the war effort. Most costly of all, nearly every family had to bid farewell to at least one of their own who answered the call to serve the nation in the military, some never to return. When troops stormed the coast of France on D-Day, June 6, 1944, over fourteen hundred Americans were counted among the dead, and casualties mounted as they made their way across Europe. Between mid-December 1944 and early January 1945, the Battle of Ardennes—also known as the Battle of the Bulge—eclipsed the Battle of Gettysburg as the bloodiest event in American history: fifty-five thousand were killed or wounded and eighteen thousand taken prisoner. In the Pacific theater, young Americans engaged in combat on a string of islands with names most had never heard of before; the intensity of warfare culminated in battles on Iwo Jima and Okinawa, where American fatalities totaled nearly twenty thousand. By the time Germany finally surrendered in May, followed by Japan in August, the United States had suffered over one million dead or wounded—more than in any other war in which Americans have participated before or since.[1]

As much as the nation yearned for peace, its arrival brought new anxieties. Experts warned that the servicemen returning home had undergone profound changes since they went away to war.[2] "He may have lost an arm or a leg," explained the surgeon general of the U.S. Army, Major General Norman T. Kirk. "His face or head may be disfigured. He may be a nervous wreck from battle fatigue and labeled psychoneurotic or psychotic."[3] Citizens also worried that the economy would slump back into a depression. It seemed inconceivable that the job market—which had been so fragile until the infusion of government spending for war mobilization—could possibly accommodate fifteen million returning veterans as well as the ten million civilians who had been employed in the war industries. But public officials had already considered postwar challenges and had made plans in advance, with the enactment of the G.I. Bill—otherwise known as the Servicemen's Readjustment Act of 1944.[4]

Today, it would seem reasonable to assume that the G.I. Bill was an extension of New Deal largesse, created for the explicit purpose of broadening access to education and facilitating movement into the middle class.[5] In fact, that was hardly the case. Though created soon after the New Deal, the G.I. Bill came about at a time when the social democratic momentum and spirit of reform associated with the period had already subsided.[6] By the early 1940s, President Franklin D. Roosevelt had distanced himself from most domestic policy-making efforts, concentrating on his role as "Dr. Win the War" rather than as "Dr. New Deal."[7] Congress had grown increasingly conservative, and interest in social legislation had declined sharply.[8]

Certainly public officials in the most progressive corner of the Roosevelt administration, the National Resources Planning Board (NRPB), did hope that the end of the war would provide the opportunity in which to expand further the New Deal vision of social rights for all citizens. Their call to arms was articulated by Roosevelt in his "Four Freedoms" speech in 1941—famously memorialized by Norman Rockwell's illustrations—which declared that the nation should guarantee to all Americans not only "freedom of speech and expression," "freedom from fear," and "freedom of worship," but also "freedom from want."[9] The NRPB carried the torch for this ambitious agenda and, focusing particularly on the last component, issued several reports that outlined bold plans for the postwar economy. The board set as a goal nothing less than "the fullest possible development of the productive potential of all of our resources, material and human, with full employment, continuity of income, [and] equal access to minimum security and living standards."[10] Most significant, the NRPB prioritized expanded access to education as a key objective, arguing that it was "essential for the exercise of citizenship in a democratic society."[11]

If the National Resources Planning Board had prevailed, we might consider the G.I. Bill as a policy intended to expand opportunities for all citizens to attain advanced education. That was not the case, however. For all its ebullient prose, the board's political star never shone very brightly, and it—as well as prospects that broad postwar plans might emanate from the Roosevelt administration—grew dimmer as the war proceeded. In fact, when NRPB head Frederick Delano urged the president to authorize planning for demobilization, Roosevelt hedged, saying, "This is no time for a public interest in or discussion of post-war problems—on the broad ground that there will not be any post-war problems if we lose this war."[12] Subsequent NRPB reports, when released to the public, were castigated by journalists and conservative groups around the nation as "fascist" and "socialist." Then, in the spring of 1943, Congress voted to terminate the board's funding, thus silencing the voices of those in the Roosevelt administration who advocated broad-based social provision in the postwar era.[13]

In the absence of the NRPB, postwar planners were motivated by the narrower and more practical goal of reincorporating returning veterans into society and, not least, by fears of social unrest. The experience of World War I veterans, who had gained little by way of government benefits, loomed in their memories: early in the Depression, during the Hoover administration, thousands of disgruntled and destitute veterans from all over the country had mobilized to march on Washington in pursuit of immediate compensation. In an incident that shocked and embarrassed the nation, federal troops, summoned by Hoover and led by General Douglas MacArthur, ran the ragtag "Bonus Army" out of town.[14] Policy makers hoped to avoid a repeat of such events by ensuring from the start that veterans of World War II would receive better treatment. They aimed, further, to "solve the bottlenecks and to get around difficulties" implicit in demobilization, to circumvent the possibilities for a return to massive unemployment rates, and at the same time to correct for educational shortages in particular occupations that had been created by the war.[15]

Public officials were also genuinely concerned about enabling veterans to retool themselves for active citizenship in peacetime. As Roosevelt himself put it when submitting the administration's proposal to Congress, "We must replenish our supply of persons qualified to discharge the heavy responsibilities of the postwar world. We have taught our youth how to wage war; we must also teach them how to live useful and happy lives in freedom, justice, and democracy."[16] Diverting veterans away from the job market and toward educational institutions and training programs appeared to constitute a possible means of addressing all of these concerns simultaneously.

Through a surprising series of events and highly paradoxical politics, the law that emerged, while limited to veterans only, was nonetheless striking for its generosity, inclusivity, and provision of social opportunity. These attributes owed not to the efforts of the ostensibly progressive Roosevelt administration, which ultimately offered only modest proposals that would have granted education to very few veterans. Rather, it was the American Legion, an organization that had a conservative reputation and had tended previously to be skeptical of public programs, that put forward the far more sweeping proposal of the G.I. Bill, then mobilized the political support necessary to its enactment.[17]

The G.I. Bill bore less resemblance to New Deal legislation—which tended to target citizens as workers—than to an older American tradition of social provision geared for citizen soldiers. In the democratic ideals so central to the nation's identity, military service had long been regarded as the utmost obligation of masculine citizenship, and the protection of the nation by ordinary citizens, as opposed to a standing army, was considered essential to maintaining self-governance.[18] In the words of George Washington, "It may be laid down as a primary position, and the basis of our system, that every Citizen who enjoys the protection of a free Government, owes not only a proportion of his property, but even of his personal services to the defence of it."[19] From the period following the Revolutionary War onward, the United States recognized those who rose to this demand of civic duty by granting increasingly generous pensions to veterans and their dependents. Initially these programs targeted only disabled veterans, but in 1890, Congress extended Civil War pensions to those who had non-service-related disabilities and to the families of deceased veterans. By the beginning of the twentieth century, such pensions had become fairly generous and widespread.[20]

Yet the G.I. Bill also represented a departure from the specific design of these prior veterans' programs. Over time, the Civil War pensions had earned a poor reputation among Progressive reformers, who associated them with corruption. They were delivered through the patronage system of party politics, which permitted a high degree of discretion to local politicians, who could in practice control the timing and targeting of benefits for political purposes.[21] With World War I, policy makers sought to create benefits that would be less expensive, less open to potential abuse, and more oriented toward the promotion of self-reliance among veterans. Rather than disability pensions, they offered veterans of the Great War merely the option of purchasing low-cost insurance, and established vocational programs and medical and hospital care for disabled veterans only.[22] This was the approach that veterans viewed as so miserly; it generated repeated demands for outright pension payments and ultimately led to the notorious treatment of the Bonus Army during the Hoover administration.

From the outset, the Roosevelt administration responded more graciously to veterans but embraced a new policy approach. President Roosevelt made his position clear when he addressed the American Legion in 1933: "No person, because he wore a uniform, must thereafter be placed in a special class of beneficiaries over and above all other citizens. The fact of wearing a uniform does not mean that he can demand and receive from his Government a benefit which no other citizen receives."[23] By executive order, he eliminated some veterans' benefits and scaled back others, instead advancing legislation that made jobs available to thousands—veterans and nonveterans alike—in the Civilian Conservation Corps and later in the Federal Emergency Relief Administration.[24] Then the New Deal proceeded, through its core pieces of social and labor legislation, to expand American social rights by bestowing them primarily on citizen workers.[25]

Once World War II was under way, the combination of Roosevelt's lack of enthusiasm for social provision limited to veterans, his focus on the war, and the withering influence of the NRPB explain why his administration offered plans for postwar veterans' benefits only in strikingly restrictive terms. First the administration's Conference on Post-War Readjustments of Civilian and Military Personnel, known as the PMC, proposed higher education benefits that would be contingent upon competitive examinations and thus restricted to a relatively small number of veterans; then it suggested that permissible programs of study should be limited to those deemed directly relevant to occupations in need of trained personnel.[26] This narrow articulation represented the confluence of viewpoints of PMC members, both the fiscal conservatism of the military officials and the cautiousness of higher education leaders about opening too widely the doors of the academy, to which few outside of the elite had access at the time.[27] A second committee, the Armed Forces Committee on Postwar Educational Opportunities for Service Personnel (called the Osborn Committee for its chairman, Brigadier General Frederick H. Osborn), made the elitist approach even more explicit. It proposed that all veterans who had served for at least six months would be able to have one year of education or training, but only a "limited number of exceptionally able ex-service personnel" who demonstrated "unusual promise and ability"—just a hundred thousand—would be assisted in pursuing education beyond one year, and their aid would combine a mix of grants and loans.[28] Roosevelt transmitted this latter plan to Congress in the fall of 1943, where it was sponsored by Senator Elbert D. Thomas of Utah, a former political science professor and loyal New Dealer who was chairman of the Committee on Education and Labor.

At this same juncture, the American Legion, a veterans' organization created in 1919, after World War I, and which by the mid-1940s had three million members in local posts across the nation and abroad, began its focus on postwar planning.[29] No doubt the Legion—both then and now—is best known for its promotion of patriotism in local communities and its involvement in community service, particularly through the support of local youth baseball leagues, Boys' State and Boys' Nation events, and Boy Scout organizations. When it came to politics, the Legion had assumed a conservative, antistatist posture. Unlike the Veterans of Foreign Wars, it had refused to lend full support to "bonus" payments for the able-bodied during the 1920s, and during the Depression, it promoted voluntary provision of aid by local Legion posts rather than expanded government benefits.[30] The Legion would have appeared an unlikely suspect for the creation and promotion of landmark social legislation.

Yet remarkably, in a period of just a few weeks, the Legion's special committee charged with planning veterans' legislation produced what became known as the G.I. Bill. John Stelle, former governor of Illinois, "a big, fighting, bulk of a man" and a leader in the American Legion, received a letter from his son in the military that described what those with whom he served hoped for after the war: "All they wanted was an opportunity from their Government to make good when they returned . . . ; an opportunity to get education or training, and to find work." This prompted him to suggest to the Legion's Executive Committee, in November 1943, the core ideas of the G.I. Bill.[31] The organization set to work, and just two months later, in January 1944, Senator Joel Bennett Clark of Missouri, one of the founders of the American Legion, introduced the organization's proposal to Congress. The speedy time frame was made possible by the Legion's ability to draw liberally on the efforts of committees and experts whose plans had begun years earlier, most notably on the Roosevelt administration's bill, which had just been considered in hearings in the Senate.[32]

But while the Legion's bill essentially replicated much of the administration's overall framework, it was the civic organization's leaders who endowed the G.I. Bill with its hallmark features, pushing vigorously for provisions that were significantly more generous and inclusive.[33] Whereas the administration's version entitled veterans to one year of education and permitted only a small percentage with "exceptional ability and skill" to receive additional training, contingent on passage of competitive examinations, the Legion-inspired bill, by contrast, offered up to four years of funding—contingent on length of service—to any veteran whose education had been interrupted.[34] The one year of guaranteed education offered by the administration's bill was promised only to those who had served at least six months, while the Legion plan offered educational benefits for all who had served at least ninety days.[35]

The Legion's G.I. Bill Committee worked intensely over a one-month period from mid-December to mid-January. Chairman Stelle stood at a large blackboard and wrote down the ideas of all in the room, which were then "kept, revised, or erased after prolonged discussion and debate."[36] The actual drafting of the bill's language fell to Legion official Harry Colmery, a lawyer from Topeka, Kansas, who, in Stelle's phrase, "jelled all our ideas into words."[37] The organization's acting director of public relations, a former newspaperman named Jack Cejnar, read the draft proposal and shrewdly dubbed it "a bill of rights for G.I. Joe and G.I. Jane." Within a few days, the name was shortened to the catchy "G.I. Bill of Rights," and publicity about the proposal began to spread.[38]

Over the next six months, the American Legion proceeded—through its vast grassroots network and public relations apparatus—to marshal critical and widespread support for the G.I. Bill. Newspaper tycoon William Randolph Hearst, acting on his personal interest in veterans' welfare, offered the Legion the assistance of three of his top reporters for the duration of the legislative battles. Besides writing feature articles, the trio canvassed members of Congress as to their positions on the bill and rallied American Legion members throughout the nation to exert pressure on those expressing indecision or opposition. The national organization mailed packets to all local posts offering them materials to help their members write letters to Congress, appear on radio talk shows in support of the legislation, organize petition drives, and encourage local journalists to write articles about the legislation. The Women's Auxiliary for the Legion joined in all such efforts. The national staff prepared a motion picture clip and sent it to local theaters around the country, and rank-and-file members barraged Congress with telegrams. The G.I. Bill quickly gained far more widespread popular support than the Roosevelt administration's plans for veterans had ever garnered.[39]

Although the Senate acted quickly, approving the Legion's bill by late March, progress slowed in the House of Representatives. There, John E. Rankin of Mississippi, chair of the Committee on World War Veterans' Legislation, argued that the educational provisions of the bill would allow federal authorities to intervene in state and local affairs. He was distrustful of higher education, certain that it yielded an "overeducated and undertrained" population, and he announced, "I would rather send my child to a red schoolhouse than to a red school teacher."[40] He saved his most vitriolic disdain for the unemployment provisions of the bill, and it was in those criticisms that it became clear that Rankin feared that the legislation threatened the racial order: "We have 50,000 negroes in the service from our State, and in my opinion, if the bill should pass in its current form, a vast majority of them would remain unemployed for at least a year."[41] The committee finally approved, and the House passed, a version of the bill that was narrower and more restrictive than the Senate's version, leading to another round of contentious proceedings in conference committee. Once again, Rankin impeded the process. Finally, in a dramatic eleventh-hour series of events, Legion officials, assisted by political leaders, managed to contact Congressman John Gibson, a committee member who had gone home to Georgia because he was ill, and arranged for a local Legionnaire to drive him to a waiting plane so that he could get to Washington in time to break the deadlock at the committee's final meeting.[42] The conference version was swiftly approved by both houses, and on June 22, 1944, President Roosevelt signed the bill into law.

Throughout the politics surrounding the G.I. Bill's passage, proponents articulated vigorous arguments about the policy's relationship to American citizenship. Importantly, these claims were voiced not as progressive demands for all citizens to enjoy broader access to economic security and welfare.[43] Rather, supporters promoted the social rights in the legislation by observing their connection to civic obligations. They stressed that potential recipients were deserving because they had already performed the ultimate act of participatory citizenship through military service. Legion official Harry Colmery explained, "We recognize that the burden of war falls upon the citizen soldier, who has gone forth, overnight, to become the answer and hope of humanity; we seek to preserve his rights, to see that he gets a square deal."[44] Equally important, supporters emphasized that the policy would enable veterans to become more active citizens in the day-to-day workings of democracy in the postwar era. As the Legion's national commander, Warren Atherton, noted, "However great may be the service of the men and women who have served on the battlefields or home front in this war, an even greater obligation will face them when peace returns. . . . The continuing duty of citizenship is to apply the lessons of this war to the establishments of a better and stronger nation. As these veterans have led in war, so must they lead in peace."[45]

Policy makers did not spell out the precise dynamics by which they anticipated that the G.I. Bill's education and training provisions might help foster civic involvement in the postwar world, but the most vocal among them made clear that they intended and hoped for such outcomes. Harry Colmery told Congress, "Now this educational provision has a much deeper significance. . . . The nation needs the trained mind and body attuned again to the peaceful pursuits of American life, because, trained in the art of destruction of both property and life in every known personal and mechanical method, the nation then will owe an obligation to them. It has to take them back sympathetically away from the horrors and stark reality of war and give them every opportunity to again become disciplined forces for peaceful progress through educational opportunity in its every aspect."[46] Still, Colmery held only modest expectations for the reach of such efforts, noting, "We do not know how many there will be. It is estimated somewhere between 10 and 20 percent." In time, the provisions would reach over 50 percent of all veterans, and former service members' experience of the bill's design, implementation, and socioeconomic effects would yield social and civic consequences beyond those Colmery could ever have imagined.

2

Citizen Soldiers

I n the late 1930s, with the nation still in the depths of the Depression, Americans hoped desperately to avoid involvement in the conflicts that were intensifying abroad. As soon as the Japanese bombed Pearl Harbor, however, support for war mobilization soared, not least among the millions of young Americans who became subject to the draft. Thus began for a generation of men the experiences that would later on qualify them for the G.I. Bill's education and training benefits.

"I thought it was a normal, natural course of events," explained Isaac Gellert, who volunteered before he could be drafted. "There was a war and everybody was needed. It wasn't a matter of patriotism, not any flag-waving patriotism. I just felt it was the appropriate thing to do, especially since the war seemed to be a good one."

Gellert had grown up in New York City, and he termed his background "middle-class . . . or lower-middle-class, by the end of the Depression." His father, a small-business owner, had died at age forty-one, which Gellert attributed to the stress of attempting to keep his business afloat after the economy soured. His mother then went to work as a secretary. As soon as Gellert graduated from high school, he volunteered for the Army, hoping that by doing so he might have the opportunity to participate in the Army Specialized Training Program (ASTP), a short-lived program geared to produce "officer material" for the Army. It enabled recruits who scored high on intelligence exams to attend universities, pursuing courses of study deemed useful to the war effort while being subject to military discipline.[1] Gellert got his wish and attended Cornell University for one semester in the autumn of 1943. At that point, however, the government—hard pressed for soldiers, with the invasion of Europe looming—terminated the program.[2] Gellert was sent to basic training in Fort Jackson, South Carolina, where he became part of the 87th Infantry Division.

"We were a bunch of eighteen-year-olds, very wet behind the ears, who didn't appreciate what was going to be demanded of us physically and emotionally," said Gellert as he recalled reporting for his assignment of duty. "The fellow who was interviewing us, each one individually, turned to me and said, 'What would you like to be, a messenger or a truck driver?' I thought to myself, a messenger is a guy I picture running across the battlefield . . . ; a truck driver sits and drives around." Gellert, who weighed barely 140 pounds, replied, "Truck driver." The man responded, "You are a little light for a truck driver. We'll make you into a rifleman." Gellert was assigned to the front lines of combat duty, where he would witness firsthand the intensity and devastation of warfare, and serve with many who would not live to return home. "I think that's how most people got to be who they were," he explained. "You didn't have a lot of choice." He continued, "Eventually [in] every squad numbering twelve people in the Army platoon, in the company, one of those people was a Browning automatic rifleman. I eventually aspired to that position. The 'virtue' of that position was that instead of carrying a ten-pound rifle, you carried a seventeen-pound light machine gun. So I was a BAR man for part of my Army career. . . . I would say it was a very unenviable position to be in."

The men of Gellert's unit, also known as the "Golden Acorn Division," joined up with the Allies as part of General George S. Patton's Third U.S. Army in Central Europe. They engaged in combat in the Alsace-Lorraine region of France, proceeded into Germany, where they captured several towns, and took part in the brutal Battle of the Bulge at Ardennes. Next, they attacked German lines, advancing first toward Belgium and then Czechoslovakia. By the time Germany surrendered, 1,109 of the division's men had been killed and 4,110 wounded.[3] Afterward, Gellert, like many others in the 87th Infantry Division, used the G.I. Bill to attend college: it paid for his bachelor's degree at Columbia University and the first year of his graduate work at Harvard.

In the world of today's all-volunteer armed forces, it may seem surprising that Gellert and so many of his comrades willingly volunteered for such life-threatening duty. Traditionally, however, America imbued male citizenship with the republican ideal of military obligation: the common man had to be willing to fight when his country called on him to do so.[4] From the post–Revolutionary War period onward, those who fulfilled such duties came to be seen as deserving of subsequent benefits from government. It was on this basis that lawmakers and citizens united in support of the sweeping legislation that became known as the G.I. Bill.

In order to understand the effects of the G.I. Bill on civic life, we must begin by considering the composition of the World War II armed forces and the nature of military service. The program benefits could be no more inclusive than the military itself, and the magnitude of their impact would be affected, first and foremost, by the scope of the potential pool of beneficiaries and their socioeconomic backgrounds. Notably, the World War II military resembled the general male population of the United States more closely than has been the case in any subsequent war.[5] Veterans' responses to the G.I. Bill would be tempered by how they experienced their time in the armed forces. While military service left some with enduring difficulties that could impede civic engagement, most gleaned from it experiences that heightened their readiness for democratic citizenship.[6]

Mobilizing Manpower

Even while the nation still hoped to avoid war, President Roosevelt took steps to prepare for possible military involvement. In 1940, he signed into law the Selective Training and Service Act, the first peacetime draft in the history of the United States.[7] The new law required all males in the United States between the ages of twenty-one and thirty-six to register for the draft; they would be called up through a lottery system. The Army drafted proportionally from each state. The president could authorize deferments for the purpose of maintaining the "public health, safety, or interest," which potentially affected many employed in agriculture or the defense industry, both of which were deemed essential to the war effort. Actual decisions regarding which individuals would qualify and which would be deferred were relegated to civilian-run draft boards at the local level.[8] Immediately, more than sixteen million men registered, and over the next year, nearly a million were inducted by these local boards, making the armed forces 1.6 million strong.[9] Mobilization accelerated rapidly after Pearl Harbor: over the next four years, nearly ten million men were drafted and another two million volunteered for military service.[10]

Among men in their late teens and twenties, military service in World War II was understood to be a fundamental obligation of citizenship. Indeed, the scope of recruitment into the military was greater than in any prior American war, with the vast majority of men between the ages of eighteen and thirty eventually joining its ranks.

Ross Flint stated simply, "It was the thing to do," a sentiment widely shared among male veterans. Interviews for this project suggest that many young men desired to volunteer, but family members—often their mothers—

dissuaded them. Richard Werner explained that he wanted to join the service during his senior year of high school, but "my mother and grandmother got a hold of me. They wanted me to wait and graduate from high school." He complied with their wishes, becoming the first member of his family to obtain a high school diploma. A few months later, Werner was, to his great relief, admitted to the military: "I think the saddest day of my life would have been if they told me I was not physically fit to be a soldier. . . . This was how everyone felt at that time." Some, such as Gellert, volunteered because they knew they might have a chance to enroll in the Army Specialized Training Program. Others, including John Mahoney, hoped to avoid being placed in the infantry. Yet as Robert Forster, already in college at the University of California at Davis, explained, a sense of loyalty was the key factor that led him and others to enlist: "It's just something that you really wanted to do, to do your bit, during that time. You'd be amazed [at] how we were. The loyalty was through all classes of society." Forster's sentiment was echoed by William Martinez, a fellow Californian who had grown up in a much poorer family. He said, "I wanted to help the country. My brother was in there already. . . . I wanted to go in and do what I could for the country. I was patriotic."[11]

Certainly a few veterans looked back on their youthful enthusiasm with skepticism. John Towey remembered, "I guess I took it as any young fellow would take adventure. I went into it all hell-bent for action, to tell you the truth." And Joe O'Leary noted, "I guess I was looking forward to it in a way. You didn't think about getting killed."

For some, joining the military was motivated not only by a collective sense of mission but also by a more specific commitment to the justness of the war. Said James Murray, "I had come to understand Hitler was a real menace." Jewish soldiers were especially cognizant of the war's purpose, knowing that their relatives were suffering persecution in Europe. Kermit Pransky recalled his family's reaction when they stopped hearing from relatives in Germany: "I was aware because my mother looked for the mailman every day . . . and no mail came. It was heartbreaking to see her; she was so disappointed all the time." As Harry Serulneck explained, "People had a good sense of what was going on, as far as Hitler [was] concerned, in killing the Jewish people; that's what drove most of us [Jewish soldiers] to enlist."

The Face of the Armed Forces

As noted above, the composition of the World War II military mirrored quite closely the male population at the time, and to the extent that it differed, servicemen on average were slightly more educated and had somewhat better health than those who stayed behind. The widespread impoverishment that had come with the Great Depression meant that many young people lacked the level of mental or physical health or educational preparation deemed desirable for military service. Early on, nearly 30 percent of those examined were rejected because they failed to pass the physical exam.[12] Contrary to the popular assumption that "flat feet" represented the most frequent cause of disqualification, it accounted for only 1 percent of rejections. Mental illness, usually defined as "psychoneurotic disorders and psychopathic personality," constituted the most frequent cause of disqualification (17 percent), followed by illiteracy— inability to read on a fourth-grade level—and lack of educational readiness, as measured by results on intelligence tests (a total of 14 percent). The remainder were disqualified due to a wide range of physical problems, ranging from hernias to syphilis to tuberculosis.[13] One in ten registrants suffered from a "manifestly disqualifying defect," such as total blindness or deafness, missing arms or legs, or chronic or severe physical or mental disorders. Over time, as the need for inductees grew more pressing, government officials opted to rehabilitate men rather than reject them. Many who would have been disqualified previously for physical reasons were provided with dental care, fitted with glasses, or treated for venereal disease, and individuals deemed to have inadequate education were no longer rejected but instead brought to special training units for several months of basic education.[14]

Overall, World War II soldiers had already attained, on average, one more year of education than their counterparts.[15] Fifty-seven percent of soldiers had completed at least one year of high school work, compared to only 41 percent of the male population of draft age. The proportion that had completed at least one year of college—12.3 percent—was equivalent to that of the general population.[16] These civilian-military differences emanated not only from the military's use of the literacy requirements, which eliminated those with little or no schooling, but also from the lack of educational deferments, which meant that by contrast to the Vietnam War, college students were not excused from duty. With the onset of World War II, representatives of the nation's colleges and universities, worried about the financial fate of their institutions as male enrollment plummeted, pleaded for student deferments.[17] Military officials opposed such deferments, viewing them as a way for those who could afford college to evade military service and thus as fundamentally undemocratic. As a compromise, they fashioned the ASTP program, in which Gellert enrolled, as well as its counterpart, the Navy College Training Program (known as V-12). Though short-lived, these programs provided an extra incentive to enlistment by those with somewhat more education prior to military service.[18]

By late 1942, policy makers, convinced that younger men were most fit for military service, lowered the draft age from twenty-one to eighteen. Young men tended to volunteer or to be drafted soon after their eighteenth birthday; a few interview subjects mentioned that they had been so eager to join up that they lied about their age and enlisted even before turning eighteen. Officials also raised the upper age limit to thirty-seven to gain additional manpower, though rejection rates increased sharply with age, with 40 percent of draftees between ages thirty and thirty-seven rejected for physical or mental defects. Early on, married men, who were likely to be older, received deferments, particularly if they had children; by 1943, as manpower demands grew, the government began to induct them regardless, unless they qualified for occupational deferments.[19] Among nonblack male respondents to the World War II Veterans Survey, year of birth ranged from 1909 to 1929, with a median of 1923 and an average of 1922. This means that on June 6, 1944, when Allied troops stormed the beaches at Normandy and began the campaign across Europe, most of these servicemen were twenty-one or twenty-two years old.

The racial and ethnic composition of the armed forces was somewhat less diverse than that of the population generally, with slightly more white Americans than their proportion in the larger population. Combined, Native Americans, Puerto Ricans, Hawaiians, and those of Mexican, Chinese, Filipino, and Japanese descent constituted 1.6 percent of the ranks. Most of these groups were represented in proportion to their presence in the general population, with the exception of Native Americans, of whom the proportion was slightly lower, and those of Chinese descent, of whom it was higher.[20] As the war began, African Americans' demand for the "right to fight"—for recognition of their willingness to fulfill the obligations of citizenship—became a rallying cry.[21] Yet despite the Selective Service Act's formal prohibitions on racial discrimination, males of African descent, though accounting for 9.5 percent of all men ages eighteen to forty in the general population, made up only 8.5 percent of those in the armed forces. Forty-one percent were disqualified because they failed to pass the physical or literacy requirements, compared to 28 percent of whites, evidence of socioeconomic disparities as well as racial bias.[22]

The most glaringly undemocratic aspect of the armed forces' treatment of men involved how African Americans were treated once inducted: they were marginalized in a manner that was overt and pervasive, in blatant contradiction to the United States' democratic posture in the battle against Nazism and fascism.[23] They served in separate, segregated units that were typically forbidden to engage in combat, relegated instead to tasks such as construction and transportation. Only after extensive and fractious congressional debate were two segregated units awarded the "right" to engage in combat.[24] And while white troops could focus on defeating the Germans, black troops experienced a more complicated mission: proving themselves as a group even as they were treated as inferior to white soldiers.[25] As Charles Dryden, a Tuskegee Airman, explained, "Oftentimes we flew missions when the birds weren't flying, the reason being that we . . . all had a deep feeling [that] we dared not fail. If a white guy failed, 'Oh, it's an individual that failed,' but [if] one of us failed, then 'None of you make it through'—the stereotyping syndrome sets in. . . . If we did not go, then we knew they would be saying, 'They are cowards—we told you they were scared of combat.' So we had to dispute that by our actions."

In terms of the composition of the World War II military, the gender barrier presented the greatest limitation to its ability to represent a cross section of the general population. Women, not being subject to the draft, constituted less than 2 percent of those who served. This was despite the fact that far more women—332,000—participated than in any prior military conflict and they were, for the first time, incorporated within units of the armed forces.[26] After considerable debate, in 1942 Congress approved the Women's Army Auxiliary Corps, a unit that would include women in a variety of noncombat roles in the Army, though without regular military status and benefits. One year later, the auxiliary corps was replaced by the Women's Army Corps (WAC), a full-fledged part of the regular Army, permitting full military status and equal benefits for women. Women gained similar treatment in the WAVES (Women Accepted for Voluntary Emergency Service), the attachment to the Navy; the Marine Corps Women Reserves; and the SPARs (meaning "Semper Paratus—Always Ready") of the Coast Guard. The exceptions were the eleven hundred Women's Air Force Service Pilots, known as WASPs, who were not granted military status until 1970, despite the fact that they risked their lives ferrying planes and teaching male cadets to fly. Nonetheless, although women constituted a larger military presence than in prior U.S. wars, their still paltry representation in the armed forces during World War II meant that the parameters of the G.I. Bill's coverage were, from the start, restricted primarily to men.[27]

The Social Worlds of Veterans' Childhoods

With the critical exception of African Americans, who were included but segregated, the military in World War II served as an institutional melting pot for young men, uniting those from all states and regions of the United States and from a diverse array of regions, ethnicities, and religious backgrounds. Overall, among nonblack male World War II Veterans Survey respondents, 18 percent had grown up on farms, 33 percent in small cities or towns, 18 percent in medium-sized cities or towns, and 19 percent in large cities. The majority had been raised Protestant (65 percent); 24 percent were Catholic, and 7 percent Jewish. As Luke LaPorta explained, in contrast to the ethnic, urban neighborhood in which he grew up, in which "we were all people of the same genre," in the military he met Jews, Poles, and countless others from different backgrounds. "It certainly wasn't homogenous. But what happened was [that] you were all in the same boat. It was a great equalizer."

The rural and small-town contingent of veterans consisted primarily of Protestants whose families had lived in the United States for several generations, often dwelling in farm communities or coal-mining or factory towns. This included people such as James Murray, who spent his childhood in New Castle, Pennsylvania, a blue-collar steel town outside Pittsburgh. His father, who had a tenth-grade education, worked as a ticket agent for the Lake Erie Railroad. Fred Windham's family had lived for several generations in Pescadero, California, where he was raised on a farm. Although his mother had attended high school, his father, who worked as a lumberman in the redwoods, had no more than an elementary education.

Veterans raised in urban environments were more likely to have grandparents or even parents who had emigrated from other countries to begin a new life in the United States.[28] Jews figured disproportionately among veterans who came from large cities, as Catholics did from midsized cities. Alphanse Antonowitz, whose parents came from Lithuania, grew up in East Chicago, Indiana. William Martinez's parents emigrated from Mexico to California. His father was employed as a stonemason and later a gardener, while his mother cared for their nine children. "It was terrible . . . we were so poor," he said, remembering when he and his siblings went without shoes, and that the family sometimes survived by eating rabbits. Harry Serulneck's Russian-born father was illiterate because, as a Jew, he had been forbidden an education in his native land; once in Brooklyn, he and his wife began their own business, operating a herring stand. They lived in a tenement, struggling during the Depression: "The house was so cold and it was dark; a meal was . . . a piece of bread and . . . cheese and some milk or something—that would have been our supper."

Indeed, for all of the differences in their family backgrounds, nearly all servicemen shared the experience of economic hardship that had been part of life in the 1930s. Most had grown up in families that started out ranging from lower- to middle-class, but almost all experienced considerably harder times during the Depression. Asked to rank their standard of living during the 1920s, nonblack male respondents to the World War II Veterans Survey answered as follows: low, 15.1 percent; low-moderate, 25.1 percent; moderate, 40.5 percent; moderate-high, 8.1 percent; and high, 0.8 percent. For the 1930s, the same individuals ranked themselves as low, 26.7 percent; low-moderate, 34.8 percent; moderate, 32.6 percent; moderate-high, 4.5 percent; and high, 0.2 percent. A high proportion of respondents—44 percent—had a father who was unemployed and seeking work during the Depression years. Anthony Miller recalled that after his father lost his job working for the railroad, "he never again was able to do the kind of thing he worked all his life to do. He sold church candles . . . and pencils and calendars and things like that, for companies for advertising." Another indicator of economic hardship was that one-quarter of the veterans' mothers were employed outside the home at some point in their childhood, despite the fact that many interview subjects were quick to explain that this was not usual for women in that era. Many veterans—77 percent—had been employed themselves during their youth, often to help support their struggling families. They worked as soda jerks, newspaper delivery boys, telegram deliverers, farmhands, stock boys in grocery stores, caddies, and doing lawn care and gardening, picking crops, or shining shoes. Such employment often interfered with their ability to earn decent grades or even to complete high school, as Richard Werner explained.

As veterans' reminiscences attest, American society had a pyramid-shaped social structure in the early twentieth century.[29] The wealthy elite included the relatively small number of families who had prospered during the Gilded Age.[30] Most Americans belonged not to the middle class, as would become the case after World War II, but rather to a less advantaged working class. After standards of living plummeted during the Depression, the pursuit of higher education sounded like a lofty dream even for those who had been born into the middle class, and for those from less advantaged backgrounds, it remained entirely out of the question. These groups, combined, constituted the vast majority of men who would find themselves eligible for the provisions of the G.I. Bill after the war. Thus, although the bill's creators had focused on meeting the needs of veterans rather than on expanding educational access among the general population, the World War II military's composition would give the policy the potential to accomplish both ends among men, while leaving the majority of women beyond its reach.

The Cost of Deservingness

Sam Marchesi, who served in the Pacific, recalled being part of the battles in 1945 to retake the Philippines, which the Japanese had occupied at the same time as they attacked Pearl Harbor. "We invaded Manila and we were going right into the city . . . and the thing I remember was General MacArthur. . . . I could see this big car driving up the highway, no roof on it, it was just an open touring car. And there he was standing up thanking us—this was actual combat now—that man was so brave, he stood right up and nothing was going to kill him—he . . . told us not to be afraid, we were doing a wonderful job for him, and to carry on. I can still hear him saying it. We kept taking the city, the city was burning, God—I forget how many days and nights—they were just destroying it, burning it all down, as they were evacuating backwards."[31] As the troops made their way into the last Japanese stronghold, the Walled City, Marchesi was seriously wounded. He was later awarded the Purple Heart.

Like Marchesi, every veteran interviewed for this study shared some of his or her memories of military service. All of them—including those who had not been directly engaged in combat—considered themselves to be profoundly influenced by their experiences in the armed forces. In one survey question, respondents were asked to check off which events, out of a list of possible responses, they considered to be "turning points," in their own lives, defined as "events that shape the course of one's life in significant ways." Presented with a list that included "growing up during the Depression," "military service in World War II," "education," "job or career-related events or opportunities," and other options, 95 percent of the respondents checked military service as a turning point, far more than the proportion checking any other response. Next, respondents were asked to rank their choices in order of importance, starting with the most important turning point. Military service ranked first in importance among 37 percent of respondents, a greater proportion than any other response. It was this life-transforming experience that served as the basis on which veterans were deemed to be deserving of the benefits of the G.I. Bill. The manner in which they would respond to the law's provisions must be understood, then, in light of their military service and how they felt they had been affected by it.

Certainly all those who engaged in combat—though their experiences varied tremendously—were touched by the horrors, devastation, and losses of war.[32] And like Marchesi, men in each of the units surveyed for the World War II Veterans Survey did take part in combat (though, as noted previously, some of the other service members interviewed did not see combat). Those serving in the two U.S. Army Air Force groups became involved relatively early, when Americans came to the aid of the British and Russians in the air war. The 379th Bomb Group, based in Kimbolton, England, began bombing German U-boats off France in May 1943.[33] James Murray was one of the 182 members of the group who were captured by the Germans and became prisoners of war. The 783rd Bomb Squadron, based in Pantanella, Italy, flew B-24s to destroy key sites in Germany's aircraft industry and oil refineries, and strategic targets in other nations that Germany occupied.[34]

The 87th, 89th, and 92nd Infantry Divisions of the U.S. Army each arrived in Europe in the months following the June 1944 invasion of Normandy and quickly became involved in combat. Members of the 89th Infantry Division, like the 87th, joined the Third Army in Central Europe, taking villages across Germany as they pressed first toward the Moselle River and then toward the Rhine, and then advancing far to the east, near to the Russian front.[35] Joining the Fifth U.S. Army in the Mediterranean theater of operations, the 92nd Infantry Division, a unit composed entirely of black enlisted personnel, was one of the only such units permitted to engage in combat; it was based in Italy.[36]

Infantrymen found themselves assigned to the most perilous duties, and just as Gellert explained of becoming a rifleman, they had no choice in the matter. Harry Serulneck, who also served in the 87th Infantry Division, remembers when he received his assignment in the military. "I was headed to the latrine, and that's where they used to put up the awards, and there it was: 'Harry Serulneck, expert marksman machine gunner.' I said, 'Oh my God.' You know what the life of a machine gunner is? Two seconds. Once he opens up the gun, he's gone. They throw everything at him: hand grenades, artillery, mortar shells. You don't last long. That was my first award. Nobody wanted it; they gave it to me. That wasn't lucky for me!"

Even in the midst of the horror of war, soldiers sometimes found inspiration, as did Richard Werner, who never forgot his company's lieutenant in the 87th Infantry Division, Bert Haskins. "Of all the officers I met, he was the only one that *asked* instead of demanded. . . . He was on the front lines with us every minute. Others would be inside, would ride in the company jeep; he was always with his men. . . . [One] night . . . during the Battle of the Bulge . . . an order came from headquarters that he was to send a sergeant and ten men on patrol. He was doing the cooking for us, and I was bringing some dishes back [to him], and he said, 'I can't send anybody, after what they've been through today; I'll have to go.' And he led the patrol, and I guess for the second time in my army career, I volunteered. And the men thought so much of him. We were dog-tired, but everybody there volunteered. And if that wasn't a perfect tribute to him." Yet it was on that very mission that Werner was hit by fire and wounded.

Some soldiers witnessed firsthand the evils of Hitler's regime. In the midst of the Central European campaign, the 89th Division together with the Fourth Armored Division liberated Ohrdruf, a Nazi concentration camp. As the Americans approached on April 4, Hitler's officers attempted to dispose of an estimated nine thousand bodies of people who had died at the camp, forcing the surviving prisoners to exhume and cremate the bodies so that they could be buried in a pit. Abandoning the task as the troops neared, SS guards machine-gunned sixty-one prisoners who were too weak to leave on their own, and fled.[37] Richard Colosimo, who served in the 89th, remembers vividly what his division found there. He recalled meeting a pair of prisoners, clad in striped pajamas, who had managed to survive the slaughter in the courtyard moments earlier. "My buddy, who spoke Polish, asked them, 'How did you survive?'" The man explained that he had fallen before he was hit and then covered his head. "Now mind you, these men were extremely frail, very skeletal, they looked like walking dead. Of course, we gave them everything we had, chocolate bars, everything . . . And he [the man who had survived] said, 'I laid there and I covered up my face, and my heart was beating so loud, I'm surprised they didn't hear it. They picked up my arm'—he demonstrated—'and I didn't move, I just stayed there and they let it drop,' and he got away."

Yet while stories of open warfare and liberation provide the most memorable reflections on the war, they were actually exceptional among servicemen, given that fewer than one out of sixteen in World War II participated in extended combat, and even for them, it occupied but a small portion of their time in the service.[38] One-quarter of the armed forces served on the home front, never venturing overseas.[39] Of those who went abroad, most were engaged in supportive functions apart from the front lines.[40] They conducted the vast array of tasks involved in keeping the military functioning, such as preparing food; repairing engines, as Alphanse Antonowitz did for the 379th Bomb Group; or delivering mail, like Joe O'Leary, who recalled, "The guys would make a beeline to me to get the letters from home before they'd get in the line to eat."[41] Fewer than one million took part in extended combat.[42]

Nonetheless, even without direct engagement in combat, military service in World War II proved momentous in veterans' lives.[43] It occurred at a key juncture, as they matured from youths into adults, and it took them to places many had never heard of before, all over the world. Not least, it lasted for a long time, averaging between three and four years among survey respondents. Over that period, individuals experienced life in an institution that contrasted dramatically with what they had known as civilians.

The military was extremely hierarchical. Ross Flint described the friction during basic training between the officers, most of whom were career army men, and the new recruits, some of whom had just left the ASTP program on college campuses. "They gave us a hard time," he remembered. "They called us 'slide rule commandos.' They were men of the world, we were children. And it's true: I was eighteen." Similarly, Richard Colosimo said, "Sometimes you'd meet officers or noncoms that were difficult to get along with. Some of them would abuse their authority— not physically, but mentally." He recalled a particular officer who didn't like him, treated him unfairly, and made efforts to get him transferred to the infantry; such stories were common.

On occasion, soldiers perceived officers' use of power to be rooted in systematic prejudice. Isaac Gellert recalled the shock of experiencing anti-Semitism for the first time in his life, when in the military he encountered "people who hated me for no reason whatsoever . . . It was occasional, but often you could perceive it, just below the surface, and although there was a degree of civility there was also a feeling of alienness. There are instances that you never forget." Kermit Pransky "got busted" by a colonel who was known for his anti-Semitic attitude; he was demoted from staff sergeant to private first class. "It was heartbreaking because I did my job," he recalled. "I went up in rank pretty fast to become staff sergeant, and it fell by the wayside."

Racial prejudice was manifested not only in personal relationships but more fundamentally in the segregated structure of the military itself. Soldiers in the 92nd Infantry Division often felt that their white officers lacked confidence in them and failed to give decisive orders.[44] Neither were they afforded the recognition and honor bestowed on other units, despite the fact that they endured similarly heavy losses.[45]

For many veterans who had been in combat, military service exacted a heavy toll, the weight of which became apparent when they returned home and tried to readjust to civilian life. One-quarter of the nonblack male respondents to the World War II Veterans survey had been wounded, and nearly as many suffered from permanent physical disabilities, including problems as disparate as hypertension, hearing difficulties caused by wearing radio headsets aboard bomber flights, and a knee that was never the same after parachuting down to the ground. Several of the men interviewed from the 87th Infantry Division mentioned that they continued to suffer from trench foot, a condition similar to frostbite, caused by exposure of the feet to cold, wet conditions, that leads to swelling, infection, and possibly gangrene.[46] As Kermit

Pransky explained, "It's from getting wet feet and [having] no place to dry them; you can't go home and change your socks, being in the foxholes, in the water." The harsh weather during the Battle of the Bulge and throughout the winter made such experiences commonplace. Anthony Miller remembered, "[I] froze my feet on Christmas night." Trench foot can cause cellular damage and lead to pain that persists for a lifetime, as one veteran after another attested. Many interview subjects felt that the Veterans Administration never adequately recognized and compensated them for such problems, some of which only worsened with age.

Professionals and society generally remained ill-prepared to understand the emotional and psychological difficulties faced by returning servicemen. As veterans themselves explained, military service profoundly affected their outlook on life. Certainly it left some with a new and positive sense of purpose. Robert Forster noted, "It made me very philosophical. . . . When you do face death and you don't suffer the consequences, you feel that you're very fortunate, and that you need to make a lot out of your life, that you're able to have it." Many, however, endured great difficulties in grappling with what they had faced in the war. As Fred Windham assessed the effects of military service on his life, he commented, "I don't know [if it changed me], but everyone around me seems to think it did. I wasn't about to be pushed around anymore." Richard Werner recalled how he wrestled with considerable anxiety once he returned home. "In those days they didn't know what it was, but [today] you would call it post-traumatic stress syndrome. I weathered the war very well; it wasn't until after all the fighting stopped and [I] started thinking about people that didn't make it—then the nightmares started." He began college on the G.I. Bill but continued to struggle. "So my first two years in school were very, very difficult. I must have failed three or four subjects. . . . A teacher might be talking in class and I'd break out in a cold sweat. At least now they recognize it. In our day I felt that I was being weak. . . . I never associated anything with the war." Another veteran, dealing with similar difficulties, recalled that his drinking problem worsened after the war, eventually leading to his divorce.[47] Certainly such difficulties might be expected to interfere with veterans' capacity and inclination to be involved in civic life.

Still, even veterans who had been in ground combat typically viewed their military service as a necessary obligation, rather than as a burdensome responsibility. They explained that they felt a sense of duty to serve but were also glad to return to civilian life. "We did go through hell," remarked Harry Serulneck, "and we froze our feet. But when we were young we didn't think about those things, only about staying alive." Some felt that military service had closed off opportunities such as advanced education to them. Said O'Leary, "It took me right at the prime of a boy's life. The best time is between the ages of eighteen and twenty-three, and there I was: nineteen to twenty-two. That's when your mind is the sharpest and your body is the strongest." Yet, even with such qualifications, veterans refrained from characterizing military service as an undue burden. Even James Murray, who spent some time as a prisoner of war, summed up his military service by saying, "There was an esprit de corps; it was fun and adventurous."

Those who did not serve in combat units may have felt equally or even more positively about their military service. Luke LaPorta, whose naval unit never left the United States, termed it "absolutely a privilege ... Certainly, as I look back, I gained a hell of a lot more than I gave." And interview subjects from groups that enjoyed less status in society at that time also depicted their experiences positively. Said Henry Hervey, an African American with the Tuskegee Airmen, "I think it was a privilege to serve and we felt that it was going to give us some status above enlisted-man status, which was all we had known prior to the war." Ann Sharp felt similarly, explaining, "I would not trade those two years for anything, even though at that time, women were considered not very chaste if you went in the service. It was very much looked down on by a lot of people."

Furthermore, nearly every veteran, infantrymen included, believed that military service in World War II had some positive long-term effects on his or her life. Several emphasized the benefits of meeting and learning to work with a far more diverse group of people than they had known prior to enlisting. Isaac Gellert explained: "Even though I grew up in a large city, I led a very sheltered life. . . . The rough-and-tumble characters that one meets in the Army were not part of my experience growing up. . . . I met . . . people who were from all over the country, whose aspirations and outlook on life was very different than those I was accustomed to seeing and being with." Richard Colosimo recalled serving with a man who asked him to read aloud the letters he received because he couldn't read or write. "I met so many people. That was an education for me in itself."

Several veterans considered themselves to have matured through their time in the armed forces. John Mahoney felt that he gained leadership skills, and George Josten a sense of responsibility and ability to solve problems. Others believed that they developed better social skills. Anthony Miller noted, "In retrospect, it's probably one of the best things that ever happened to me. . . . My brothers were a lot older [than me] and I grew up kind of an only child. I was introverted. I had never been away from home, so it socialized me." Robert Forster concurred, "I think I developed quite a bit of self-esteem. I was very shy . . . but that experience brought me out a lot more and a lot more rapidly." Through such effects, military service transformed individuals in ways that readied them to be active members of society in peacetime, and poised to assume leadership roles.

The cost of deservingness for the G.I. Bill's generous provisions was substantial. All veterans—even those without injuries and without readjustment problems—found their lives permanently altered by their experiences in the military. Even those who remained far away from the front went through a long period, at a critical juncture in life, when they were not in charge of their own destiny, and when they were forced to comply with routines that diverged sharply from those of civilian life. And those who had been in combat were left with injuries, memories, and losses that would forever haunt them. At the same time, veterans generally appeared unresentful of what had been demanded of them, and they typically felt that military service had benefited them personally. Not least, the experience had socialized many veterans for more active citizenship in the postwar world; this readiness, once ignited by the experience of the education and training benefits of the G.I. Bill, would help spur their civic involvement.

A Citizen Soldier Returns Home

James Johnson, who served in I Company, 345th Regiment, 87th Infantry Division, spoke of his military service in a way that summed up the sentiments of many World War II veterans: "I wouldn't take a million dollars for my experiences, but I wouldn't give a penny for any more of them." Like most veterans, he had grown up in hard times, when opportunities were few, and the Army introduced him to a broader world. He came from a small town in South Carolina, where his father and grandfather ran a country store. Typically, customers were granted credit and paid their tab monthly, but during the Depression, many could no longer afford to pay what they owed. Johnson remembered seeing a man come into the store to buy his groceries, and another man turned to his father and said, "You better not let that man charge because he never will pay you." Johnson's father replied, "We can't see him starve, you know." As debts accumulated, however, the family lost the store, and they spent the Depression years moving from place to place, trying to make ends meet. "I was pretty depressed about it," he remembered. After completing high school, he found work in a federal government job, until he was drafted into the Army.

Johnson clearly recalled the wide-ranging travels of his tour of duty, which began with basic training in Mississippi. "Out in the boonies, sure enough!" he laughed. After more extensive training at several locations in the states, he and his unit shipped out on the *Queen Elizabeth,* landing in Scotland before being sent to England and then across the Channel to France and the front.

All told, Johnson spent three years in the military, predominantly in the rifle company. Like so many others, he commented on the value of "learning to get along with others, suffering the same as they did from the environment and the fatigues of battle. I'm just fortunate for my condition; some men couldn't stand it—I mean, they couldn't stand it physically or mentally." Though barely out of his teenage years, Johnson found himself advancing through the ranks to leadership roles. "With each platoon you have a platoon leader and a platoon sergeant and on down the line. Our platoon leader got wounded and was sent back and so did our platoon sergeant, so I had the platoon by myself for a big portion of the action." Time in the infantry took its toll: Johnson came down with jaundice and was hospitalized for a long time, both in Europe and after returning to the States.

When asked in the interview about his attitude toward his years of military service, James Johnson's voice broke and his eyes filled with tears. "It was a privilege for me to serve," he said, "because I love this country." He explained that traveling abroad in the service had given him a special appreciation for American citizenship. A good citizen, he noted, was someone who "stands up for his rights and serves his country," through both "volunteer work and military service."

After Johnson was discharged and came home, he used the G.I. Bill's vocational training benefits. While employed, he spent one year attending classes at night, after work. He raved about the bill, which enabled him to collect a subsistence allowance at the same time that he was earning a paycheck, and which helped him to advance in his job and later to switch to a second career. Like Johnson, the majority of other returning veterans found their transition to civilian life eased by use of the G.I. Bill's education and training benefits.

3

Beyond All Expectations

I doubt very many kids in my [high] school ever considered college," explained Richard Werner, "because in those days you had to be very well off to go. . . . And at the time, America was still in the web of the Depression, so I looked upon a college education [as] about as likely as my owning a Rolls-Royce with a chauffeur." Growing up far removed from such luxury, Werner knew about chauffeurs only because his father had been employed as one, and that was before the Depression hit; after he lost that job, the family had to move to a cold-water flat in Queens. Werner dreamed of attending college but doubted he would have the opportunity. The G.I. Bill made it possible.

Just as Werner had presumed it improbable that he could attend college, so too did most public officials consider it unlikely that many veterans would utilize the education and training provisions of the G.I. Bill. During the summer of 1943, before the bill's enactment, the Army surveyed white enlisted men about their postwar educational plans and found that only 7 percent of the troops expected to go back to school full time after being discharged, and an additional 17 percent anticipated continuing their schooling on a part-time basis.[1] Even after the highly publicized passage of the G.I. Bill, new surveys suggested that at most 8 to 12 percent of all veterans would choose to pursue education on a full-time basis. Government officials and educational leaders interpreted these results cautiously, suspecting that the actual percentage of veterans who would return to school would be even lower.[2] Early enrollment figures seemed to confirm administrators' expectations: by September 1945, fifteen months after the bill had been enacted, only fifteen thousand veterans had enrolled in colleges and universities.[3] *Saturday Evening Post* contributor Stanley Frank proclaimed the G.I. Bill a failure, declaring, "It is a splendid bill, a wonderful bill, with only one conspicuous drawback. The guys aren't buying it. They say 'education' means 'books,' any way you slice it, and that's for somebody else."[4]

Yet within a year, the pace of veterans' enrollment began to climb exponentially, as more veterans were discharged and understanding of the opportunities offered by the bill spread. Government officials quickly changed their message, alerting the nation that a "flood of students" would soon overwhelm educational institutions.[5] Even their revised expectations drastically underestimated G.I. Bill usage. Ultimately, more than twice as many veterans used the higher education provisions than the most daring predictions officials had forecast, and more than twenty times as many attended vocational training schools than anticipated. By 1947, the number of veterans enrolled in colleges swiftly escalated over the one million mark, up from just two hundred thousand the year before, and accounting for 49 percent of enrolled students; by 1949, over two million veterans had used the G.I. Bill to pursue higher education.[6] Meanwhile, more than two and a half million veterans enrolled in schools below the college level, and their numbers continued to soar.[7] Among the eight thousand schools approved by the government to provide such training, fifty-six hundred opened their doors just after the enactment of the G.I. Bill.[8] By the time World War II veterans' eligibility period for G.I. Bill use ended, a stunning total of 7.8 million veterans—fully 51 percent of all who had served in the military—had attended school or obtained training on the G.I. Bill. Among them, 2.2 million veterans attended colleges and universities, and 5.6 million pursued vocational training, on-the-job training, or other subcollege education.[9]

Certainly the impressive rates at which veterans took advantage of the education and training benefits owe in part to their inclusive design.[10] To be eligible, a veteran needed only to have a discharge status other than dishonorable and to have served for at least ninety days of active duty, a requirement that could be waived in the case of a service-incurred disability.[11] In 1945, responding to pressure from the public and veterans' organizations, Congress further liberalized the provisions, eliminating an age requirement that would have put usage off-limits to older veterans.[12] Veterans could use the benefits to attend any college, university, or approved subcollege program to which they could gain admission.

To what extent did this program, for which usage so surpassed expectations, actually expand veterans' access to advanced education and training, enabling them to further their schooling regardless of their socioeconomic background and other aspects of status? Conversely, did it, as critics charge, actually perpetuate or even exacerbate divisions of class, race, and other forms of privilege among American citizens?[13] The answers to these questions are essential to understanding how the G.I. Bill influenced civic engagement. If the law reached only those who would have been educated anyway, then it likely did little to expand the scope of participation in American democracy. Conversely, if it did widen access to education and training, veterans' perceptions about those effects may help illuminate why they felt inclined to become such active citizens later.

Reopening the Question

Scholars seeking to explain whether the G.I. Bill broadened access to education draw frequently on a study of college students conducted in 1946–47 that asked veterans to evaluate whether they would have furthered their education without the aid of the G.I. Bill.[14] The Frederiksen-Schrader survey, as it is known, which was administered by the Educational Testing Service to students at sixteen universities, found that 20 percent of veterans in college reported that they probably or definitely would not have attended college if they had not had the financial aid provided by the veterans' benefits.[15] This result, which implies that the G.I. Bill increased educational opportunities among one-fifth of the group, is typically presented as clear evidence that the policy did little to expand access to education.

Yet, for several reasons, we should be skeptical about overemphasis on the results of the Frederiksen-Schrader survey. The survey was created for aims other than evaluating G.I. Bill usage, and several limitations render it insufficient for that purpose.[16] There is no indication that the institutions surveyed were representative of the full array of institutions of higher education that veterans attended.[17] Nor do the authors assess how well the respondents mirrored the broader universe of students in programs of higher education under the G.I. Bill, and it appears likely that they may have oversampled better-off veterans.[18] The much-publicized findings rely on answers to one generally worded survey question and do not shed light on nuances that may lie beneath veterans' responses.[19] And those responses reveal only veterans' perceptions, with no gauge of their objective circumstances. Most problematic, the study included none of the subcollege programs, those through which the majority of G.I. Bill beneficiaries used their benefits, and thus it tells us nothing about the extent to which that group of programs broadened veterans' opportunities.

Even if we could overlook these problems and assume that Frederiksen and Schrader's finding does offer an accurate estimate of how the higher education provisions affected the general population, still it makes little sense to interpret such results as evidence of only modest effects. To have made college attendance possible for one out of five veterans who enrolled, or one out of ten college students at that time, is actually quite an impressive record; that 440,000 out of the 2.2 million veterans who pursued higher education could not have done so if the G.I. Bill had not existed offers verification of its redistributive effects, not the reverse. Indeed, Frederiksen and Schrader perceived their findings as indicating the effectiveness of financial aid, through which "a substantial pool of academic talent could be tapped by lowering economic barriers to education."[20] It is difficult to think of other social programs that have made such a marked difference in the lives of so many. Today, for example, the Pell grant program, the chief U.S. higher education program that assists students from less advantaged backgrounds, reaches 22 percent of all college students but finances only 40 percent of each student's costs for tuition, room, and board at the average public four-year institution and only 15 percent of those costs at the average private four-year institution.[21] The G.I. Bill, by contrast, covered outright the cost of tuition at any institution and lent considerable assistance with other living costs, making it far more possible for students from less advantaged backgrounds to enroll in college and to complete their degrees.

Veterans' Perceptions

The World War II Veterans Survey of 1998, conducted for this project, draws on a representative sample of nonblack male veterans and allows us to examine questions about veterans' usage of both the higher education benefits and the subcollege programs.[22] In assessing whether the G.I. Bill expanded access to education or training, we will begin by considering veterans' own perceptions of the matter, and then proceed to more rigorous means of measuring the G.I. Bill's actual impact. We draw on several survey questions that probed beneficiaries' beliefs about whether they would have attained the same education or training in the absence of the G.I. Bill.

First, veterans were asked the extent to which they agreed with the statement "If the G.I. Bill or Public Law 16 had not existed, I could not have afforded the education or job training that I acquired after military service";[23] they could indicate responses on a four-point scale, from "strongly disagree" to "strongly agree."[24] As shown in Figure 3.1, among

Figure 3.1. Level of Agreement Among Nonblack Male G.I. Bill Users: Could Not Have Afforded Education/Training Without G.I. Bill

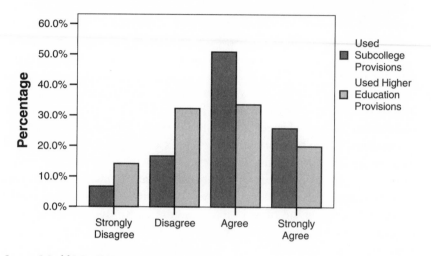

Source: World War II Veterans Survey, 1998

nonblack male higher education beneficiaries, more than half—54 percent—felt that the G.I. Bill made college accessible to them, with 20 percent of veterans strongly agreeing and 34 percent agreeing.[25] While it is possible that individuals might have answered such questions differently when this study was conducted than they would have fifty years previously, interview subjects responded very thoughtfully and carefully. Some who grew up in middle-class homes replied as George Josten did: "Well, let me put it this way. I would have gotten a college education without the G.I. Bill, whatever it would have cost. I would somehow have paid for it, whether I committed myself to a job for several years after, or a loan, or something, because I was going to get that education." But those who had grown up fairly poor were more likely to respond as Richard Werner did in his quote at the beginning of this chapter, indicating that they perceived it as highly unlikely.

Even more striking, among survey respondents who used the G.I. Bill for vocational training, 77 percent concurred that they could not have afforded such training in the absence of the program: 26 percent strongly agreed and 51 percent agreed. Jerome Dribin, who used the benefits to acquire training as a television repairman, answered, "Definitely not. I couldn't afford it. I was only working part time. We were married and had a child. I had to quit a job working for my uncle at a machine shop to go back to TV school."

When asked how they viewed the statement "If the G.I. Bill or Public Law 16 had not existed, I would not have considered acquiring education or job training after military service," those who attended college on the G.I. Bill took a more skeptical view. In this case, only 23 percent agreed or strongly agreed, as seen in Figure 3.2. Yet, while this explanation was less typical, it is still impressive to consider that for a not insignificant proportion of beneficiaries, the G.I. Bill's existence presented them with an option that they never even would have imagined previously. Luke LaPorta was certain that he would not have attended college had the G.I. Bill not existed, "for a lot of reasons: I didn't think I had the brainpower, I didn't have the money." He explained that military service itself had made him acquire a sense of "self-worth," which made him more open to the possibility of advanced education once it arose. James Murray, similarly, had served in the Air Force with college-educated men and had begun for the first time to imagine pursuing more education himself. After coming home from the war, however, he returned to his former job at a steel mill in his hometown in Pennsylvania, where he expects he would have continued working if his wife had not encouraged him to use the benefits to attend Penn State. "If someone had pushed me, I probably could have gone to night school, but I don't think I would have had the incentive," he explained. "The G.I. Bill opened the door. It

Figure 3.2. Level of Agreement Among Nonblack Male G.I. Bill Users: Would Not Have Considered Education/Training Without G.I. Bill

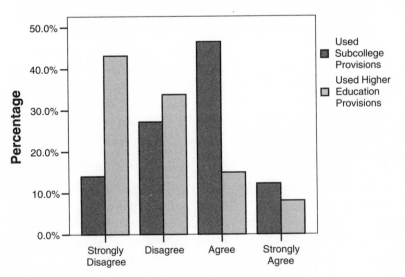

Source: World War II Veterans Survey, 1998

was there, 'take advantage of it,' as my wife said." Interestingly, users of the vocational provisions were much more likely to agree that they would not have considered further training in the G.I. Bill's absence: 12 percent strongly agreed and 47 percent agreed. As we will see in the next chapter, the G.I. Bill actually prompted the creation of the majority of the vocational schools and on-the-job training programs that served veterans; most simply had not existed previously.

A high proportion of program beneficiaries felt that they would have acquired education or training even without the G.I. Bill, but under different circumstances. Fully 75 percent of college-goers and 69 percent of subcollege users agreed or strongly agreed that it would have taken them longer. As several veterans explained in the interviews, had the G.I. Bill not existed, they would have had to attend night school or to have gone to school part time so that they could work a regular job and provide for their dependents. John Mink imagined that he would have gone on to college, but "it would have been under very strange circumstances, I'm sure. We were not aware, in our small town, of scholarships or that sort of thing. There's just no information that was passed on. They didn't have such things as counselors. So we had no knowledge of what could have been available." Of course, this raises the question of how changed circumstances might have affected actual degree completion rates; we can only speculate that in the absence of the program, many of those who would have had to pursue education on a part-time basis instead likely would never have finished. Furthermore, 59 percent of higher education users and 64 percent of subcollege users agreed or strongly agreed that while they could have obtained education or training without the G.I. Bill, they would have to have done so in a program "of lesser cost, quality, or reputation." Some interview subjects noted that because the G.I. Bill paid for tuition at any institution to which they were accepted, they were able to attend a university that was more expensive and prestigious than they ever would have considered. For example, Isaac Gellert grew up in a middle-class home that fell on hard times during the Depression, when his father struggled to keep his small business afloat and subsequently died prematurely. He explained, "I had the opportunity to go to Columbia University for the simple reason that the G.I. Bill paid everything. I probably would have—in the absence of any financial support—gone off to City College. But Columbia was essentially free; the G.I. Bill paid for most of my expenses. The support lasted even into graduate school: the first year [toward his doctorate] at Harvard was paid for by the G.I. Bill."

This evidence suggests that the G.I. Bill may have played a more powerful role in broadening access to education and training than previously thought. Perhaps more important, it reveals that the majority of veterans who used the Bill themselves believed that the benefits helped make education or training accessible and affordable to them. Later we will explore whether veterans' own interpretations of the policy's effectiveness might have influenced their inclination to be involved in public life.

We still need to consider why nearly half of all World War II veterans, 49 percent, did not use the G.I. Bill. Among nonblack male respondents to the World War II Veterans Survey of 1998, the most common reason, cited by 51 percent of nonusers, is that they "preferred work to school." Less common reasons included "lack of money to be a student," mentioned by 25 percent of nonusers; "had not decided what to do next," noted by 19 percent; "had all the education or training I needed," 12 percent; and "other," 16 percent.[26] Those citing "lack of money to be a student" were likely those who already had a responsibility to support others, such as wives, children, and in some cases infirm parents. Similarly, among those who checked "other," the majority wrote in that they were married and had children—some noting as many as three or four children already—and thus could not afford to return to school.[27] The possibility exists that some form of bias may underlie these explanations—for instance, that nonusage, especially when attributed to reasons such as "preferred to work," actually meant that such individuals came from less advantaged socioeconomic backgrounds and program usage was not a meaningful option for them. In order to assess whether a class bias underlay G.I. Bill usage, we turn to more objective means of assessing whether provisions were broadly accessible.

Privileging the Privileged?

Rather than relying solely on veterans' perceptions of how the G.I. Bill affected their opportunities to pursue education or training, we can consider their program usage in light of their socioeconomic background in childhood. First, we can examine the veterans' rates of usage by their family's standard of living in the 1920s, as shown in Figure 3.3.[28]

The bars indicate the percentage of veterans with various standards of living who used the G.I. Bill for either higher education or any of the subcollege programs. Not surprisingly, usage rates were greatest among those with the highest standard of living in childhood, among whom 83 percent received education at government expense. But this point should not obscure the fact that usage was also remarkably high among veterans who had a lower standard of living as children. Even among veter-

Figure 3.3. Rates of G.I. Bill Usage and Nonusage Among Nonblack Male Veterans by Standard of Living in Childhood

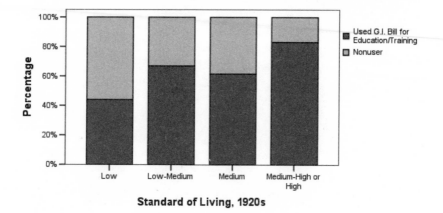

Source: World War II Veterans Survey, 1998

ans from the poorest backgrounds, 44 percent used the benefits; usage levels surpassed 60 percent at both the low-medium and medium levels.[29] In terms of sheer numbers, the majority of veterans—including 90 percent of survey respondents—came from low- and moderate-income strata rather than from the most privileged group, such that the bulk of the benefits served a redistributive function.

Figure 3.4 illustrates how veterans' perceptions of the difference the G.I. Bill made in their lives related to their childhood socioeconomic circumstances. The lower a veteran's standard of living in the 1920s, the greater the likelihood that he agreed or strongly agreed that he could not have afforded the education or job training acquired after military service had the G.I. Bill not existed. This was the case among the majority of beneficiaries who had a low or low-medium standard of living in childhood, who concurred at rates of 67 percent and 58 percent, respectively. For such individuals, the availability of the G.I. Bill provided opportunities that simply would not have been available without it.

It is possible, however, that many other influences also played a role in determining whether individuals used the program or not. We need to be able to account for the impact of factors widely regarded to be the chief determinants of whether individuals pursue advanced education, including socialization in childhood (that is, having been encouraged to pursue an education while growing up) and various socioeconomic factors.[30] Only on this basis can we assess the extent to which usage of the

Figure 3.4. Nonblack Male Veterans' Views Regarding Whether They Could Have Afforded Education/Training Without the G.I. Bill, by Childhood Standard of Living

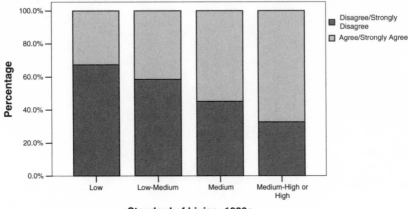

Source: World War II Veterans Survey, 1998

G.I. Bill's education and training provisions proved genuinely accessible to veterans regardless of their class background.[31]

Considering nine different factors that could have been expected to have some bearing on whether veterans used the higher education provisions, three emerge as highly significant.[32] First, a veteran's level of education prior to military service influenced program usage; not surprisingly, those who already had higher levels of education were best positioned and likely most inclined to acquire yet more education. Second, socialization in childhood also mattered, as those who had been strongly encouraged to pursue advanced education proved more likely to use the benefits. Again, this is to be expected, both intuitively and as shown in studies.[33] Third, age made a difference: younger veterans were far more likely to use the provisions. As many noted in the interviews, the war interfered with the normal course of their lives, and once they returned home, some—especially those who were already married and had children, who tended to be older—were more likely to feel that the opportunity to pursue additional education had passed them by.

Two socioeconomic factors, standard of living in childhood and parents' level of education, proved to have only a mild effect on which veterans used the G.I. Bill for higher education, much less so than the aforementioned variables. Because the G.I. Bill did aid some veterans who had already begun college at their own expense before the war and who returned to finish their studies, it is not surprising that these factors would be of at least modest significance; they were, after all, the chief determinants of attending college in the era prior to the war.[34] What is most striking, however, is that among influences on G.I. Bill usage for higher education, these indicators of privilege pale in significance next to those discussed above.[35]

When the same type of analysis is applied to usage of the G.I. Bill for subcollege education or training, fewer patterns emerge.[36] A veteran's level of education prior to military service did play a significant role, but through the reverse of the relationship it bore to higher education program usage: veterans with less education before military service were especially likely to use the subcollege programs, with the average beneficiary having not quite completed high school.[37] Vocational education users tended to have parents who were less well educated, though this explained less of the variation between users and nonusers than did their own level of education before joining the military. None of the other factors—including age, socialization, and standard of living in childhood—bore a significant relationship to vocational training usage. This means, in short, that the vocational training programs attracted a diverse array of veterans whose only common characteristic was that they had acquired less formal education than others before they entered military service.

An appropriately skeptical reader might wonder whether some of the factors that have emerged as highly influential in determining G.I. Bill usage might themselves be strongly related to veterans' socioeconomic backgrounds. We might ask, for example, whether those veterans who attained more education prior to military service were able to do so precisely because they spent their childhoods in more privileged families.[38] As it turns out, the prominent indicators of G.I. Bill usage for higher education are not strongly associated with socioeconomic factors, and thus they are unlikely to be reducible to them.[39]

In fact, secondary school enrollment and high school graduation rates rose dramatically in the United States during the early twentieth century. These trends, which were most pronounced in nonsouthern states with greater wealth and less economic disparity, help explain why veterans' educational attainment prior to military service was not strongly biased by their socioeconomic status in childhood. Ironically, the Great Depression sharply boosted high school graduation rates by eliminating many of the jobs teenage males otherwise would have filled, leaving them nothing to do but attend school.[40] Therefore, many of those who enlisted, regardless of their standard of living during childhood, had attained or nearly completed high school degrees.

Neither did the experience of having been encouraged during childhood to pursue advanced education correspond closely to having grown up in a more privileged home. Survey participants' responses showed that families across the socioeconomic spectrum encouraged children to seek an education. Veterans who grew up in the most well-to-do families were, as we would expect, most likely to be encouraged to pursue education: 85 percent reported that they had been encouraged or strongly encouraged to do so. Yet majorities of veterans from less advantaged backgrounds also received such encouragement: 76 percent of those from the medium level, 66 percent from the low-medium level, and 53 percent from the lowest level.[41] The socialization factor, therefore, cannot be reduced to or identified exclusively with measures of economic well-being.

Several interview respondents who had used the G.I. Bill raised this point themselves, noting that while they had grown up very poor, a parent or other mentor had encouraged them to obtain as much education as possible. As Richard Colosimo put it, "I would have made every effort to [go to college] because that is one of the things my father instilled [in] me.... My father said, 'Dick, I don't know how I can ever help you, but *get an education*—that's the most important thing.' That was the cry of those immigrants at that time. They tried to instill the educational aspect in their children because they didn't have the opportunity and they were all working as domestics or laborers. They didn't want their children to do that." Similarly, John Mulravey, who grew up in a working-class family, said "My mother was so determined that we go to college." Showing the height of a small child with his hand, he added, "I knew that [I would go to college] from this big." Conversely, even some who had grown up in middle-class homes felt they had not been encouraged to pursue education. John Towey's father had left high school one year short of graduating but nonetheless had a good job as wire chief for New England Telephone Company, not an unusual outcome in a period when occupational status was much less closely tied to educational level than now. In explaining why he had not used the G.I. Bill, Towey said, "You see, I didn't have that pressure or push from my family because none of them had any thought to do that.... In fact, I couldn't even tell you if there was any particular college I wanted to go to. I just know I was sorry afterwards because I didn't go to college." Another veteran, who grew up quite poor, felt that his family put little emphasis on education when he was young, and pressured him to help his father, an aspiring small-business owner, rather than use the G.I. Bill to further his education.

All told, the higher education provisions of the G.I. Bill proved relatively accessible to nonblack male veterans, and their usage was influenced only slightly by their economic backgrounds. Because it did not make eligibility contingent on financial need, the G.I. Bill financed the college tuition of some veterans who came from higher socioeconomic levels, had more educated parents, and could have paid their own way. At the same time, for numerous middle-class veterans, the G.I. Bill offered the opportunity to pursue college under better circumstances—full time, or at more expensive institutions—than would have been possible otherwise. And most impressive, the program truly opened the doors to higher education for many from the lower and lower middle classes. Meanwhile, the G.I. Bill's vocational training provisions featured especially broad accessibility, being utilized by veterans regardless of socioeconomic background, socialization, age, or other demographic factors. Those who had less prior education embraced such subcollege programs at a ratio of two-and-a-half to one over those who enrolled in institutions of higher education.

Opening Doors

Prior to the war, many colleges and universities adhered to practices, both official and unofficial, that restricted admission on religious grounds. Following the waves of immigration at the turn of the century, the proportion of Jews at Ivy League universities increased rapidly. University officials, fearing that their schools would fail to attract their traditional clientele—the sons of wealthy, native-born white Protestants—adopted quota systems aimed at limiting the enrollment of Jewish students. Relatively few Catholics numbered among college students nationwide, predominantly because of their class background: they were more likely to have grown up with a lower standard of living and thus were far less likely to be able to afford advanced education.[42]

Through the G.I. Bill, both Jewish and Catholic veterans gained greater access to higher education.[43] Through its class inclusivity, the program expanded the reach of higher education to Catholics, as well as to lower-status white Protestants.[44] Educational institutions also opened their doors to Jewish veterans through a relaxing or dismantling of quota rules, as we will see in Chapter 4. In fact, among nonblack male G.I. Bill beneficiaries who responded to the World War II Veterans Survey, college attendance was especially high among the Jewish G.I. Bill beneficiaries, followed by Protestants and then by Catholic users.[45]

Among the veterans interviewed for this study was Anthony Miller, a Catholic priest. He felt that if the G.I. Bill had not existed, he "would have kept working for the insurance company" that employed him prior to the war, and he would not have attained the college degree that led him to the seminary. "I think the two most influential moments in the

American Catholic Church," he commented, "were the second Vatican Council [and] also the G.I. Bill." By extending higher education to many veterans, he reasoned, the G.I. Bill helped stimulate Catholic intellectual life, which had previously been limited to priests and nuns. A careful study in the late 1960s found that after the end of World War II, the long-established gap between the college education rates of Protestants and Catholics disappeared among young adults.[46] Among veterans, the G.I. Bill appears to have played a role in facilitating this greater social inclusion.

Prior to the war, the ranks of higher education had also been dominated by those who descended from old-stock native-born Americans. By contrast, among nonblack male respondents to the World War II Veterans Survey, 31 percent had at least one parent born outside of the United States. Strikingly, G.I. Bill usage patterns differed little between such individuals and veterans with two native-born parents: majorities of both groups used the benefits,[47] and they were as likely to use the higher education benefits as the subcollege benefits.

The bill's benefits were also relatively accessible to veterans regardless of the type of community they were from. While suburbanites were most likely to use the provisions, with 74 percent doing so, even among those who had grown up in the country who were least likely to use them, 48 percent did so. Majorities of those from all other locales—including small towns, farms, medium-sized towns, and cities—utilized the benefits. In the interviews, one male veteran after another related that without access to the G.I. Bill, he would have returned to the farm, mining town, or small village in which he had grown up. The G.I. Bill made new opportunities nearly as accessible to veterans from such provincial backgrounds as it did for those from more populous areas.[48]

Across the Color Line

Comprehensive information has been especially lacking about the extent to which the G.I. Bill's benefits reached African American service members.[49] In the absence of such data, black veterans' access to the education and training provisions has been heavily disputed. Some have argued that the bill played a significant role in fostering the development of a black middle class.[50] Others contend that African Americans' use of the provisions was thwarted by such formidable obstacles as persistent segregation at universities across the nation and overcrowding in historically black colleges.[51] Both of these contradictory claims rely primarily on anecdotal evidence and leave unanswered the question of black veterans' program usage.[52]

In considering the racial inclusivity of the G.I. Bill's education and training benefits, it is important to recall, as noted in Chapter 2, that African Americans were somewhat underrepresented in the military during World War II. The bounds of eligibility for G.I. Bill benefits could be no broader than the military selection process itself had been. Within those parameters, we utilize recently located evidence to assess whether usage of the education and training provisions was as commonplace among black veterans as it was among whites.

"Every black we knew used the G.I. Bill," said Celeste Torian, whose husband served in the 92nd Infantry Division and later used the G.I. Bill to finance his college education.[53] Indeed, a survey conducted nationwide by the Veterans Administration in 1950 verifies that higher proportions of nonwhites than whites used the education and training benefits.[54] As shown in Figure 3.5, nationwide, 49 percent of nonwhite veterans (640,920 out of 1,308,000) had used the benefits by 1950, compared to 43 percent of white veterans. Rates were especially high in the South, where 51 percent of all veterans had begun some type of education or training by 1950. Strikingly, nonwhite southern veterans' usage of the provisions surpassed that of white veterans in the region, at 56 percent compared to 50 percent. Similarly, in the West, 46 percent of

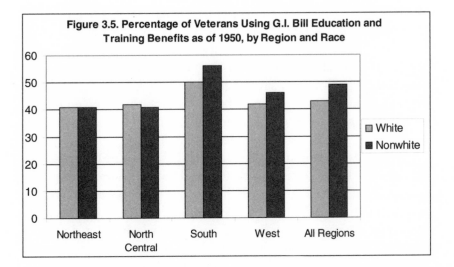

Figure 3.5. Percentage of Veterans Using G.I. Bill Education and Training Benefits as of 1950, by Region and Race

Source: Veterans Administration, Research Division, Coordination Services, "Benefits and Services Received by World War II Veterans Under the Major Veterans Administration Programs," Records of Office of Management and Budget (RG 51), ser. 39.20a, box 9, National Archives, Washington, D.C., 27. Data show total usage rates as of August 1950, when the survey was conducted.

nonwhite veterans went to school on the G.I. Bill, compared to 42 percent of white veterans.[55]

Importantly, African American veterans had less education than whites prior to military service and thus were less likely to use the G.I. Bill to attend college, but they were also more likely to utilize its subcollege benefits. Among the Army troops in World War II, only 17 percent of black soldiers had graduated from high school, compared to 41 percent of white soldiers.[56] Hence, among veterans born from 1923 to 1928, only 12 percent of black G.I. Bill users pursued higher education, compared to 28 percent of whites.[57] Of the subcollege programs, blacks were particularly likely to utilize the vocational training benefits and the opportunity to complete high school.[58]

What factors influenced individual black veterans' ability to utilize the G.I. Bill's education and training benefits? Interestingly, evidence from the 92nd Infantry Division suggests that the only significant determinant of program usage was their parents' level of education: those with more highly educated parents were especially likely to take advantage of the G.I. Bill.[59] It is likely that veterans' parents' educational level had important implications for both their well-being and their expectations while growing up, influencing their capacity and predisposition to acquire more education if they had the opportunity to do so. As we have seen, nonblack veterans' G.I. Bill usage was qualified by a wider array of personal factors, such as age and prior level of education. African American veterans, by contrast, appear not to have let those obstacles stand in their way: they seized the opportunity to acquire more education regardless of how old they were and how much schooling they had had previously. Notably, black survey respondents were more than twice as likely as nonblack respondents to report that they had grown up poor; nonetheless, just as in the case of nonblack veterans, standard of living in childhood did not determine their program usage.

African Americans in the 92nd Infantry Division were far more likely than white veterans to report that they had been encouraged to pursue an education: 55 percent reported that family members strongly encouraged them, compared to 31 percent of white veterans. As one black veteran explained in an interview, at midcentury "education [was] the number one project in the South in the black community. I mean, if you [had] any possibility of going to college, you [were] going to take it." African American veterans were deeply committed to acquiring more education if they had the chance; the G.I. Bill was the means that made it possible for many to act on those inclinations, and they seized the opportunity.

Even as racial segregation persisted in the United States, therefore, the G.I. Bill gave African Americans greater opportunities to acquire education and training than they had ever known. The question of which institutions black veterans were able to attend and how they were treated within them will be addressed in Chapter 4. Apparent here is that black veterans ignored the kinds of personal obstacles that discouraged many white veterans from seeking further education. Although they were less well positioned than white veterans to pursue higher education, black veterans who were prepared for college seized the chance to attend, and others took advantage of the subcollege programs at greater rates than white veterans.

A Magnanimous Law

Richard Colosimo, who served in the 89th Infantry Division, explained, "I'm a child of the Depression. We had a very poor life. . . . [My] father and mother . . . both worked hard. We didn't have all the meals during the day you were supposed to have." When the economy soured, Colosimo's father lost his job. "His brother (my uncle) had a tailor shop, and my dad would help him occasionally, but there certainly wasn't enough business for two families to be supported," he explained. Colosimo had grown up in Pittsburgh, in a neighborhood full of children. "We played a lot of ball. It was a way out in the Depression: you played ball or you went to sleep so that you weren't hungry."

Upon returning from the war, Colosimo felt that he wanted to "further all this knowledge I had gained" through his military experience. Looking for a school to attend, he heard about the American Television Institute, a vocational training school in Chicago. He thought, "Well, television is a coming thing," and decided to use his G.I. Bill benefits and enroll. After several months, though, he decided that he wanted more than a technical certificate, and matriculated at the University of Illinois at Navy Pier. Then Colette, the woman he had fallen in love with in France during the war, came to the United States, and they were married. They moved to Colosimo's hometown of Pittsburgh, and he transferred to the University of Pittsburgh. There, he earned his bachelor's degree on the G.I. Bill, while the program's subsistence allowance helped them pay for their apartment.

Colosimo's experience attests to the inclusivity of the G.I. Bill, not only for veterans such as himself who came from less privileged backgrounds, but also for those who belonged to ethnic, racial, and religious groups that had previously had little hope of such opportunities for education and training. Colosimo felt that for members of his generation, so many of whom had grown up poor, the G.I. Bill provided "a way out . . . a route to go . . . an opportunity. I think anybody that didn't take advantage of it missed on an opportunity, because it was rather magnanimous." His opinion of the value and generosity of the benefits exemplified the views of many others, who felt that the program had significantly improved the options available to them and treated them as honored citizens. They carried these impressions with them into the postwar era.

4

Conveying Messages

Describing the actual delivery of the G.I. Bill's education and training benefits, Richard Colosimo said, "It was quite simple, actually. If you went to the Veterans Administration and said, 'I want to go to school,' they said, 'Go to your school and make application and refer that application to the [local branch office of the] Veterans Administration—they will then set it up.'" Colosimo praised the VA as "diligent" in administering the program. "When I was in Chicago, going to the University of Illinois, I was living in a rooming house [where] they would take your mail and just put it on the table. Someone got my check from the school, my G.I. Bill check, and cashed it. [When] I reported it stolen, [the VA] gave me another one. They subsequently wrote me a letter that they did find the check and it was an obvious forgery." Such experiences of responsiveness from the government in a public program impressed Colosimo. "For me, [the G.I. Bill] was ideal. They made it easy for you. You could go to trade schools, barber schools, any kind of schools."

Like Colosimo, veterans typically found the G.I. Bill's benefits to be readily accessible and smoothly administered. Program implementation conveyed to them powerful messages not only about the value of one particular program but also, more broadly, about government's responsiveness to people like them. Their experience of the G.I. Bill functioned as a microcosm of their relationship to government: from it, they derived crucial lessons about the role of government generally and about their own worth as citizens in the polity. This suggests that the way in which government implements social programs can have a direct effect on the kind of citizens it produces.

Implementation and Citizenship

Among political scientists, policy implementation is regarded as an inherently political process, one involving different players than policy creation but equally consequential.[1] In making such claims, however, scholars usually overlook how citizens themselves participate in and are affected by the implementation process. They tend to focus on organizational arrangements and political actors, from agency heads all the way down to "street-level bureaucrats," who cleave to their own institutional imperatives and standard operating procedures, even when charged with administering a very different program than in the past.[2]

Citizens themselves appear only in oblique references to "clients" or "beneficiaries," if at all.[3] Certainly these accounts take note of such facts as the number of individuals who benefit from a government program, the duration of benefits for the average user, and the cost of benefits. But while the value of resources provided by goods and services is important to citizens—and is the primary focus of Chapters 3 and 5 in this book—so too are the signals citizens receive from the manner in which they are treated through the rules and procedures that characterize implementation.

During policy implementation, citizens receive important political messages from a program's ease of use, or lack thereof; from the process of qualifying for benefits; from the extent to which they feel privileged versus scrutinized; and from whether the procedures appear to be routinely applied to all citizens or applied differently to some. These encounters may tell them a great deal about whether government is legitimate, how well it functions, how people like them are regarded in the political community, what their rights are, and what their obligations are. Such interpretive messages may shape citizens' support for government, their inclination to be engaged in civic life, and their subsequent participation in public affairs. Indeed, without analysis of such effects, public officials may miss some of the most important effects of public programs or may incorrectly identify policy success or failure.

Expanding the Scope

"We weren't surprised to find bugs in our G.I. Bill of Rights," wrote an American Legion staffer just thirteen months after the law's passage, referring to veterans' complaints about a few restrictive features of the law. "They appear no matter how sturdy the tree. But they have to be wiped out, before they can multiply and cause real trouble. The American Legion, after carefully observing the G.I. Bill of Rights in action, has gone right to work on the bug-hunt."[4] At its national convention in September 1944, the American Legion resolved to promote "prompt and sympathetic administration" of the law, "with red tape eliminated."[5] National commander Edward N. Scheiberling commissioned a nationwide survey of the bill's operations, to be conducted by Legion officials nationwide who were "in daily contact with the returning veterans [and] know their hopes, their fears, their problems and their needs," and who were thus well positioned to ask them "how the G.I. Bill is actually working."[6] Three Legion committees studied the bill's implementation, and by April 1945—before Germany had surrendered and while war still raged in the Pacific—the organization called upon Congress to pass the amendments that liberalized various features of the law.

Based on what veterans who sought to use the education and training provisions were experiencing, the American Legion proposed—and quickly obtained—several changes in them. First, it called for dropping the age restriction that deemed veterans eligible only if they were under twenty-five years of age, on the presumption that their education had been delayed or interrupted by war. Second, the Legion demanded higher subsistence allowances, noting that its national survey had revealed the benefits to be inadequate.[7] In amendments enacted in December 1945, Congress not only met these requests but also stretched the bill's coverage further by extending the period for initiating education or training from two years after discharge to four years, and lengthening the maximum period during which such benefits could be used from seven years after the war to nine years. Policy makers raised the level of subsistence allowances for both single veterans and those with dependents, and included provisions to permit veterans to attain G.I. Bill coverage for short-term courses and correspondence courses, neither of which had been covered by the initial law.[8]

Various factors made Congress willing to enact such major alterations in the G.I. Bill only eighteen months after it was enacted. Though planning committees in the Roosevelt administration had wished for a slow and orderly demobilization, unanticipated events dictated otherwise. The war ended in both Europe and the Pacific within a period of less than four months. Between V-J Day in August 1945 and the end of that year, 5.4 million service members were discharged, twice as many as officials had expected to be released within the entire year.[9] By November, only three out of five veterans in the labor force had found a job.[10] Thus, Members of Congress, concerned about economic stability and social unrest, and mindful of ambiguities in the original law, readily liberalized it.[11] Henceforth, veterans could cease job hunting and pursue education or training instead.

Opening the Floodgates

While use of the education and training provisions had started as a trickle—only 216,000 had begun to use the benefits before the passage of the 1945 amendments—the torrent soon began.[12] Veterans entered some programs more rapidly than others. The college program achieved immediate popularity, with annual enrollment reaching its apex of nearly 900,000 in 1948. Demand for vocational training and education in other schools below the college level materialized more slowly, not peaking until 1950 and then dropping off gradually. Job training crested early, in 1947, and then declined rapidly, whereas on-the-farm training did not reach its highest level until 1950.[13]

The massive use of the program provoked close scrutiny by public officials. A critical essay in *School and Society,* a magazine for education professionals, was titled "How Many Wrongs Make a G.I. Bill of Rights?" It cited vast sums that were being used to support veterans' enrollment in courses such as ballroom dancing or horsemanship, the lack of extensive educational and vocational counseling for program beneficiaries, and a high number of dropouts.[14] Representative Olin Teague (D-TX), chair of a special congressional committee charged with reviewing the educational provisions, lambasted officials in the Veterans Administration and told Congress that there were a number of abuses of the program: "We wasted millions and millions of dollars on the thing." Senator Paul Douglas (D-IL) concurred: "They certified a lot of fake schools and some of the schools milked the system."[15]

That the implementation of a brand-new program utilized by nearly eight million people over a nine-year period produced some administrative problems and fraud is hardly surprising. As one early analysis noted, "The Veterans Administration had barely had time to disseminate information and instructions within its existing organization relative to the amendatory provisions of the law before hundreds of thousands of recently demobilized veterans began applying for the various liberalized benefits."[16] The VA had been established as an independent agency in 1930, combining the Veterans Bureau, the Bureau of Pensions, and the National Home for Disabled Volunteer Soldiers. As soon as veterans began to return from World War II and to press their claims, it became apparent that the agency's administrative arrangements—a centralized, hierarchical structure in which each executive leader was charged with administering a particular function of the organization— was outmoded.

Besieged by the avalanche of applications for the G.I. Bill, the Veterans Administration modified its structure in 1945, creating additional layers of decentralized authority so that it could respond more readily to veterans. The new organization included thirteen branch offices throughout the nation, each charged with overseeing programs; seventy regional offices, each required to administer federal programs for veterans within a specific geographic vicinity; and in some cases subregional offices and contact field offices as well.[17] Besides handling such an immense alteration in its structure and functions, the VA simultaneously assimilated a vast number of new personnel. Between December 1945 and February 1947, the total number of individuals employed by the VA tripled, growing from 72,607 to 226,131.[18]

Within each regional office, the Vocational Rehabilitation and Education Division was charged with administering the G.I. Bill's education and training programs. The Registration and Research section determined veterans' eligibility and authorized their benefits. The Training Facilities section, which dealt directly with state-level approval agencies and with educational institutions in matters pertaining to tuition levels and fees, permitted the Veterans Administration to publish a complete listing of institutions and programs in which the G.I. Bill benefits could be used, and the number of students to be admitted to each.[19] The Advisement and Guidance section provided professional counseling primarily, though not exclusively, to disabled veterans, and the Educational and Training section oversaw training of disabled veterans.[20]

While the Veterans Administration made an easy target for disgruntled public officials, the rapid pace at which the agency had been required to adapt would have stretched most any organization, public or private. As noted in a management study of the agency conducted by Booz-Allen-Hamilton: "Faced with an overwhelming influx of veterans seeking training benefits, an immediate expansion in operations and a tremendous increase in staff, [the] Veterans' Administration was handicapped in administering the program by frequent and unanticipated changes in legislation, inadequate training facilities, groups of unduly self-interested people, and drastic, recurring changes in the agency's overall organizational structure."[21]

Interestingly, however, veterans interviewed for this study almost never mentioned the role of the Veterans Administration when they spoke of the implementation of the G.I. Bill. Neither did they speak about the state agencies that assessed the quality of courses in educational institutions and prepared lists of approved institutions that veterans could attend on the G.I. Bill. From veterans' point of view, the program was implemented primarily by the educational institutions they attended. Congress could conduct oversight of the Veterans Administration itself, but its authority over the other far-flung institutions engaged in day-to-day implementation was fairly remote. As a result, veterans' experiences varied with the type of education they pursued, the state in which they pursued it, and more specifically the individual institution or program in which they enrolled. Therefore, in order to assess the content of the messages veterans received from the G.I. Bill, we need to consider its implementation in the context of each of those specific settings.

Storming the Colleges and Universities

Soon after the G.I. Bill was written, University of Chicago president Robert M. Hutchins predicted that it would promote opportunism by institutions of higher education, which had suffered from low enrollments throughout the war, and would lead to the degradation of higher education generally, to the disservice of veterans. "The G.I. Bill gives [the colleges and universities] the chance to get more money than they have ever dreamed of, and to do it in the name of patriotism," he warned. "They will not want to keep out unqualified veterans; they will not want to expel those who fail. Even if they should want to, they will not be allowed to, for the public and the veterans' organizations will not stand for it. Colleges and universities will find themselves converted into educational hobo jungles. And veterans, unable to get work and equally unable to resist putting pressure on the colleges and universities, will find themselves educational hoboes."[22] The title of an article in *Newsweek* warned, "Bursars Rub Hands over G.I. Bill but College Standards May Suffer," envisaging that veterans might reject liberal arts training for courses of immediate practical value, and colleges might be all too willing to turn away from traditional standards. As program usage began, Harvard University dean Wilbur J. Bender voiced concerns about new students that the policy brought to campus: "There is a kind of unhealthy determination to get ahead, a grim competitive spirit, an emphasis on individual careerism and success which is disturbing . . . the lights are burning very late and there is not much leisurely talk or fellowship or group spirit."[23]

From the perspective of nonblack college-bound veterans, however, the experience of qualifying for the G.I. Bill benefits and commencing their studies bestowed upon most veterans the status of privileged citizens. In practice, the verification of their eligibility—confirming that they had served at least ninety days and had an other-than-dishonorable discharge—and the distribution of benefits were administered, with relatively few exceptions, smoothly and efficiently. The Veterans Administration produced numerous pamphlets informing veterans in clear language about their benefits and how to activate them.[24] Veterans could use the G.I. Bill at any approved institution of higher education to which they could gain admission through regular procedures. The list of approved institutions was long and diverse, given that colleges and universities were so well established in the United States, with private institutions having emerged steadily since the colonial era and public institutions, especially since the Morrill Act of 1862 created the land grant system.[25] Once admitted to a college or university, veterans obtained G.I. Bill benefits through minimal effort, first filing a request for eligibility that noted length of service, type of discharge, and marital status, and then having their status verified by a public official who inspected and copied their discharge papers and informed them of the level of subsistence payments for which they qualified.[26] George Josten remembered, "We had to apply. It was processed through some regional offices . . . and then we simply got a check. I got a check for $75 and the school was paid directly. It was an extremely convenient arrangement." Similarly, Ann Sharp explained, "You had to bring your discharge papers to an office where they check them through, make copies, and certify that you were able to get your $90 a month to live on while you were going to school. . . . And every single semester you had to check in again and make sure you were still eligible." Though Sharp, a student at Auburn University in Alabama, recalled having to walk into town to go to the appropriate office ("none of us had cars"), Ross Flint remembered streamlined procedures at Ohio State: "I got my books at one counter, and the G.I. Bill at another. . . . The G.I. Bill paid for the whole [degree]." Anthony Miller concurred: "You just enrolled—I didn't have to do anything. I got $75 a month in addition to that. Pretty good!" Noted James Murray, "It wasn't a big deal. I think they did it with less of the commotion than with Medicare these days." The fact that the program's procedures are remembered so positively even five decades later underscores the potential power of participants' interpretations of such programs.

In a tragic exception to this general pattern, veterans who had been released from the military with what became known as "blue discharges," particularly for reasons related to homosexuality, encountered procedures that appeared exclusive, arbitrary, and unfair. Such discharges—formally considered neither honorable nor dishonorable—were reserved, generally, for those deemed unfit for military service because of "undesirable habits or traits of character," including "criminalism, chronic alcoholism, drug addiction, pathological lying, or homosexuality."[27] Although policy makers had explicitly written the G.I. Bill's eligibility rules to extend benefits to all veterans with any discharge status aside from an outright dishonorable, in April 1945 the Veterans Administration issued an instruction that blue discharges pertaining to homosexual "acts or tendencies" should be considered the same as dishonorable discharges. Veterans with such discharges found themselves turned away when they sought to use their benefits.[28] In 1946, the Committee on Military Affairs in the House of Representatives reviewed these procedures and issued a scathing report, noting that "nothing could more clearly prove the anomalous and illogical and disingenuous nature of the blue discharge than this policy of the Veterans Administration." It lambasted the agency for assuming "the right to separate the sheep from the goats," taking it upon itself to reinterpret such discharges as "dishonorable," and "passing moral verdicts on the history of any soldier."[29] Nonetheless, the VA reissued its instructions in 1949, prompting Congress to revisit the issue throughout the next decade. The treatment of the blue-discharged veterans likely conveyed harshly negative interpretive messages to these individuals, and communicated to the broader public that government was neither representative of nor responsive to homosexuals.[30]

Making Room for Veterans

Even as the war was ending, many states and individual colleges and universities braced themselves for demobilization, anticipating increased enrollments and students whose personal and academic needs differed from those of their traditional clientele. Given the long period of drought in higher education, most (though not all) were pleased to welcome the veterans, whom they readily treated with gratitude and respect. To accommodate veterans immediately after discharge, some institutions established "vestibule schools," special courses and tutoring to help veterans ready themselves for regular coursework once the next semester began.[31] Many colleges also expressed willingness to admit promising students who had not completed high school. They used guidelines from the Armed Forces Institute and American Council of Education to establish how military service and education in the military could be counted in terms of credits and semester hours, typically through the newly created General Education Development (GED) tests.[32] The New York State Education Department announced special procedures for admitting veterans to college, permitting those who had not completed high school to be considered for admission if their military service itself and any coursework that was part of it could be considered the equivalent of completion of a standard secondary school program. The state also mandated that colleges and universities cooperate with local high schools to offer secondary schools on their campuses on a noncredit basis, enabling veterans with strong academic records to complete the necessary requirements for admission.[33] Syracuse University announced a nine-point program that offered veterans vocational and educational guidance and personalized curricula. Rather than being limited to high school graduates, the program welcomed qualified veterans who appeared, on the basis of their military record and aptitude tests, to be ready for college work. Barnard College made similar plans to welcome women veterans.[34]

Institutions also developed other special programs to signal their openness to veterans. The University of Illinois established a division to offer academic and occupational advising to veterans and to meet their other special needs; similarly, Boston College opened a full-time guidance clinic for the veterans.[35] Minnesota, aiming to make college education available to all students seeking it, set up a clearinghouse to "help direct the traffic jam of applications" for admission to colleges in the state.[36] Many universities and colleges began offering courses throughout the entire year rather than only during the traditional nine-month schedule, thus permitting veterans to complete their degrees in less than the typical four years.[37]

None of these arrangements was sufficient to handle the throngs of veterans who utilized the G.I. Bill for higher education. By 1947, veterans accounted for half of enrolled college students, doubling the number of males registered in prewar times, and increasing overall enrollment by 75 percent. Instantaneously, the student body more than doubled at numerous institutions, growing, for example, from 7,000 before the war to 16,000 in 1948 at Rutgers, from 4,800 to 7,200 at Stanford, and by comparable rates at Boston College, the University of Georgia, and the University of Maine.[38] At the University of Minnesota, enrollment of veterans hit the highest level in the country, as registration climbed from 14,986 in 1940 to 27,103 in 1946.[39]

Universities and colleges varied in the extent to which they deliberately increased their enrollment to accommodate veterans, with the average institution planning an expansion of 25 percent, and many others 50 or 100 percent or more.[40] The alumni in the Class of 1949 Survey, drawn from public and private institutions from all regions of the nation, including some chosen for racial, ethnic, and religious diversity, illustrate such variation, as shown in Table 4.1 below.[41] The lower level of G.I. Bill use at Morehouse College is likely due to the fact that black veterans, as we saw in Chapter 3, had less prior education and were less

Table 4.1. G.I. Bill Users and Their Experiences, at Selected Institutions of Higher Education, Class of 1949 Survey

	Percentage of Survey Respondents Who Used G.I. Bill for for Education	Percentage of Users Ranking G.I. Bill as Turning Point in Their Lives	Percentage of Users Who Agree or Strongly Agree They Couldn't Afford College Without G.I. Bill
Brooklyn College	73%	70%	51%
Boston College	76	66	39
Syracuse University	83	86	54
University of Georgia	94	89	50
University of Texas at Austin	91	84	53
Vanderbilt University	84	77	58
Morehouse College	59	80	52
Wayne State University	81	72	46
Northwestern University	84	74	46
Washington State University	84	74	51
Pomona College	83	66	47
Total	81	76	50

likely to use the G.I. Bill for higher education, and to lower life expectancy among African Americans than among nonblacks, with a greater percentage having died by the time of this survey.[42] Program usage soared highest in the South, accounting for the levels of veteran enrollment at the University of Georgia and at the University of Texas at Austin.[43] Junior colleges, though not included in this sample, opened their doors wide to veterans. They attracted many who found the two-year program preferable to a four-year course of study and who appreciated their greater willingness to permit the combination of vocational training with a liberal arts curriculum.[44]

Interestingly, none of the veterans interviewed for this project complained about the overcrowding that ensued on college campuses. Administrators struggled to find enough instructors to teach brimming classes and to procure adequate space for classrooms and housing.[45] They hired graduate students to serve as instructors, scheduled multiple extra sections of classes from early in the morning until late in the evening, and adopted new procedures of mechanical grading. Students were housed in crowded accommodations, sometimes miles from campus. Yet veterans mentioned overcrowding only as an aside, usually in the context of conveying the sense of excitement on campuses at the time. John Mink explained, "[Going to college on the G.I. Bill] was great. There was such a swarm of veterans returning. We were dominant. We brought a great deal of experience to the campus." When asked explicitly whether overcrowding had presented a problem, Isaac Gellert, who attended Columbia University, replied: "Oh God, yes. The first year we were put up in Army Hall, which is up in City College. City College had a unit of the Army stationed up there for some time and they had a large Quonset type of structure. At the end of the war the structure was still there, [and] Columbia was very overcrowded with students, so they sent part of the freshman class to live at Army Hall. We were crowded, yes, but it wasn't bad."

Like Gellert, other veterans expressed more awe than exasperation about the ways in which colleges and universities managed, despite the record number of individuals attending. The only negative comments came from a veteran who had begun his studies at Syracuse University before military service and who was aghast at the crowded conditions he encountered upon returning to complete his degree, after the war.[46] His reaction was hardly surprising: the university enrolled more veterans than any other institution of higher education in New York State, ranked seventeenth nationwide in the number of veteran students, and, perhaps most significant, grew at an exponential rate, as enrollment soared from 3,000 students in 1943 to 19,698 in 1948. Certainly students accustomed to the more tranquil environment on campuses previously might have been less than pleased to find themselves in classes that had expanded in size by 650 percent. Nonetheless, the Class of 1949 Survey revealed that 86 percent of the G.I. Bill beneficiaries at Syracuse University considered the use of the bill's educational provisions to be a turning point in their lives, as seen in the second column of Table 4.1. In fact, majorities of the users at each of the universities in the sample considered G.I. Bill use to be a life turning point, suggesting that they had positive experiences even under crowded conditions.

Veterans generally seemed to perceive that government and the educational institutions were doing their best to handle the heightened demand. Public officials engaged in a creative form of demilitarization, in 1945 amending the Lanham Act of 1940—which had authorized the construction of public housing to aid the war effort—and transforming it into the Veterans' Reuse Program. The new law offered over one hundred thousand Quonset huts, military surplus buildings that had been used at Army bases and at airfields during the war, and allocated nearly $5 million to move them and convert them into housing. Syracuse University, for example, held classes in military-issue metal prefabricated buildings located temporarily in the heart of the campus.[47] The government also offered to colleges, on a no-cost lease basis, the use of "in-place" military installations or converted facilities, such as barracks and hospitals, that were located in proximity to their campuses.[48] Thus at Stanford, a former military hospital was converted to one- and two-bedroom apartments.[49]

These measures not only changed the appearance of existing colleges but also introduced new campuses, some temporary and others that became permanent. For example, George Josten began his studies at the University of Illinois at the new Navy Pier branch in Chicago, and later finished his degree at the established downstate Champaign-Urbana campus.[50] James Murray was admitted to Pennsylvania State University on the condition that he attend classes at a Jesuit college in Erie, Pennsylvania, for the first year of his studies.[51]

Whereas higher education had long been the domain of young, single individuals, the G.I. Bill enabled veterans with families to enroll: 30 percent of all veteran college students had spouses, and 10 percent had one or more children.[52] Such families typically lived in sprawling communities of government-provided trailer homes or Quonset huts. These nontraditional students captivated the public's interest. In a photo essay titled "Veterans at College: They Go Back to Studies with Wives and Children," *Life* magazine depicted veterans and their families at the University of Wisconsin pushing baby carriages near their trailer homes and hanging out clothes washed at the common laundry. In one image that captures the civic culture of the era, several couples are shown bowling together, with the caption "YWCA girls watch the baby."[53] Another issue highlighted married veterans at the University of Iowa: "Packed into his tiny trailer home with his wife and child, he has a hard enough time living on the GI subsistence pay and an even harder time getting his studies done. . . . For about $25 a month they get a furnished trailer, electric light and the right to use the common baths and washrooms."[54]

Ann Sharp and her husband, both veterans, attended Auburn University on the G.I. Bill, living in a trailer park established for veterans' families. She explained, "We were all in one group: all of us were veterans or married to veterans, none of us had more than $90 a month, [and] most were pregnant or had small children because they were newly married." She spoke with pride about the ability of veterans' families to manage under crowded circumstances, and expressed gratitude for the accommodations provided. "Just to show you how we were treated: either the Rotarians or the Optimists Club, one of those two, gave money for all the supplies to put in a playground for the children of the veterans. The veterans just had to pour the cement and put it up, but all the supplies were donated." To Sharp, such treatment underscored the positive nature of her experience on the G.I. Bill.

Veterans as Students

Similarly, when asked how administrators, faculty, and fellow students treated them, veterans answered positively, sometimes conveying a sense of a special status accrued to them. Said Colosimo, "We were treated with . . . respect. They'd say, 'That guy was in the war, he was in the Army.'" For some such as Robert Forster, who had been an officer, "to go back and have these people telling you what to do was a little hard to take." Still, veterans felt that they challenged the traditional style of classroom learning. As George Josten explained, "The professors liked us very much because we demanded them to give us very, very substantial answers and responses to our questions. We didn't buy off, let's say, with the pacifiers; we wanted some meat and potatoes with our education. They had to respond because they all felt we were . . . pushing them, we were urging them, we had to hurry up and get done and get on with our life. We were trying to make up for times gone by."

Indeed, those who had worried that veteran students would lead to the demise of academic standards were proven mistaken. Studies revealed that veterans earned better grades than nonveterans at the same institutions, and married veterans outperformed single veterans.[55] Faculty praised the veteran students, noting, "They have that one priceless quality which is the answer of every teacher's prayer: they want to learn."[56] Richard Werner commented, "Most of the professors . . . were very friendly and had a lot of respect for the veterans. Some, of course, lived in their ivory towers. I remember some of . . . [them] saying, 'Why should we take these veterans in? Their marks aren't as good as some of the other kids; their performance is horrible compared [to the others] . . . ,' [but] actually, when it came to all the awards when I graduated, most of them [went to] veterans."[57]

Veterans proved themselves to be serious students, with little time for the frivolous traditions that had long marked college life. As one Harvard official quoted in *Time* observed, "These fellows knocked out the playboy era of American colleges."[58] Isaac Gellert recalled that among his classmates at Columbia, the vast majority of whom were veterans, "there was no interest whatsoever" in the old annual campus ritual in which freshman and sophomores competed to climb a greased pole to retrieve an object from the top.[59] Veterans pursued more practical fields than students of the past, gravitating especially toward business administration, followed by professional fields such as law, medicine, dentistry, and teaching, and then, in almost equal numbers, engineering, architecture, the physical sciences, the humanities, and the social sciences.[60]

Many, such as James Murray, discovered abilities and opportunities they had been unaware of previously: "When I first went [to college], it took a few weeks until I found out I could do everything everybody else could do. . . . I worked at it and applied myself, I [found I] could do it. The required courses were tough, but I got through them. Once I got through that first year, I really started to enjoy college. The college life really opened things up for me. The work became easy and I enjoyed it, which surprised me to some extent. . . . We got in on all the social occasions in [the department where my wife worked], with the graduate students who were older. These people were very well educated and they exposed us to things we hadn't thought of before."

Just over one-quarter of all veterans who used the G.I. Bill to attend colleges or universities (26 percent) did not complete their entire degree.[61] Although some nonveterans complained that veterans' withdrawals from programs indicated a lack of seriousness, in fact veterans' overall noncompletion rate is hardly unusual. Contemporary data show that 39 percent of college students today fail to complete their degree; by comparison, the veterans were relatively successful.[62] Exit interviews with students who withdrew from the University of Minnesota revealed that insufficient subsistence payments constituted the single largest reason why veterans left before completing their degrees. As the cost of living rose, students were more likely to leave the university prematurely and to seek employment instead. Delayed arrival of checks constituted a major reason for withdrawal only among a minority of veterans.[63] While veterans perceived the G.I. Bill benefits to be generous, making ends meet could still prove challenging, especially for married veterans. This was the case despite the fact that veterans frequently worked part time while pursuing their degrees: at Wayne State in 1947, for example, three-quarters of the G.I. Bill recipients held some form of employment.[64] Some critics believed that the lack of sufficient counseling for veterans who used the program meant that many pursued fields for which they were ill-suited, leading them to drop out of their studies.[65] Only disabled veterans specifically qualified for such counseling, financed under Public Law 16 rather than the G.I. Bill itself.[66] Other veterans received academic and career counseling through a government agency only if they requested it.[67] Still, studies found that veterans were generally pleased overall with the counseling they received under either of the laws.[68]

Barriers Lifted and Barriers Left

By offering tuition support to all returning veterans, the G.I. Bill allowed them—regardless of their ethnic or religious background—to attend the best universities and colleges that admitted them. This raises the question of how academic institutions would administer the bill, given their long-standing exclusivity in admissions, whether by custom, institutional rules, or law. Prior to the war, quota systems limiting the number of Jewish and African American students had been well entrenched at elite institutions in the North.[69] Seventeen southern states and the District of Columbia mandated separate schools for whites and blacks through formal legalized segregation, and segregated schools were permitted in numerous other states, even some that had enacted legal prohibitions against such practices.[70] Certainly this could send highly negative messages to veterans about their status as citizens, particularly if veterans perceived the discrimination as indistinguishable from the G.I. Bill's education and training benefits.

The G.I. Bill was implemented amid growing pressure on government and educational institutions to remove barriers to equal educational opportunity. Immediately following the enactment of the legislation, Walter White, executive secretary of the National Association for the Advancement of Colored People, informed President Roosevelt, "One of the most important instrumentalities toward assurance of equality of opportunity without regard to race, creed, color or national origin will be the Veterans Bureau and the implementation by the Bureau of the . . . G.I. Bill of Rights Act."[71] Later, leaders of the National Education Association and related groups, alarmed by the emergence of new quotas at major universities aimed at limiting Jewish enrollment, pressed Roosevelt to eliminate "quotas and other forms of racial and religious discrimination in the nation's colleges, especially in relation to returning servicemen seeking education under the G.I. Bill of Rights."[72] While the Roosevelt administration responded to such requests with polite letters but little in the way of action, a more dramatic response came in 1947, when President Truman's Commission on Higher Education published *Higher Education for American Democracy*, a scathing report that detailed the racial and religious barriers to educational opportunity in the United States.[73]

A series of court decisions signaled the first cracks in the wall of racial segregation in higher education.[74] In *Sipuel v. Board of Regents* (1948), the Supreme Court ruled against the state of Oklahoma for refusing to admit a qualified student to its state law school on the basis of race.[75] Two years later, a unanimous Supreme Court ruled in *Sweatt v. Painter* that a black law school failed to meet the demands of the equal protection clause of the Fourteenth Amendment.[76] Among the bevy of amicus curiae briefs, one submitted by the American Veterans Committee, a veterans' service organization founded in 1944, argued for an end to segregation so that African American veterans could use their G.I. Bill provisions fully.[77] Next, in *McLaurin v. Oklahoma State Regents*, the Court declared that the segregation of a single black student within a graduate school was unconstitutional.[78] Though the wider implications of the Court's decisions only became evident in the 1954 decision *Brown v. Board of Education of Topeka*, the earlier decisions may have signaled to institutions of higher education that a change from the old practices might be necessary.[79]

Whatever the reason, as the G.I. Bill was implemented, many institutions of higher education in the North and West dismantled their most overtly discriminatory barriers. The program fostered a climate in which colleges and universities were inundated with applications and could seize the opportunity to adopt more competitive admissions policies rather than adhere to their traditional norms of exclusivity.[80] Many schools began to drop their quota systems.[81] A perusal of the institutions that members of the 92nd Infantry Division attended reveals that black veterans outside the South—though they attended some historically black institutions such as Wilberforce University in Ohio and Lincoln in Pennsylvania—attended primarily integrated institutions, including Delphi, Wayne State, the University of Iowa, Fisk, Ohio State, the University of Chicago, Purdue, the University of California at Berkeley, San Francisco State, San Jose State, Pasadena Community College, City College of New York, Penn State, Queens College, and many others.

As educational institutions in the North and West eradicated obstacles to admission, hundreds of thousands of African Americans continued to migrate to those regions. The postwar years, in fact, marked the culmination of the relocation of blacks from sharecropping and rural and small-town life in the South to urban centers elsewhere.[82] Strikingly, by 1947, one out of every ten black veterans who had lived in the South prior to the war had migrated to the North or West.[83]

The confluence of black migration and the demise of quotas produced results that stunned educational professionals. Indeed, analysts in the late 1940s observed that "an almost unbelievable increase has taken place" in the enrollment of blacks at universities in the North and West, "probably totaling some four or five thousand students as contrasted with two or two and a half thousand formerly."[84] The outcomes were pronounced in the context of individual institutions and especially individual lives. Reginald Wilson reports that one-third of the veterans at his alma mater, Wayne State University in Detroit, were African American.[85] Henry Hervey, a black Tuskegee Airman who was able to attend his first-choice institution, Northwestern University, explained that without the G.I. Bill, "I possibly would have continued [my education] but it would have been at a local [junior] college . . . [where] the tuition was $60 a semester. . . . So there's a possibility I would have [gone to college] but it would have taken much longer." Given the availability of G.I. Bill funds, combined with nondiscriminatory admissions procedures at Northwestern, he—like thousands of other African American veterans— was able to attend a well-established, highly regarded, and increasingly integrated institution to obtain his education.

Still, in 1947 nearly two-thirds of all black veterans (65 percent) were living in the South, where most institutions of higher education—with the exception of historically black institutions—remained formally closed to them. A few black respondents from the 92nd Infantry enrolled at integrated institutions such as the University of Maryland, Catholic University, George Washington University, Georgetown University, and American University. But most—especially in the Deep South, where no other options existed—attended schools for blacks only, such as North Carolina A&T State, Tuskegee University (Alabama), Delaware State, Morgan State (Maryland), Howard University, Morehouse College, Tougaloo College (Mississippi), Florida A&M University, and Prairie View A&M University (Texas).[86] These findings mirror a 1947 analysis in the *Journal of Negro Education*, which surmised, "Throughout the entire southern region Negroes are now attending public colleges and universities organized primarily for white persons in only 2 states (Maryland and West Virginia) and private institutions in only 2 states (Maryland and Missouri) and the District of Columbia."[87] The value of the higher education provisions of the G.I. Bill for black veterans in the South, therefore, was contingent on the ability of historically black colleges and universities to accommodate them.

Although black institutions of higher education had improved immensely over the preceding decades, severely inadequate budgets still hindered their quality. Thus, while overcrowding was the norm at institutions of higher education in the postwar years, black institutions bore a greater burden than most. Between 1946 and 1947, while enrollment at universities and colleges increased generally by 13 percent, black institutions expanded by 26 percent, growing from 29,000 in 1940 to 58,000 in 1946 and 73,174 in 1947.[88] While veterans composed smaller percentages of the student body at black institutions than at white ones—in 1947, 41 percent at black colleges, compared to 52 percent at white colleges— accumulated deficiencies resulted in severe space shortages in black institutions.[89] Martin Jenkins added a personal note to his analysis of these overwhelmed colleges: "The writer has observed . . . English composition classes of 80 students and elementary language classes of 60 students taught by a single teacher, without assistants. He has seen classes in history and education in which students sat in the window sills because there was no space for additional chairs in the classroom. He has seen students enrolled, taught, failed, and dropped, without an interview, even by a trained counselor and without an evaluation by the college. . . . He has seen as many as six students sleeping and studying (?) in a dormitory room designed for two."[90]

As it did for other institutions of higher education, the federal government responded to historically black colleges' needs for increased space and enhancement of existing facilities. Staff in the office of the commissioner on education estimated black colleges' new floor space needs to be more than double those of the white institutions in the region.[91] Still, the additional facilities did not begin to meet demands.[92]

Aside from physical space shortages, black institutions of higher education also faced especially severe difficulties in hiring sufficient numbers of instructors. The war had displaced a generation of individuals who might have become professors. Many who might have taught at black colleges either used the G.I. Bill to further their own education or took newly available jobs at universities and colleges in the North and West or in government service instead. The opportunities for better pay and working conditions elsewhere meant that black colleges suffered, essentially, from "brain drain."[93] As a result, African American veterans seeking to use the G.I. Bill for higher education in the South faced severely restricted options.

In sum, while the G.I. Bill did not prohibit schools or states from discriminating on the basis of religious background or race, various factors began to attenuate the power of such practices. Change was not perceptible in the deep South, where many thousands of black veterans crowded into the historically black institutions, increasing enrollment by 50 percent compared to the beginning of the 1940s.[94] Universities and colleges in the North, however, began to drop their prejudices in favor of more open admissions. And most strikingly, thousands of southern black veterans joined the Great Migration, heading for parts of the nation where they found many schools increasingly willing to accept qualified students on a color-blind basis.

In Favor of the Veteran

When congressional committees and presidential commissions reviewed the implementation of the G.I. Bill's higher education provisions, none of the topics discussed thus far came within their purview. They focused instead on the handful of universities and colleges that seized the opportunity to amass federal funds. The fact that the G.I. Bill covered tuition and fees up to $500 per year lured some institutions to instantly raise tuition without a commensurate increase in services. A few state universities and colleges managed to charge the VA nonresident tuition even for resident veterans; one state military school mistakenly refunded veterans themselves for overpayment by the VA, and G.I. Bill payments to land-grant colleges sometimes duplicated other federal funds paid to them. Elsewhere, the General Accounting Office detected payment errors such as reimbursements to colleges after a veteran had ceased to attend, when the student's entitlement had ended, or when a veteran failed to attend classes.[95] College administrators argued that the multitudes of veterans taxed their facilities and faculties, and that the government's contribution did not begin to pay the average cost of educating the individual student.[96]

Nonetheless, from the veterans' point of view, the G.I. Bill's higher education provisions permitted them to enjoy the advantages of well-established institutions. Although colleges and universities were overwhelmed by postwar enrollments, they proved quite flexible in meeting veterans' needs, because doing so did not change their tasks fundamentally but rather challenged them to do more of what they already did, by serving a larger clientele. The President's Commission on Veterans' Pensions, otherwise known as the Bradley Commission, reported, "Compared with the other types of training pursued by veterans, the program at the college level has operated more satisfactorily. The problems were less serious, largely because the institutions were better equipped than other schools and industries to meet immediately the needs of the new, adult students."[97] Furthermore, to the extent that the VA made errors, it appeared to have done so "consistently and perhaps often without justification . . . *in favor of the veteran*."[98] Though such patterns understandably provoked public officials, they produced highly favorable responses from G.I. Bill beneficiaries. The veterans perceived themselves to be well treated, suggesting that program implementation yielded interpretive effects that might, in turn, foster inclination for civic involvement.

Creating New Opportunities for the Non-College-Bound

The G.I. Bill did not mark the first instance of federal funding for vocational training and related programs in the United States, but it was by far the largest and most comprehensive to date. Since the turn of the century, educational reformers had sought to expand vocational training opportunities for American youth and adults. The Smith-Hughes

Act of 1917 signified the beginning of U.S. federal involvement in postsecondary education, providing funding for teachers in programs offering training in agriculture, trades and industry, and home economics.[99] In the same year, the War Risk Insurance Act offered vocational rehabilitation for disabled World War I veterans.[100] Yet both of these programs and later extensions of Smith-Hughes served relatively small numbers of students and allocated, at most, $15 million per year.[101] The G.I. Bill, by contrast, attracted 3.5 million veterans to vocational training, 1.4 million to on-the-job training, and 700,000 to on-the-farm training.[102] Combining direct payments to schools for tuition and subsistence payments to veteran students, these subcollege-level programs cost the government $9 billion over a ten-year period, an average of $900 million annually.[103] Instantly, the number of trade schools in the nation tripled to meet the new demand: fifty-six hundred of the eight thousand approved schools veterans attended below the college level were established after the enactment of the G.I. Bill.[104] Such programs stood poised to convey, through program implementation, critical messages to the vast majority of G.I. Bill recipients.

Administrative challenges emerged—not surprising given the overwhelming demand for education and training programs below the college level, the spontaneous establishment of so many new schools and facilities, and the lack of institutional capacity for overseeing such developments. In keeping with the tradition that education was regarded as a state-level responsibility in the United States, policy makers had divided authority for all of the educational and training programs between the Veterans Administration, which was held responsible for the proper use of federal funds, and state-level agencies, which retained the authority to approve educational and training facilities. Public officials were chagrined to learn that in many states, such agencies lacked the ability to oversee the quickly expanding subcollege-level programs. Claims were rampant that the G.I. Bill sanctioned the development of "fly-by-night" schools.[105] Nationwide, state-level administrators operated in the absence of clear federal guidelines for program approval.[106] Members of Congress became especially concerned that G.I. Bill funds were being used for some "avocational" or recreational courses such as "bartending," "calisthenics," and "personality development."[107] Public officials worried that the quality of training in many schools and on-the-job training programs was highly questionable.

Yet veterans' own experiences of the vocational training provisions and other G.I. Bill–funded programs below the college level barely surfaced in the government studies or congressional hearings regarding implementation. Neither did the popular press devote the attention to veterans in such programs that it had given to those on college campuses. Scholarly literature on the implementation of such programs does not exist. In short, though more than a third of all World War II veterans—a sizable portion of the "civic generation"—benefited from such government programs, to date we have known little about their experiences.

World War II Veterans Survey respondents used the G.I. Bill for a wide variety of educational programs and forms of training, as evidenced by Table 4.2. Vocational or trade school programs and on-the-job training proved most popular. Veterans using such programs mentioned training they received in a plethora of skills, including carpet installation, construction and architecture, telephone repair work, pipefitting, tailoring, carpentry, electrical work, auto repair, meatcutting, welding, glasswork, radio and television work, horticulture, barbering, cabinetmaking, auto mechanics, electronic repair work, sheet metal work, printmaking, refrigeration, aircraft engine repair, plumbing, refrigeration and air-conditioning, wood pattern making, gunsmithing, and small

Table 4.2. Nonblack Male Veterans' Experiences of G.I. Bill-Financed Education and Training Programs Below College Level, World War II Veterans Survey

Type of Training	Percentage of Subcollege G.I. Bill Users per Program*	Percentage of Users Ranking G.I. Bill as Turning Point in Their Lives	Percentage of Users Who Agree or Strongly Agree They Couldn't Afford Training Without G.I. Bill	Average Time in Program on G.I. Bill	Percentage Graduating from Course of Study or Completing Program on G.I. Bill
Vocational or trade school	31%	70%	82%	1–2 years	84%
Apprenticeship or on-the-job training	25	56	72	1–2 years	74
Business school	9	77	100	1–2 years	54
On-the-farm training	7	33	88	1–2 years	75
Correspondence course	8	46	60	6–12 months	80
Other (except high school)	17	52	73	1–2 years	86

*Note: The first column does not add to 100% because of rounding and because the small number of high school users was dropped, being too small to evaluate.

engine repair. Several also noted that they attended business school or flight school, or received agricultural training.[108]

How valuable was the below-college-level training that veterans received on the G.I. Bill? The second column in Table 4.2 depicts the percentage of nonblack male veterans using each type of training who regarded it as a turning point in their lives. Interestingly, a majority of veterans in each of the most popular programs ranked the G.I. Bill as a turning point. In fact, veterans' experiences of the most frequently utilized programs, the vocational training schools, rivaled those of the higher education program users, with 70 percent ranking benefit usage a turning point compared to 76 percent of the college and university graduates, as noted earlier. Even more striking, veterans who used the G.I. Bill for programs below college level were far more likely to agree or strongly agree that they could not have afforded the training they received without the benefits. By contrast to the 54 percent of nonblack male higher education beneficiaries who believed they could not have afforded college without the G.I. Bill, a full 82 percent of vocational training participants and 72 percent of on-the-job training program users credited the benefits with making their training possible.[109] These results suggest that participation in the programs below the college level constituted highly positive experiences of government, with salutary attitudinal effects.

Among African American veterans who used the subcollege programs, 89 percent ranked them as a turning point in their lives and 53 percent reported that they could not have afforded the training they acquired in the absence of the G.I. Bill. Certainly, black veterans who sought to use subcollege programs in the South encountered problems similar to those of black veterans pursuing higher education in the region, as southern states insisted upon developing segregated programs. Nonetheless, as we saw in Chapter 3, black veterans in the South utilized the education and training provisions at higher rates than black or white veterans elsewhere, and the vast majority did so in subcollege programs.

Vocational Schools

Given the oversight difficulties with new programs, the quality of training differed considerably from one trade or vocational school to another. As the Bradley Commission noted, "The length and content of courses varied so greatly between States that a trade school course in auto mechanics ranged in length from 28 to 117 weeks and radio and television courses from 14 to 111 weeks."[110] Owing to the rapid pace of developments, government agencies sometimes resorted to granting approval on a "mail-order basis," using only mail or phone contact and avoiding "the formality of inspection of facilities or courses of instruction unless there were reasons to believe something was amiss."[111] Nonetheless, veterans found most of the programs—whether new or established—to be extremely useful.

Sam Marchesi, who had an eighth-grade education prior to the war, used the G.I. Bill benefits to learn architectural drawing, blueprint reading, and estimating at the Alfred Leonard School in New Rochelle, New York, as well as for on-the-job training. Marchesi explained that his training under the G.I. Bill allowed him to gain what would today be the equivalent of a four-year college degree in architectural drawing and estimating. "I was actually working as an apprentice carpenter and going to school four nights a week and getting my education in," he explained. "I was getting both field training and the education part." Marchesi marveled at the program's quality: "The schoolteachers were great. You were either going to learn or please get out: that was their attitude." Thanks to his training, Marchesi pursued a lifelong career as a custom builder.

The vocational training benefits proved useful as well for Jerome Dribin, who attended television repair school in Chicago. He began his studies at American Television but, finding the program to be insufficiently practical, switched to DeVry, where he continued for one and a half to two more years. "I learned circuitry and things like that.... I had never worked with my hands before. It gave me incentive to try things." The training enabled Dribin to become a television repairman, a job he held for seven years, and then to switch to more lucrative electrical work. The skills he had learned at DeVry, specifically in working with circuitry, helped him make the transition to his new field. Dribin emphasized the value of the G.I. Bill subsistence allowances, especially given that he was already married. He sighed and said, "It was great. It paid for my schooling, paid for my upkeep. We had our own little apartment and I was able to keep it up." Dribin and his wife had their first child while he attended the program; he then took a part-time job but was still able to complete his training under the G.I. Bill.

Certainly some veterans used the G.I. Bill vocational training simply because it was available rather than as a path toward a career. Alphanse Antonowitz was already employed full time at U.S. Steel in Chicago when he decided to utilize the benefits to learn radio and television repair skills at Coyne Electrical School. "[The G.I. Bill] was getting near expiration so I said, 'I might as well take it.' If I was real ambitious, I might have jumped in right away; ... since I dragged it on, you might say it was hit-and-miss.... I expected it would be useful, [though] I didn't expect to be a TV repairman all my life, or anything." Nonetheless, the benefits did allow Antonowitz to earn a second income: "When I worked at U.S. Steel . . . instead of going home [at five], I'd fix a TV or two."

Public officials worried continually that federal dollars were being wasted amid the unfettered development of the vocational programs.[112] They found that schools of all varieties resorted to advertisements aimed at luring veterans to enroll in programs in order to gain the subsistence allowances and equipment available through the G.I. Bill; some even promised to pay bonuses to veteran students as a means of gaining their government-sponsored tuition payments.[113] State authorities in the South insisted—contrary to the aims of federal administrators—on establishing brand-new segregated programs catering specifically to "white veterans" or "colored veterans."[114] And nonprofit schools below the college level often charged the VA more than the cost of veterans' training, garnering federal funds for the construction of new buildings and purchase of new equipment. Subsequently, the VA adopted new procedures and recovered approximately $5.5 million in surplus funds from such schools. After detecting price gouging by the new for-profit schools, in 1948 the VA began to require them to submit financial statements, and declared that 58 percent were charging rates in excess of fair and reasonable amounts.[115] Despite all of these shortcomings, veterans typically considered the vocational schools to be deeply consequential for their lives, delivering high-quality training and endowing them with useful skills that enhanced their occupational opportunities.

On-the-Job Training

In 1946, Veterans Administration head Omar N. Bradley warned the nation that in on-the-job training programs, "a national scandal may be in the making involving millions in Federal funds." Bradley pointed the finger at "unscrupulous persons" who were taking advantage of the program.[116] Indeed, government studies detected numerous abuses: businesses paying lower wages to veterans than nonveterans because the veterans were receiving subsistence allowances, lack of adequate classroom instruction, programs providing trainees with unnecessary tools at government expense, and programs offering training that either duplicated veterans' proficiencies or failed to coincide with job objectives.[117] Certainly some interview subjects testified to such difficulties. The worst indictment of the program came from Fred Windham, who found the mechanics training program he attended for three to four years in California to be useless. Though the program was intended to function as an apprenticeship, "I was practically forgotten," said Windham. "There was no school, no testing, nothing." Joe O'Leary had no complaints about the quality of his laundry and dry cleaning apprenticeship, but after learning those skills for two years—"until the money ran out"—he proceeded to work for the railroad, which he would have done sooner had the G.I. Bill benefits not been available. Most egregious, the on-the-job programs in the South also were segregated by race.[118]

Still, many veterans found on-the-job training to be a positive experience. Kermit Pransky, for example, attended a program for several months in Boston where he learned about motors and small engine repair, enabling him to go into business with his brother-in-law. Subsequently, as a small-business owner himself, he became involved in training other veterans. "I thought the government did a great job that way, in trying to get the people into something that they liked," he commented.

In response to early excesses in the program, Congress enacted amendments that stipulated a nationwide limit of two years for veterans in job training programs, authorized aid to the states to facilitate greater program supervision, and placed limits on overall payments to veterans. As a result, veterans in the job training programs encountered more cumbersome bureaucratic procedures than veterans in the other programs.[119] Pransky remembered, "There was a lot of paperwork involved. Once you were in . . . you had to fill out [forms]: first the teacher had to fill out instructions and then you had to abide by the instructions. It was a lot of red tape involved, a necessary evil."

James Johnson was already employed at the Atlanta Gas Light Company when he had the opportunity to apprentice for the company to acquire further training. "I ended up as a first-class journeyman. I was a troubleshooter. I was trained in all phases of it, from a Bunsen burner to a boiler." The training was extensive, he noted. "I took it at night and after work, and it went on for a year or better." In the absence of the G.I. Bill, Johnson explained, the company would have had to pay the entire cost of the training, whereas with the benefits, the federal government partially offset expenses. "But the G.I. Bill helped them to get good employees," he added. Johnson evaluated the quality of the program as "great," explaining that "we had a laboratory that we worked in. We did the actual things, like calibrating thermostats, insulation, things of that sort. I used the training I got for the next ten years in that job. It also helped me into my next job as an industrial supply salesman." Like Pransky, Johnson encountered "a good bit of paperwork." "You had to take these tests. First, I went as an apprentice, then I was moved up to a second-class journeyman, and then moved from there to a first-class journeyman . . . pass[ing] all the tests. I was very lucky—I passed it the first time. Some of the men had to take it four to five times. I wanted to pass it because the pay scale was better."

Other Programs

Notably, the only G.I. Bill-financed training programs that less than half of beneficiaries ranked as a turning point in their lives—on-the-farm training and correspondence courses—were those that proved especially difficult for administrators to regulate. More than half of all veterans utilizing the farm program resided in the South, where the resistance to federal control combined with the retention of program authority by local advisory committees yielded notorious instances of program implementation. A General Accounting Office study uncovered numerous examples of abuse, typically involving veterans who received little or no training for their farm labor, and occasional instances of funding for veterans who already owned farms and had substantial backgrounds in agriculture. Over a hundred thousand veterans dropped the program without finishing.[120] While low levels of usage of on-the-farm training among black veterans may have resulted in part from their desire to leave agriculture behind, discrimination by local whites who administered training and controlled access to farm loans is a more likely explanation of the discrepancy.[121] The VA did not conduct extensive oversight of correspondence courses but found that only 10.7 percent of veterans who chose such programs completed their course of study; it suggested that "many of the courses taken were of little subsequent use to the veterans."[122] Nonetheless, even in these programs, some veterans attained valuable training, as suggested by the turning-point data in Table 4.2 above.[123]

Best Years

Reflecting back on how he felt about using the G.I. Bill at Penn State, James Murray, who said he never would have considered going to college were it not for the G.I. Bill, paused and his eyes filled with tears. "We were driving out of State College after I graduated and got the job in Washington, and I stopped the car. My wife asked why. . . . I said I just wanted to look [back] at the college. We'd been there for four and a half years. I said, 'These have been the best years of our lives.' She said, 'You're right.'"

By the time World War II veterans' eligibility for G.I. Bill benefits ended in the mid-1950s, 7.8 million veterans had acquired education or training. Government expenditures for the provisions totaled $14.5 billion, including $10 billion for subsistence allowances to veterans and $3.9 billion in tuition and fees paid directly to the schools and colleges.[124] Not surprisingly for a brand-new program that met with overwhelming demand, implementation presented significant challenges. Complexities had been foreordained in the institutional arrangements, with public funding channeled to many private institutions, and federal administrators reliant on ground-level supervision by state and local authorities. Fortunately, the higher education provisions could be implemented through the existing network of institutions, though administrators struggled to find enough instructors, classrooms, and housing to accommodate the massive enrollments of students. The vocational training programs forced the instant emergence of thousands of new schools and institutes, and the job training and on-the-farm programs required government officials to establish unprecedented, and often thorny, relationships with individual employers. Given these gargantuan obstacles, program implementation—especially from the viewpoint of most citizens benefiting from the program—proved a stunning success.

With few exceptions, veterans experienced these provisions of the bill in a highly positive manner. The college-educated veterans felt that they were regarded with respect and were guaranteed generous benefits that were easily accessible through routinized procedures. Though veterans using the programs below the college level met with somewhat more cumbersome administrative procedures, most found the training they received to be highly useful, and they also felt they were well treated. The cognitive effects of the experience of program implementation, marked primarily by fairness and ease of accessibility, proved powerful for many veterans. These characterizations appear to have held true for African American beneficiaries, who distinguished between the effects of the G.I. Bill itself and the segregated schools and programs in which many had to use its benefits.

At the same time, the manner of the G.I. Bill's delivery made government's role plainly manifest. Through the administration of eligibility rules, as well as tuition payments and stipend allocations, veterans were continually reminded that government had sponsored their education. Scholars have suggested that the visibility and traceability of government programs have an important bearing on their civic consequences among mass publics.[125] The fact that veterans readily identified the G.I. Bill as a government program was evidenced by responses to the interview question "What does the American government owe veterans? How well has government done in this regard?"[126] Veterans typically responded that government had treated World War II veterans well, and they frequently mentioned their own usage of the G.I. Bill's education and training benefits as a chief example. Richard Colosimo remarked: "As far as World War II veterans, they did well. I must admit if it wasn't for government and subsidizing our education I never would have gotten my degree, both degrees." Sam Marchesi said, "The government made many opportunities for us . . . for a man such as myself with a lack of education to better myself." Veterans routinely credited government with the benefits they received from the G.I. Bill, and they experienced those benefits as granting them an elevated status in American society. Conceivably, these effects would, in turn, spur them to become more involved in public life.

5

Fostering Social Opportunity

John Mulravey grew up on the edge of Boston, "in a section of Brookline called Wishing Point." Most adults in the neighborhood, he explained, were employed as "chauffeurs [or] housekeepers on the big estates. The affluent people didn't go for civil service jobs, so most of our family . . . and friends . . . became policemen, firemen, and worked in the towns. . . . The G.I. Bill was the thing that saved all of us," emphasized Mulravey. "It was the best thing that happened to the military men that were low-income at that time. They became all very, very successful people in different positions in big companies. But they got their start through the G.I. Bill."

Social scientists have long known that in the lives of many veterans, World War II marked a critical turning point, shaping the subsequent course of their lives in significant ways, but how the G.I. Bill might have figured into such outcomes has been unclear.[1] Scholarly studies and government reports have suggested that veterans enjoyed academic, occupational, and economic success that surpassed that of nonveterans.[2] Yet most of these fail to control for G.I. Bill usage, and those that do consider it tend to limit their analysis to the effects on income alone.

When given the option of including the G.I. Bill among life turning points, a majority of those who used the education and training provisions identified it as such, along with such life-transforming events as growing up in the Depression, military service during World War II, education, job opportunities, and marriage. Among nonblack male respondents to the World War II Veterans Survey, fully 78 percent of those who used the G.I. Bill for higher education and 58 percent of those who used subcollege-level programs regarded the G.I. Bill as a turning point in their lives.[3] Rates were even higher among African American male veterans in the 92nd Infantry Division, of whom 92 percent of the higher education beneficiaries and 89 percent of the subcollege beneficiaries considered the bill a turning point.

Asked to identify how the G.I. Bill made such a difference in their lives, the higher education beneficiaries offered a resounding chorus about its profound effects. They stated, over and over, that it made college possible or affordable for them, or shortened the time it took to complete their degree. Some spoke of more subtle or far-reaching effects. A few emphasized the long-term effects on their careers, saying that it "led to a good job with a major corporation from which I retired after forty years of service with a good pension," or that it "gave me the opportunity to have a career (thirty-eight years) as a teacher." Others praised the bill for permitting them to combine being a student with family life, as the free tuition and subsistence allowances enabled them to marry while in college, or to attend college if they were already married and had children. Several explained that the education they received led to personal growth, enhancing their self-image and enabling them to develop a more sophisticated personal philosophy and worldview: they noted that it "opened my potential to achieve," "eliminated [an] inferiority complex of not having a college education," "helped to engage my mind in learning; helped me to become more self-assured and confident," and "broadened my outlook and philosophy of life." One man wrote that in his case, the G.I. Bill "broadened my scope of knowledge, making me hireable, interesting; increased my friendships, which now, fifty years later, still permeate my life—just last week [I] spent five days rafting and fishing with eight others from my college days." Some answers from African American veterans of the 92nd Infantry Division spoke of effects of the policy that were especially striking given the segregation in so many facets of life at the time: "[It] prepared me for [a] position I never dreamed possible," "Despite [the] racism of [the] country [I] was able to gain job opportunities because of college education," and "[It] enabled me to attain college of my choice."

Those who used the G.I. Bill for vocational training or other subcollege programs also emphasized the program's wide-ranging and transformative effects on their lives. Some credited it with enhancing their employment prospects and standard of living, saying that it "got me off the farm," "helped me get a job with General Motors," "helped me learn new farming methods," "gave me a chance to try other venues of work," or "helped me make a decent living for my family." A few elaborated in statements such as "My tool-making apprenticeship and related schooling helped me advance into manufacturing engineering, where I worked for thirty years," "It put me in position to acquire a career ladder job with the Social Security Administration, [which] provided me with a good retirement with the [federal] government," and "[I] became an optician [and] owned my own business for forty-one years." As with the higher education beneficiaries, some pointed to even more personal ways in which the program affected them: "[gave me] ability to function well in society," "made me feel better about myself," and "enhanced [my] self-confidence." Through hundreds of such responses, veterans affirmed the value of the same subcollege programs that had been frequently maligned in congressional hearings and by presidential commissions, and which have never received much attention from journalists or scholars.

That veterans credited the G.I. Bill with changing their lives so substantially is evidence of yet another way, in addition to those we have seen previously, in which the policy conveyed messages to citizens that they were full-fledged and honored citizens, and that government was for and about people like them. First, though, we must consider what the G.I. Bill's perceived socioeconomic effects actually amounted to. Scholars have argued that various forms of social and economic advancement—for example, higher levels of education or occupational status—may prompt higher rates of involvement in civic life and politics.[4] Evaluating the extent to which these purported first-order effects actually materialized for G.I. Bill users will allow us to assess what difference they might have made for veterans' subsequent civic participation.

Educational Attainment

Individuals who are more highly educated are more likely to participate in civic organizations and politics, and thus we can expect that to the extent the G.I. Bill's education and training benefits actually elevated veterans' levels of education, they also may have increased their likelihood of participating in civic life.[5] Scholars reason that advanced levels of education stimulate the development of the skills, resources, and networks that help facilitate civic capacity.[6] For example, college-educated people typically develop advanced writing skills and confidence in public speaking, both through their education and also in their later employment, and they can use such abilities to make their concerns known to elected officials or to speak up at public meetings. These effects are thought to accrue over time, amplifying the influence of education on civic engagement over a lifetime. Economists have also found that greater educational attainment extends individuals' lives, promotes better health, and reduces early childbearing and single parenthood, any of which might also facilitate the well-being and time available for engaging more in public life.[7]

Did usage of the G.I. Bill's education and training provisions elevate beneficiaries' educational levels above what they would have been if it had not existed? Here, rather than focusing on veterans' access to the program, as we did in Chapter 3, we are asking about how far it actually took them in terms of formal education. Certainly majorities of veterans believed they attained more education through G.I. Bill use than they would have in its absence. The differences between veteran and nonveteran students graduating from the same colleges and universities in 1949, revealed by the Class of 1949 Survey, also suggest that the G.I. Bill aided less privileged individuals. Compared to nonveterans, veteran students came from families in which parents had less education and in which they had received less encouragement to pursue an education. Studies of the student body at other universities and colleges also found that veteran students came from less privileged backgrounds.[8] Neither these descriptions nor veterans' own perceptions tell us definitively, however, whether the G.I. Bill actually enabled individuals to acquire more education than they would have otherwise.

Several scholars have used statistical tools to compare the strength of various factors that may have influenced the highest level of education attained by G.I. Bill users, while holding others constant. Some taking this approach suggest that the provisions yielded a mildly positive effect: other things being equal, the G.I. Bill user acquired between one-third and one-half year more in education than the nonuser.[9] Such studies are limited, however, by their inability to account for factors widely regarded to be the chief determinants of educational attainment, namely, socioeconomic background factors from childhood and socialization factors such as having been encouraged to pursue an education while growing up.[10] Thus, they cannot tell us the extent to which differences in educational attainment are attributable to G.I. Bill usage versus other distinctions between users and nonusers.[11]

Two exceptional studies used data sources that enabled them to overcome such obstacles so that they could control effectively for socioeconomic background factors. Neil Fligstein, using the Occupational Changes in a Generation Survey, a 1973 survey of 33,614 men between the ages of twenty and sixty-five, both veterans and nonveterans, shows that G.I. Bill users gained between 2.7 and 2.9 more years of education than they would have otherwise.[12] Jere Behrman and his coauthors, drawing on data samples of white male veteran twins and their offspring, also found that G.I. Bill usage had a similarly pronounced effect.[13] Notably, when compared to others that failed to account for such factors, both of these studies offer evidence that the G.I. Bill had a much more powerful effect on extending educational attainment.[14]

While we will defer to these studies for actual estimates of the extent to which the G.I. Bill extended users' levels of education, the World War II Veterans Survey includes measures of socioeconomic background and socialization, and thus it is helpful for examining the *relative* significance of the G.I. Bill in extending educational levels among nonblack male veterans. Holding steady several other determinants of educational attainment, we can assess the relative influence of the G.I. Bill's higher education provisions.[15] This analysis reveals that benefit usage proved to be the most influential factor in determining respondents' educational attainment, exerting an even stronger influence than level of education prior to military service, although both factors are highly significant. The power of the G.I. Bill's provisions to further veterans' educational level becomes all the more striking when we consider the insignificance of a number of factors that would typically have influenced such outcomes in the early twentieth century. For instance, it is surprising that age is not a significant determinant, given that veterans had missed the chance to attend college at the typical point in their lives because of military service. Yet, whereas before the war college students had nearly always been young and single, the subsistence allotments for veterans and their families, combined with the new family housing erected on many campuses, made college newly accessible for older individuals, who often were already married.[16] Even more impressive is the impotence of socioeconomic, socialization, and religious factors, each traditionally so important in determining how much education individuals pursued. In effect, then, the G.I. Bill mitigated the ability of these factors to determine how much education veterans acquired; rather, it allowed less advantaged individuals who had been socialized to pursue education to do so successfully.

Besides enabling beneficiaries to advance toward their dream careers and a higher standard of living, the G.I. Bill's higher education benefits also may have produced a stronger sense of civic duty and other attitudes conducive to civic involvement. Noted Ann Sharp of the G.I. Bill's benefits, "It enabled me to become a teacher and to fulfill a dream I had. It rounded out my thinking . . . it exposed me to ideas and other ways of looking at things. My mother used to say [that] I only saw black or white; I never realized there was gray. . . . Going to college helped me see there were other ways to look at things. The G.I. Bill made that possible." More highly educated individuals are known to be more tolerant in their attitudes, as well as more likely to participate in political activities.[17] While the effect of education on civic responsibility may wax and wane depending on the period discussed, studies regarding the impact of college education in the postwar United States found that between the freshman and senior years students' values changed: they became less supportive of authoritarianism, dogmatism, and prejudice, and more tolerant in their views.[18] Many felt that the education they received on the G.I. Bill opened their minds and gave them a broader view of life. Thus, the very content of higher education may have produced cognitive effects that would later be conducive to democratic citizenship.

As for the beneficiaries of the subcollege programs, all else being equal, they actually acquired less formal education than they would have without program usage. This is because most of the kinds of training that were offered have no effect on formal educational level as it is typically measured. Rather, the extent of users' level of education achieved before joining the military proved highly influential in determining their educational attainment, and so did many of the other more traditional determinants (albeit to a lesser extent): youth, having been encouraged to pursue education while growing up, standard of living in childhood, and parents' level of education. If use of the subcollege programs elevated veterans' civic involvement, then, it was not because of elevated educational attainment.

Occupational Advancement

While income may be, for most people, the most valuable product of their employment, jobs have considerably more meaning to us than simply the paycheck they generate. Jobs vary in the extent to which they feature variety in work assignments and tasks and the extent to which they offer employees opportunities to use creative skills and intellectual abilities, routes toward promotion, and chances to make decisions or exercise authority. On the basis of such variation, occupations are thought to differ in the status attributed to them by society. Government reports in the 1950s suggested that World War II veterans pursued occupations with higher statuses than did their nonveteran peers, but they were not able to specify why.[19] Whether such outcomes pertained to G.I. Bill usage is important because individuals' occupational status is known to be related to their civic involvement: the kinds of jobs people have make a difference in terms of the skills that enable them to participate actively in public life. For instance, teachers and lawyers have far more opportunities to organize meetings and make presentations than fast-food workers or meatcutters, and this makes them better prepared to take a role in civic organizations or politics.[20] Thus, we need to know whether G.I. Bill usage itself affected veterans' job status.

In the 1960s and 1970s, sociologists noticed a striking development under way in the United States.[21] Previously, a man's job status had been determined primarily by the kind of job in which his father and grandfather had been employed.[22] In the middle of the twentieth century, by contrast, many American men seemed to be experiencing dramatic upward mobility in this regard.[23] Liberated from the more rigid occupational patterns of the past, they found employment in jobs with significantly higher statuses than those in which their fathers had been employed.[24]

Certainly World War II veterans themselves viewed the G.I. Bill as a critical factor in facilitating their occupational opportunities, as evidenced by the survey responses about turning points and frequent comments throughout the interviews. In fact, occupational opportunities ranked second only to educational attainment as reasons veterans provided for considering the G.I. Bill as a turning point in their lives. In interviews, some veterans stressed the status aspects of occupational advancement and commented that they would have returned to the same types of jobs that their fathers had—in farming, mining, at steel mills, or with the railroad—had the G.I. Bill not made other opportunities available to them. John Mulravey said the G.I. Bill "made my whole life. Without it I wouldn't have been able to get into the FBI and everything else that happened after that." Similarly, Sam Marchesi, who became a builder of custom homes after completing vocational training on the G.I. Bill, said, "I became very successful at the field I chose. I have to credit the G.I. Bill for sending me to school."

Veterans not only valued the prestige and status associated with some occupations but also relished having had the opportunity to choose how they would spend their lives, to select a career that they found meaningful and fulfilling. Educator Richard Werner noted that the G.I. Bill "put me in a profession I love. I always felt that it was a gift to be able to be with young people and be able to teach them. I've never enjoyed anything else I've done as much as teaching."

Over the years, scholars have devised a multitude of scales that assign status rankings to occupations.[25] Two studies used such scales to examine how G.I. Bill usage affected socioeconomic achievement generally and occupational status in particular. One found that while occupational status among non-G.I. Bill users—veterans and nonveterans alike—could be explained by traditional background characteristics such as fathers' education, farm background, and age, the same features failed to explain the status of G.I. Bill users. The author concluded, "This evidence is quite compelling and it suggests that if one controls for level of educational attainment, the G.I. Bill user is still able to escape the effects of social background and has attained a certain amount of social mobility."[26] Another study, which focused on socioeconomic outcomes of men who grew up in poor neighborhoods of Boston during the Depression, found G.I. Bill usage to be highly significant in boosting occupational status, especially among those with a delinquent past, even when controlling for numerous individual characteristics including childhood antisocial behavior, family socioeconomic background, and IQ. Over time, G.I. Bill users emerged as more likely to have experienced a transformation in their life circumstances and to be leading more secure lives than in their youth.[27]

Using the World War II Veterans Survey, we can consider how individual veterans' occupational status in 1960, when they were in their late thirties, compared to that of their fathers, back when they were children.[28] First we will consider the experiences of nonblack males. Among those who did not use the G.I. Bill's education and training provisions, veterans' occupations typically mirrored those of their fathers'. The son of a farmer became a farmer; an autoworker's son went into the auto industry himself; a salesman begat a salesman, and a lawyer another lawyer. The majority of the fathers of nonusers of the G.I. Bill worked in jobs that fit one of three categories: skilled manual work (for instance, as a postal worker or streetcar conductor), semiskilled work (e.g. steamfitter, steelworker, or chauffeur), or unskilled jobs (for example, as a stevedore, peddler, or concrete worker). Some limited upward mobility was apparent, as some sons of unskilled workers made their way into the ranks of semiskilled workers, and other sons of semiskilled workers became skilled workers. A few sons emerged, by 1960, as self-employed owners of small businesses or gained responsibility for overseeing others in factories or small businesses. Still, the relatively few non-G.I. Bill users who became stockbrokers, business executives, and attorneys typically were the sons of men who had similarly prestigious occupations; these individuals were likely to have acquired their college degrees prior to military service, at their own expense. The occupational mobility associated with the postwar era was barely apparent among these non-G.I. Bill beneficiaries.

Veterans who used the G.I. Bill for vocational training and related subcollege programs, a random sampling of whom is shown in Table 5.1, enjoyed more frequent and greater leaps of social mobility than nonbeneficiaries.[29] Many fathers in this group had worked as laborers, coal miners, farmers, and mechanics, or in factories or on the railroad; others had been employed as bank tellers, furriers, loggers, cotton mill workers, bakers, and bricklayers. After G.I. Bill usage, some of their sons worked as skilled manual employees, but more often they became the

Table 5.1. Nonblack Male Subcollege Users of G.I. Bill, World War II Veterans Survey (Random Sampling of Responses)

Father's Occupation During Veteran's Childhood	Veteran's Occupation, 1960
Carpenter	Production manager, glass machinery manufacturer
Manager, lumberyard	Manager, lumberyard
Salesman, International Harvester	Auditor, Air Force Audit Agency
Cooper	Claim authorizer, Social Security Administration
Farmer	Mechanic
High school teacher and principal, farmer	Senior partner, public accounting practice
Coal miner	Technician, appliance repair store
Farmer	Pilot, U.S. Air Force
Farmhand	Watch repairman
Train conductor, railroad	President, insurance agency
Machinist, auto industry	Assistant professor of military science and tactics, university
Farmer	Civil service, education specialist
Bricklayer	Carpenter
Insurance salesman	U.S. Army, head of ROTC on university campus
Farmer and blacksmith	Logger
Farmer	Sales manager, tire and rubber company

owners of small or medium-sized businesses, took jobs in a supervisory or managerial capacity, or advanced to become commissioned officers in the military. For many, their G.I. Bill training helped them to get hired or promoted, especially in the technical trades. In the postwar economy, such jobs offered a high degree of employment security and a middle-class standard of living. They commanded not only relatively strong wages but also employer-provided health and pension benefits and enhanced status.[30] Far from being inferior substitutes for the higher education provisions, then, the subcollege benefits facilitated a meaningful advancement in the quality of life enjoyed by these veterans and their families.[31]

Among those who used the G.I. Bill for higher education were many who experienced breathtaking transformation in their life circumstances. A random sampling from the full array of responses, shown in Table 5.2, offers a glimpse of the kind of occupational change experienced from one generation to the next. Here are the son of the shoe salesman who became a chief of seismological services for the U.S. government before he was forty years old, the upholsterer's son who became a teacher, the postal employee's son who became a school principal, the longshoreman's son who became an attorney in private practice, the coal miner's son who became a geologist, the cobbler's son who became an engineer, and

Table 5.2. Nonblack Male Higher Education Users of G.I. Bill, World War II Veterans Survey (Random Sampling of Responses)

Father's Occupation During Veteran's Childhood	Veteran's Occupation, 1960
Coal miner	Superintendent of maintenance
Plumber	Plumber
Postal service employee	Industrial district sales manager
Credit manager	Accountant, manager of forecasting
Barber	Attorney
Rubber worker	Manager, plant engineer
Accountant	Regional sales manager
Ambulance driver	High school teacher
Tool grinder	Doctor of podiatry
Auto salesman	Schedule manager, 1960 presidential campaign, Republican Party
Coal miner	Mining engineer
Laborer, foundry	Teacher
Fireman and engineer, Southern Railway	Self-employed builder-developer
Farmer	Manager, commercial research, manufacturing company
Owner/manager, real estate development and furniture factory	Television producer
Baker	Optometrist, self-employed
Manager, farmers' mercantile and farmer	Design engineer, nuclear industry

the window cleaner's son who became a chemist. Certainly some college users, with greater frequency than nonusers, had fathers who worked in high-status professions, and they typically acquired occupations of similar status: a lawyer begat a microbiologist, an accountant's son grew into a professor of mathematics, an investment banker's son became a mechanical engineer. Just as it was not surprising that individuals from upper-class families would be more likely to take advantage of the higher education provisions than others, and just as it was to be expected that those whose fathers had more education would themselves attain more education, neither is it surprising that the sons of high-status fathers would themselves attain high status after using the G.I. Bill. What is so astonishing, though, is that so many other G.I. Bill users did achieve upward social mobility, often by several leaps along any scale of occupational status. Veterans appeared less impressed with the prestige that sociologists attach to such transitions than to the fact that they and their friends were able to find jobs that matched their passions and interests and gave them more freedom, more decision-making authority, and more ability to use their intellectual and creative powers than their fathers had enjoyed.

Black male veterans' occupations in 1960 and their fathers' occupations during their childhood reveal different patterns than those of the nonblack males, and the disparities illuminate the boundaries of institutionalized racism that persisted in most jobs and professions.[32] Nearly all of the fathers of black veterans had worked as semiskilled or unskilled laborers—janitors, masons, bricklayers, dry cleaners, stevedores, factory workers, coal miners, and railroad workers—with only a handful in highly skilled professions such as law, medicine, or education. Their sons did experience upward mobility in employment, typically to extents that varied according to the level of advanced education they obtained through the G.I. Bill, but their occupational advancement was clearly more limited than that of white men. Some of the black non–G.I. Bill users gained positions with greater leadership responsibility than their fathers, often as foremen in industry or as master sergeants in the U.S. Army. The G.I. Bill users generally achieved higher occupational statuses, but in different jobs than their nonblack cohorts did. Those who used the vocational training programs frequently continued in military service or found civil service jobs as policemen, mail carriers, and clerks. They do not appear to have moved into the highly technical industrial jobs that their nonblack peers did. Similarly, by 1960 the black higher education beneficiaries typically worked in the public sector as teachers or civil servants or in the military; they were less likely than white veterans to have secured higher-status jobs in the private sector, for example, as executives, proprietors of large concerns, and professionals. Their jobs point to both the scope and the limits of antidiscrimination provisions that were applied to government employment beginning with the Fair Employment Practices Commission in the 1940s and through subsequent reforms preceding the Civil Rights Act of 1964.[33]

Many African American veterans who used the higher education provisions of the G.I. Bill found that afterward, the job market to which they returned, degrees in hand, remained highly segmented. Gentry Torian, who served in the 92nd Infantry Division, used the G.I. Bill to attend college but was unable to find a job in teaching, his chosen profession, for many years. He worked in a factory until finally he achieved his dream and began to teach. After the war, explained his wife, Celeste Torian, "the only good thing was the G.I. Bill." One survey respondent wrote of the G.I. Bill, "It changed my outlook on how to live, but I couldn't change my color." Indeed, another respondent wrote "equal employment laws" in the blank next to "other turning point." For African Americans, the G.I. Bill appears to have gone far in preparing them for jobs of higher status than their fathers enjoyed, but racial discrimination in the job market continued to thwart their chances for social mobility.[34]

The G.I. Bill served as a vehicle though which the occupational status of men—both nonblacks and blacks—was elevated in the course of a generation, although racial biases limited African American beneficiaries' ascendance in the job hierarchy.[35] To the extent that the education and training provisions moved veterans toward jobs that involved greater interaction with others and use of written and oral analytical skills, they are likely to have improved beneficiaries' capacity for civic engagement.

Income

Veterans themselves certainly credited the G.I. Bill's education and training provisions with boosting their earnings, as evidenced by the World War II Veterans Survey. Scholars have found that veterans who served in the wars of the mid-twentieth century, particularly those from socially disadvantaged groups, enjoyed higher subsequent incomes than nonveterans. They explain veterans' elevated earnings by suggesting that military experience offered a "bridging environment" that conferred new skills and abilities on individuals, and that employers used veteran status as a screening device in hiring decisions.[36] But this leaves unanswered the question of whether the G.I. Bill itself actually raised veterans' incomes beyond what they would have been otherwise.[37] If so, such outcomes might help explain beneficiaries' higher rates of civic involvement. Not surprisingly, people with higher incomes are much more likely than others to make financial contributions to political campaigns. But higher-income people also participate at higher rates in a wide array of political activities, in part because they are more frequently recruited or asked to become involved.[38]

Certainly given the impact of the G.I. Bill on educational attainment, a subsequent boost in earnings might seem like an obvious result today. The effectiveness of advanced education in fostering higher incomes must be viewed, however, in historical context. Although an individual's educational level is a strong predictor of his or her earnings in the contemporary United States, the relationship between education and income was not as dramatic at midcentury. The 1940s through the early 1970s marked an era of "wage compression" in the United States relative to the earlier decades of the twentieth century and to the decades since that time.[39] The percentage of Americans with a high school education had increased sharply, especially during the Depression, and labor markets became flooded with applicants for white-collar jobs. As a result, education offered less of a premium to workers than it had earlier in the century.[40] Simultaneously, several factors also helped raise the earnings of less-skilled workers, including the demand for their labor in the wartime economy, the establishment of the minimum wage in 1938, the strength of organized labor throughout the era, and the postwar demand for construction workers.[41] Thus, in 1950, the income gap between the least well paid and most well paid workers diminished to its lowest point in the entire twentieth century. Inequality remained fairly low over the next two decades until it ascended dramatically once again beginning in the mid-1970s.[42]

As a result, the education and training attained through the G.I. Bill did raise incomes, but in different ways than might be expected today. A careful study of its effects on income among World War II and Korean War veterans found that in 1955, veterans who had used the benefits earned $56 per month more, on average, than nonusers.[43] These distinctions varied considerably by veterans' age group, the length of time they had worked in the same occupation, and the type of job they held before entering the service. Among younger veterans, G.I. Bill users tended to have higher wages than nonusers in their age bracket; those who saw the greatest boost in their incomes had worked in semiskilled jobs previously (as factory operatives and in related positions), and their training under the G.I. Bill enabled them to advance to higher-paying positions. Such individuals experienced a large increase in their earnings, making $459 more annually than those who had worked alongside them before the war but who opted not to use the G.I. Bill benefits.[44] By contrast, among veterans age thirty-five and older, those who returned to the jobs in which they had worked prior to the war actually enjoyed higher incomes than G.I. Bill users. Their jobs were protected through both the preferential treatment afforded to veterans and the efforts of labor unions to perpetuate the privileges associated with seniority.[45] As a result, they earned relatively high wages—considerably more than their peers who opted to return to school. Given that the bulk of G.I. Bill users came from the younger age bracket, however, the majority of program beneficiaries did reap income gains from their program usage.[46]

African American G.I. Bill users experienced less of an income boost after program usage than white beneficiaries. While those who achieved higher levels of education did earn larger paychecks in 1960 than those with less schooling, prevailing discrimination in employment and the racially segmented nature of labor markets meant that advanced education offered a smaller income return to nonwhites than to whites. Among whites in 1960, those with some college earned an average of $1,300 more annually than high school graduates, whereas blacks with some college received only $300 more than blacks with high school diplomas. And though earnings for both whites and nonwhites were lower in the South than elsewhere, the racial wage gap ratio was similar in all regions.[47]

Later in the twentieth century, incomes in the United States became more closely related to educational attainment, and thus by late in their lives, veterans who had achieved the highest levels of education through the G.I. Bill stood poised to reap the greatest income gains. After 1970, highly educated nonblack males, especially those employed in scientific and technical fields, saw their real incomes increase, whereas those in blue-collar jobs witnessed declines in the value of their earnings.[48] Those who had used the G.I. Bill for higher education were thus especially likely to see the greatest income boost from their education at that juncture.[49] By contrast, many of the vocational training beneficiaries and non-college-educated nonusers of the program likely experienced stagnating wages in the last decades of the century. Indeed, among survey respondents, considerably greater income disparity emerged between the most and least well educated veterans by 1997 than had existed in 1960.

In sum, the immediate income effects of the G.I. Bill appear to have been greatest among young veterans who used the subcollege provisions of the bill, though such gains were restricted primarily to white beneficiaries. Only later on would those who had gained higher education through the program experience substantial income advantages.

Home Ownership

American home ownership soared in the postwar era. While the G.I. Bill's loan guarantee program, which offered veterans government-backed credit to buy a home (or, alternatively, a business or farm), is often assumed to have played a critical role in the process, the booming economy, favorable tax laws, public programs, and a revived home-building industry all contributed to putting ownership within the reach of far more families.[50] From around 1900 until the Great Depression, an average of 47 percent of Americans owned their own homes; rates declined to 44 percent by 1940. After the war new financing arrangements facilitated and backed by the government, permitted banks to lower the required 50-percent down payment and allowed mortgages to be paid off over periods longer than the previous standard of five to ten years.[51] In many locations, it became cheaper to buy a home than to rent an apartment.[52] By 1960, 62 percent of Americans claimed a house of their own, a rate that held fairly constant throughout the remainder of the century.[53] Scholars have suggested that those who own homes are more rooted in their communities and are more likely to be active in politics and community affairs as a result, especially at the local level.[54] If the G.I. Bill's loan guarantee provisions truly did expand home ownership, that outcome might help explain enhanced rates of civic engagement.

In fact, among nonblack veterans who responded to the World War II Veterans Survey, the G.I. Bill's loan guarantee provisions did boost home ownership rates.[55] Veterans were granted home loans with a term of up to thirty years and a maximum interest rate of 4.5 percent. Several interview subjects remembered the exact interest rate and down payment on their first home. The government guaranteed up to 60 percent of the loan, to a maximum of $7,500. Veterans could use the loan anytime within ten years of the end of the war.[56] Overall, 29 percent of all World War II veterans took advantage of the loan guarantee provisions, compared to 51 percent who used the education and training benefits. Among borrowers, 93 percent purchased homes, 5 percent acquired businesses, and 2 percent bought farms.[57] Purchases of first homes among veterans peaked during the late 1940s and early 1950s, the era when they enjoyed access to the G.I. Bill provisions.

Interestingly, the education and training provisions of the G.I. Bill did not themselves affect rates of home ownership. Neither did the group of veterans who utilized the home mortgage program overlap significantly with those who used the educational benefits.[58] Not all education beneficiaries were positioned to use the loan program; as Isaac Gellert explained, "I was not at that stage in my life," given that he was pursuing his studies, culminating in a doctorate, during much of the eligibility period.

While home ownership itself might have boosted civic engagement, it is unlikely that veterans' experience of the G.I. Bill provisions helped generate such outcomes. By contrast to the education and training provisions, the loan provisions did not convey the same powerful messages to veterans about how government mattered in their lives. Likely this owed in part to the fact that the Federal Housing Administration (FHA) offered loans with rates comparable to the G.I. Bill, and banks offered rates that averaged only about one percentage point higher.[59] Though a few veterans specified the use of the G.I. Bill's loan guarantee program as a turning point, most did not attach the same significance to that program as they did to the education and training provisions, which they experienced as an investment in their lives, one that was far more personally transformative than home ownership.

Perhaps one reason the loan program made less of a lasting and favorable impression on veterans is because it lacked the inclusive character of the G.I. Bill's education and training provisions. Despite the federal government's willingness to guarantee the loans, veterans had to find a bank or lending agency that would agree to lend to them. This could prove difficult for those with an insufficient history of good credit, particularly lower-income veterans.[60] And more than any other feature of the G.I. Bill, the loan program was vulnerable to racism because it required African American veterans to pass through a gauntlet of local banks that were often unwilling to make loans to them. Unlike the education and training provisions, to which African Americans had access (but had to use in segregated programs if they lived in the South), in the case of the loan provisions they were often denied benefit usage outright. Experiences in the South were notorious: for example, *Ebony* magazine found that among 3,229 VA-backed loans granted in Mississippi cities in 1947, black veterans received only 2. As Harry Wright, an African American veteran himself and a field agent for the Southern Regional Council, observed: "To Negro veterans in Mississippi, getting a G.I. loan is similar to seeking 'The Holy Grail.'"[61] In fact, racial exclusion in real estate markets was a nationwide phenomenon, owing to federal policies. The Home Owners' Loan Corporation, signed into law by Roosevelt in 1933, had systematized uniform appraisal methods across the nation, in part through the creation of "residential security maps" that classified neighborhoods. These maps were used routinely by financial institutions to refuse loans for home purchases in "redlined" neighborhoods, those categorized as "definitely declining" or "hazardous" either because they appeared to be physically deteriorating or because members of minority groups resided there. Such procedures effectively encouraged white migration to suburban neighborhoods and relegated African Americans to decaying urban areas. The Federal Housing Administration, established as part of the National Housing Act of 1934, had exacerbated the problem by conveying criteria to underwriters that effectively devalued urban neighborhoods and encouraged mortgage loans for suburban homes.[62] The G.I. Bill loan guarantee provisions were administered through procedures similar to those for FHA mortgages, and while neither program overtly sanctioned discrimination, the guidelines used by local lenders and the discretion they retained led, in many areas, to that result.[63] Indeed, one black survey respondent wrote, "I was required to make a 10 percent down payment because I was told that colored G.I.s were a bad risk." The treatment of African American veterans under the loan guarantee provisions stood in contrast to what they encountered under most aspects of the education and training provisions. Those who experienced such discrimination received clear messages that despite their military service on behalf of the nation, they were unworthy of the treatment afforded to white citizens.

Suburbanization

The pace of suburbanization in the United States intensified dramatically after World War II. Many young Americans moved away from the farms and urban areas where they had been raised; nonblacks, especially, took up residence in new homes built in subdivisions outside the nation's cities. Veterans and their families were prominent among the throngs who moved to the inexpensive, mass-built homes of the Levittowns on Long Island and outside Philadelphia, and to similar communities across the nation.[64] Such neighborhoods, developed on the periphery of urban areas, featured lower density of population, detached homes with yards, and similarity in architecture, including Capes, split-level, ranch-style, and modified colonial-style homes. Initially, as suburbs grew in the 1950s and 1960s, they were touted as havens for "joiners."[65] Potentially, then, if the G.I. Bill did facilitate suburbanization, that may help explain why beneficiaries became more involved in civic life.

Certainly numerous nonblack respondents to the World War II Veterans Survey moved from rural or urban areas to the suburbs during the postwar era. Overall, the proportion of respondents who lived on farms declined from 17 percent in childhood to 5 percent by 1960, and the proportion living in large cities dropped from 20 percent to 16 percent. Suburbs, from which only 7 percent of veterans hailed before the war, absorbed most of the transients, becoming home to 24 percent after the war. Yet, although vast numbers of veterans shifted to the suburbs, those who used the G.I. Bill for education or training were only slightly more likely to make the move: 18 percent more lived in suburbs in 1960 than had lived there during their childhood, compared to 15 percent for nonusers of the G.I. Bill. Neither was use of the loan guarantee program highly correlated with suburbanization: the greatest percentage of beneficiaries—31 percent—bought homes in towns or small cities, followed by the 29 percent who chose homes in suburban neighborhoods.[66]

In the postwar years, African Americans, veterans included, continued to participate in the Great Migration—which had already been under way for decades—leaving behind sharecropping and rural and small-town life in the South to move to the North.[67] But rather than locating in the newly emergent suburbs, African Americans moved to the cities, and not by choice. The federal lending guidelines effectively relegated African Americans to deteriorating urban neighborhoods while facilitating "white flight" to what became homogenous suburbs. Firms such as the Levitt organization flatly refused to sell homes to African Americans: in 1960 not a single one of the eighty-two thousand residents of Long Island's Levittown was black.[68] Among veterans of the

92nd Infantry Division, the proportion living in large cities nearly doubled during the period, growing from 26 percent who had lived there in childhood to 51 percent in 1960. Meanwhile, the proportion of African Americans living in suburbs actually declined by a percentage point, from 12 to 11 percent, evidence of the rigid new patterns of segregation that emerged in areas far away from the Jim Crow South. Black G.I. Bill users themselves led the way toward urban areas, suggesting that the education they gained enabled them to leave behind the life of the old South.

The G.I. Bill's provisions did not, then, serve as a catalyst for the suburbanization that intensified during the postwar era, among either nonblack or black veterans. And in any case, recent research suggests that the effects of suburbanization on civic engagement are mixed. Today, at least, the time that suburbanites spend commuting and the social segregation of their neighborhoods act as disincentives to involvement in public life.[69] These findings cast doubt on the extent to which suburbanization itself—even apart from G.I. Bill usage— explains the public involvement of the civic generation.

The Long Reach of Social Rights

The G.I. Bill's education and training provisions extended highly consequential social rights to a broad cross section of nonblack male veterans of the WW II generation. The higher education provisions fostered impressive increases in beneficiaries' educational attainment, with eventual effects on their occupational status and income; the subcollege provisions yielded more immediate strong effects on users' job status and income. The program has also been credited with enabling white Catholics, who previously had been thought to lack the values necessary for socioeconomic success, to leapfrog over white Protestants in educational attainment and to move ahead in occupational status and income.[70] Many hundreds of thousands of Protestants and Jews from working-class homes were also among those whose lives were transformed by the law. Meanwhile, the loan guarantee program facilitated home ownership.

The socioeconomic effects of the G.I. Bill's education and training provisions reached across the color line, but their impact for African Americans was curtailed by the persistence of racial discrimination in employment. The benefits represented what was likely the most egalitarian and generous twentieth-century government program black Americans had experienced up to that point, more inclusive than New Deal social programs and implemented more fairly than the G.I. Bill's own loan guarantee programs.[71] The program did significantly elevate formal educational attainment among African Americans veterans outside of the South and, through the vocational training programs, boosted the job skills of African Americans nationwide, but once black G.I. Bill beneficiaries sought jobs, they encountered the same barriers to advancement that they had faced before. Enduring discrimination, both de jure and de facto, limited the return on their advanced education and training.

Nonetheless, among both black and nonblack beneficiaries of the G.I. Bill's education and training provisions, elevated educational levels, occupational statuses, and incomes could be expected to enhance their capacity to participate in civic life. As well, the law left many of them with a strong appreciation of its high value in their lives and generated attitudes that might have facilitated their strong inclination to participate in civic life. As one recipient wrote in his survey, the G.I. Bill "renewed my faith in government."

Veterans credited the G.I. Bill with some social and economic effects beyond what we have been able to evaluate here. Perhaps most compelling is that several interview subjects remarked on what they considered to be the program's effects for the next generations, noting the rate at which their children and grandchildren attended college. One survey respondent wrote that the G.I. Bill "gave our family a 'boost' that has allowed us to help our children go to college more than I had expected, i.e., G.I. Bill benefits have been passed to a second generation!"[72]

6

Creating Active Citizens

After describing his experiences using the G.I. Bill, John Mink commented, "Those who became the movers and shakers came from backgrounds that had been oppressed before the war. It created a whole new United States. It really changed the dynamics." Military service itself had broadened the outlook of men of his generation, he reasoned, by taking them out of the "isolated environments" in which they had grown up and "thrusting everyone into situations they would never have experienced before, dealing with people, different people." Upon his return home, the G.I. Bill's education and training benefits were "probably one of the greatest advantages I ever experienced, as our whole generation did." Somehow that sequence of events, Mink reasoned, prepared his generation to become active participants in postwar democracy.

What was it about the G.I. Bill that made recipients more likely to participate in the activities of self-governance and community life? We now come to the crux of our investigation, to assess how the education and training benefits—through their actual and perceived effects, which we have observed over the last few chapters—affected veterans' subsequent participation in public affairs.

Through the program's inclusive design, its fair manner of implementation, and its transformative socioeconomic effects, it communicated to beneficiaries that government was for and about people like them, and thus it incorporated them more fully as citizens. Beneficiaries responded by embracing the duties and obligations of active citizenship. Such effects were most pronounced, as we shall see, among particular groups whose inclusion signified the expansion of social opportunity.

Igniting a Civic Era

We begin by assessing how the G.I. Bill's influence compared to that of other important factors in shaping nonblack male veterans' involvement in civic life during the immediate postwar era, 1950 to 1964, when they were young adults. Individuals' civic participation at this point in their lives is known to be highly determined by their socioeconomic well-being in childhood and by the influence of their parents as role models, as well as by their own educational attainment and standard of living.[1] Statistical analysis permits us to examine the impact of each of these factors while holding the others constant.[2] Throughout this analysis, we will be looking at the determinants of the rate of veterans' participation in two different types of civic activity. The first is their membership in a wide array of civic organizations, including fraternal groups (e.g., Masons, Lions, Elks), neighborhood or homeowners' organizations, Parent-Teacher Association (PTA) or other school-support groups, or the category "any other civic or community organization."[3] The second is their political activity, including memberships in political organizations—both clubs and party committees—and participation in a wide range of other political activities, including contacting a political official to communicate concerns about some problem or issue; working on a campaign for a candidate running for national, state, or local office; serving on any official local government board or council that deals with community problems or issues; contributing money to an individual candidate, party, or other organization that supports candidates; and participating in a protest, march, or demonstration.

It is through such analysis that it becomes evident that veterans who used the G.I. Bill's education and training provisions became especially active citizens in the postwar era. The program benefits themselves emerge as highly significant in determining both the number of civic organizations that veterans joined and the number of political organizations and political activities in which they took part.[4] All else being equal, veterans who benefited from the provisions were members of a significantly greater number of civic organizations—approximately 50 percent more—than nonusers, and they were involved in about 30 percent more political activities.

Certainly the G.I. Bill did not act alone in prompting veterans' civic involvement. As we would expect, some preexisting personal characteristics mattered as well. Specifically, veterans whose parents had been active in civic life were likely to become members of more civic organizations themselves, and those whose parents had been involved politically also became highly active in politics.[5] They had been powerfully socialized for such participation by their parents' examples as role models. Conversely, however, veterans' standard of living during the 1920s, a measure of their socioeconomic status in childhood, did not affect the rate at which they joined civic groups.[6] Importantly, the G.I. Bill's influence on civic involvement is not merely a function of such preexisting differences between individuals.

It would be reasonable to assume that the secret of the G.I. Bill's influence on civic engagement lay in the fact that the resource it offered—advanced education—is widely regarded to be the most powerful determinant of civic activity. The greater income, social networks, and skills accrued by those with more education are known to reap a considerable harvest of greater civic involvement.[7] As well, the institutions of formal education produce a more tolerant and informed citizenry, and the content of such education itself, such as civics courses, may help impart such knowledge.[8]

Yet the G.I. Bill's effect on civic involvement was not reducible simply to the formal education that it promoted. It is the case that veterans who had achieved higher levels of education joined more civic organizations than others. At the same time, even among veterans who had the same level of education, those who had used the G.I. Bill became members of more such organizations, and the relationship between G.I. Bill usage and joining was stronger than that between educational level and joining. And in the case of getting involved in political organizations and activities, once we control for G.I. Bill usage, veterans' level of education actually appears not to have made a difference. This is an unorthodox finding, to be sure, and we will probe it later in this chapter. Both of these findings make it evident that the G.I. Bill's role in prompting active citizenship was not simply a function of the degree to which it elevated educational attainment.[9]

Similarly, neither can the G.I. Bill be understood as a mere vehicle for enhanced socioeconomic well-being, which in turn generated greater civic involvement. It is the case, as we saw in the last chapter, that veterans who benefited from the education and training provisions experienced enhanced incomes and occupational status in the postwar era. Individuals who are better off in such terms are known to participate more in civic life, and our analysis shows that veterans who enjoyed higher standards of living did in fact join more civic organizations. Yet, once again, that G.I. Bill usage remains significant even when controlling for standard of living means that the actual instrument of public provision through which beneficiaries obtained their education or training—the policy itself, not just the resources it conveyed—must be responsible, in part, for stimulating their subsequent civic involvement.

Still, one might wonder whether the G.I. Bill's education and train-ing provisions, though they appear to have prompted civic involvement, might actually be disguising an underlying factor that affected both pro-gram usage and civic participation. If so, variation in the rate at which users and nonusers joined civic organizations could have arisen simply because they differed fundamentally from each other from the outset. For instance, presumably aspects of military experience—being in com-bat, or being wounded, or length of service—could be expected to have acted as a deterrent to veterans' subsequent G.I. Bill usage, as well as to their later civic participation. Yet when these factors are substituted for G.I. Bill usage, none of them proves to be a significant determinant of either form of involvement.[10] Alternatively, we might expect that those who volunteered for military service rather than being drafted are people who possess greater motivation and energy generally, and they may have both seized the chance to use the G.I. Bill and later participated at high levels in civic life.[11] But this factor does not exhibit any discernable in-fluence either.[12] Similarly, when we substitute several other factors that are unrelated to military service, none emerges to explain veterans' rates of involvement in the postwar era: neither veterans' age, nor being a first-generation American, nor living in the suburbs in the postwar era, nor the timing of becoming a home owner.[13] Veterans who had been most encouraged to pursue an education did become significantly more active in politics, possibly indicating that G.I. Bill beneficiaries were people who had been raised to take initiative in life, to seize opportuni-ties and get involved.[14] Importantly, however, this socialization factor was not as significant as G.I. Bill usage itself, and when both are ac-counted for, its significance diminishes to a marginal level.[15] Most im-portant, analyses that omit G.I. Bill usage fail to explain as much about the determinants of civic involvement as those that account for which veterans utilized the bill's education and training provisions.[16]

Even more rigorous tests confirm that the G.I. Bill's impact is not reducible to beneficiaries' other characteristics.[17] Neither can the bill's effect on civic involvement be discarded as a proxy for veteran status or belonging to the World War II generation, given that users and nonusers had these characteristics in common. Something about the program it-self prompted increased participation in civic groups.

Some scholars and political leaders have suggested that public poli-cies themselves might have a bearing on civic engagement, but generally they have emphasized ways that policies might deter active citizenship. They argue that the expansion of social rights weakens civil society and fosters dependency among citizens by advancing a rights-claiming ori-entation that displaces attention from civic obligations.[18] Clearly, very different dynamics appear to be at work in the case of the G.I. Bill, since it had the effect of elevating rather than diminishing civic involvement.

The G.I. Bill generated what can be considered an independent "feedback" effect on veterans' civic involvement. Its impact was distinct from that of preexisting personal characteristics that had prompted veterans to utilize the program, and it was in addition to the bill's effects on beneficiaries' educational attainment and standard of living, which we have been able to measure separately. Possibly, the G.I. Bill's civic impact may also have been transmitted through some resource effects that we have been unable to measure, such as enhanced occupational status, which might not be fully encapsulated by our measure of standard of living. In the main, however, these findings imply that the bill's power in generating civic involvement operated especially through its interpretive effects, the messages it conveyed to recipients, which prompted them to become more inclined to participate.

Feedback Dynamics

The G.I. Bill's education and training benefits spoke volumes to beneficiaries about the role of government in their lives and their inclusion as full citizens. First, the program's design, through which usage became widely accessible, made veterans perceive that the bill made a marked difference in their opportunity to acquire education or training. Second, beneficiaries experienced its implementation as fair and efficient, managed through procedures that made them feel treated as respected citizens. Third, the bill's socioeconomic effects left many with highly positive views about how government had played a role in transforming their life circumstances. These attitudinal effects coalesced to make recipients more cognizant that government was for and about people like them, and they responded by participating as more active citizens. The program, in other words, produced effects that subsequently transformed citizens and their likelihood of expressing their political voice, and that could in turn affect the political system itself.

The power of the G.I. Bill's feedback effects were likely exacerbated by the fact that military service had already taken young people out of their ordinary environments, exposed them to a broader world, and given them opportunities to learn to get along with those of different social backgrounds. These experiences had readied them for leadership development and civic involvement; the education and training offered by the G.I. Bill then offered the actual skills that enabled them to take the next steps.

As well, the G.I. Bill's impact may have been especially pronounced among veterans because it came as so unexpected. One interview question asked veterans to discuss how they thought about the G.I. Bill, asking whether they considered it a right or a privilege and whether they felt they owed something to American society after receiving it.[19] Nearly all respondents answered unequivocally that they did not regard the G.I. Bill as something to which they were entitled. The most common sentiments are summed up in the response of Richard Colosimo: "I considered it a privilege, a sign of gratitude. I thought, they didn't have to do that. They could have just did like they . . . did in World War I, where they gave them a bonus and that was it. They could have done that. I think this was a really smart idea and I took it with appreciation. . . . It was an opportunity. I think anybody that didn't take advantage of it missed out on an opportunity because it was rather magnanimous." Veterans explained that the G.I. Bill could not be considered a right because military service was an obligation of citizenship for which no recompense was owed. As Robert Forster articulated, "I think it was more of a way of appreciation than a right. We did what we were supposed to do and we really didn't plan on anything special. It was, of course, a very desirable thing when it came along."

From a contemporary perspective, this view might seem hard to believe, even incomprehensible. But, as we saw in Chapter 2, men of the World War II generation experienced military service as something commonplace and obligatory. And despite its difficulties, they returned home feeling, for the most part, that they had done what was required—their civic duty—and they did not expect much, if anything, in return. In fact, those with political knowledge of World War I veterans' experiences—often shaped by the experience of their fathers and uncles—knew that they had received very little from the nation upon their return. Furthermore, the World War II veterans had grown up in an era of deprivation, and while many aspired to gain more education and achieve a better life, they did not anticipate that such opportunities would be readily or easily available to them. All of these effects may have had a particularly pronounced impact among specific groups of users, through dynamics that we will now explore, focusing on the experiences of nonblack male veterans.

Critical Effects for the Less Privileged

Veterans who came from less privileged backgrounds before the war stood poised to have their lives altered most dramatically by the G.I. Bill and to be most impressed by its effects.[20] The program's generous terms of eligibility were particularly consequential for those who would not otherwise have had the opportunity to advance their education or training, and its socioeconomic effects were most pronounced for such veterans. Similarly, the ease of access and fairness associated with program implementation may have been especially striking to individuals from less privileged backgrounds, who were likely more accustomed to the invasive scrutiny and demeaning means testing associated with public assistance programs.

Indeed, veterans' praise for the procedures through which the education and training benefits were administered contrasted sharply with their portrayal of social programs targeted for the poor. When asked, "During the Depression, did any New Deal programs affect your family directly?" some who had grown up fairly poor stressed how their families attempted to avoid reliance on such programs. Richard Colosimo commented, "My father did not want to take welfare. He didn't want people to say, 'That foreigner had to come here and take welfare.'" Richard Werner, whose family lost their home after his father became unemployed in the Depression, explained, "We were pretty proud. We may have been poor, but nobody wanted any of the home relief or any of that." Later, when these same veterans used the G.I. Bill, they experienced a program administered according to standardized procedures that were applied uniformly to all recipients, regardless of their socioeconomic background. These broadly inclusive eligibility rules and impersonal, routinized procedures may have produced particularly strong cognitive effects among less advantaged beneficiaries. The fact that they received treatment equal to that given any other veteran may have struck them as an elevation of their civic status and their full inclusion as privileged members of the nation.[21]

Thus, it is reasonable to expect that G.I. Bill users from low to moderate socioeconomic backgrounds may have had their civic capacity and predisposition for participation accentuated most dramatically, in turn yielding an especially large impact on their civic involvement.[22] In fact, our analysis reveals that G.I. Bill usage did boost significantly the rate of joining civic organizations among those from low-medium and medium standards of living in childhood, and the rate of political involvement of those from a low-medium standard of living.[23] Given that civic involvement is usually biased toward those who enjoy social and economic advantages, this is a striking finding, implying that the G.I. Bill helped to level not only the playing field of educational opportunity but that of citizenship as well.

The civic impact of the education and training benefits varied among other groups. Although, as we have seen, benefit usage appears to have improved, in socioeconomic terms, the lives of those who had grown up with the very lowest standard of living, the experience did not prove powerful enough to make a pronounced difference in their civic activity. Arguably, even greater interventions in the lives of such individuals would have been necessary to compensate for the impediments to participation imposed by an impoverished childhood. Among those who came from the most privileged groups, those with medium-high and high standards of living during childhood, G.I. Bill usage had no special effect on civic joining. Presumably because the program's benefits did not dramatically alter their life circumstances, it did not affect their civic capacity or inclination. Program usage did foster higher rates of political activity among the most well-off, but this is not surprising. What stands out as most impressive is that the G.I. Bill's effects broke with the usual pattern of bestowing participatory advantages primarily on the already privileged.

Program-Specific Effects

So far, our analyses have lumped together the effects of both the higher education and subcollege benefits of the G.I. Bill. This might leave one to wonder whether in fact only the provisions that enabled veterans to attend colleges or universities actually enhanced recipients' civic involvement. Given that three times as many veterans used the subcollege provisions, it is imperative that we evaluate how those benefits in particular affected civic involvement.

Our investigation of the coverage, implementation, and socioeconomic effects of the subcollege programs has suggested that they produced resource and cognitive effects that were only slightly less impressive than those associated with the higher education provisions. Given the lack of prerequisites for enrollment, the vocational training schools, on-the-job training, and related programs actually proved more accessible to veterans than the higher education provisions, and thus usage might be expected to have generated positive attitudinal effects. In terms of implementation, beneficiaries of the subcollege programs experienced somewhat more cumbersome procedures; conceivably these dynamics may have generated less positive cognitive effects than the more smoothly administered higher education provisions. The socioeconomic effects of the subcollege programs, though less dramatic than those of the higher education provisions, nonetheless did lead to increases in recipients' incomes and occupational statuses.[24]

Remarkably, our analyses reveal that use of the G.I. Bill for subcollege programs functioned as an especially powerful and significant determinant of both veterans' civic memberships and their political involvement in the postwar era, even more so than use of the higher education benefits.[25] The higher education provisions appeared slightly less instrumental than the subcollege programs in prompting recipients to join civic organizations, and they actually failed to increase their participation in political activities.[26] Interestingly, once we control for which type of provisions veterans used, their level of education is shown to be irrelevant to their rate of political involvement. This surprising result suggests that in the immediate postwar era, usage of the subcollege-level programs of the G.I. Bill had positive effects on political participation that overwhelmed the influence of the factor that is typically considered the most important determinant of such activity. Evidently the value that veterans found in these programs transformed both their socioeconomic well-being and their relationship to government sufficiently to prompt their heightened participation as citizens.

Time Spent on the G.I. Bill

Like many other types of social programs, the G.I. Bill permitted beneficiaries to utilize different amounts of resources, specifically by attending education and training programs and collecting subsistence allowances for different amounts of time. Possibly variations in the duration of veterans' benefits might have influenced the extent to which they participated subsequently in civic organizations and politics.

Notably, the length of time that veterans spent using the provisions was not simply a function of whether they pursued higher education versus subcollege training. As seen in Table 6.1, both types of beneficiaries varied considerably in the duration of their program use. Although for some who entered college after the war, time spent on the G.I. Bill

Table 6.1. Time Spent on G.I. Bill, by Usage Type, Among Nonblack Veterans

Time Spent	Subcollege Programs	Higher Education
Less than 6 months	10.4%	2.1%
6–12 months	28.4	5.1
1–2 years	32.8	13.5
2–3 years	16.4	26.2
More than 3 years	11.9	53.2

Source: World War II Veterans Survey

might be a measure analogous to level of education, others used the program only to finish up a college degree that they had begun previously. By the same token, beneficiaries of vocational training programs sometimes used the provisions just as long as higher education users, yet the program did not affect their formal level of educational attainment.[27] It should be noted also that some survey respondents were highly educated but never used G.I. Bill assistance, primarily because they had acquired their college degrees prior to military service.

Veterans who used the education or training provisions for particularly long periods of time emerged as especially active citizens. This disparity held among veterans who were alike in other key regards, including level of education.[28] The longer a veteran benefited from the provisions, the more political organizations he joined and the more political activities he engaged in during later years. Of course, veterans who stayed on the G.I. Bill for longer durations accrued more value from the program, and with each passing month or semester, they became more highly skilled or educated, thus enhancing their employment prospects. The likelihood that veterans considered program usage to have been a turning point in their lives also increased with the amount of time they spent on the bill, as seen in Figure 6.1, below.

In turn, those who spent the most time on the G.I. Bill felt the strongest sense of obligation afterward, believing that they owed something back to American society.[29] In interviews, although veterans generally conveyed that they regarded the G.I. Bill as a privilege rather than something owed in exchange for military service, they diverged in their responses

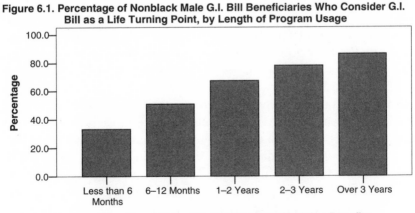

Figure 6.1. Percentage of Nonblack Male G.I. Bill Beneficiaries Who Consider G.I. Bill as a Life Turning Point, by Length of Program Usage

Source: World War II Veterans Survey

to the question "After receiving the G.I. Bill benefits, did you think you owed anything back to society?" James Murray, who had been a prisoner of war, replied, "I have to be honest, I didn't think about it in those terms. I felt more of it as a reward than [as something for which I] owed back. I figured I'd paid for it. Being there, I saw my friends killed." Yet some suggested that they did feel a sense of owing back, although they emphasized that it was not in the form of an explicit quid pro quo. Isaac Gellert, whose G.I. Bill-sponsored higher education enabled him to become a chemist and college professor, responded that he felt he owed something back "in the normal sense in which good citizenship demands that you live in the society and make a contribution to it . . . a contribution not only in your community but also in whatever professional life you have. I regard teaching as an important calling." Asked his views on how government has treated veterans, Luke LaPorta said, "I'm one of the beneficiaries. I feel that American government really, really went the limit to deal with the people who were in the service [in World War II]." During the interview, LaPorta wondered aloud whether his lifetime of extensive voluntary participation in numerous civic organizations might have been his own attempt to give something back to society after receiving the benefits.

Contrary to our assumptions today that time spent using government programs may produce less vibrant citizens, those who collected the benefits of the G.I. Bill over the longest duration became more active in politics, not less so. Men who received three or four years' worth of free tuition and monthly payments for themselves and their families joined the ranks of the politically active at higher levels than their other characteristics would lead us to expect. Throughout the postwar era, they joined political organizations, worked on campaigns, served on local town boards and councils, and participated in a range of other political activities. The impetus for such heightened levels of involvement emanated not only from the more extensive resources they received but also from the more potent messages they gleaned from them. Long-term beneficiaries gained an especially strong sense that government had made a difference in their lives, and they were more likely both to regard its influence as transformative for their circumstances and to feel that it was their responsibility to give something back to American society. They did so, bolstering the vibrancy of democracy in the postwar era.

We have seen three distinct dynamics through which the G.I. Bill's education and training benefits generated civic and political involvement in the postwar era. These processes represent diverse and cross-cutting pathways toward active citizenship. Combined, they underscore the power of a program that affected different individuals in different ways, but in each case stimulated their greater involvement in public life.

Other Policies

The G.I. Bill's education and training benefits constituted but one piece of the full panoply of government social programs that emerged in the New Deal and postwar eras. Perhaps the enlarged presence of government in citizens' lives during this era, through other programs as well, contributed to the civic-spiritedness of the generation that reached young adulthood at that time. While we lack the means to evaluate the impact of the vast array of these programs, we can assess the effect of the G.I. Bill's low-interest loan guarantee program.

Among veterans, usage of the loans emerged as a significant determinant of rates of joining organizations, though at the most modest level, and it did not make any discernible difference in their rates of political activity.[30] This outcome points to a marked difference in the civic impact of the loans versus the education and training provisions, despite the fact that both were included under the same comprehensive piece of legislation. Despite their shared eligibility criteria and target group, the two offered distinct resources and did so through different kinds of mechanisms. The loans, as we saw in Chapter 5, seemed to make less of an impression on veterans than the education and training benefits, and to alter their lives less fundamentally. The outright payments offered to veteran students made government's role more obvious and visible. The difference in the measurable impact of the two programs suggests that while the education and training benefits were not alone in influencing the civic generation, they may have been especially potent as facilitators of civic involvement.

Over Time

For how long would usage of the education and training provisions affect veterans' political involvement? While our analyses thus far have focused on the immediate postwar era, now we explore effects among the nonblack male veterans when they reached middle age (1965 to 1979) and during their senior years (1980 to 1998).[31]

Over time, as veterans' experience of the G.I. Bill became more remote, its cognitive effects faded, but its resource effects, from which the higher education beneficiaries had gained the most, became more powerful.[32] Thus, the bill's influence on political involvement waned.[33] At the same time, the more typical determinants of political participation assumed greater importance as veterans' lives continued. Veterans' educational level—which had been so conspicuously absent as a determinant in the 1950–64 period—emerged as highly significant, increasingly so over time; by late in veterans' lives, it proved by far the most powerful predictor of their rates of political activity. And veterans' standard of living—also notable for its absence as a significant determinant in the 1950–64 period, when the G.I. Bill's influence was so strong—asserted itself as a strong predictor in 1965–79 and became increasingly influential in 1980–98.

Notably, in middle adulthood, the most powerful and significant determinant of political participation was the extent to which veterans had been involved in civic organizations during early adulthood. The civic joiners of the 1950–64 period emerged as the political activists of the 1965–79 period; this supports scholars' findings of a connection between the civic and political realms. In later adulthood, the power of educational attainment transcended that of prior civic involvement in explaining political participation, though both remained important.

Thus, the cross-class nature of veterans' political activity in the immediate postwar era dissipated as those with higher standards of living and more formal education gained a stronger voice in the political realm than others. The growing influence over time of veterans' educational attainment on their political participation paralleled the gradual civic disengagement of those with less formal education, such as the vocational training beneficiaries who had been so active in the postwar years. As the messages that G.I. Bill usage had conveyed across the spectrum of program experiences receded, the resources gained by the higher education users became increasingly valuable sources of political mobilization.

Inasmuch as the G.I. Bill had expanded the formal education of some veterans, those individuals continued to reap the benefits of usage through enhanced political involvement even late in life. The effects of advanced formal education for participation accumulated over time as its beneficiaries gained even more of the skills, networks, and income that help to foster civic engagement. The heightened sense of civic duty that comes with higher education may also help explain why their participation only intensified. Thus, as time passed, they remained ensconced within the political community, whereas the presence of the subcollege users, whose educational level had not been influenced by the program, receded. The more level playing field of political activity seen at midcentury was increasingly replaced by one tilted toward the participation of the most highly educated.[34]

From Social Rights to Civic Engagement

In recent years, matters of citizenship have received considerable attention in academic and public debate, but typically, two separate conversations have ensued. One dwells on citizens themselves and the extent to which they participate—or, more likely, fail to participate—in civic and political life. The other focuses on government and the extent to which it bestows—or fails to bestow—rights on citizens in the form of social, civil, and political guarantees.

Our findings here suggest that these conversations must be conjoined. Through the bestowal of social rights, citizens may become more fully incorporated as members of the political community.[35] The extension of social provision may not only ensure them some modicum of well-being but also convey to them a sense of dignity and value as citizens.[36] If coverage is broad and inclusive, it may promote a shared sense of civic identity and solidarity among beneficiaries. In response, they may become more fully engaged citizens, more active in civic and political life.[37]

Indeed, the G.I. Bill's education and training provisions fostered an incorporation dynamic among World War II veterans and thus served as a stimulus for the high levels of civic and political involvement that characterized the postwar era. The benefits enhanced beneficiaries' socioeconomic circumstances and skills in ways that heightened their capacity and predisposition for civic involvement. As well, they generated strong cognitive effects by offering beneficiaries a highly positive experience of government, one that provided them with resources they judged to be valuable, and treated them with respect in the process. The effects coalesced to incorporate recipients more fully as citizens, intensifying their predisposition to participate by joining civic organizations and engaging in a wide range of political activities.

To be sure, the G.I. Bill cannot be said to be the sole cause of the civic-spiritedness of the "greatest generation." Given that their lives continued to coincide with the development of America's most successful policies, no doubt other factors also helped to boost their civic involvement.[38] And some measure of their exemplary participation undoubtedly derives from experiences quite apart from public policy. We have examined some of these in our analysis here, but others remain unmeasurable. For instance, it may be significant that the vast majority of those in this active generation served in the military and that they defended the nation in the last armed conflict widely perceived to be a "good war." Nonetheless, the G.I. Bill's education and training benefits were clearly powerful, and they offer us an instructive example of the potential of public programs.

The case of the G.I. Bill illustrates how a public policy can function, like any institution, in promoting norms; in this case, it fostered participatory norms and civic engagement. By contrast to most determinants of participation, the G.I. Bill stimulated involvement especially among groups that were somewhat less advantaged in the typical prerequisites for such activity. It functioned not only through programs that advanced formal education but, most strikingly, through those offering job training skills, although their civic impact faded over time. And remarkably, the longer a veteran benefited from the provisions, the more involved he became in politics subsequently. Through each of these dynamics, as beneficiaries became more fully incorporated as citizens through social policy, they responded through more active forms of participatory citizenship. Perhaps in calling the G.I. Bill the "legislation of the century," John Mink had it right.

7

Making Democracy

After using the G.I. Bill, veterans fanned out across the nation and became the active citizens in peacetime for which the bill's author, Harry Colmery, had hoped. In Atlanta, Georgia, James Johnson joined the American Legion, the Veterans of Foreign Wars, the Methodist Church, and the Masons. In Indiana, George Josten became a devout member of the Knights of Columbus, a Catholic fraternal organization, which gave him the chance to "socialize with people who have a sense of morals and responsibilities," and the Society of Mechanical Engineers. Near Boston, Massachusetts, Kermit Pransky coached Little League baseball and basketball, formed a Babe Ruth baseball league in his town, and started another baseball league for his temple, as well as joining the Veterans of Foreign Wars. In terms of political involvement, each man acquired a lifetime habit of voting, one widely shared among their generation. James Johnson voted "every time the poll opens," and Josten noted that he never missed a primary or any other type of election. Both of them also wrote letters on occasion to their elected officials, and Josten served as a town trustee. Pransky, who worked in the electrical motor repair business, traveled to Washington, D.C., with others in his trade organization so that they could lobby members of Congress about issues concerning their industry. While these men's involvements exemplified the most common balance of civic and political activities pursued by G.I. Bill beneficiaries, some spent less time on civic associations but became considerably more immersed in politics. John Mink, for example, grew intensely involved in working on political campaigns from the 1950s onward. He noted that many of those who actually ran for statewide public office during that time were G.I. Bill-educated veterans.

Would the kinds of civic involvement pursued so intensely by G.I. Bill beneficiaries help make American society and politics more democratic? Most of veterans' civic energies were applied to civic associations, groups whose primary purpose was not first and foremost political. Nonetheless, involvement in such groups did help to politicize citizens and draw them closer to the political process, and it unified them in ways that could help shorten the distance between elected officials and the average citizen. In turn, many veterans who became active in politics brought with them a zeal to make the system more responsive to ordinary Americans. The policies of the era suggest that in many ways they succeeded. Our focus in this chapter will be on the involvement of nonblacks; in the next chapter we turn to the activism of African American beneficiaries.

The Politics of the Postwar Era

Though all Americans had, for the sake of democracy, united in the war effort, afterward the nation continued to deny the promises of equal citizenship to African Americans and to women generally. African American men returned from military service to find Jim Crow segregation still firmly entrenched in the South and labor markets nationwide as permeated as ever by discriminatory practices.[1] Women who had been employed in good-paying jobs for the war effort found themselves forced to relinquish those positions to male veterans and either go back to lower-status jobs or return home.[2]

At the same time, other features of the politics of the era showed democratic vibrancy. Citizens exhibited high levels of interest and engagement in politics. They kept up with the political news on a daily basis. Voter turnout rates hit twentieth-century peaks, and compared to the present, citizens were more likely to work for political parties, attend public meetings and rallies, sign petitions, run for political office, and engage in a wide array of other activities.[3] In turn, public officials were more responsive to the needs and concerns of the average citizen, of people belonging to the working and middle classes. Indeed, national government played a major role in facilitating economic security and opportunity, helping to make the postwar era the most egalitarian period of the twentieth century.[4]

During the presidency of Republican president Dwight Eisenhower, for instance, the social programs established in the New Deal not only remained intact but were improved and expanded upon.[5] Social Security coverage was broadened, the minimum wage was raised, and the construction of forty-five thousand units of new public housing was approved.[6] Eisenhower founded the new cabinet-level Department of Health, Education, and Welfare; ushered in the largest public works project in history, the federal interstate highway program; and signed into law the National Defense Education Act, which granted federal aid to educational institutions at all levels.[7] And though Eisenhower was not a vocal advocate of organized labor, like other American presidents throughout the period, he offered at least tacit support for trade unions.

Owing to such policies and myriad others, the fruits of the rapidly growing U.S. postwar economy were distributed broadly across the population.[8] The "rising tide" of economic growth "lifted all boats," as John F. Kennedy put it: everyone was better off, especially those who had the lowest standards of living. As the middle class grew, the American social structure changed in shape from a pyramid to a diamond. Before the crash in 1929, 80 percent of all American families had earned less than $4,000 a year in 1950 dollars; by 1953, by contrast, over 58 percent of households enjoyed incomes from $4,000 to $10,000 in 1950 dollars.[9] Between 1945 and 1970, factory employees witnessed a doubling of their real weekly earnings, far more workers gained access to employer-provided hospitalization insurance, and private pension funds quadrupled.[10] Rates of home ownership and college attendance soared higher than ever before, with both increasingly coming within the reach of average citizens. The question is whether the vibrant civic associationalism of the era, spurred in part by G.I. Bill usage, in any way helped facilitate government's role in promoting such outcomes.

The Civic Universe

When World War II veterans were asked to name the civic organizations in which they had been most involved, the most frequently cited groups were often those most popular among American adults generally in 1955.[11] Veterans' organizations headed the list, most notably large, federated groups such as the American Legion and Veterans of Foreign Wars, which included 5.5 and 2.1 percent of all American males in 1955, respectively.[12] Numerous churches and religious groups followed—not surprisingly, given that the United States, distinct from other nations, experienced a surge in religious membership during the postwar era. Americans with a religious affiliation rose from 49 percent of the population in 1940 to 69 percent two decades later; indeed, a higher proportion of Americans possessed a formal affiliation with a church in the 1950s than during any other decade of the twentieth century.[13]

Cross-class fraternal groups flourished during the postwar years, and veterans became devout and long-term members. They flocked to the Masons and the Benevolent and Protective Order of Elks, which encompassed, respectively, 7.9 percent and 2.3 percent of the U.S. adult male population in 1955. Other fraternal organizations that also were popular among veterans and included more than 1 percent of the eligible population were the Order of the Eastern Star, Fraternal Order of Eagles, Loyal Order of Moose, Knights of Columbus, and Nobles of the Mystic Shrine (Shriners).[14] Veterans also swelled the ranks of the Red Cross, a national service organization, as well as those of smaller, elite service groups such as the Lions, Kiwanis, Rotary, and Exchange, which courted business and professional members.[15]

The fact that veterans were parents of the baby boomers helped to explain a good share of their civic involvement. PTA membership surged to 9 percent of the adult population in 1955 and climbed still higher in subsequent years as parents became involved in their children's education.[16] Adults also took an active role in youth groups, including the Boy Scouts of America, which involved 1.29 percent of all American adults in 1955 in leadership positions, and Little League.[17]

Highly educated veterans belonged to a vast number of professional, trade, and business organizations. Such organizations, most of which had been established in the late nineteenth century, flourished in the post–World War II era, as the number of professionals increased dramatically and as they gained a more central role in the political economy.[18] Indeed, veterans listed groups representing nearly every conceivable profession. The Chamber of Commerce and American Chemical Society each included more than 1 percent of all survey respondents; these were followed by the American Medical Association, American Society of Civil Engineers, American Institute of Certified Public Accountants, American Bar Association, and hundreds of others.

Less highly educated veterans frequently joined labor organizations. Although the Cold War climate presented challenges to labor, in U.S. historical perspective it was the best of times, with about one-quarter of all workers unionized.[19] Two labor organizations ranked high among respondents' memberships: the American Federation of Labor–Congress of Industrial Organizations (AFL-CIO), which included 12.05 percent of the adult population at that time, and the smaller United Auto Workers (UAW).

We will now analyze the social and political significance of belonging to such groups. Interestingly, despite what we have found about G.I. Bill users' higher *rates* of involvement overall compared to nonusers, almost no differences emerged in the *types* of organizations they joined.[20]

This suggests that the education and training benefits—though serving as a lubricant for greater levels of civic activity generally—did not promote a different form of such involvement. As a result, our discussion revolves around veterans generally, not distinguished by program usage.

Empowering Citizens

The most fundamental feature of the vast majority of organizations to which veterans belonged in the postwar era is that they promoted interaction among individual members. As seen in Figure 7.1 below, veterans from all educational levels were highly involved in membership groups, especially in those that, being neither professional organizations nor trade unions, were not job-related. As members of such groups, individuals not only paid dues but took an active role in a local post or chapter, in which they met face-to-face with other members on a regular basis. They socialized, carried out organizational rituals, and engaged in such varied events as making elaborate floats for local parades, organizing chicken barbecues and turkey dinners, sponsoring dances, screening movies in towns that did not yet have theaters, and promoting patriotism through essay contests and other events. Some raised money for special causes involving needy members of the local community and beyond by hosting fund-raisers that ranged from horse-pulling contests to minstrel shows, talent nights to pancake breakfasts, and, in one rural community, contests to guess the number of "cow pies" per acre in a farmer's field.[21]

In all of these ways, as Theda Skocpol has demonstrated, such membership organizations differed dramatically from the professionally run, advocacy-style organizations that have become increasingly prevalent and prominent in the last thirty years. These groups, such as the Children's Coalition, Sierra Club, National Abortion Rights Action League, and National Right to Life Committee, lack a base of active, grassroots members. Individuals may write checks to such organizations and send them to offices in Washington, D.C., or other faraway places, but paid staff employees usually perform the day-to-day tasks.[22] Foundations, commissions, and boards, each involving only a small number of participating individuals, also qualify as nonmembership groups. The hallmark of all such groups is that elite leaders engage in activities on behalf of a collective interest rather than associating with a broad array and large number of members. Typically, highly educated specialists might testify before legislatures on behalf of particular groups of less advantaged citizens, or raise money on behalf of some worthy cause.[23] These organizations—in which, to use Skocpol's terms, "management" replaced "membership"—have become increasingly common, especially since the late 1960s and 1970s.[24]

In the postwar era, as Figure 7.1 makes apparent, these nonmembership groups were already garnering organizational energies disproportionately from the most well educated of the veterans. Interestingly, the one minor difference in types of civic joining that emerged between G.I. Bill users and nonusers was that those who used the provisions for higher education were more likely than nonusers to take part in these nonmembership organizations.[25] Many G.I. Bill users perceived themselves to be beneficiaries of a program that changed their lives significantly and thus believed that they owed something back to society. Conceivably, as a result, they may have been especially attracted to associations geared toward improving the community by acting on behalf of individuals deemed less fortunate. In any case, besides being just as active in cross-class organizations as other veterans with comparable levels of education, they assumed leadership responsibilities on boards and commissions through which they could advocate for their fellow citizens.

Nonetheless, during the postwar era, individual membership organizations, in which people from across the educational spectrum actively associated with one another, remained vibrant and dominant. As a result, individuals with moderate amounts of education remained at

Figure 7.1. Average Number of Nonblack Male Veterans' Memberships in Types of Organizations, 1950–64, by Level of Education

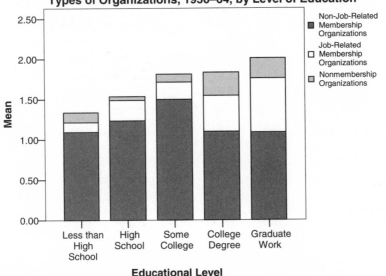

Source: World War II Veterans Survey

Flanked by congressional leaders and representatives of the American Legion, President Franklin D. Roosevelt signs into law the Servicemen's Readjustment Act of 1944, otherwise known as the G.I. Bill. The Legion crafted the bill's most generous and inclusive features, and mobilized grassroots support nationwide, which helped ensure its passage. (OWI, Franklin D. Roosevelt Library)

One of the 7.8 million beneficiaries of the G.I. Bill, Luke LaPorta devoted his adult life to community involvement, starting youth baseball leagues throughout central New York. LaPorta is shown here with two young players at ceremonies commemorating the fiftieth anniversary of the founding of Little League, 1989. (Craig Jackson/*Post-Standard*)

African Americans served in segregated units during World War II. Among them, Tuskegee Airman First Lieutenant Henry P. Hervey (far right), shown here training with his crew, the 477th Bomb Group, 616th Bomb Squadron, at Godman Field in Kentucky, 1945, later used the G.I. Bill to earn his college degree at Northwestern University. (From the collection of Henry P. Hervey)

Richard Colosimo (right) and Walter Irla, of the 89th Infantry Division, relaxing during time on leave in Nice, France. When their unit liberated the Ohrdruf concentration camp, Irla, who spoke Polish, was able to communicate with two Russians who had managed to survive. (From the collection of Richard Colosimo)

A member of the 92nd Infantry Division, one of the only all-black units of enlisted personnel permitted to engage in combat, William Perry (left) in Genoa, Italy, 1945. Perry later attended Case Western Reserve University on the G.I. Bill. (From the collection of William Perry)

Among those soldiers who began college courses through the Army Specialized Training Program, Gentry Torian (right), of the 92nd Infantry Division, attended the historically black Hampton Institute in Virginia on the ASTP. Later he used the G.I. Bill to complete bachelor's and master's degrees at Fenn College, Cleveland State University, and went on to become an English teacher. (From the collection of Celeste Torian)

Richard Colosimo, who grew up in poverty, used the G.I. Bill first for vocational training and then to attend the University of Pittsburgh, where he graduated with a degree in business and engineering in 1952. Already married with one child, he both worked and took classes full time. (From the collection of Richard Colosimo)

Above, Left During discharge procedures, fewer efforts were made to inform women of their access to the G.I. Bill. One of many women veterans who did not realize that she qualified and never applied for benefits, this woman served in the Women's Army Corps, playing clarinet in a band that performed for injured soldiers returning to American cities for further hospital treatment.

Above, Right Following his service in the 87th Infantry Division, Kermit Pransky used the G.I. Bill to obtain on-the-job training in electric motor repair. Afterward, he and his brother-in-law started a business and offered training to other veterans using the bill. (From the collection of Shirley Pransky)

Ann (Vino) Bertini's unit of the Army Nurse Corps in training. Bertini used the G.I. Bill's benefits only briefly when she took an additional course in nursing after the war. Like many female veterans, she returned for additional schooling years later, after her children were grown, but unfortunately this was after her G.I. Bill eligibility had expired. (From the collection of Ann Bertini)

Students acquiring training in welding at Morehead City Technical Institute in 1949, in a one-year, shop-oriented program pioneered by North Carolina State University. The subcollege provisions of the G.I. Bill attracted more than twice as many veterans as the higher education provisions. (Copyright © 1949 North Carolina State University. Used with permission.)

Veterans training to be chefs at the Restaurant Institute of Connecticut in New Haven, 1949. Now called the Culinary Institute of America and located in Hyde Park, New York, it was one of fifty-six hundred new programs that opened their doors to offer vocational training to veterans. Veterans accounted for 98 percent of its student body immediately after the war. (The Culinary Institute of America)

Veterans registering for classes at Indiana University in September 1947, by which point they constituted 49 percent of all enrolled college students nationwide. (Indiana University Archives, PS 47-1254)

Jubilant veterans celebrating after registering for college classes on the G.I. Bill at Indiana University in September 1947. (Indiana University Archives, PS 47-1082)

Veterans and their families attending the grand opening of the University of Minnesota Village playground in the late 1940s. The University of Minnesota, where enrollment doubled to over twenty-seven thousand under the G.I. Bill, boasted the greatest number of veteran students anywhere in the nation. (University of Minnesota Archives)

The Woodlawn Trailer Courts, affectionately nicknamed "Fertile Acres," at Indiana University, 1946. After the war, universities nationwide faced severe space shortages, and many put up temporary housing such as this development, which housed married students only and included a central co-op store and bathroom and shower facilities. (Indiana University Archives, PS 46-136)

Left   Keith Peterson, who had served in the Navy as a cook, later studied physical education at the University of Iowa on the G.I. Bill. There, he lived with his wife and young son in their cramped trailer, which had no plumbing. (Margaret Bourke-White/Getty Images)

Above, Right   Charles Smayda, a graduate student in geology at the University of Iowa, tries to study and hold his daughter Sue while his wife, Ginny, irons. Combining student and family life proved challenging, and women of the World War II generation, the majority of whom were civilians and did not qualify for the G.I. Bill, made it work. (Margaret Bourke-White/Getty Images)

Syracuse University's Crouse College looming over prefab structures that were used as temporary classrooms when student enrollment grew by over 600 percent under the G.I. Bill. Responding to universities' space shortages, the federal government transferred military surplus buildings to campuses nationwide. (Syracuse University Archives)

least as active in civic associations as the most highly educated individuals, if not more so. Among veterans, this included especially those who had used the G.I. Bill for the subcollege programs, as well as those who had acquired only some college education.

Participation in such civic organizations was conducive in several ways to political involvement. Such groups provided ample opportunities for the development of leadership at the grassroots level: every local chapter of an organization needed officers and committees for specific purposes, and members tended to serve on a rotating basis, so a fairly large number had a chance to acquire civic skills. Often, individuals had the opportunity to represent their local post at regional, state, or even national conventions. These experiences not only granted some measure of organizational authority to citizens of modest means but also endowed them with valuable skills for the practice of democracy. Certainly they enabled them to accomplish things collectively in their own communities. In one rural area of upstate New York, for instance, the American Legion helped organize a community rescue squad, staffed entirely by World War II veterans who volunteered their time; the Legion purchased the squad's first ambulance.[26]

Interestingly, the G.I. Bill's subcollege training benefits appear to have played a particularly important role in democratizing the nature of organizational leadership among men of the World War II generation. All else being equal, veterans who used the G.I. Bill for vocational training and related programs were more likely to hold office or serve on a committee for a civic organization.[27] Apparently, inclusion in these programs—which the majority of beneficiaries deemed a turning point in their lives—helped promote both the inclination and the capacity to serve as leaders. As Robert Wuthnow comments, "Leadership skills, the ability to speak comfortably in medium-sized groups, familiarity with organizational rules, and the capacity to make small talk about the right subjects" are all critical to civic involvement.[28] In the late twentieth century and the present, leadership has become strongly associated with educational level, favoring more-affluent individuals. That the G.I. Bill's vocational training benefits extended the skills and confidence necessary for leadership among those without college degrees suggests their far-reaching effects in enhancing American democracy.

Though most civic organizations existed primarily for nonpolitical purposes, many nonetheless took it upon themselves to encourage political involvement. Groups ranging from the Methodist Woman's Society of Christian Service to the Parent-Teacher Association and the Lions Club held sessions to inform and educate citizens on public issues. An even broader array of organizations exhorted their members to be informed and to vote.[29] Some organized meet-the-candidates events for their members and others in the community, or hosted Election Day dinners.

Such associations also politicized their members through their organizational structures, which typically paralleled the arrangements of American federalism. Fully 90 percent of veterans' memberships were in organizations with a wide, translocal reach, most often in chapters or local posts of a national or international federation, as well as in other national, regional, or state-level organizations. Only 10 percent of their memberships were in strictly local groups, such as most sports or hobby clubs, or in singular institutions such as libraries or schools. Members of federated organizations ranging from the Farm Bureau to the American Legion to the AFL-CIO deliberated about political issues at national or regional meetings and agreed on official positions. In many cases, the organization then mobilized around such issues: leaders informed the larger membership through newsletters, encouraged local posts to contact elected officials and write letters to the editor, and represented the group's position nationally.[30]

As membership organizations, then, civic associations empowered their members in ways that helped to promote political participation, and in so doing, they brought citizens closer to government. Even if the predominant activities of an organization involved mostly social activities such as hunters' suppers and cake walks or conducting secret rituals among their own members, still they offered means through which citizens could learn to work together to accomplish things collectively in their own communities. Moreover, members routinely gained leadership skills, along with knowledge of public issues and the expectations and obligations of active citizens. Thus, for G.I. Bill beneficiaries, who were especially active in these groups, such memberships pointed the way toward active political citizenship.

Joining Citizens Together

Civic organizations are widely thought to be conducive to what scholars call "social capital," meaning that they foster connections between people, facilitating the development of social networks, norms of reciprocity, and social trust. Yet groups vary in whether they lead individuals to associate only with people like themselves or somehow link them to a broader and more diverse group of citizens. Robert Putnam observes that organizations promote a "bonding" form of social capital if their membership is quite homogenous and their mission is "inward looking." Such groups can help build community among those who already have a shared identity, but they are unlikely to build bridges toward people different from themselves. Conversely, other groups promote "bridging" or inclusive social capital; such groups are "outward looking and encompass people across diverse social cleavages."[31]

Certainly many of the widespread organizations of the postwar era restricted membership by sex, race, or ethnicity. With the exception of churches, many of the other groups—including fraternal organizations, hobby and sport groups, and veterans' organizations—limited membership exclusively to men. As well, some organizations, especially men's groups, refused to admit African Americans or Latinos, leaving them to begin their own, separate organizations.[32] Latino veterans, for instance, after being denied membership in local chapters of the Veterans of Foreign Wars, formed their own vibrant organization known as G.I. Forum, and also participated in high rates in the federated League of United Latin American Citizens (LULAC), Community Service Organization (CSO), and others that flourished in the postwar era.[33]

At the same time, the civic associations of the postwar era were remarkably diverse to the extent to which they brought citizens together across class lines.[34] Through such groups, the most highly educated veterans— many of whom had attained their education on the G.I. Bill—found opportunities to associate with people whose needs and circumstances differed from their own, and vice versa.[35] As seen in Figure 7.2, rates of belonging to such groups peaked among those who had only some college. Granted, veterans at the two ends of the educational spectrum belonged to some groups—namely, labor unions (in the case of those with less education) and business or professional associations and elite service groups (in the case of those with the most education)—in which they associated only with similarly situated individuals. Yet even among veterans with graduate education, half of their memberships were in elite groups and half in cross-class groups, and the average individual belonged to one of each type of group. Only about 20 percent of veterans with college or graduate education were active only in organizations with other elites, while fully 80 percent or more counted cross-class organizations among their memberships. Such associational patterns kept those who had reached upper-middle-class or upper-class status associating with fellow citizens who were less well-heeled.[36]

Veterans' organizations proved especially significant in this regard. While such organizations were especially popular among those with less education, accounting for half of the cross-class memberships of the veterans who had not completed high school, they made up nearly a quarter of such memberships among those with some college, a college

Figure 7.2. Average Number of Nonblack Male Veterans' Memberships by Class Scope, 1950–64, by Level of Education

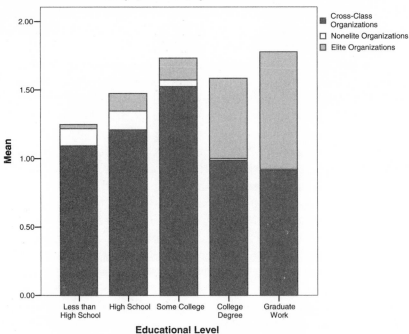

Source: World War II Veterans Survey

degree, and even graduate education. Their shared past of military service linked veterans of distinct social strata, and veterans' organizations gave them a continuing means of connecting with one another even years later.

The widespread civic associations brought people together not only by virtue of their cross-class composition but also through their organizational structures, given that they were predominantly translocal. Belonging to an organization with wider ties made citizens "part of something bigger," as Theda Skocpol notes: "The genius of classic American associational life was that joining something small connected members of local chapters to much grander organized endeavors." Delegates of local chapters attended district meetings, or state or national conventions, and returned back home with reports from the larger organization. The federated model of organization stimulated the creation of local chapters and sustained them, while offering members the sense of being linked to others beyond their local community.

Thus, civic associations did much to give their members a sense of common citizenship and mutual understanding of those with circumstances different from their own, and this too may have affected the character of postwar politics. Granted, to the extent that organizations limited their membership by race or sex, they remained exclusive and discriminatory. At the same time, they brought together individuals of diverse means and connected them to others across their region, in their state, or across the nation. For highly educated people, associating in such groups likely helped them to better understand the needs, concerns, and perspectives of citizens less well-off than themselves. Such associationalism may help explain why public officials of the postwar era, who were themselves active in such organizations, were more responsive to the needs of average Americans than has been the case in recent decades.[37]

Revitalizing Politics

For some veterans, political involvement followed directly from G.I. Bill usage; for others, the bill prompted their participation in civic associations, which in turn encouraged and trained them to take a more active role in politics. Whichever route they took, we might wonder about the attitudes and voting patterns they brought to politics, and the nature of their political achievements. Although, unfortunately, the evidence that would allow us to specify G.I. Bill users' politics is lacking, we can engage in some informed speculation based on what we know about veterans generally.

As active citizens, most veterans are likely to have been fairly moderate in their politics. Despite the constraints on civil liberties that were born of the virulent anticommunism of Senator Joseph McCarthy and other political elites, most Americans in the postwar era tended to have fairly moderate views on most matters.[38] Surveys at the time found that veterans, generally, held views similar to their contemporaries, and certainly were not more conservative.[39] A survey conducted by *Fortune* in 1946 found that a majority of veterans disapproved of either General MacArthur or General Eisenhower becoming a candidate for president in 1948, suggesting that they would have preferred a political leader without a military background. Veterans supported union activity more than the general public did, and they were less willing than other citizens to support banning strikes. Though they gave business higher marks than labor for its role in the war effort, they also tended to think that business executives were compensated too generously.[40] Over time, study after study found veterans' political attitudes—whether on political trust, foreign policy, or a wider range of attitudes—to be generally indistinguishable from those of comparable nonveterans of the same age group.[41]

Inasmuch as usage of the G.I. Bill's higher education provisions permitted individuals to further their formal education, they may have adopted values conducive to liberal democracy. Advanced education is known to develop in citizens greater levels of political knowledge, a greater recognition of government's role, a more developed sense of the interdependence between citizens, and a higher value on justice and fairness.[42] Studies conducted in the postwar era found that between the freshman and senior years, college students became "less authoritarian, less dogmatic, less ethnocentric, and less prejudiced," and the experience of higher education appeared to have prompted students toward political liberalism and away from political conservatism.[43]

Besides becoming active in the basic duties of political citizenship, veterans also ran for public office at a far greater rate than their presence in the population would have suggested. By all accounts, G.I. Bill users led the way, claiming positions at every level and at each branch of government.[44] Veterans generally are reported to have brought a reformist spirit to politics.[45] One author notes that after the war, "a wave of G.I. revolts swept city politics ... as bright young veterans ... marched against complacent civic leaders and self-satisfied politicians in towns from the South Atlantic coast to the Rockies."[46] Veterans in some municipalities in the South attempted to capitalize on their public image and staged challenges to what they perceived as "politics as usual." Amid a complicated controversy about how to reform city government in Nashville, Tennessee, eight veterans entered the fray and formed a "G.I. Joe" ticket. Though all but one of them lost, their presence was credited with pushing their opponents to make good on promises to improve local governance.[47] The movement spread across the nation in the late 1940s. As political scientist V. O. Key explained in 1950, "Not all G.I. leaders were white knights leading crusades against wicked local machines. . . . Nevertheless, the movement, if it can be called that, included a number of men of extraordinary idealism coupled with [skill] and coolness in the hard-boiled tactics of politics."[48]

By 1960, veterans accounted for about 60 percent of the membership of the U.S. House of Representatives and an even higher percentage of cabinet posts.[49] Studies found that voters at the time did not actually show a preference for veterans compared to nonveterans; rather, the overrepresentation of veterans in the House owed to the fact that both political parties, and especially Republicans, were inclined to nominate veterans over nonveterans. After they became candidates, Republican veterans outperformed their party in the South and West, though Democratic veterans did not fare as well.[50]

Once elected, the ways in which G.I. Bill beneficiaries governed were likely influenced by their social backgrounds, military service, and experience of a generous government program. Veterans' presence is known to have made a difference in terms of U.S. foreign policy. Congresses containing high proportions of veterans have proven less willing to use American troops than Congresses with fewer veterans, though once the nation has committed itself to armed conflict, the veteran-populated legislatures have supported higher degrees of force in the conflict.[51] Possibly, too, the fact that many veterans themselves came from less-advantaged or middle-class backgrounds and had seen their lives transformed by the G.I. Bill may have made them supportive of policies that aided those in the lower and middle classes to gain more opportunities. Certainly the major social policy achievements on the national level from the later 1950s through the early 1970s—such as aid for higher education and K–12 education, Medicare and Medicaid, and the War on Poverty—epitomized that spirit.[52] Through such creations, policy makers responded to the needs of ordinary citizens, both lower- and middle-income Americans.

A Virtuous Circle

Relatively speaking, in the postwar era Americans felt optimistic about their society and liked their government. Compared to their predecessors, they were highly and increasingly trusting of each other, believed themselves to be happier, and anticipated a bright future. During the Eisenhower era, 90 percent of the public concurred that they "usually have confidence that the government will do what is right." In 1960, 85 percent reported that they were aware of government's impact on their lives, and 76 percent agreed that the effects of such intervention were positive.[53] In cross-national perspective, Americans reported a high degree of pride in their political institutions.[54] These attitudes are particularly striking in historical perspective, given that trust in government and citizens' sense that public officials cared about people like them fell precipitously later on.[55]

In the mid-twentieth century, a virtuous circle emerged that dramatically reduced the distance between government and citizens, and it is exemplified by the story of the G.I Bill. Through the education and training provisions, a large number of Americans found new opportunities that improved their life circumstances. They then participated more in civic life and in politics, thus democratizing the active citizenry and making those in public office become more representative of the general public. The civic organizations that swelled with members from across the socioeconomic spectrum offered leadership training and civic education, further prompting a wider cross section of the citizenry to make their voices heard in politics. As well, they provided a means through which those who went on to serve in public office could retain a shared form of association with those less well-off than themselves, and thus be more responsive to them. For a time, it seemed, the people came closer to government, and government closer to the people.

Policy developments reflected the period's highly representative politics. The most enduring policies that had been created in the New Deal bore their most plentiful fruit after policy makers in the 1950s through the early 1970s bolstered their initial terms of coverage or benefits. They raised the real value of the minimum wage, thus enhancing the wages of low-wage workers. Owing to the enforcement of the National Labor Relations Act, organized labor grew to its highest levels, comprising over 20 percent of the workforce from the early 1940s through the 1970s. Both policies helped boost the pay collected by ordinary citizens. Congress extended Social Security to more sectors of the workforce and to the disabled, and raised the value of program benefits. Korean War veterans gained G.I. Bill benefits that were nearly as generous as those offered after World War II.[56] As well, home ownership came within reach of increasing numbers of Americans through later versions of the G.I. Bill, FHA loans, and other government programs. It was thanks in part to such programs that the tremendous economic growth of those decades was widely distributed, helping to facilitate the growth of a large middle class.

Such programs may have, like the G.I. Bill, contributed further to the soaring levels of civic engagement among the "greatest generation." The resources they offered were likely also instrumental in enhancing civic skills and networks, prompting citizens to be more interested in politics, and stimulating political parties and interest groups to mobilize such individuals politically. By featuring highly universalistic and visible policy designs, they may have further enhanced individuals' perception of the extent to which government included people like them, and thus promoted in beneficiaries a yet greater sense of belonging to a public, greater confidence in their ability to effect change, and heightened motivation to participate politically.

Thus, for the civic generation, while the G.I. Bill's education and training provisions provided a stunning example—to many, the ultimate example—of a successful and highly effective government program, it was not a mere lone instance of good governance. Rather, the federal government's role in promoting economic security and opportunity continued to flourish in tandem with their generation, just as it had in their childhood and young adulthood. Time and again, they experienced policies that helped improve the well-being of ordinary citizens and likely helped expand and intensify their generation's steadfast participation in the nation's civic and political life. Postwar policies, organizational involvement, and a representative and responsive politics took the form of a virtuous circle of processes that both expanded and deepened American democracy.

8

Mobilizing for Equal Rights

Hosea Williams, son of blind African American parents, grew up in poverty in the segregated South, working as a cleaner, caretaker, and farm worker before the war began and he joined the Army. When his platoon of thirteen men was hit by a shell in France, Williams alone survived. He spent over a year in the hospital and endured permanent disabilities, walking with a limp the rest of his life. Upon returning home, he dared to drink from a whites-only water fountain at a segregated bus station and was beaten nearly to death by a mob of whites. The incident proved a turning point in the making of a civil rights activist. After he recovered from his injuries, Williams both joined the National Association for the Advancement of Colored People (NAACP) and resumed his education, using the G.I. Bill to complete high school and then bachelor's and master's degrees in chemistry from Morris Brown College and Atlanta University. He was hired by the U.S. Department of Agriculture as a research chemist, becoming one of the first blacks to hold such a position in the South. Meanwhile, Williams grew increasingly involved in the struggle for equal rights, emerging as a leader in demonstrations throughout the later 1950s; over the years he was arrested at least 124 times. Martin Luther King Jr. recruited him, first to join the Southern Christian Leadership Council and later to join his staff. On March 7, 1956, Williams led a march from Selma to Montgomery for voting rights. A national audience of television viewers watched as the participants knelt in prayer and state troopers attacked them with whips, tear gas, and nightsticks; Williams himself was beaten unconscious and left with a severe concussion and fractured skull. It was this infamous "Bloody Sunday" that prompted President Lyndon B. Johnson to send to Congress the legislation that would at last guarantee voting rights regardless of race.[1] Like Williams, many other G.I. Bill–educated African American veterans also assumed positions on the front lines of the struggle for racial equality in the 1950s and 1960s.

The experience of the Second World War has long been considered the fuel that helped to ignite the civil rights movement in the 1950s. The standard story is that African American veterans, having put themselves in harm's way for the nation, returned home with heightened expectations, no longer willing to accept legalized racial segregation, and hence took up the struggle for equal rights.[2] The precise mechanisms through which this occurred, however, have been unclear.[3] In fact, the G.I. Bill's education and training benefits played a crucial role in mobilizing black veterans.[4] Just as it had among nonblack veterans, the bill sparked high rates of civic engagement among black beneficiaries. They, too, joined more civic organizations and participated in politics at considerably higher rates than nonbeneficiaries. Yet the same program that had prompted white veterans to be especially involved in conventional civic organizations and political activities enabled black veterans to mobilize against existing political structures, demonstrating and marching for change.[5]

Organizing for Change and Claiming New Rights

Many black civic organizations already had a long history of working for the betterment of the black community, and in the postwar era, such groups directed their attention specifically to the cause of civil rights.[6] They provided vital leadership, a communications network, financial support, places to meet, and other factors essential to the emergence of the movement. Black churches and the NAACP led the way, and other organizations played a part as well.[7]

Following their usage of the G.I. Bill's education and training benefits, black beneficiaries devoted themselves to organizations that made the pursuit of social and political change a central objective.[8] Among respondents to the World War II Veterans Survey, black G.I. Bill users, compared to whites, belonged to a greater number of ethnic or nationality groups and to more organizations that served or advocated on behalf of vulnerable populations; both types of groups actively pursued racial equality. They also filled the ranks of black college and professional fraternities, groups that played a supporting role in the civil rights movement through their financial contributions to the NAACP during the 1950s and by taking leadership roles in demonstrations during the 1960s.[9] The political organizations they joined at the highest levels, especially the

NAACP and Urban League, stood at the forefront of the civil rights movement. Conversely, these same black beneficiaries were less likely than whites to belong to fraternal organizations, groups that emphasized rituals and social activities rather than social and political change.

The Supreme Court's *Brown v. Board of Education* decision in 1954 emboldened the organizations that steered the nascent civil rights movement. The boycott of the bus system in Montgomery, Alabama, which began in December 1955 and lasted eleven months, succeeded in ending segregation, and stimulated similar efforts in town and cities all over the South. Martin Luther King Jr. emerged as the movement's primary leader. Thirty-five thousand people attended the 1957 Prayer Pilgrimage he led in Washington, D.C., making it the largest civil rights demonstration in U.S. history until that time.[10]

Black G.I. Bill users immersed themselves in confrontational political activity, challenging politics as usual in order to gain the rights of equal citizenship.[11] Here, too, their involvement dramatically surpassed that of black non–G.I. Bill users, particularly in protests, marches, and demonstrations. During the height of the civil rights era, 1950 to 1964, 35 percent of black users participated in such activities compared to 8 percent of black nonusers and 2 percent of white users; rates in the 1965 to 1979 period were comparable. Black survey respondents noted again and again that "civil rights" was the purpose of such activity; some offered specifics, such as "civil rights sit-ins," "against Jim Crow," "1963 March on Washington," "antidiscrimination march with NAACP," "desegregation," "open housing," "petitioning for right to vote, which had been denied to us," "better schools/fair employment," and "job rights/ opportunities." Among these veterans of the 92nd Infantry Division, G.I. Bill users led the way toward political change.

Years of struggle culminated in the enactment of two landmark policies, both signed into law by President Lyndon B. Johnson. The Civil Rights Act of 1964 outlawed discrimination in employment, permitted the federal government to withhold funding from programs that discriminated, and brought an end to legalized segregation in the South. The Voting Rights Act of 1965 paved the way toward political equality. It suspended literacy tests and other such barriers to voting, mandated that federal registrars conduct voter registration in areas in which blacks were underrepresented on the rolls, and stipulated that those interfering with voting rights could be penalized. By creating the formal, legal framework for equal citizenship, these laws ushered in a whole new era of black political involvement.

Soon after the passage of the civil rights legislation, black G.I. Bill beneficiaries proceeded to claim their newly guaranteed rights by participating at strikingly high levels in a wide range of formal political activities.[12] During the period from 1965 to 1979, they became especially active in working on campaigns, serving on local government boards or councils that dealt with community problems and issues, and contributing money to political candidates, parties, or groups. Their participation contrasted sharply with that of black non-G.I. Bill users, especially in political campaign activity, in which 30 percent of users took part compared to 21 percent of nonusers, and in local government, in which 31 percent served, compared to 4 percent. Hosea Williams, for instance, was elected to the Georgia General Assembly in 1974.[13] As well, the rates of black G.I. Bill users' membership in political clubs and party committees, which had equaled those of white users in the 1950–64 period, grew considerably. Thus, G.I. Bill usage facilitated black veterans' political action for social change, first by prompting civil rights activism and later by enabling active use of newly won political rights.

The Sequence of Events

If we had considered only the kinds of civic engagement pursued by nonblack G.I. Bill users, it might have seemed that receiving such generous government benefits necessarily steered citizens toward activities that supported the status quo. One might have expected, then, that black G.I. Bill beneficiaries would not show particularly elevated levels of involvement in the civil rights movement. To the contrary, not only did they engage in political resistance, but many stepped forward as leaders in that effort.

The sequencing of black and white veterans' particular experiences of government illuminates why their usage of the G.I. Bill prompted such different forms of activity.[14] For white veterans, the education and training benefits typically stood as the most significant in a series of positive interactions with government. Many remembered that when they were children, New Deal programs rescued their families from the hardships of the Great Depression. However painful their memories of military service, they typically felt that they had been treated fairly in the course of the draft, enlistment, and time in uniform. Afterward, they encountered what for many were overwhelmingly affirmative experiences of the G.I. Bill, finding it to be readily accessible, generally well administered, and the source of beneficial socioeconomic effects in their lives. The society that they entered with their new training and education welcomed them. As John Mink said, "I felt I was a Roman in the early Roman Empire: at the top of the world, so to speak." Opportunities abounded for such men, and they seized them. Thus, it is not surprising that when white veterans became involved in politics, they did so in a fairly conventional manner. Certainly their involvement broadened the scope of who participated in politics and to whom public officials responded, but taking part did not require them to fundamentally change existing laws and procedures of government.

Conversely, for black veterans, their positive experience of access to the G.I. Bill's education and training provisions represented a rare but influential moment amid a succession of highly negative interactions with American government. As children, they had known legalized segregation in schools, on public transportation, and in other public as well as private facilities.[15] New Deal social programs routinely excluded their families, whether through occupational exclusions or the retention of discretion by local elites.[16] Military service, too, proved stigmatizing, as they were relegated to segregated units, often forbidden the "privilege" of engaging in combat, and denied many of the honors and forms of recognition typically bestowed on their white comrades. Charles Dryden was one of the Tuskegee Airmen, the unit that escorted the Allied B-17 and B-25 bomber planes, which usually carried crews of ten white servicemen, on their missions. He explained, "We turned out to be the best pilots the air corps ever had: in two hundred escort missions we never lost a friendly bomber to any aircraft, never." And yet, he continued, "when you came back home you couldn't even be buried in the town cemetery, you had to be segregated. And if you lived, wherever you shopped . . . or went to school, you were treated like a second-class citizen. That was painful, very painful." Even some federal policies, after the war, still marginalized black veterans, as in the case of the federal mortgage loan assistance programs and the G.I. Bill's own loan guarantee provisions, to the extent that they were administered by local banks or lending institutions that relied on redlining and other discriminatory guidelines in making loan decisions.[17]

Interrupting this long series of negative interactions with government, the G.I. Bill's education and training benefits actually demonstrated that government does have the capacity to treat blacks and whites equally and to bestow generous resources on both. As we have seen, African American veterans gained full access to the benefits, using them at higher rates than white veterans nationwide. They enrolled in educational programs at especially high rates in the South, where the bill's inclusivity likely provided a jarring contrast to the segregated institutions in which they had to utilize the benefits. And while black veterans in other regions sometimes encountered instances of informal discrimination in colleges and training programs, they found the G.I. Bill's provisions to be administered in an even-handed manner. One black veteran of the 92nd Infantry Division who used the G.I. Bill to learn watchmaking described his treatment in the vocational program as "very accessible and very valuable" and "fair," separating it from what he had experienced in the military. Another, William Perry, who attended Case Western Reserve University on the G.I. Bill, described gaining entrance to the program as "fairly easy" and administration as "pretty fair" in contrast to some instances of informal discrimination he encountered during the course of his studies. These men experienced it as the most inclusive and valuable policy they had known up until that point in their lives. Most important, through such education and training, they—like other beneficiaries—gained not only the chance for greater socioeconomic status but also the skills, resources, and networks that are widely regarded as making political action possible.[18] For black veterans in particular, that opportunity would prove pivotal, preparing them to serve as leaders for social change.

Finally, the experience that typically followed after black veterans completed their studies under the G.I. Bill served, for many, as the ultimate catalyst for their political mobilization: they returned to a job market that remained as hostile and discriminatory as ever. Seeking employment, college diploma or training certificate in hand, they found that they were offered the same low-level positions that they would have gotten even without the additional schooling. The fundamental unfairness of such treatment likely felt intolerable following the experience of G.I. Bill usage. As Henry Hervey noted, explaining his reaction to employment discrimination after obtaining his college degree on the G.I. Bill, "By that time you learn that you can fight city hall, and you have to fight, and there are ways you can bring pressure to make changes." Black G.I. Bill users thus took to the streets, demanding fundamental social and political changes in American society.[19]

Whereas an overwhelmingly positive experience of government in a string of affirmative encounters led white veterans to conventional politics, the G.I. Bill's status as an exception to the rule in the experience of black veterans impelled them toward involvement that challenged the system. The benefits helped spur their heightened political activity and to direct it toward the struggle for improved circumstances for blacks generally.[20] Critically, too, the education and training programs had equipped them for their role in the vanguard of the civil rights movement. As one survey respondent noted, the G.I. Bill marked a life turning point because it gave him the "educational background to give leadership," stimulating his later involvement in the civil rights movement.[21]

Creating a Vanguard for the Movement

Medgar Evers was born in the age of segregation in Mississippi, his father a sawmill worker and his mother a laundress. So too was Aaron Henry, whose parents were sharecroppers, and W. W. Law, who lived in Georgia and began working at age ten to help support the family after his father died. All three served in the military in World War II and then returned to the South. Though little had changed, they did have access to the G.I. Bill, and each one used it. Medgar Evers enrolled at Alcorn A&M College in Mississippi, where he was able to first complete his high school degree and then go on to a college degree in business administration. He became class president, yearbook editor, and editor of the student newspaper; most important, he gained exposure to the emerging civil rights movement when, in his senior year, he participated monthly in an interracial seminar in Jackson, through which he became aware of and joined the NAACP. Henry studied pharmacy science at Xavier University in New Orleans and served as president of his junior and senior classes. Law obtained a bachelor's degree in biology at Georgia State College.

Before long, each man emerged as a leader in the civil rights movement. Evers began organizing NAACP chapters all over the state and then confronted segregation head-on by becoming the first black applicant to the all-white University of Mississippi law school. Though university officials quickly rejected him on a supposed technicality, Evers's profile as a leader only grew larger, and he became the NAACP's state field secretary, helping to double the organizational membership over the next three years. On June 12, 1963, Evers was assassinated outside his home. Henry became president of the NAACP in Mississippi in 1959 and also led the formation of the more militant Mississippi Freedom Democratic Party and the Council of Federated Organizations. He was jailed on thirty-three occasions for his activism. Law became president of the Savannah chapter of NAACP in 1950, and by 1962 he and others had begun to press the lawsuits that subsequently led the courts to order the desegregation of public schools in Savannah. Both Henry and Law led numerous boycotts of stores that refused to hire black workers and discriminated against black customers, and they also organized sit-ins at public libraries and store lunch counters.[22]

The point is not that the G.I. Bill alone explains the civil rights movement; certainly most who took to the streets were not veterans, and a wide range of organizational, social, economic, and political factors coalesced to prompt the broader mobilization. Rather, black veterans who obtained advanced education—available to them through the G.I. Bill—

were especially likely to become activists and to participate intensely in the political struggles through which civil rights were won. They populated the civic organizations that became the engines for social change, joined the crowds that took to the streets to protest, and took part in the sit-ins. Then, once new rights were at last achieved, they were among the first to exercise them in the realm of formal politics. The G.I. Bill's education and training benefits, being democratic in application, subsequently helped facilitate the development of a more democratic America.

9

Created with the Men in Mind

Whena asked about the G.I. Bill, Ann Bertini, who had served in the Army Nurse Corps, replied, "Oh, I think we viewed it as a policy for the men. I mean, they really created it with the men in mind, didn't they?" Indeed, the story of the G.I. Bill's effects is, in the main, the story of men of the World War II generation, just as our predominant image of the "greatest generation" is essentially masculine, captured by scenes of male soldiers in the trenches or of Shriners, Moose, Masons, and veterans marching in hometown Memorial Day parades. Though more women served in World War II than in any prior U.S. war, still they constituted only 2 percent of the armed forces, and a mere 132,000 women were among the 7.8 million veterans who utilized the G.I. Bill's education and training benefits.[1] The benefits themselves were not inherently sexist so much as the social norms and other policies of the era which encouraged male veterans' usage while discouraging females.

Furthermore, the vast majority of women of their generation remained civilians and thus were ineligible for the G.I. Bill. Rosie the Riveter, revered as she was, was not offered the chance to utilize the benefits. Certainly to the extent that millions of civilian women married veterans who used the program, they benefited from it indirectly, through the heightened standard of living that it enabled their families to enjoy. But unlike Civil War veterans' pension programs, which had included generous benefits for soldiers' widows and dependents, the G.I. Bill covered only veterans, save for the extra amounts in subsistence allowances for married veteran students.[2] The story of how women fared under the G.I. Bill deserves our careful consideration because it bears lessons about how a group's marginalization from generous social rights can hinder, for decades, their capacity and inclination to participate as active citizens.

Gender and Program Usage

While 51 percent of male veterans of World War II used the G.I. Bill's education and training benefits, only 40 percent of females did so. While this difference is not very large—only nine percentage points—the fact that it exists at all raises the question of whether, aside from the overwhelming presence of men in the eligibility pool, the G.I. Bill may have been designed or implemented in a way that deterred women from using its benefits at rates comparable to men.

A small portion of the women who had served in the World War II military were formally and systematically disqualified from using the G.I. Bill. The eleven hundred Women Air Force Service Pilots (WASPs)—the women's unit attached to the Army Air Force—were not granted military status until the 1970s and thus did not qualify for program benefits.[3] The nation's recognition of the WASPs was long overdue: they had performed daring missions throughout the war, ferried planes under all sorts of conditions, and taught cadets to fly; some had lost their lives in the service.[4] Nonetheless, they constituted less than one-half of 1 percent of all women who served in the military.[5] Other women who served, all in the larger units—the Women's Army Corps (WACs), the Navy (WAVES), the Coast Guard (SPARs), the Marines (MCWR), and the nurse corps attached to each branch—did qualify for the same education and training benefits as men, and the same subsistence allowances if single. Some ambiguity revolved around the status of women who had served in the Army early in the war, in what was then called the Women's Army Auxiliary Corps (WAAC). After Congress opted to remove the word *auxiliary* in 1943, the WACs became part of the regular Army, with benefits equal to those of men.[6] While women who had served in the WAAC previously could have encountered difficulties in qualifying for the G.I. Bill, those who responded to the World War II Veterans' Survey had routinely continued on under the WAC and thus did gain eligibility for G.I. Bill benefits, which many of them utilized.[7] One systematic disparity that did emerge in women's treatment was that whereas male veterans routinely garnered an additional allowance for dependents (a total of $105 if they had one dependent, $120 for two or more), female veterans were denied such payments on the theory that their husbands should be able to provide for themselves.[8]

The importance of these issues notwithstanding, they do not in themselves explain gender bias in the G.I. Bill. At least one group of men who served in World War II was also systematically excluded from G.I. Bill coverage: the 215,000 who served in the merchant marine, also risking their lives, never received veteran status either, and thus were ineligible for veterans' benefits.[9] They constituted close to 1.5 percent of the World War II military. It would be a mistake, therefore, to interpret the G.I. Bill as sexist on the basis of the exclusion of the WASPs and some WAAC members. Excessive focus on their situation misses more central issues about how and why women were so underrepresented among beneficiaries and why it matters.

The average male and female veteran differed in many other ways besides sex. Most men had been recruited into the armed forces through the draft, whereas all women who served were volunteers. Higher enlistment standards were required of women, who were sought particularly for their skills and prior training. Thus, 62 percent of enlisted women had completed at least a high school education, compared to only 39 percent of enlisted men.[10] And while men in the service represented a remarkably broad and representative cross section of the general population, women came from a narrower, relatively elite group; they were less likely to have grown up in poverty and more likely to have been strongly encouraged during childhood to pursue advanced education.

Taking into account these differences, it becomes even more apparent that the G.I. Bill, in practice, was far less inclusive of female veterans: all else being equal, women were much less likely to use the bill's benefits.[11] Indeed, the seemingly minor disparity in male and female veterans' G.I. Bill usage (9 percent) is actually more significant given the characteristics, other than sex, of the particular women who served. If gender dynamics had been missing, the female veterans would likely have utilized the provisions at higher rates than male veterans, because they tended to be from more privileged backgrounds: they had experienced higher standards of living in childhood, had received more encouragement to pursue education, attained a higher level of education prior to military service, had more highly educated parents, and were more likely to be Protestant. The female veterans were comparable to a narrow subset of male veterans who used the education and training benefits at particularly high rates, typically for higher education, and who likely would have continued their education even if the G.I. Bill did not exist. In short, had the female veterans been different in only one regard—sex—they would have used the G.I. Bill at higher average rates than male veterans did. Gender was the sole factor that stood in the way of their G.I. Bill usage.[12]

How did gender play such a powerful role in determining which veterans utilized the G.I. Bill's education and training provisions? First and most important, use of those provisions fit neatly with how an increasing number of young men in the middle of the twentieth century understood their gender role, whereas it contradicted the prevalent understanding of women's role. To put it plainly, women were expected to be at home raising children, and this was not viewed as requiring higher education. In some instances, gendered reasons also explained men's choices not to use the program, most often if their expected role as bread-winner meant that they had to work full time to support their families, instead of taking time to further their schooling. The most common reason men cited for nonusage, noted by 51 percent, was that they "pre-ferred work to school," and many qualified this reason by writing in the margin that they had wives and children to support. More typically, how-ever, men's gender roles promoted their usage of its resources. Though in the past, advanced education had been viewed largely as a luxury, increasingly it came to be considered an essential route—especially for men—toward being able to support oneself and one's family success-fully, particularly as white-collar jobs became increasingly prevalent in American society.[13] For men, higher educational attainment became the route to upward social mobility. Among male veterans who chose to use the benefits, the opportunity to improve their employment prospects and socioeconomic standing figured prominently as a way to better sup-port their families.

Female nonusers' most frequent explanation for forgoing the ben-efits, checked by 38 percent of survey respondents, was "other," after which they most frequently wrote in some type of reason involving familial obligations, such as caring for children or supporting a husband's breadwinning role. One woman explained that she "got married and helped my husband operate a bakery," another that "Mother passed away, [and I] took care of Dad until I married." Others wrote "got married," "planned to marry," "raising family," "married and moved," "husband still in service; [I] followed him till his twenty-one years [were] up," and so forth.

These reasons cohere with the facts of most young women's lives in the postwar era, which, more than at any other time prior or since in the twentieth century, revolved around marriage and child rearing. Elaine Tyler May reports, "Those who came of age during and after World War II were the most marrying generation on record: 96.4 percent of the women and 94.1 percent of the men." Marriage rates soared, reaching the century's all-time high. And, reversing a trend of declining fertility rates, once married, young women proceeded to have more children, to bear them sooner (throughout their twenties), and to space them closer together than had their own parents' generation.[14] Some have character-ized the trend—which produced the baby boom generation—as a "head-long rush into domesticity."[15] Indeed, such developments were surprising on the heels of decades of increasing employment rates by married women, and particularly in the wake of World War II, during which 50 percent more women held down jobs.[16] By contrast, the gender role assigned to women in the postwar years placed heavy emphasis on women's roles as homemakers: having babies, being at home to raise them, living up to heightened norms of home maintenance, and purchasing goods for the home from the vast cornucopia of the postwar "consumers' republic."[17]

A confluence of factors—economic, cultural, and political—produced the renewed emphasis on women's domestic roles in the postwar era. Fears of recession once veterans returned home and flooded the labor market prompted policy makers and union officials alike to urge women to leave their wartime jobs and go "back to the kitchen." Some preferential hiring procedures for male veterans were inscribed in the Selective Service Act, and others were adopted voluntarily by companies. Unions' seniority rules and special contract clauses privileged the returning male veterans over more recently hired women. Combined, these factors presented obstacles to women who sought jobs.[18] Public opinion surveys also revealed widespread desires among Americans, men and women, for a sharp division of labor between the sexes: men were expected to be the breadwinners and women to take care of the home.[19] Furthermore, Congress revised the federal income tax in 1948 such that married couples could file jointly and receive a considerable advantage, especially if one spouse was the sole or primary wage earner. Remaining in place until 1969, this system provided economic incentives for married women to stay out of the labor force.[20] The power of these myriad forces helps explain why so many women veterans felt after the war that their primary responsibilities involved being in the home, as wives and mothers.

Yet to portray women as belonging only to the domestic realm is to miss the complexity of the postwar era.[21] After women veterans pointed to marriage and family to explain why they did not use the G.I. Bill, the next most frequently cited reason was that they "preferred to work," noted by 28 percent. Before the end of the war, a survey of WACs' future plans found that while 29 percent wished to be housewives, 48 percent sought full-time employment or to start their own business.[22] Indeed, given the new skills and job experience they had acquired, military women had reason to expect such a future.[23] In the postwar years, women were more likely to participate in the labor force than prevalent images might suggest, and female veterans were no exception. Despite the fact that many women workers had been laid off during the reconversion period and women's labor force participation rates dipped slightly as male veterans reclaimed their old jobs, by 1950 more women were employed than ever before, continuing a long-term trend.[24]

Nonetheless, although many women had secured employment in better-paying, higher-status jobs during the war, afterward the old patterns of occupational segregation were reestablished and women once again experienced routine discrimination in job placement and pay scales.[25] Women veterans found that employers, often unaware that they had full military status, were unwilling to grant them the special treatment afforded to male veterans.[26] They were usually relegated to low-paying, low-status jobs that utilized none of the new skills they had acquired during their military service.[27]

Married women's labor force participation in the postwar era most typically served to support husbands in their breadwinning role and upward mobility. In fact, one of the explanations for rising employment rates among married women at the time was that they were helping support husbands who were full-time students under the G.I. Bill, as did many female veterans.[28] In sum, women's employment, like their domestic responsibilities, tended to be understood as a component of their gender role, and as such, it interfered with their usage of the education and training provisions.

To what extent did women's likelihood of pursuing additional education explain their lesser usage of the G.I. Bill? Next to domestic reasons and work, women's most common explanation for nonusage, noted by another 20 percent, was "had all the education or training I needed." This reason might be attributable both to female veterans' higher educational attainment prior to military service, compared to their male counterparts, and to cultural assumptions that women did not require as much education to fulfill their expected roles in society. At the same time, many women veterans did continue their education after the war, but without G.I. Bill assistance. A Harris poll found that a full 60 percent of female veterans participated in some kind of post-military-service education program, but only 58 percent of that group used the G.I. Bill to pay for their education.[29] By this measure, they contrasted sharply with male veterans, among whom postwar education was, for all intents and purposes, synonymous with G.I. Bill usage.

Women's lesser use of the G.I. Bill benefits even when they did pursue additional education or training emanated from ways in which the program's design and delivery effectively circumvented them. Women were less likely to be made aware of the provisions. Whereas men were routinely informed of them in the course of discharge, women were not. Vocational counseling, routinely available to men as they separated from the military, was provided only sporadically to women, and counselors were ill-prepared to advise women on their postwar plans for education or employment. The War Department's pamphlet *Going Back to Civilian Life,* which apprised servicemen of their rights and the assistance available to them, contained no reference to women.[30] One of the female veterans interviewed returned to nursing school for two years after the war, but she did not use the G.I. Bill to assist her with tuition payments. Asked why she did not draw upon its benefits, she replied, "I don't know why. ... My father had died, and I don't know if my mother understood it, or I didn't ... but ... it would have helped if I had [used it]." Even women who were aware of the G.I. Bill sometimes were reluctant to utilize the benefits because, as Ann Bertini said, they viewed it as being "for the men."[31] Perhaps most important, women were more likely—due to their gender roles—to pursue additional education later in life, after their G.I. Bill benefits had expired. Bertini herself, for instance, returned to school at age fifty, after her children were grown, and trained for a new career as a funeral director.[32] Women's gender roles steered them toward delaying additional education while they attended to domestic pursuits and related employment. The same nine-year limit on G.I. bill entitlements that fused fairly seamlessly with expectations of men's life course in the postwar era actually disadvantaged women.

On balance, then, although the reasons for women's lesser use of the G.I. Bill education and training benefits are somewhat related to how the law was designed and implemented, the predominant causes lie in the larger cultural and political milieu of the postwar era. Granted, the education and training benefits might have benefited women veterans more if they had been structured to accommodate their gender roles— for example, by permitting usage over a longer period (so that women could use them once their children were older) or by offering child care benefits and facilities (as had been provided for women workers in defense plants during the war) so that they could attend school even when their children were young.[33] When creating the program and even when amending it later on, however, policy makers had "the men in mind," not the ways that female veterans might have been more effectively included.

Gender and the Effects of Usage

Research about the postwar era has shown again and again that despite several decades of political rights, women remained considerably less involved in politics than men.[34] Strikingly, being female remained a strong negative influence on political involvement even among women who used the G.I. Bill, an experience that had mobilized male veterans—especially those from less advantaged backgrounds—so powerfully.[35]

What could explain women's lesser degree of involvement in civic and political life even after they benefited from a program that so clearly boosted such participation among men? In short, it appears that neither the resource effects nor the cognitive effects of the G.I. Bill's education and training provisions were sufficiently powerful in women's lives to produce such outcomes. Given that the cultural and political environment was structured against high levels of civic engagement by women, comparable civic outcomes would have required the G.I. Bill to transform women's lives even more powerfully than men's. But, as we shall see, even when women veterans gained valuable resources from program usage, they did not experience the life-altering effects or perceive the affirming messages of inclusion that so enhanced the participation rates of male beneficiaries.

Certainly women G.I. Bill beneficiaries, like men, gained valuable resources. In terms of the type of education they obtained through program usage, they appear—from the World War II Veterans Survey, the only existing source of such data—to have been equally as likely as male beneficiaries to attend college versus using the subcollege programs. Men and women varied in their top choices among subcollege programs: men most frequently chose vocational training, while women were especially likely to attend business school for accounting or clerical skills, or to further their training in nursing. And when we control for several determinants of advanced education, G.I. Bill users of both sexes appear to have gained comparable levels of formal education through the program; its effectiveness proved highly significant for women's educational attainment, just as it did among male users.[36]

In naming the G.I. Bill's effects on their lives, women emphasized many of the same outcomes as men. In open-ended survey responses, several jotted down ways in which the program furthered their education (e.g., "enabled me to finish college, which was my mother's dream for me"). Others suggested that it enhanced their job opportunities. One reported that it had "provided the foundation for a very successful teaching career." Another noted that it "enabled me to resume college and become a professional," and some stressed how it subsequently made it possible for them to have an important impact on society ("I taught five thousand children to read and write"). Finally, a few mentioned how G.I. Bill usage enabled them to grow personally and intellectually (e.g., "opened up the doors to a liberal education and a quest for more knowledge and the ability to weigh values and think through problems," "made several friendships which have continued through the years.")

The G.I. Bill's effects, though, proved less transformative and conveyed less powerful messages among female veterans than had been the case among males. The fact that the women tended to come from privileged backgrounds meant that their usage of the bill was stripped of some of its interpretive potential for them. As well, the World War II Veterans Survey reveals that they actually received less in benefits than the male veterans: they spent less total time in school or training on the G.I. Bill (one to two years, on average, compared to over three years among male users), and they were considerably less likely to complete their degree programs (only 63 percent did so, compared to 79 percent of the men). Just as gendered roles and expectations had kept the majority of women veterans from taking advantage of the G.I. Bill's education and training benefits, they also hindered those women who did utilize the program from using it as fully as most male veterans did.

Further, women beneficiaries who attended college or training programs on the G.I. Bill often faced herculean challenges, given their multiple domestic responsibilities. It is true that the availability of free tuition enabled some to continue their education despite their roles as wives and mothers. Several wrote that they were already married but that the G.I. Bill gave them the opportunity to attend college anyway, sometimes at the same institution as their veteran husbands. In addition, a few mentioned that they bore their first children soon after the war, and while they had expected to delay advanced education for several years, the G.I. Bill enabled them to continue on immediately. One survey respondent wrote, "I was married with two small children. I would have had to delay my education toward a degree in sociology and may never have devoted my professional career to social work, both as a welfare worker then later as a child welfare worker, working up to a [position as a] supervisor." Another explained, "I had two children when I started college. I needed an education . . . small towns do not have many job opportunities. The G.I. Bill really was a lifesaver."

At the same time, these women clearly obtained their education or training against the odds, given that they needed to find some form of child care for the periods while they were in classes, and because they had to squeeze time for studying in between their domestic responsibilities. In a sense, the exception proves the rule, as highlighted by the story of Ann Sharp. She and her veteran husband moved to a trailer in married student housing at Auburn University when he decided to attend college, and she gave birth to their first child there. Subsequently, Ann chose to become a student as well. She explained that she would not have gone to college so promptly if the G.I. Bill had not been available. "I think I would have, eventually after my children had grown, because I felt a definite need. But there was no way I could have done it when I did or had the years in teaching that I had because of it if it hadn't been for the G.I. Bill." She explained that her brother, also a veteran, came to live with them, and the three managed a collective child care arrangement: "It was hysterical: we took separate classes so there would always be one of us with the child. I'd rush to campus and my husband or brother would meet me and take the child." For most women, the societal assumption that taking care of their children was their primary responsibility likely preempted such arrangements as this from even being considered, making their lives as students—even if financed by the government—very taxing indeed. In short, for student mothers to have experienced the education and training benefits to be as transformative of their lives as men had found them to be, they would have required more resources—targeted toward child care, for instance—to aid them.

Female veterans were also less inclined than males to think of themselves as rightful beneficiaries of the G.I. Bill, and thus they were less likely to experience the program as transforming their status into that of first-class citizens. In receiving the benefits, male veterans felt that government bestowed generous resources on them and treated them with dignity and respect. They felt more fully incorporated in the polity as a result, and thus began to participate more actively. Female veterans, by contrast, thought of the G.I. Bill as targeted primarily toward males, and perceived themselves as fortunate secondary beneficiaries. As such, the program paled in its ability to more fully incorporate them as active citizens.

Finally, usage of the bill's education and training benefits had less dramatic socioeconomic effects on women's lives than on men's, thus further curtailing its effects on their views of it. The G.I. Bill liberated many male veterans from the occupational paths they had assumed they would follow, allowing them to obtain training in newly emergent fields and subsequently to collect higher salaries than they would have otherwise. By contrast, even women who attained high levels of education through the program found themselves restricted to a small array of occupational opportunities. In 1960, one-third of female survey respondents who had used the provisions reported themselves to be housewives. For those who were employed outside the home, the list of their occupations in 1960 includes only a tiny number of the sorts of professions that appeared frequently among male survey respondents: one physician, one editor and publisher of a newspaper, and two professors. The vast majority worked as nurses, teachers, secretaries, or clerks, or had positions in retail or social services. Given that many females had been recruited into the military because they already had a nursing background, it is not surprising that many of them used the G.I. Bill to gain more advanced nursing degrees; several such women achieved supervisory positions. Nonetheless, women in the postwar era, whether or not they used the G.I. Bill to finance their degrees, experienced considerable restrictions in terms of the fields in which they were permitted to study and to obtain degrees and licenses. "Most of the women students at that time were going into home economics or elementary education . . . certainly not in medicine or dentistry or law," commented Ann Sharp. "[Those] fields were not as open then as they are now." Medical schools, for instance, imposed a 5 percent maximum quota on female admissions. Whatever their training, once women sought employment, they faced rigid occupational segregation and were routinely denied higher-status jobs. Wage differentials between men and women, even for the same jobs, remained the norm, and in industries in which women constituted more than half of all employees, particularly low wages prevailed.[37]

For all of these reasons, the G.I. Bill's education and training benefits failed to have the same powerful effects among female users that they had generated among male users. Women genuinely valued the education they received from the G.I. Bill, but given the structure of family life, education, and employment, the program affected their lives far less dramatically than men's. Not surprisingly, then, the program's effects on their civic engagement were also more limited. Its influence became evident only in the fact that in the period 1965 to 1979, women who had become highly educated—in part through the G.I. Bill—participated more intensely in politics.[38] This means that the G.I. Bill did have a resource effect among women, but it failed to convey the more powerful interpretive effects that had so affected men's lives. The "private roots of public action" that for so long had thwarted women's participation in politics were barely disturbed by the policy's impact on female veterans.[39]

Gendered Effects of the G.I. Bill
Across Veterans and Civilians

Given that most women of the World War II generation were civilians and therefore did not even qualify for the G.I. Bill's education and training benefits, we must consider the broader impact of their exclusion. We will begin by examining the consequences of the G.I. Bill for educational attainment among members of the civic generation generally, veterans and nonveterans alike, comparing men to women.

If civilian widows of World War II veterans had been treated in a manner comparable to the widows of Civil War veterans, the G.I. Bill would have been extended to them as well.[40] The absence of such provisions did not result from a lack of effort. In 1947, the Gold Star Wives of America, a military widows' organization, testified before Congress in support of extending the education and training benefits of the G.I. Bill to widows and dependents of those who had given their lives in service to their country. As Helen Gooden explained to the Committee on Veterans' Affairs:

> In justice, the widow who has taken her husband's place as head of the family, and who must now provide food, clothing, and shelter for herself and that family, should have the same opportunity which he would have had to secure the necessary training to fit herself for her tremendous job.... Since it is necessary that these widows work outside their homes, it is sensible and economical to give them an opportunity to fit themselves for some gainful occupation in order that they may become trained, useful workers, rather than odd-job seekers. In the business world, women do not have, as yet, equal opportunities with men.[41]

Congress did not enact such provisions until 1956, however, and those were written in a manner that excluded the families of World War II veterans from coverage.[42]

With the G.I. Bill's provisions advantaging primarily men, the pursuit of higher education grew more biased toward men. The gender gap among new recipients of college degrees—which had been narrowing since the 1870s—widened sharply once again.[43] The proportion of women among recipients of bachelor's or first professional degrees had grown steadily from 19 percent in 1900 to 41 percent in 1940. As male veterans stormed the colleges and universities with their G.I. Bill benefits, women's enrollment rates declined precipitously to 24 percent of graduates in 1950, nearly the same level as in 1910. Not until 1970 did the proportion of women among college graduates return to its prewar levels.[44] During the Cold War era, these trends sparked some concern, as policy makers became aware that in the Soviet Union, women accounted for 69 percent of medical students and 39 percent of engineers, whereas in the United States, they made up only 20 percent of all math and science majors.[45] Seeking ways to redress the resulting loss in human capital development, studies during the era examined whether the liberal arts curriculum should be adapted in particular ways for women, and how the patterns of women's lives, including bearing and raising children, could be better accommodated by institutions of higher education.[46]

The educational gender gap resulted not from a decline in women's enrollments but rather from the tremendous upsurge in men's enrollment facilitated by the G.I. Bill itself. Without the bill, it would be reasonable to expect that both male and female students would have gradually continued to increase their numbers in the halls of higher education. This is, in fact, what women did, as seen in Figure 9.1: in absolute terms, the number of female college graduates increased by 25 percent between 1940 and 1950, a rate comparable to that of previous decades. Over the same period, however, men's numbers grew by 66 percent, a stark aberration from prior periods.

The disparity between male and female graduation rates also may have resulted in part from the ways in which universities' treatment of veterans disadvantaged civilian women. As early as 1946, federal officials realized that women who sought admission to college during the "G.I. bulge" would have their chances impeded. A report from the U.S. Office of War Mobilization and Reconversion noted that the war had interrupted the normal course of women's lives just as it had for men, but lamented, "Facilities for the accommodation of women students are proportionately shorter and more difficult to expand on a temporary basis than those of men. A disproportionate number of the nonveteran students who will be turned away this fall will therefore be women."[47] In fact, as one male veteran interviewed for this project remarked, "The only women students who got in were the straight-A students."

Several universities and colleges were known to have granted preferences to veteran applicants in the immediate postwar years, to the detriment of civilians, especially women.[48] Some, such as Cornell, went further, placing limits on female enrollment as an explicit means of

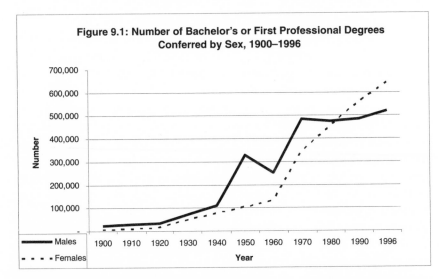

Figure 9.1: Number of Bachelor's or First Professional Degrees Conferred by Sex, 1900–1996

Source: George Thomas Kurian, ed., *Datapedia of the United States, 1790–2005* (Lanham, MD: Bernan, 2001), 176–77; United States Bureau of the Census, *Historical Statistics of the United States, Colonial Times to 1970*, Part 1 (Washington, DC: GPO, 1975), 383.

making room for veterans.[49] At Penn State, no women were admitted to the main campus as freshmen until a sufficient number of veterans graduated in 1949.[50] The University of Wisconsin first limited enrollment of out-of-state women and then banned their admission altogether.[51] At some elite universities, bars to women's admission long predated the G.I. Bill and endured beyond it: neither Yale nor Princeton, for instance, admitted female undergraduates until the late 1960s.[52] Other private universities and colleges, though they dismantled existing racial and religious barriers, continued to apply their long-standing quotas on the proportion or number of women they would admit.[53]

Yet in explaining the source of the gender gap in college graduation rates in 1950, the importance of discriminatory practices pales by comparison to the impact of the overwhelming advantages bestowed on men through the resources of the G.I. Bill. In the late 1940s, fully half of all college students in the nation had their studies financed by the law's provisions, and the availability of tuition coverage and subsistence allowances appears to have persuaded hundreds of thousands of male veterans who would not otherwise have attended college to do so.[54] Discrimination against women most likely explains much about where they received their degrees (more often in women's colleges or in public universities, the latter being more gender-blind in admissions than private colleges and universities) and what they studied but little about the gender gap in college graduation rates.[55] Rather, the advantaging of men through the G.I. Bill is essential to explaining why their numbers in the academy spiked in the postwar era.

The gender disparity in college graduation rates that followed from the G.I. Bill precipitated additional inequities in the achievement of graduate education. The proportion of women among those attaining master's or second professional degrees declined from 38 percent in 1940 to 29 percent in 1950, and did not return to the former level until 1970. Similarly, whereas women had earned 13 percent of all doctorates and equivalent professional degrees in 1940, they received slightly less than 10 percent of such degrees in 1950.[56] The proportion of women among recipients of both types of degrees had peaked in 1930 and then began to fall over the next two decades, starting well in advance of the G.I. Bill. Conceivably, during the Depression years, families and individuals found it more reasonable to spend scarce resources on tuition for males rather than females, given the sharp disparity in subsequent wages between the two and the greater likelihood that women, given their gender roles, would not use the training they had received.[57] Then, with the G.I. Bill, not only did men gain extra opportunities to pursue graduate and professional training, but the extent to which they outnumbered women at the undergraduate level further skewed the pool of potential candidates for postgraduate study.[58]

The gap in men's and women's education and training that followed from the G.I. Bill may well have promulgated enduring inequalities. Such disparities likely helped perpetuate the dominance of men in the professions and in emergent fields in the sciences, engineering, and technology. Given the dip in women's presence in graduate programs, it is no surprise that they were so underrepresented in such fields.[59] As well, the gendered nature of G.I. Bill usage begs the question of the implications for women's participatory citizenship generally, not just among female veterans. While over a third of all men in the World War II generation actually benefited from the education and training provisions of the program, only a very few women could even consider using the bill's benefits. What would be the civic consequences of such gendered social provision?

Wives of G.I. Bill beneficiaries are unlikely to have accrued much in the way of enhanced civic capacity and inclination from the program, given that they lacked the firsthand experience of the program that was so crucial to its interpretive effects. It is even less likely that other civilian women of their cohort would have gained from its civic impact. Certainly, there may have been some generational effects of the program beyond those who used the bill's benefits. Civilians who attended college at the same time as the G.I. Bill beneficiaries may have been inspired by their presence and by the fact that many of them would not have gained such education otherwise. Simply being alive in a period of highly visible and popular government programs may well have had an impact on citizens' views of the importance of public life and the efficacy of political action. While these possibilities cannot be discounted, it is unlikely that they could compare to the impact of the G.I. Bill's benefits in the lives of those individuals who actually used them.

The G.I. Bill itself contributed, then, to the gender inequality that persisted in American citizenship during the middle of the twentieth century. Women of the "greatest generation" did not experience incorporation as citizens through the G.I. Bill, and they were deprived of its mobilizing effects for civic and political involvement. Even for female veterans, the G.I. Bill lacked the transformative power it had for men. The gendered expectations that shaped their lives, by contrast to those affecting men, did not fuse well with the design of the G.I. Bill, and thus women were much less likely to use it or to use it as fully. Neither did usage of it alter their lives as dramatically as was the case among male beneficiaries. The vast majority of women, not having served in the armed forces, were ineligible for the benefits, and even if they were married to men who used the program, they did not derive the same benefits from it.

Thus, in absolute terms, women's status in the polity remained much the same as it had been before the war, but relative to men's position, they had effectively been demoted. Men of their generation had become elevated in public life—not only through the G.I. Bill, but also through a wide array of social and labor policies of the New Deal that treated them as first-class citizens. Through the Social Security Act of 1935, the National Labor Relations Act of 1935, and the Fair Labor Standards Act of 1938, government granted men, primarily, an array of nationally guaranteed and nationally administered social rights that had been unknown previously to American citizens.[60] Atop these social provisions, the G.I. Bill's education and training benefits stood as the example par excellence of the privileging of males as citizens. Granted, qualification for the G.I. Bill rested, as veterans' benefits always had, on the willingness to perform the utmost obligation of citizenship: military service. By putting their lives at risk for the nation, men had been deemed worthy of the country's most generous social benefits. The trouble, of course, was that women were not granted the privilege of being charged with such duties.[61]

These generous forms of social provision granted to men suggest a powerful explanation for why men consistently participated in political activities at higher rates than women in the postwar polity. Voting rates differed between the sexes by about ten percentage points, though the disparity was greatest between men and women of lower socioeconomic status and least among those of higher status.[62] In the latter decades of the twentieth century, the gender gap in voter turnout disappeared (in fact, female turnout has surpassed male turnout recently), but the disparity persisted in other forms of participation, such as affiliating with a political organization, contacting a government official, and making campaign contributions.[63] Some scholars have suggested that perhaps women made up the difference by participating in civic organizations more than in more overtly political activities.[64] Indeed, many women's civic organizations active in the 1950s schooled their members in principles of good citizenship, and they often took a stand on a wide range of policy issues at all levels of government. For example, Methodist women's organizations supported the expansion of Social Security to agricultural and domestic workers, civil rights legislation, and federal aid to education; the General Federation of Women's Clubs advocated the deductibility of child care expenses from the taxable income of employed mothers, funding for library services in rural areas, regulation to control water pollution, and tougher enforcement of narcotics laws.[65] Nonetheless, evidence from the World War II Veterans Survey suggests that in the postwar era, women participated less than men in the widespread, federated organizations that were most likely to assume such political roles. Rather, they were far more likely to be involved in local, community-based organizations, which were less apt to involve their members politically.[66]

Uncovering the Public Roots of Private Action

Given the considerable gender inequity prompted by the G.I. Bill, today it might seem appropriate simply to dismiss the policy as an artifact of a bygone era that bears no positive or constructive messages for our own times. To do so would be a mistake. Unless we can appreciate and understand the specific and powerful ways that the G.I. Bill not only bestowed social rights on men but also fostered their civic involvement, we will fail to realize the full and grave consequences of women's exclusion. By the same token, we would miss the opportunity to garner valuable lessons about how policies could be fashioned in the future to be more fully inclusive across gender lines and to empower both men and women to exercise political voice.

Following the slogan of second-wave feminism that "the personal is political," research on gender and politics has exposed sources of inequality in political participation that emanate from the nonpolitical institutions of everyday life, especially the family and the workplace. Scholars have noted that while women's participation in the workplace generally boosts their political involvement, inequality in the family depresses it.[67] Meanwhile, men, particularly white men, are multiply advantaged by their gender roles, which place them in circumstances—whether in the workplace or in voluntary organizations—in which they are more likely to be recruited for political activity and in which they are more likely to have the necessary resources and skills to take part.[68] But such scholarship overlooks the role that public policies may play in perpetuating participatory inequality.

Conversely, those who study gender and public policy tend not to consider effects for civic engagement.[69] Some policy scholars focus on the extent to which policies extend social citizenship, meaning access to economic security and well-being, and typically challenge treatments of it that neglect to consider gender.[70] Yet they overlook the subsequent implications for civic engagement.

Lessons of history have shown us that the inscription of gender in-equality in law and public policy does matter for civic engagement. Women's exclusion from political rights in the late nineteenth and early twentieth centuries fostered gender-specific forms of civic organizing and political activism. The United States was exceptional in granting what is called "universal manhood suffrage" well before comparable nations. By the 1830s, virtually all white men had the right to vote, regardless of whether they owned property. Unlike in Europe, where class had a major role in defining political status, in the United States gender and race became critical cleavages. White men, including new immigrants, became incorporated politically through patronage party politics, often via lively rituals that became identified with masculinity: they joined local party organizations, attended political rallies, wore campaign paraphernalia, placed bets on election results, and on Election Day turned out in droves at polling places located in saloons, barber shops, and other bastions of male sociability.[71] Conversely, through the delineation that cast them as the out-group, women organized as well, often in ways explicitly identified in terms of gender, by taking up different issues than men did, and by organizing according to distinct strategies. This distinct stream of activism led eventually to the enactment of "maternalist" social programs, Prohibition, and other reforms. The gender-exclusive characteristics of political rights thus prompted gender-specific and gender-identified forms of political and civic activity.[72]

In 1920, after seventy-two years of struggle, the women's suffrage movement finally succeeded when the Nineteenth Amendment to the Constitution was ratified, thus guaranteeing the right to vote regardless of sex. Political rights, at long last, became equalized—at least formally speaking—in terms of gender. Yet within a decade and a half, the New Deal began to extend new social rights to citizens in ways that stratified the citizenry once again, with white men incorporated into mostly nationally administered programs and women and minority men left to the states.[73] This raises the question of whether the gendered extension of social rights would matter politically in a manner comparable to the earlier gendered character of political rights.

In the case of the G.I. Bill, the divide in social citizenship did indeed encourage unequal political citizenship. Through increased access to education, a new form of identity was established among American men, overcoming prior divisions of class, ethnicity, and religion. As men attained further education through this broad, generous program, they became more fully incorporated as citizens, and they subsequently participated in politics at greater levels as a result. Once again, rights that differed by gender elevated men's participation.

Varying degrees of incorporation of different groups of citizens throughout American political history have had marked effects on their relative degrees of trust in government, sense of political efficacy, support of government, and participation in a wide range of political activities. Virginia Sapiro notes, "Participation in the governance of one's community is participation in the governance of oneself. Those who are governed but do not govern are not citizens but subjects."[74] The historic bias toward men in various public policies may have curtailed the promises of democracy in ways that we have barely begun to unravel. Likewise, any social right that treats groups differently, privileging the status of some while ignoring others, may have long-term consequences for the scope of democratic citizenship.

10

The Unfinished Work

T he men who benefited from the G.I. Bill have been, at least until recently, all around us in every walk of life.[1] Legions of famous Americans rank among those who used the education and training provisions after military service in either World War II or the Korean War, including former U.S. presidents George H. W. Bush and Gerald Ford; Chief Justice William H. Rehnquist and Justices John Paul Stevens and Byron R. White; Senators Dale Bumpers, John Glenn, Ernest Hollings, Daniel K. Inouye, Spark Matsunaga, George Mitchell, Daniel Patrick Moynihan,[2] Bob Dole, and Alan K. Simpson; numerous U.S. representatives including John Conyers, Ronald Dellums, Bill McCollum, G. V. "Sonny" Montgomery, Charles Rangel, and Gerald Solomon; Virginia governor Douglas Wilder; Secretary of State Warren Christopher; journalists and commentators David Brinkley, Art Buchwald, and John Chancellor; entertainers Harry Belafonte, Johnny Cash, Ossie Davis, Clint Eastwood, Paul Newman, Jonathan Winters, and Walter Matthau; and scholars Clifford Geertz and Howard Zinn, just to name a few.[3] For every one of these high-profile beneficiaries of the G.I. Bill, there are tens of thousands more whose names are unrecognizable to a national audience but who were often well known within their local communities for their active and lifelong participation in civic life. They threw themselves into civic associations, took politics seriously, and treated the right to vote as a hallowed obligation. They cared deeply about the public good and considered participation in American democracy to be both a privilege and a duty.

While the G.I. Bill had helped expand and intensify civic engagement among men from a wide array of backgrounds, later on in the postwar years American society became yet more fully democratized.

The achievements of the civil rights and feminist movements dismantled central pillars in the systems of racial hierarchy and gender privilege that had curtailed the reach of the bill's education and training provisions. Finally, the racial segregation and workplace discrimination that African American veterans had faced after World War II became outlawed, and political rights were extended to all citizens regardless of race or ethnicity. Women at last gained formal rights to participate in society on a level playing field, as new laws proscribed the overt practices that had limited their educational opportunities and employment prospects in the postwar era. As the United States entered the 1970s, the nation seemed ever closer to becoming the fully inclusive and highly participatory democracy implicit in its highest ideals.

At that very juncture, however, circumstances coalesced that rattled the very underpinnings of the American polity. Beginning with the first oil shock in 1973, the economy, which had been growing at a rapid pace throughout the postwar decades, slowed considerably. Jobs that had long guaranteed strong wages and benefits to less highly educated workers began to disappear. Over the next couple of decades, lower- and middle-income families saw little real growth in their incomes, while the wealthiest reaped considerable advantage. At the same time, a conservative political coalition began to gather steam, advancing a political philosophy that treats government itself as the problem. Thus, by contrast to those who governed in the middle of the twentieth century, public officials of recent decades have been largely unwilling to use public social provision to ameliorate growing inequality. Many public programs have been left to wither, and government has become considerably less present in the lives of ordinary Americans, particularly the young. As a result, economic inequality, which had remained relatively low since about 1950, began to escalate and has continued to do so, returning American society to the disparities that marked the Gilded Age.[4] Further, the fault lines of the new inequality have reinforced many of the old racial and gendered cleavages that the rights revolution had meant to eradicate. Granted, today women and African American men who are highly educated professionals occupy positions in society that would not have been conceivable in the postwar era. For the vast majority, however, growing economic inequality has sharply curtailed the hope of equality.[5]

Over the same period, we in younger generations have come to feel much more alienated from government, and public life has grown considerably less robust and less inclusive of ordinary Americans.[6] We fail to join broad-based civic organizations at anywhere near the same levels as those whose late youth or early adulthood coincided with World War II.[7] Local chapters of most cross-class civic organizations, including the

Elks, the Masons, the Veterans of Foreign Wars, and most others, hobble along with ever-diminishing numbers from the faithful ranks of the civic generation; when too few members remain, such units fold. Highly educated members of younger generations have taken up advocacy work instead, serving on boards and commissions that allow them to do something on behalf of the less advantaged, rather than actually joining in fellowship with them.[8] Less privileged Americans are left without thriving organizations to join, and they are considerably less active in public life than their forebears.[9] Citizens' rates of political participation are highly stratified: the more affluent exercise considerably more political voice than the less advantaged.[10] Since the 1970s, voter turnout has declined most precipitously among members of post–New Deal generations who have less than a high school diploma; they vote at much lower levels than those with the same education in the earlier generation, even at the same point in their lives.[11] And despite the victories of the rights revolution, participatory inequality persists, as African Americans and Latinos participate in political activities at lower rates overall than whites, and women in each group participate with less frequency than men.[12]

These developments raise profound concerns about the well-being and future of American democracy. The danger is that as social and economic disparities intensify, the political playing field will become increasingly tilted to favor the participation of the affluent, and public officials will respond mostly to their voices, ignoring those of ordinary Americans who have been left behind. As this happens, our political system may become less and less a real democracy.

Today we have no comparable successor to the World War II version of the G.I. Bill: no policy that encompasses a broad cross section of younger citizens, transforms their social and economic opportunities, and in the process incorporates them as citizens ready to engage more actively in the nation's public life. The modern-day G.I. Bill, though a highly laudable policy in its own right, reaches only the much smaller ranks of today's all-volunteer force. We need to recall what it was about the G.I. Bill that generated such pronounced effects on civic engagement among ordinary citizens and consider what the lessons are for our own time.

Reciprocal Obligations

The G.I. Bill stands as a premier example of how government can, through public policy, provide social opportunity, and, at the same time, promote active citizenship, making America more democratic. As such, it flies in the face of our contemporary prejudice against government programs and our expectation that social policies only exacerbate dependency on government. As well, it thwarts our assumption that policies that emphasize individualism must be preferable to those based on social principles, and it refutes the reigning ideology that the unfettered forces of the market must be more effective than policies rooted in political principles.

The fundamental idea behind the G.I. Bill, and the key to the program's stunning success, was that in a democracy, reciprocal obligations bind citizens and government. Beneficiaries' deservingness was premised on their willingness to fulfill their civic duty, their commitments toward the polity; it bestowed honor on them for giving of themselves for the common good. The bill's provisions thus reinforced the notion that recipients of government benefits are first and foremost citizens, members of a shared community to which we all have responsibilities and in which we are interdependent. By contrast to today's policymakers' inclination to emphasize individual self-sufficiency and workplace participation as the behaviors to be rewarded (this is the case in policies ranging from welfare reform to the earned-income tax credit and privatized individual retirement accounts), the G.I. Bill underscored our common citizenship and collective bonds.

Simultaneously, the G.I. Bill emphasized the obligations we all have, as members of the larger political community, to offer, through government, social provision and opportunity. The bill was built on the idea that through the public realm, which reflects the authority and will of all citizens, we can grant our fellow citizens not simply the assurance of economic security but also equal opportunity, the kind of social provision that breathes life into the American dream. In doing so, government effectively invests in citizenship, incorporating individuals as full members of the polity who have a stake in its existence. Social rights that are derived from citizens' mutual interdependence as members of a political community and which make recipients more able to enjoy the full fruits of membership can, in turn, beckon them into yet greater civic participation in the polity.

In an era when advanced education seemed out of reach for most Americans, the G.I. Bill's education and training provisions made it accessible, and did so through broadly inclusive eligibility features and implementation that treated recipients with dignity and respect, as rights-bearing beneficiaries. Both of these aspects conveyed to citizens that government is for and about people like them, buttressing further the idea of a common citizenship. Driving home the bill's message of civic inclusion, the education and training provisions enhanced life opportunities and standard of living particularly among recipients from middle-

and working-class backgrounds, thus elevating their civic involvement most of all. Government's role in the process was clear and unambiguous. Through all of these dynamics, the bill expanded the bounds of the actively engaged citizenry.

Generations and Government

The "greatest generation" has continued to flourish in tandem with social policies built on these reciprocal obligations between citizens and government. In their senior years, members of this generation have benefited from Social Security, Medicare, and Medicaid, all programs that have maintained their real benefit levels even amid fiscal austerity.[13] Through such benefits, seniors have gained the resources that to this day facilitate their political participation and provoke their interest in politics.[14] Like the usage of the G.I. Bill's education and training benefits by members of the civic generation early in their lives, their receipt of Social Security and Medicare later in life seems to have again fostered a "virtuous circle" of enhanced social well-being and heightened and more widespread civic engagement.

Nonelderly citizens, by contrast, today experience government quite differently than did members of the World War II generation, and the manner in which they do depends on their socioeconomic status and has important implications for their civic engagement. For relatively well-off citizens, the federal government offers social provision, but does so through means that make its redistributive role far less obvious: tax breaks for home mortgage interest, state and local income tax payments, charitable contributions, real estate taxes, and medical expenses.[15] In addition, many with full-time jobs receive from their employers retirement benefits and health insurance that are effectively subsidized by government, as they also permit a reduced payment of taxes.[16] Such programs do convey to recipients that they have a strong stake in government and thus may help explain why advantaged members of younger generations continue to participate in politics at high levels.[17] At the same time, however, they advance the notion that we are separate individuals, actors in a marketplace, and they undercut principles of common citizenship and mutual obligation to the commonweal.[18]

Most important, since the early 1970s, government has in effect receded from the lives of less advantaged, nonelderly citizens, even as they have borne the brunt of stagnating wages and diminished employee benefits. Unionization rates have plummeted, as has the real value of the minimum wage, unemployment benefits, food stamps, and welfare or public assistance.[19] Granted, there are some exceptions to these patterns, including the expansion during the 1990s of the earned-income tax credit (a program that supplements the low wages of the working poor) and increased coverage for low-income parents and children under Medicaid.[20] Nonetheless, the cumulative effect of policy developments is that the role of government has, in powerful ways, diminished in the lives of ordinary citizens. This retreat of government is bound to have civic and political consequences among those affected by it. Lack of support for unionization has directly undermined one form of organizational involvement that in the past played a critical role in linking the less advantaged to politics.[21] As benefits in other policies such as Pell grants and food stamps have declined in real terms, citizens gain less of the resources that in prior decades helped foster civic capacity.

Among younger generations, then, policy development may shed light on why participation is strongly tilted toward more advantaged citizens.[22] The demise of resources in programs for the less advantaged, coupled with the application of more invasive and restrictive rules in programs directed to them, may explain much about why they do not perceive government to be responsive to or representative of people like them, and why they have increasingly withdrawn from participating in the political process.

The Lack of an Equal Successor

Most conspicuous by its absence in the lives of younger generations is a program that could carry on, with comparable impact, the legacy of the World War II version of the G.I. Bill. Over recent decades, having a college degree has become much more critical to individuals' job prospects and earning potential: the "college premium" has grown tremendously, as college graduates witnessed a 5 percent increase in their weekly earnings between 1979 and 1994, whereas high school graduates' earnings fell by 20 percent.[23] Given that an individual's educational level is the most powerful predictor of his or her political participation,[24] this means that government's role in providing access to higher education is essential to maintaining some modicum of political equality. Yet since the 1970s, public funding for higher education has failed to keep pace with tuition increases. No single policy, or even the full array of existing programs, performs as ably as did the G.I. Bill, in expanding access to advanced education and in fostering political equality.

The G.I. Bill has been reinvented time and again, but although the recent iterations continue to provide educational opportunity to less advantaged Americans, they reach much smaller segments of the population than the original bill did. The version of the law that was established for Vietnam veterans, in 1967, was more restrictive than those for either World War II or Korean War veterans, requiring a minimum of eighteen months of service before veterans could qualify.[25] Still, the program was well utilized: 41 percent of veterans drew on the education or training provisions, and a much higher percentage of users, 57 percent, pursued higher education, compared to only 28 percent of World War II beneficiaries.[26] The provisions were extremely beneficial to those who used them, extending their educational attainment by 1.4 years, boosting their annual earnings by approximately 6 percent, and, in the case of the vocational training programs, raising earnings especially among African Americans.[27] Nonetheless, overall the program reached only about 1.5 percent of the total U.S. population, whereas the World War II version reached 5 percent of all Americans.[28]

In the early 1970s, the nation ceased to view military service as a fundamental obligation of male citizenship. After an all-volunteer force was established in 1973, some policy makers opposed the notion of offering G.I. Bill-style benefits, arguing that they had been meant to provide for those who had fulfilled their civic obligation, a rationale that no longer applied in the same sense.[29] Only very modest benefits were extended to the newly enlisted.[30] Quickly, though, it became evident that even these served as the all-volunteer force's most powerful recruitment tool, one that was mentioned as a most important or very important factor in enlistment by 78 percent of soldiers.[31] In 1984, policy makers endorsed the more generous Montgomery G.I. Bill, which persists to the present. The program is financed in part by service members' own contributions and requires two years of active duty before qualifying for the benefits. By the late 1980s, over 90 percent of all eligible active-duty soldiers in the Army were contributing toward it, as well as large proportions of the other branches and Army reservists.[32] Now, as of the latest increases in 2003, it offers a maximum of $35,460 per individual, allocated over thirty-six months, and enjoys great popularity among service members.[33] This Montgomery version continues in the tradition of the original bill inasmuch as it provides educational opportunity to those who would not otherwise have it.[34] Yet because the military is so much smaller today—just 1.4 million Americans, less than one-half of 1 percent of the general population—the program's capacity to grant social opportunity and broaden democratic citizenship is but a glimmer of that of the World War II version.[35]

Back in the postwar period, besides continuing to help finance veterans' advanced education, the nation expanded access to higher education for all citizens, regardless of whether or not they had served in the military. At the federal level, policy makers established guaranteed student loans, the College Work-Study Program, and various grants for lower-income students.[36] The Higher Education Amendments of 1972 included Pell grants (named in honor of their champion, Senator Claiborne Pell), which came to be the primary source of federal aid for undergraduate students who exhibit financial need and have not yet earned their bachelor's or professional degree.[37] States also poured extensive resources into higher education, particularly by expanding public universities and colleges. In 1940, less than half (46 percent) of all college students attended public institutions; by 1970, 75 percent opted for public over private institutions.[38]

For a brief period in the 1970s, these federal and state programs worked effectively to broaden access to higher education to those of lesser means. Since then, however, many policies offering financial assistance to students have diminished in real terms, at the same time as tuition costs have increased. Accounting for all sources of public aid, support per student has just kept pace with inflation, but real costs per student have grown by about 40 percent.[39] At the federal level, though the number of Pell grant recipients has grown steadily, the grants' value has diminished, with the maximum value per student peaking at $4,205 in 1975 (in 1999 dollars), then declining steadily to $2,500 in the mid-1990s, rebounding only slightly in recent years. In 1975, a Pell grant covered about 80 percent of a student's tuition, fees, and room and board at the average public four-year institution and 40 percent at the average private four-year institution; by 1999, such coverage had fallen to about 40 percent and 15 percent, respectively.[40] After federal funding stagnated, states initially continued to increase their contributions to higher education, but more recently considerable fiscal pressures have constrained their capacity to do so.[41] Overall, while states' average financial support per student has grown since the 1980s, tuition costs have increased more rapidly.[42]

Over the past decade, the G.I. Bill's example has become increasingly remote, as the latest new policies for higher education entirely fail to expand access to less advantaged students. The federal HOPE Scholarship and Lifetime Learning Tax Credits, created in 1997, have surpassed Pell grants as the largest federal source of higher education funding, but to date they are underutilized, and low-income families typically do not participate due to insufficient tax liability.[43] Several states, meanwhile, have shifted away from subsidizing tuition at public colleges and toward merit-based scholarships, both of which stymie the possibilities for expanded enrollment among students who would not otherwise attend college.[44]

A college education has become more difficult to afford, then, at precisely the same time as its value has become more pronounced. While enrollment in four-year colleges has grown sharply in recent years among individuals from high-income families, it has increased much less among those from middle-class families and has actually declined slightly among those from the least advantaged families.[45] In addition, among those who enroll, college completion rates have declined, with the lowest completion rates among underrepresented minority groups.[46] In sum, even as higher education has become more clearly the road to economic success in the United States, those from less advantaged and even middle-class backgrounds find their chances of attending college to be far less than those of their wealthy peers, and diminishing. In a climate of rising tuition costs, current public programs fail to broaden access to higher education in the manner achieved by the G.I. Bill.

Meanwhile, the United States has failed to develop alternatives for non-college-bound students that would compare in value to the vocational training and other subcollege programs that were utilized by the majority of G.I. Bill beneficiaries. Policy makers and educators have neglected to consider ways to make high school education a more effective bridge to employment, for instance through the creation of more systematic technical preparation and cooperative education programs to serve those who are not college-bound.[47]

The outcomes of exacerbated inequality can seem inevitable, generated by technological and economic forces beyond our control, unless we stop to consider that a half century ago, public policy did help generate very different results. A careful study finds that by contrast to the middle of the twentieth century, when most individuals gained higher levels of education than their own parents, in more recent decades that trend has tapered off.[48] Certainly many factors underlay the expansion of high school and college graduation rates of the postwar era. Among them, the education and training provisions of the G.I. Bill stand out as a stunning example of a program that broadened social opportunity not only for those prepared to attend college but also for millions of others who utilized the subcollege provisions. Many of the veterans interviewed for this study marveled at how, thanks to the G.I. Bill, they were the first person in their family to attend college, and their success subsequently allowed them to send their children to college; their grandchildren have become even more highly educated. Such are the long-run consequences of the G.I. Bill.[49] The tragedy is that this policy, which expanded social opportunity so powerfully a half century ago, lacks a successor with comparable impact today. The losses accrue not only in terms of forfeited educational advancement and enhanced socioeconomic status for many lower- and middle-class Americans but also in terms of their civic engagement and political participation, the very lifeblood of American democracy itself.

Generating Future Citizens

The lessons of the G.I. Bill do not offer us a precise blueprint for policy making today so much as they challenge us, as citizens, policy makers, and policy analysts, to address a range of questions and concerns that are missing in contemporary political discourse. The results of another recent study of the G.I. Bill offer a poignant illustration of the possibilities that we have forfeited as a nation in departing from the logic that underscored the program. Sociologists Robert J. Sampson and John H. Laub studied one thousand men, all of whom were raised in poverty-stricken areas of Boston during the Great Depression, and half of whom had a record of official delinquency in their past. Controlling for childhood differences and socioeconomic background, they found that the education and training benefits of the G.I. Bill, as well as overseas service and schooling during military service, worked to enhance individuals' subsequent occupational status, job stability, and economic well-being. Strikingly, these results were most pronounced among veterans with past delinquency, suggesting that the G.I. Bill, as well as the other factors, intervened in their lives and helped move them toward substantially better futures. Furthermore, these men were especially likely to use the subcollege programs of the G.I. Bill, and the training they received offered them long-term advancement in the job market. The authors emphasize that their study underscores the potential of "large-scale structural interventions in the lives of disadvantaged youths."[50]

Today, young men who both grow up in poor neighborhoods and have a record of delinquency are also likely to experience the role of government in their lives, but in a far different way: through the corrections system. Indeed, the number of Americans in prison quadrupled between 1980 and 2000. The United States now holds the world record for incarceration, having a larger portion of its population behind bars than any other nation. Three percent of Americans are either in prison or on parole.[51]

It is incumbent on us as a society to ask how things could have turned out differently. The majority of those who are in prison come from poor neighborhoods: areas in which work opportunities are few and where pay and benefits are poor, where large numbers of citizens languish in ill health, and where educators struggle to respond to the multiple needs of children in their classrooms.[52] As income inequality has grown over the last quarter century, so too has the economic disparity between neighborhoods; rich people increasingly live surrounded mostly by other rich people, and poor people near only poor people.[53] Racial segregation of school districts has increased as well, an outcome especially harmful to minority students' chances of academic achievement.[54]

Our recent and current public policies fail to invest in making social opportunity more accessible. At the same time as higher education has become more determinative of socioeconomic well-being than ever before, the increase in college enrollments has lagged behind the growth in incarceration rates. The point is illustrated by the circumstances of young black males, the majority of whom still grow up in poor neighborhoods: today, they are more likely to be incarcerated than to be in college. As recently as 1980, black men were three times as likely to be attending universities and colleges than to be imprisoned; in 2000, by contrast, four sat in prison for every three enrolled in an institution of higher education.[55] The problem is not so simple as the lack of sufficient public funds to support education; indeed, the building and staffing of prisons draw heavily on scarce resources. Whereas tuition at four-year public colleges has fluctuated recently between $2,986 and $7,331, the cost of prison per inmate hovers between $20,000 and $25,000 annually. Between 1977 and 1995, the increase in U.S. spending on corrections grew by 823 percent, dwarfing a 374 percent increase in higher education spending.[56] The point is not that these choices represent a clear trade-off, as if we could simply shut down the prisons and send all inmates straight to college instead; rather, we need to consider where decades of missed opportunities for government to make a difference in the lives of less well-off citizens have brought us, particularly in light of the vastly different outcomes achieved for an earlier generation under the G.I. Bill's education and training benefits.

While the fate of the least advantaged amid such circumstances may be most evident, the middle class is also struggling. Although by contrast to the postwar era, most middle-class households now have the benefit of incomes from two working adults, this has come with the stresses and strains of spending a considerably greater number of hours in the workplace. Moreover, even with additional income, families struggle to hold their own, paying at high rates for child care, home ownership in better school districts, health care, and higher education for their children while hoping to save for retirement, a goal out of reach for many.[57] Recent tax cuts further advantage the wealthy and boost the national debt such that the creation of new or improved government programs to assist the middle class in these areas becomes all the less likely to emerge.[58]

The implications of such policy choices for American democracy are vast and troubling. Whereas the G.I. Bill and other policies of the postwar era incorporated less advantaged and middle-class individuals and families, advancing their socioeconomic well-being and treating them as deserving citizens, current policies have the opposite effect. As inequality grows, the lives of wealthy citizens become increasingly distinct from those of the poor and the middle class, and individuals' fates become more predetermined by their family background. Such circumstances imperil the tremendous sense of hope that buoyed past generations. Equally disturbing, the withering of government support in the lives of ordinary citizens, apart from seniors, threatens to undermine their capacity and inclination for civic involvement. As the stratification of political voice and influence grows ever more disparate, the political system will, increasingly, represent primarily the most advantaged citizens.[59]

In the face of such developments, the story of the G.I. Bill challenges us to alter our thinking dramatically. For the sake of democracy itself, we need to consider how public programs could foster social inclusion, increase opportunity, and stimulate civic engagement. Policies are often subjected to economic cost-benefit analyses, but their political implications are typically ignored. Henceforth, the civic effects of programs should be probed as well by assessing what kinds of resource and civic effects they are likely to generate and how those might affect civic engagement. The policy alternatives to be pursued today are not obvious, but it is imperative that we begin to deliberate about what they might be.

Policies that invest in the young and programs that enhance educational opportunity are most likely to have the greatest payoff, not only in terms of fostering socioeconomic advancement but also for boosting civic involvement.[60] By contrast to the G.I. Bill, new programs must be as accessible to women as they are to men, and the terms of eligibility must be fully inclusive of citizens regardless of sexuality. And like the bill, they should reach across lines of race and class to incorporate individuals as part of a common citizenry.

In terms of program design, the strongest civic impact is likely to be gained if the role of government is unambiguous. This recommendation is at odds with the trend in new policies, which tend to be shrouded in the tax code or offered as privately administered loans.[61] The former approach helps remind us that we are citizens of a shared political community, whereas the latter advances the logic of the marketplace, conveying the idea that we are separate individuals whose fates rely strictly on our place in the economy and who lack mutual obligations.

We should, as a society, think expansively about the kinds of activities that help contribute to the well-being of democratic governance. We should not limit our purview to participation in the military alone; certainly the ways of contributing as citizens are considerably more varied. One hundred years ago, policy makers recognized that the raising of future citizens had a vast civic impact, and thus they fashioned social provision that recognized mothers for caregiving.[62] In part because their ways of doing so were based on gender roles that have become antiquated, we have abandoned such approaches. This means, however, that those who do such work—still largely women—are not recognized for their efforts. We have restricted our considerations of the ways in which we can invest, effectively, in democratic citizenship.

A promising approach to considering the duties of citizenship broadly has been taken recently by some policy makers who propose establishing a new form of national service for the general population, not only to boost the numbers of those engaged in military service but also to provide a force prepared to conduct service for domestic needs, such as teaching in schools in low-income neighborhoods.[63] Such an approach might help replenish citizens' sense of civic commitment and nationhood and provide a fair basis on which to offer social provision in the tradition of the G.I. Bill.

From their service during World War II through their civic engagement even late in life, members of the civic generation have proven unceasing in their commitment to participation in self-governance. They have given much to the nation, and they have benefited much from it as well. Those of us who follow must now do our part to preserve the ideal of democratic citizenship, for which they sacrificed and through which they thrived. The lessons of the G.I. Bill offer us powerful evidence that through public investment that acknowledges civic obligation with expanded social opportunity, democracy itself may be revitalized. The challenge before us is to find out how to foster democracy in our own time. To recall again words that hold precious meaning for the civic generation: "it is for us the living . . . to be dedicated . . . to the unfinished work which they . . . so nobly advanced . . . that this nation . . . shall have a new birth of freedom, and that government of the people, by the people, for the people shall not perish from the earth."[64]

Appendices

Appendix A:
Overall Research Design

Certainly many other factors besides G.I. Bill usage can be expected to have shaped veterans' rates of civic engagement after the war. Therefore, in order to discern whether the education and training benefits themselves made a difference, we need to be able to compare veterans who resemble each other closely in terms of their family backgrounds and life circumstances but differ in one critical regard: whether or not they used the G.I. Bill to attain their education or training. Put differently, we need to be able to control for the "usual suspects" that are widely regarded to affect civic involvement, such as standard of living in childhood and adulthood, parents' level of involvement in civic life, and highest level of education. As well, we need to know some specifics about veterans' usage of the benefits and about the nature and extent of their later civic and political involvement. Most important, we must have such information from a group of veterans that is sufficiently large and sufficiently representative of the relevant subgroups (non-G.I. Bill users, subcollege program users, and higher education program users) in the original population to permit us to analyze them and to make general inferences about larger trends.[1]

No survey has ever been conducted in the past that fulfills these qualifications. For this study, therefore, it was necessary to collect fresh data from living veterans. Mailing lists from several male veterans' organizations provided the primary source of research subjects. I gathered information through mail surveys, in procedures outlined in Appendix B.

The data I collected from nonblack male veterans of World War II, who served in separate units from African Americans, meet these essential criteria.[2] The sample includes individuals from a full range of socioeconomic backgrounds and levels of educational attainment, and sufficient numbers of both program nonusers and users, and higher education beneficiaries and subcollege program beneficiaries. Most important, the subgroupings sufficiently resemble the corresponding members of the original population for me to generalize about the findings. (See Appendix C.) Still, given the retrospective nature of these data, I interpret them as indicative of general patterns rather than as the source of precise measures. Finally, I also surveyed other members of the World War II generation, namely, black male veterans, women veterans generally, and male graduates of the Class of 1949 at selected universities and colleges (given that the greatest number of G.I. Bill beneficiaries graduated from college in that year); from them, I obtained data that are useful for specific purposes but also are more limited, and so I use them more sparingly and cautiously. (See Appendix D.)

Understanding veterans' experiences of G.I. Bill usage and nonusage also required that I be able to examine them in a more in-depth way, in the context of individual lives. Accordingly, I conducted a smaller number of personal, semistructured interviews with veterans in all regions of the country.[3] I used the interviews together with the survey data in an interactive way: they suggested possible dynamics that could be explored in the survey data, and they shed light on the meaning of aggregate trends that emerged in the survey data.[4]

Appendix B:
Survey Design and Procedures

Survey design involves making numerous decisions about whom to survey, what format to use, and the types of questions to include. The primary goal throughout is to obtain reliable data drawn from a random sample that sufficiently represents the original population, using procedures that elicit valid answers.

Given that no means of access to a national, random sample of World War veterans was available, I had to design an inventive approach to reach them. Many survivors from specific military units have formed their own veterans' organizations, groups that typically have mailing lists, generate newsletters, and hold reunions. I contacted several such groups, seeking access to mailing lists from a few that would represent a wide range of personal backgrounds, military ranks, and wartime experiences, and ultimately settled on the ones described here and in Appendix C.

I considered the possible sources of bias inherent in this approach. The strategy does elicit a national sample: the World War II military drew members of individual units from across the nation rather than from a particular region; moreover, veterans who served in such units and who belong to their associations lived throughout the nation in the subsequent course of their lives. I considered whether this approach might target veterans who were predisposed to active participation in civic life, given that they were already members of an organization. Interviews revealed, however, that membership in the unit associations does not demand active involvement, and not all members even initiated their own membership status. The groups have made a considerable effort to get as many survivors as possible on their lists, but the percentage that attends reunions and participates actively as members is small. Survey questions about participation in each veterans' organization confirmed the wide disparity in degrees of involvement.

I prepared a twelve-page booklet of questions covering a wide variety of topics, including experience in the military, education, socioeconomic well-being, participation in civic and political activities in various time periods, and G.I. Bill usage.[5] Given that I sought to obtain data from elderly individuals about events that happened long ago, I had to be particularly attentive to issues of bias. The finding that salience matters in terms of what individuals can remember alleviates these concerns considerably: people will recall events or activities that were important to them, known as "landmark events."[6] Participation in the war and the pursuit of education thereafter constitute landmark events in the autobiographical knowledge of most veterans.[7] Furthermore, in designing and implementing the survey, I took several steps to minimize sources of error related to memory and recall, using techniques known to improve accuracy of survey responses.

Specifically, I chose to use the mail survey approach as a means to limit problems related to memory and recall. Mail surveys are actually more expensive to conduct than telephone surveys and require considerably more administrative involvement and time to implement. But they are not reliant on individuals' hearing—a factor important given the older population being studied—and they give respondents as much time to answer questions as they would like, which has been found to stimulate memory and thus to increase the reliability of answers.[8] Recipients could respond at their leisure, taking time to remember past activities.

I limited survey questions to fairly general characteristics of individuals' childhood and early adult circumstances. Generally, I did not need to ascertain specific details from individuals' pasts, such as the number of meetings of the Lions Club or Parent-Teacher Association meetings that a person attended in a given year, or the years of the particular elections in which they voted. Rather, I wanted to know whether the subjects were generally active participants or not. While data regarding some specific details, such as grades in high school or scores on aptitude tests, would have been useful, I ruled out such questions given the obvious difficulties of remembering such facts with any degree of accuracy. Neither did I ask respondents much about past attitudes, given that such responses would likely be influenced by intervening circumstances and present attitudes; rather, the survey focused on events in individuals' lives. Because voting is such a commonplace activity among members of the generation I was studying, and one which they widely view as a fundamental obligation, I omitted questions about frequency of voting on the basis that such data would likely be of questionable value; rather, I focused on less typical political activities. Before designing the survey, I conducted several of the open-ended interviews with veterans. This process helped me to design the survey instrument, limiting questions to those that veterans answered readily and with confidence.

In the actual survey instrument, I organized questions in a framework that facilitated both forward (chronological) and backward recall.[9] Survey researchers have found that greater accuracy is obtained by framing questions for a specific time period; for this purpose, specific responses were requested for each of three periods: 1950–64, 1965–79, and 1980–present. This grouping of questions is intended to prompt respondents to consider how their activities might have changed, if at all, thus enabling them to respond to the questions about the earlier period as clearly and thoughtfully as possible. Also, asking a number of questions about a given time period has proven to facilitate memory; the many questions about the immediate postwar years in the survey should have yielded a cumulative effect.

In the summer of 1998, I pretested the survey instrument with a small group of individuals whose names appeared on the mailing lists I had collected; these individuals completed the survey individually and then participated in a focus group to address areas for improvement and clarification regarding question wording, directions, and overall appearance. Then names of survey respondents were randomly selected from the lists to be used, in ratios noted in the appendices below. In order to limit bias from early respondents, each subject received as many as three mailings: an initial one followed by two subsequent mailings sent to nonrespondents one and two months later. Copies of the survey instrument are available at the following Web site: http://faculty.maxwell.syr.edu/sbmettler/research.htm.

Appendix C:
Representativeness of the Nonblack Male Veteran Sample

The sample of nonblack male veterans who participated in the World War II Veterans Survey included members of two U.S. Army units and two Army Air Force units.[10] From the four thousand on the lists of their military unit organizations, I randomly selected the names of one thousand veterans. This grouping yielded 716 completed surveys, a 74-percent response rate. The sample featured considerable variation among subjects generally and within relevant subgroups. Notably, for instance, within the groups of respondents who used the G.I. Bill for higher education, those who used it for subcollege programs, and those who did not use either type of provision, each group included respondents who, prior to military service, came from each of the nine different educational levels.

While the high response rate and degree of variation among respondents are positive signs, the particular means of reaching veterans—through military unit organization mailing lists—and the timing of the survey, so late in veterans' lives and so long after the experience of the program, meant that the representativeness of the sample needed to be assessed carefully. I needed to consider the extent to which it mirrored the original population, and to the extent that it deviated, to conduct analyses in a way that took such disparities into account.

Those in the sample of nonblack male veteran respondents were somewhat more likely to use the G.I. Bill's education and training benefits than members of the original population: 60.8 percent in the sample did so, compared to 51 percent in the original population. A greater disparity existed in terms of type of program usage, whether for higher education or subcollege programs: among the original population of World War II veterans, 28.6 percent of those who used the provisions pursued higher education, whereas this same survey sample included 63.5 percent such users. Death rates may account in part for these differences between the original population and the sample. When World War II Veterans were surveyed in 1998, the average veteran—born in 1923—would have been seventy-five years old; this is precisely the average life expectancy for white males born in that year. Slightly less than two-thirds of World War II veterans were deceased when the survey was conducted in 1998.[11] Studies show that in the United States, being better educated is associated with better health and hence with longer life expectancy.[12] Demographers report a recent increase in longevity among American males that some suspect may be attributable to the effects of the G.I. Bill, inasmuch as it enhanced individuals' socioeconomic well-being. The higher rate of higher education beneficiaries among respondents may also be a reflection of the fact that younger veterans were more likely to use those provisions originally, and they are more likely to have still been alive in 1998, thus tilting the response rate toward college users.[13]

Importantly, however, for the purposes of this study, it is unnecessary for either the ratio of G.I. Bill users to nonusers or the ratio of higher education users to vocational training users to mirror that of the original population of World War II veterans. Meaningful results are still attainable as long as *each subgroup* reflects characteristics of the same group in the original population, and if they do, that we consider the groups separately and in regression analyses control for level of education. To make such assessments of comparability, we can compare the subgroups in the sample used here with results from a government survey conducted in 1956, relatively shortly after G.I. Bill use and drawn from a nationwide random sample of veterans.

This analysis reveals that the respondents who used the G.I. Bill for the subcollege programs very closely resemble those in the original population.[14] In terms of education before joining the military, 28 percent of both samples had completed elementary school or less and 4 percent of both samples had four years of college or more. In the World War II Veterans Survey, 57 percent of the subcollege users had completed high school, compared to 60 percent in the government study, and 11 percent had one to three years of college, compared to 8 percent. The data's underrepresentation of vocational training participants relative to higher education participants necessitates separating them and analyzing the distinct consequences of each type of program usage, as is done on several occasions throughout this book.

A comparison of veterans who used the G.I. Bill's higher education benefits in both studies revealed that the respondents to the World War II Veterans' Survey had more education prior to military service than those in the 1956 survey. Only 1 percent had elementary school or less education, compared to 4 percent in the government study; 47 percent had finished high school, compared to 68 percent; 45 percent had completed one to three years of college, compared to 21 percent; and 6 percent had completed four years of college or more, compared to 7 percent.[15] The higher levels of pre-military-service education among subjects in the World War II Veterans Survey suggests that they may have been, on average, from somewhat different backgrounds than the original universe of veterans who used the G.I. Bill benefits for higher education. Notably, this disparity implies that to the extent a discrepancy may exist between the behavior of the survey respondents and the original population, this study errs on the conservative side and may understate its claims: given that we find that the benefits proved particularly inclusive of less advantaged veterans, they may actually have made a larger difference than implied both in extending advanced education and in raising civic engagement rates. In other words, the G.I. Bill may have had even stronger salutary effects than suggested here.

Appendix D:
Additional Survey Samples Collected for and Used in This Study

Using the same survey format and procedures as those outlined in Appendix A above, I also reached additional groups that are analyzed in this study. First, given that the military remained segregated during World War II, in order to reach black veterans it was necessary to survey members of a separate division that consisted entirely of black rank-and-file members. The 92nd Infantry Division provided the source of this data. I surveyed its members on two occasions, in 2000 and in 2001, using different (and mutually exclusive) lists; these yielded responses of 42 and 53 percent, respectively, for a combined total of 104 respondents.

The average life expectancy for African American males born in 1923 was sixty-eight years, seven years less than that of white males. Thus, to the extent that a mortality bias exists, it is likely to have been more pronounced among African American men, who were not surveyed until a decade after their average life expectancy had passed. While white respondents may have been slightly more privileged than whites in the original veteran population, black respondents are likely to have differed more sharply relative to the original universe of black veterans.

The task of comparing black survey respondents from the World War II Veterans Survey to the original population of black servicemen is facilitated by archival data presented by Paula Fass.[16] This allows for comparison of level of education prior to joining the military between the survey respondents and black soldiers in the World War II military more generally. As was the case among nonblack veterans, black survey respondents had more education prior to military service than black World War II servicemen generally, and not surprisingly, the difference is more exaggerated in the case of the black veterans. The majority of black survey respondents—78 percent—had completed high school prior to military service, compared to only 17 percent of the original population; 15 percent had only some high school, compared to 26 percent; and 7 percent had completed elementary school or less, compared to 57 percent. These facts alone need not thwart the data analysis if each of the subgroups within the data—nonusers, vocational education users, and higher education users—still resembles its original cohort sufficiently, as was the case among nonblack respondents. Unfortunately, data are not available to permit such comparisons.[17] Thus, I interpret the data on black veterans in a more cautious manner than the data on nonblack veterans, and consider it indicative only of the sample here and not as representative of the original universe of black veterans' experiences.

To assess veterans' experiences of G.I. Bill implementation at different institutions of higher education and their characteristics relative to nonusers at those institutions, I chose to study college graduates in the Class of 1949, the peak year of veteran graduates, from a combination of 11 public and private institutions of higher education in all regions of the United States, including some chosen for racial, ethnic and religious diversity. The small set of universities and colleges from which I drew the Class of 1949 survey recipients was not meant to be representative of all institutions of higher education in the United States; rather, my intention was to sample from a variety of schools that would have attracted and admitted students with a variety of different backgrounds, and provided distinct environments in which they would be educated. I reached a large number of Catholics by surveying Boston College alumni, Jewish graduates through the inclusion of Brooklyn College, and African Americans through surveying Morehouse College alumni. The remaining public institutions whose alumni participated included Washington State University, Wayne State in Michigan, the University of Georgia, and the University of Texas; private institutions included Syracuse University, Vanderbilt University, Northwestern University, and Pomona College. The Class of 1949 lists included approximately six thousand men; from those, one thousand were randomly selected to be survey recipients. In addition, in order to obtain adequate data from members of minority racial, ethnic, and religious groups, I oversampled alumni from particular institutions by selecting 150 more names from them. This survey yielded 792 completed surveys, a 69 percent response rate.[18]

From Women in Military Service for America, Inc. (WIMSA), in Washington, D.C., I obtained a separate nationwide list of women who served in World War II from all branches of the service. The survey of women veterans, conducted in 2000, yielded 222 completed surveys, a response rate of 80 percent.

Appendix E:
Model and Variables Regarding G.I. Bill Usage

I analyzed the determinants of usage of either type of the G.I. Bill's education and training provisions, with the higher education and subcollege provisions treated separately. This is done through logistic regression that allows us to control for and compare the significance of the relevant factors in explaining such outcomes. The first analysis utilizes a dummy variable in which 1 = higher education training users and 0 = all other veterans, and in the next, 1 = subcollege program users and 0 = all other veterans. Year of birth, an inverse measure of age, is included because in the postwar era men who were older were more likely to be married and to refrain from additional education because of responsibilities to support a family.[19] Having one or both parents born outside of the United States (1/0), is included to allow for consideration of whether new immigrants and first generation Americans were more likely to pursue education than those in the ranks of the longer-term, native-born working class.[20] A series of dummy variables is used to denote religion, namely, Catholic, Jewish, and no religion or other religion; Protestant is the excluded dummy variable and represents the reference or baseline category.[21] Two more independent variables allow us to control for socioeconomic background in childhood. These are parent's level of education, measured on a scale ranging from no formal schooling to graduate or professional degree (1 to 7),[22] and standard of living during childhood in the 1920s, indicated on a five-point scale (from low to high).[23] In addition, a socialization variable measures the extent to which individuals were encouraged while growing up to pursue an education by family members or others, from strongly discouraged to strongly encouraged (1 to 5). Lastly, we account for veterans' level of education prior to military service, as measured on a nine-point scale from elementary school only (1) to advanced graduate work or doctorate (9).

Appendix F:
Supplementary Tables

The following tables provide some of the major results on which the analyses in the book are based. The tables are numbered to correspond to the chapters in which the results are discussed: for example, Table F.3.1 is the first appendix table mentioned in Chapter 3.

Table F.3.1. Determinants of G.I. Bill Usage for Education Among Nonblack Male Veterans

Independent Variables	Vocational Training G.I. Bill Usage	Higher Education G.I. Bill Usage
Parent's level of education	−.196*	.185*
	(.083)	(.075)
Standard of living in childhood, 1920s	.029	.322*
	(.137)	(.137)
Year of birth	−.028	.389***
	(.041)	(.057)
Education encouraged	−.183	.487**
	(.144)	(.146)
Level of education before military service	−.347**	.771***
	(.126)	(.136)
At least one parent born outside of U.S. (1 = yes)	.057	.226
	(.280)	(.287)
Catholic (1 = yes)	.005	−.162
	(.285)	(.290)
Jewish (1 = yes)	.144	−.592
	(.514)	(.481)
No religion or other (1 = yes)	1.37	−.442
	(.815)	(1.16)
−2 log likelihood	475.034	475.527
Chi-square goodness of fit	**	***
N	469	469

Source: World War II Veterans Survey
Note: Figures in cells are logistic regression coefficients (* $p < 0.05$; ** $p < 0.01$; ***$p < 0.001$); standard errors are in parentheses.

Table F.3.2. Bivariate Correlations Between Key Selected Independent Variables, Among Nonblack Male Veterans

	(1)	(2)	(3)	(4)
(1) Standard of living, 1920s	—	.26**	.28*	.23**
(2) Level of education prior to military service	—	.16**	.31**	
(3) Parent's level of education	—	.16**		
(4) Education encouraged while growing up	—			

Source: World War II Veterans Survey
Note: *p < .05, **p < .01, two-tailed test; N = 433

Table F.3.3. Level of Encouragement by Family Members or Others to Pursue Education, by Standard of Living in Childhood, Nonblack Male Veterans

Standard of Living, 1920s	Strongly Discouraged or Discouraged	Neutral	Strongly Encouraged or Encouraged	N
Low	3.8%	43.3%	52.8%	104
Low-medium	2.4	31.6	66.1	171
Medium	4.0	20.4	75.7	280
Medium-high or high	—	14.8	85.3	61

Source: World War II Veterans Survey

Table F.3.4. Determinants of G.I. Bill Usage for Education or Training, Black Male Veterans

Independent Variables	G.I. Bill Usage
Parent's level of education	.510**
	(.246)
Standard of living in childhood, 1920s	−.718
	(.437)
Education encouraged	.393
	(.550)
Level of education before military service	.283
	(.306)
Year of Birth	.063
	(.092)
−2 log likelihood	50.04
Chi-square goodness of fit	*
N	54

Source: World War II Veterans Survey
Note: Figures in cells are logistic regression coefficients (*p < 0.10; **p < 0.05); standard errors are in parentheses.

Table F.5.1. Determinants of Educational Attainment Among Nonblack Male Veterans Depending on G.I. Bill Usage Type

Variable	Higher Education	Subcollege Programs
Year of birth	.022	.161***
	(.027)	(.199)
Level of education prior to military service	.830***	1.05***
	(.413)	(.523)
Used G.I. Bill for higher education (1 = yes)	2.73***	
	(.577)	
Used G.I. Bill for vocational training (1 = yes)		−.909***
		(−.169)
Parent(s) born outside of U.S. (1 = yes)	.117	.231
	(.024)	(.048)
Catholic (1 = yes)	−.003	−.120
	(−.001)	(−.022)
Jewish (1 = yes)	.468	.291
	(.057)	(.035)
No religion or other (1 = yes)	−.461	−.213
	(−.026)	(−.012)
Parent's level of education	.063	.117*
	(.042)	(.078)
Standard of living in childhood, 1920s	.081	.246*
	(.032)	(.097)
Education encouraged	.125	.381***
	(.047)	(.143)
R^2	.729	.503
Adjusted R^2	.723	.491
N	423	423

Source: World War II Veterans Survey
Note: Cell entries represent unstandardized coefficients for ordinary least squares regression. (* $p < 0.05$; ** $p < 0.01$; *** $p < 0.001$); standardized coefficients in parentheses

Table F.5.2. Determinants of Home Ownership Among Nonblack Male Veterans

Independent Variables	Coefficient
Income 1960	−.245
	(.151)
Used G.I Bill for education	−.761
	(.491)
Used G.I. Bill home loan guarantee program	1.037*
	(.460)
Educational level	−.049
	(.174)
−2 log likelihood	177.057
Chi-square goodness of fit	**
N	388

Source: World War II Veterans Survey
Note: Figures in cells are logistic regression coefficients (* $p < 0.05$; ** $p < 0.01$); standard errors in parentheses

Table F.6.1. **Determinants of Civic Involvement Among Nonblack Male Veterans, 1950–64**

Independent Variable	Civic Memberships	Political Participation
Level of education completed	0.92*	0.13
	(.129)	(0.25)
Parent's level of education	.002	−.003
	(.002)	(−.004)
Used G.I. Bill for education or training	.471**	.384**
	(.140)	(.155)
Parents' Civic or Political Activity	.275***	.181***
	(.209)	(.169)
Standard of living, 1920	0.72	.112
	(.039)	(.082)
Standard of living, 1960	.233	.058
	(.093)	(.032)
R^2	.14	.08
Adjusted R^2	.13	.06
Sample size	393	379

Source: World War II Veterans Survey
Note: Cell entries represent unstandardized coefficients for ordinary least squares regression (* $p < 0.05$; ** $p < 0.01$; *** $p < 0.001$); standardized coefficients in parentheses.

Table F.6.2. **Considering Rival Explanations of Civic Involvement Among Nonblack Male Veterans, 1950–64: Variations on Civic and Political Model with G.I. Bill Usage Variable Replaced**

Variable Replacing G.I. Bill Usage	Civic Model	Political Model
None	.12	.06
In combat	.02	−.26
	(.37)	(.28)
	.12	.06
Wounded in military	.07	.00
	(.18)	(.14)
	.12	.06
Disabled in military	.09	−.04
	(.19)	(.14)
	.12	.06
Length of time, active military duty	.10	−.11
	(.11)	(.08)
	.13	.06
Drafted into military	.00	−.00
	(.07)	(.05)
	.12	.06
Year of birth	.02	−.00
	(.03)	(.02)
	.12	.06
Had foreign-born parent	−.08	−.00
	(.16)	(.02)
	.12	.06
Lived in suburb, 1960	−.20	−.14
	(.18)	(.14)
	.12	.06

Table continues on next page

Table F.6.2. Considering Rival Explanations of Civic Involvement Among Nonblack Male Veterans, 1950–64: Variations on Civic and Political Model with G.I. Bill Usage Variable Replaced (*continued*)

Variable Replacing G.I. Bill Usage	Civic Model	Political Model
Year of first home purchase	−.09	−.00
	(.00)	(.00)
	.12	.05
Religion (4 types; Catholic is noted)	−.35*	.08
	(.19)	(.14)
	.12	.06
Encouraged to pursue education while growing up	−.05	.16**
	(.10)	(.08)
	.12	.07

Source: World War II Veterans Survey
Note: The cells each summarize results of ordinary least-squares regression. The top row contains the adjusted R^2 for the model when all variables included in Table F.6.1 are present except G.I. Bill usage. All other rows present results of analyses in which one additional variable is used to substitute for G.I. Bill usage. The results presented for each include: the unstandardized coefficient for the new variable and its significance (*p <. 10; **p <. 05); the standard error in parentheses; and the adjusted R^2 for the model.

Table F.6.3. Critical Effects Model of Determinants of Civic Involvement Among Nonblack Male Veterans, 1950–64

Independent Variable	Civic Memberships	Political Participation
Level of education completed	.093**	.016
	(.131)	(.030
Parent's level of education	.004	.002
	(.003)	(.002)
Low standard of living, 1920,* G.I. Bill use+	.347	.172
	(.054)	(.035)
Low-medium standard of living, 1920,* G.I. Bill use	.473**	.397**
	(.113)	(.128)
Medium standard of living, 1920,* G.I. Bill use	.465**	.272
	(.126)	(.099)
Medium-high or high standard of living, 1920,* G.I. Bill use	.706*	1.220***
	(.121)	(.276)
Parents' civic or political activity	.278***	.191***
	(.211)	(.179)
Standard of living, 1920	.014	−.043
	(.008)	(−.031)
Standard of living, 1960	.238*	.085
	(.095)	(.047)
R^2	.14	.11
Adjusted R^2	.12	.09
Sample size	393	379

Source: World War II Veterans Survey
Note: Cells show results of interactive equation, ordinary least-squares regression: unstandardized coefficients (* p < .10; ** p < .05; *** p < .01); standardized coefficient shown in parentheses.
+ This interactive dummy variable was constructed by multiplying standard of living in the 1920s, where low = 1 and all other values = 0, by G.I. Bill use (coded as 1 = use, 0 = nonuse). The three variables below were constructed similarly, in each case with the named standard of living level coded as 1 and all others as 0. The missing dummy variable, which serves as the reference category, is nonuse of the G.I. Bill.

Table F.6.4. Determinants of Civic Involvement Among Nonblack Male Veterans, 1950–64, by G.I. Bill Usage Type

Independent Variable	Civic Memberships	Political Participation
Level of education completed	.089*	.019
	(.124)	(.035)
Parent's level of education	−.007	.011
	(−.007)	(.014)
Used G.I. Bill for higher education	.492*	.321
	(.146)	(.129)
Used G.I. Bill for subcollege education or training	.475**	.423**
	(.121)	(.144)
Parents' civic or political activity	.277***	.173***
	(.207)	(.159)
Standard of living, 1920	.080	.113
	(.043)	(.081)
Standard of living, 1960	.252**	.082
	(.100)	(.044)
R^2	.14	.07
Adjusted R^2	.13	.06
Sample size	383	369

Source: World War II Veterans Survey
Note: Cells show results of ordinary least-squares regression: unstandardized coefficients (* $p < .10$; ** $p < .05$; *** $p < .01$); standardized coefficient shown in parentheses.

Table F.6.5. Determinants of Civic Involvement Among Nonblack Male Veterans, 1950–64, by Length of Time on G.I. Bill

Independent Variable	Civic Memberships	Political Participation
Level of education completed	.103**	.004
	(.144)	(.008)
Parent's level of education	−.020	−.001
	(−.019)	(−.002)
Length of time on G.I. Bill	.073	.085**
	(.091)	(.145)
Parents' civic or political activity	.298***	.181***
	(.225)	(.170)
Standard of living, 1920	.081	.122
	(.044)	(.089)
Standard of living, 1960	.254**	.063
	(.101)	(.035)
R^2	.14	.07
Adjusted R^2	.13	.06
Sample size	393	381

Source: World War II Veterans Survey
Note: Cells show results of ordinary least-squares regression: unstandardized coefficients (* $p < .10$; ** $p < .05$; *** $p < .01$); standardized coefficient shown in parentheses.

Table F.6.6.   Determinants of Civic and Political Involvement Among Nonblack Male Veterans, 1950–64, by G.I. Bill Education and Training and G.I. Bill Low-Interest Mortgage Benefits

Independent Variable	Civic Memberships	Political Participation
Level of education completed	.092**	.006
	(.128)	(.012)
Parent's level of education	.006	−.003
	(.007)	(−.004)
Usage of G.I. Bill for education or training	.532***	.444***
	(.157)	(.177)
Usage of G.I. Bill for low-interest mortgage for purchase of home, farm, or business	.303*	−.213
	(.091)	(−.085)
Parent's civic or political activity	.265****	.179***
	(.198)	(.165)
Standard of living, 1920	.057	.112
	(.031)	(.081)
Standard of living, 1960	.296**	.078
	(.117)	(.042)
Lived in suburb, 1960	−.233	−.124
	(−.062)	(−.043)
R^2	.16	.09
Adjusted R^2	.14	.06
Sample size	366	353

Source: Source: World War II Veterans Survey
Note: Cells show results of ordinary least-squares regression: unstandardized coefficients (* $p < .10$; ** $p < .05$; *** $p < .01$; **** $p < .001$); standardized coefficient shown in parentheses.

Table F.6.7.   Determinants of Political Participation Among Nonblack Male Veterans, 1965–79 and 1980–98

Independent Variable	1965–79	1980–98
Level of education completed	.100***	.152***
	(.149)	(.253)
Combined memberships in civic organization in prior period (1950–64 or 1965–79)	.213***	.122**
	(.230)	(.157)
Usage of G.I. Bill for education or training	.223	.268*
	(.071)	(.096)
Standard of living (1960 or 1998)	.228**	.245***
	(.097)	(.136)
Lived in suburb (1960 or 1998)	−.107	−.292*
	(−.030)	(−.087)
R^2	.14	.20
Adjusted R^2	.13	.19
Sample size	386	390

Source: World War II Veterans Survey
Note: Cells show results of ordinary least-squares regression: unstandardized coefficients (* $p < .10$; ** $p < .05$; *** $p < .01$); standardized coefficient shown in parentheses.

Table F.7.1. Determinants of Activity in Nonmembership Civic Organizations, 1950–64, Among Nonblack Male Veterans

Independent Variable	Active in Nonmembership Organizations
Level of education completed	−.002
	(−.013)
Parent's level of education	−.005
	(−.017)
Used G.I. Bill vocational training benefits	.043
	(.041)
Used G.I. Bill higher education benefits	.206**
	(.232)
Parents' civic activity	.038**
	(.110)
Lived in suburb, 1960	−.084*
	(−.087)
Standard of living, 1960	.026
	(.038)
Year of birth	−.008
	(−.054)
R^2	.06
Adjusted R^2	.04
Sample size	363

Source: World War II Veterans Survey
Note: Cells show results of ordinary least-squares regression: unstandardized coefficients (* $p < .10$; ** $p < .05$; *** $p < .01$); standardized coefficient shown in parentheses.

Table F.7.2. Determinants of Serving as an Officer or on a Committee of an Organization, 1950–98, Among Nonblack Male Veterans

Independent Variable	Served as Officer/Committee Member
Level of education completed	.162**
	(.260)
Parent's level of education	.047
	(.049)
Used G.I. Bill vocational training benefits	.364*
	(.107)
Used G.I. Bill higher education benefits	.259
	(.088)
Standard of living, 1960	.027
	(.012)
Year of birth	−.056**
	(−.111)
Lived in suburb, 1960	−.053
	(−.016)
R^2	.11
Adjusted R^2	.09
Sample size	375

Source: World War II Veterans Survey
Note: Cells show results of ordinary least-squares regression: unstandardized coefficients (* $p < .10$; ** $p < .05$; *** $p < .01$); standardized coefficient shown in parentheses.

Table F.8.1. Mean Level of Involvement in Selected Organizations, Users vs. Non-Users of G.I. Bill Education and Training Benefits, African American and White Male Veterans

Type of Activity and Time Period	African American Veterans		White Veterans	
	G.I. Bill Non-Users	G.I. Bill Users	G.I. Bill Non-Users	G. I. Bill Users
Memberships in civic organizations, 1950–64	1.26 (3.41)	2.00 (2.25)	.92* (.163)	1.51* (1.76)
Memberships in civic organizations, 1965–79	1.42 (3.70)	2.37 (2.67)	1.05* (1.96)	1.58* (1.94)
Memberships in political organizations, 1950–64	0* (0)	.17* (.43)	.13 (.64)	.17 (.65)
Memberships in political organizations, 1965–79	0* (0)	.25* (.56)	.15 (.76)	.17 (.65)
N	75		557	

Source: World War II Veterans Survey
Note: Cells show means (* marks relationships significant at $p < .05$); standard deviations in parentheses.

Table F.8.2. Rates of Political Activity Among G.I. Bill Education and Training Benefits Users and Non-Users, African American and White Veterans

Type of Activity and Time Period	African American Veterans		White Veterans	
	G.I. Bill Non-Users	G.I. Bill Users	G.I. Bill Non-Users	G. I. Bill Users
Participated in protest, march, demonstration, 1950–64	8%	35%	1%	2%
Participated in protest, march, demonstration, 1965–79	4	33	3	4
Contacted political official, 1950–64	12	31	12	20
Contacted political official, 1965–79	15	41	22	41
Worked on political campaign, 1950–64	17	25	7	14
Worked on political campaign, 1965–79	21	30	7	17
Served in local government, 1950–64	4	15	6	11
Served in local government, 1965–79	20	31	12	15
Contributed money to political candidate, party or group, 1950–64	0	25	9	21
Contributed money to political candidate, party or group, 1965–79	29	46	26	41
Average	13	31	11	19
Average w/o protest	15	31	13	23

Source: World War II Veterans Survey

Table F.9.1. Determinants of Use of G.I. Bill for Education Among Nonblack Male and Female Veterans

Independent Variables	G.I. Bill Usage
Parent's level of education	.062
	(.058)
Standard of living in childhood, 1920s	.287**
	(.106)
Year of birth	.198***
	(.033)
Education encouraged	.215*
	(.108)
Level of education before military service	.214**
	(.082)
At least one parent born outside of U.S. (1 = yes)	.197
	(.216)
Catholic (1 = yes)	−.124
	(.220)
Jewish (1 = yes)	−.197
	(.420)
No religion or other (1 = yes)	1.327*
	(.662)
Female (1 = yes)	−1.036***
	(.228)
−2 log likelihood	761.27
Chi-square goodness of fit	***
N	627

Source: World War II Veterans Survey
Note: Figures in cells are logistic regression coefficients (*p < 0.05; **p < 0.01; ***p < 0.001); standard errors are in parentheses.

Table F.9.2. Determinants of Combined Political Activities and Memberships Among Nonblack Male and Female Veterans, 1965–79

Independent Variable	Political Participation
Level of education completed	.139***
	(.261)
Used G.I. Bill for education	.141
	(.060)
Standard of living, 1960	.226**
	(.122)
Female	−.244*
	(−.087)
R^2	.12
Adjusted R^2	.11
Sample size	577

Source: World War II Veterans Survey
Note: Cells show results of ordinary least-squares regression: unstandardized coefficients (* p < .10; ** p < .05; *** p < .01); standardized coefficient shown in parentheses.

**Table F.9.3. Determinants of Educational Attainment: Nonblack Male and
Female Veterans Compared**

Variable	Male Veterans	Female Veterans
Year of birth	.090**	.000
	(.110)	(.004)
Level of education before military service	1.040***	.677***
	(.519)	(.474)
Used G.I. Bill for education (1 = yes)	1.508***	1.99***
	(.327)	(.470)
Parent(s) born outside of U.S. (1 = yes)	.140	−.251
	(.029)	(−.056)
Catholic (1 = yes)	−.035	.288
	(−.006)	(.061)
Jewish (1 = yes)	.353	.329
	(.042)	(.020)
No religion or other (1 = yes)	−.963	−.051
	(−.053)	(−.005)
Parent's level of education	.132**	−.009
	(.089)	(−.008)
Standard of living in childhood, 1920s	.104	.134
	(.041)	(.057)
Education encouraged	.293**	.398*
	(.111)	(.172)
R^2	.57	.61
Adjusted R^2	.56	.58
N	433	123

Source: World War II Veterans Survey
Note: Cells show results of ordinary least-squares regression: unstandardized coefficients
(* $p < 0.05$; ** $p < 0.01$; *** $p < 0.001$); standardized coefficient shown in parentheses.

Notes

Introduction

1. Tom Brokaw, *The Greatest Generation* (New York: Random House, 1998); Stephen E. Ambrose, *Citizen Soldiers* (New York: Simon and Schuster, 1997); Robert D. Putnam, *Bowling Alone: The Collapse and Revival of American Community* (New York: Simon and Schuster, 2000), chap. 14; William Strauss and Neil Howe, *Generations: The History of America's Future, 1584–2069* (New York: William Morrow, 1991), 261–78.
2. Brokaw, *The Greatest Generation*, xix.
3. For example, see John Ellis, *The Sharp End: The Fighting Man in World War II* (New York: Charles Scribner's Sons, 1980); Gerald F. Linderman, *The World Within War: America's Combat Experience in World War II* (Cambridge, MA: Harvard University Press, 1997); Ambrose, *Citizen Soldiers*.
4. William L. O'Neill, *A Democracy at War: America's Fight at Home and Abroad in World War II* (New York: Free Press, 1993), chap. 7; Geoffrey Perrett, *Days of Sadness, Years of Triumph: The American People, 1939–1945* (Madison: University of Wisconsin Press, 1993), chap. 19; Meg Jacobs, "'How About Some Meat?': The Office of Price Administration, Consumption Politics, and State Building from the Bottom Up, 1941–1946," *Journal of American History* 84, 3 (1997): 910–41; Lawrence R. Samuel, *Pledging Allegiance: American Identity and the Bond Drive of World War II* (Washington, DC: Smithsonian Institution Press, 1997), chap. 2.
5. Putnam, *Bowling Alone*.
6. Theda Skocpol, *Diminished Democracy: From Membership to Management in American Civic Life* (Norman: University of Oklahoma Press, 2003), 67, 130–31.
7. Also, while voter participation was not as high among eligible voters as it had been during the late nineteenth century, it involved far more of the populace given the expansions of political rights to women and to African American men. Jerrold G. Rusk, *A Statistical History of the American Electorate* (Washington, DC: CQ Press, 2001), 52; Putnam, *Bowling Alone*, 32.
8. Putnam, *Bowling Alone*, chaps. 1, 14.
9. Michael Schudson, *The Good Citizen: A History of American Civic Life* (Cambridge, MA: Harvard University Press, 1998); Virginia Sapiro, "Toward a History of Political Action in the United States," available at http://polisci.wisc.edu/users/sapiro/research.htm.
10. Alexis de Tocqueville, *Democracy in America* (New York: Knopf, 1945), 2:114; Gerald Gamm and Robert D. Putnam, "The Growth of Voluntary Associations in America, 1840–1940," *Journal of Interdisciplinary History* 29, 4 (1999): 511–57.

11. Recent studies of political participation verify that participation in civic organizations helps to facilitate political participation. See Sidney Verba, Kay Lehman Schlozman, and Henry E. Brady, *Voice and Equality: Civic Voluntarism in American Politics* (Cambridge, MA: Harvard University Press, 1995).

12. Skocpol, *Diminished Democracy,* chap. 3; Theda Skocpol, *Protecting Soldiers and Mothers: The Political Origins of Social Policy in the United States* (Cambridge, MA: Harvard University Press, 1998); A. Lanethea Mathews-Gardner, "From Women's Club to NGO: The Changing Terrain of Women's Civic Engagement in the Mid-20th Century United States," Ph.D. dissertation, Syracuse University, 2003; Linda Gordon, *Pitied but Not Entitled: Single Mothers and the History of Welfare, 1890–1935* (New York: Free Press, 1994), chap. 5; Aldon D. Morris, *The Origins of the Civil Rights Movement: Black Communities Organizing for Change* (New York: Free Press, 1984).

13. Martin P. Wattenberg, *Where Have All the Voters Gone?* (Cambridge, MA: Harvard University Press, 2002); Ruy A. Teixeira, *The Disappearing American Voter* (Washington, DC: Brookings, 1992); Theda Skocpol, *Diminished Democracy: From Membership to Management in American Civic Life* (Norman: University of Oklahoma Press, 2003); Robert Wuthnow, *Loose Connections: Joining Together in America's Fragmented Communities* (Cambridge, MA: Harvard University Press, 1998); M. Kent Jennings and Laura Stoker, "Social Trust and Civic Engagement Across Time and Generations," Acta Politica 39 (2004): 342–79; John E. Hughes and M. Margaret Conway, "Public Opinion and Political Participation," in *Understanding Public Opinion,* ed. Barbara Norrander and Clyde Wilcox (Washington, DC: Congressional Quarterly Press, 1997), 191–210.

14. Warren E. Miller and J. Merrill Shanks, *The New American Voter* (Cambridge, MA: Harvard University Press, 1996), chaps. 2, 5, 7; Putnam, *Bowling Alone,* chaps. 2, 14; Jennings and Stoker, "Social Trust and Civic Engagement." After forty years of nearly uninterrupted declining voter turnout, turnout in 2004 rose to the level of 1968; time will tell whether this election represents a reversal of the trend or merely an aberration.

15. Putnam, *Bowling Alone,* 268–72.

16. Ibid., 485, n. 41; M. Kent Jennings and Gregory B. Markus, "The Effect of Military Service on Political Attitudes: A Panel Study," *American Political Science Review* 71, 1 (1977): 131–47; M. Kent Jennings and Gregory B. Markus, "Political Participation and Vietnam War Veterans: A Longitudinal Study," in *The Social Psychology of Military Service,* ed. Nancy L. Goldman and David R. Segal (Beverly Hills, CA: Sage Publications, 1976), 175–201. Ellison did find higher rates of high-initiative political activity among black male veterans than nonveterans, but his study does not control for G.I. Bill usage. See Christopher G. Ellison, "Military Background, Racial Orientations, and Political Participation Among Black Adult Males," *Social Science Quarterly* 73 (1992): 360–78.

17. Richard Polenberg, *War and Society: The United States, 1941–1945* (Philadelphia: J. B. Lippincott, 1972), chap. 5.

18. This observation is also made by Strauss and Howe in *Generations,* 256–57.

19. Walter I. Trattner, *From Poor Law to Welfare State: A History of Social Welfare in America,* 5th ed. (New York: Free Press, 1994); Michael Katz, *In the Shadow of the Poorhouse: A Social History of Welfare in America,* 2nd ed. (New York: Basic Books, 1996).

20. Edwin S. Corwin, "The Passing of Dual Federalism," *Virginia Law Review* 36 (1965): 1–24.

21. Skocpol, *Protecting Soldiers and Mothers,* chap. 2; see 132 for estimate of pensions' reach.

22. The federal Sheppard-Towner Act, which channeled maternal health funding through public health agencies, represents an important exception to this pattern, but it was short-lived. See ibid., chaps. 6–9; on the limits of these programs prior to the New Deal for social citizenship, see Suzanne Mettler, "Social Citizens of Separate Sovereignties: Governance in the New Deal Welfare State," in *The New Deal and the Triumph of Liberalism,* ed. Sidney M. Milkis and Jerome M. Mileur (Amherst: University of Massachusetts Press, 2002), 231–71.

23. See, for example, Edwin Amenta, *Bold Relief* (Princeton, NJ: Princeton University Press, 1998); Suzanne Mettler, *Dividing Citizens: Gender and Federalism in New Deal Public Policy* (Ithaca, NY: Cornell University Press, 1998); Karen Orren, *Belated Feudalism: Labor, the Law, and Liberal Development in the United States* (New York: Cambridge University Press, 1991).

24. President's Commission on Veterans' Pensions, *Veterans' Benefits in the United States* (Washington, DC: GPO, 1956), 275, 300–304.

25. Ibid., 287.

26. In 1948–49, the average cost of tuition, books, and supplies was only $234 at a four-year public institution and $418 at a four-year private institution; two-year colleges and vocational programs cost substantially less. If expenses did exceed $500 per year, veterans could use the tuition allowance at an accelerated rate. U.S. Congress, Senate, Committee on Veterans' Affairs, "Final Report on Educational Assistance to Veterans: A Comparative Study of Three G.I. Bills," 93rd Cong., 1st Sess., Senate Committee Print No. 18 (Washington, DC: GPO, 1973), 20, 29.

27. Ibid., 289. Current dollars are calculated using Consumer Price Index for All Urban Consumers, 1950, from U.S. Department of Labor, Bureau of Labor Statistics, as recommended by John J. McCusker, *How Much Is That in Real Money?: A Historical Commodity Price Index for Use as a Deflator of Money Values in the Economy of the United States* (Worcester, MA: American Antiquarian Society, 2001).

28. Putnam, *Bowling Alone*, 268.

29. U.S. Congress, Senate, Committee on Veterans' Affairs, "Final Report on Educational Assistance to Veterans," 161.

30. Book-length studies of the G.I. Bill are few, and they include little analysis of the policy's effects among World War II veterans. Two classic studies focus predominantly on how the G.I. Bill came to be enacted: see Keith W. Olson, *The G.I. Bill, the Veterans, and the Colleges* (Lexington: University of Kentucky Press, 1974); Davis R. B. Ross, *Preparing for Ulysses: Politics and Veterans During World War II* (New York: Columbia University Press, 1969). Two more recent books offer syntheses of existing knowledge: Michael J. Bennett, *When Dreams Came True: The GI Bill and the Making of Modern America* (Washington, DC: Brassey's, 1996); Milton Greenberg, *The G.I. Bill: The Law That Changed America* (New York: Lickle Publishing, 1997). Another book assesses primarily the effects of the Vietnam-era program: Sar A. Levitan and Joyce K. Zickler, *Swords into Plowshares: Our GI Bill* (Salt Lake City: Olympus, 1973.)

31. American Council on Education, "The G.I. Bill's Lasting Legacy," special issue of *Educational Record* 75, 4 (1994); Edwin Kiester Jr., "The G.I. Bill May Be the Best Deal Ever Made by Uncle Sam," *Smithsonian*, November 1994, 129–39.

32. For an especially thoughtful treatment of this point that addresses how the G.I. Bill acquired its lauded stature even without supporting evidence, see Robert C. Serow, "Policy as Symbol: Title II of the 1944 G.I. Bill," *The Review of Higher Education* 27 (2004): 481–99.

33. Glen H. Elder Jr., "Military Times and Turning Points in Men's Lives," *Developmental Psychology* 22 (1986): 233–45; Glen H. Elder Jr., Cynthia Gimbel, and Rachel Ivie, "Turning Points in Life: The Case of Military Service and War," *Military Psychology* 3 (1991): 215–31; Yu Xie, "The Socioeconomic Status of Young Male Veterans, 1964–1984," *Social Science Quarterly* 73 (1992): 379–96; Wayne J. Villemez and John D. Kasarda, "Veteran Status and Socioeconomic Achievement," *Armed Forces and Society* 2 (1976): 407–20; Harley L. Browning, Sally C. Lopreato, and Dudley L. Poston Jr., "Income and Veteran Status: Variations Among Mexican Americans, Blacks, and Anglos," *American Sociological Review* 38 (1973): 74–85; John Modell, Marc Goulden, and Sigurdur Magnusson, "World War II in the Lives of Black Americans: Some Findings and an Interpretation," *Journal of American History* 76 (1989): 838–48.

34. Thrainn Eggertsson, "Economic Aspects of Higher Education Taken Under the World War II G.I. Bill of Rights," Ph.D. dissertation, Ohio State University, 1972; Carl Curtis Brown, "An Economic Analysis of the G.I. Bill Educational Benefits: A Study of Korean and Post-Korean Veterans," Ph.D. dissertation, Oklahoma State University, 1979; John Bound and

Sarah Turner, "Going to War and Going to College: Did World War II and the G.I. Bill Increase Educational Attainment for Returning Veterans?" *Journal of Labor Economics* 20, 4 (2002): 784–815; C. B. Nam, "Impact of the 'G.I. Bills' on the Educational Level of the Male Population," *American Education* 1 (1964): 26–32.

35. Jere Behrman, Robert Pollack, and Paul Taubman, "Family Resources, Family Size, and Access to Financing for College Education," *Journal of Political Economy* 97 (1989): 398–419; Neil Fligstein, "The G.I. Bill: Its Effects on the Educational and Occupational Attainment of U.S. Males: 1940–1973," CDE Working Paper 76-9, Center for Demography and Ecology, University of Wisconsin, Madison, 1976.

36. Only a couple of studies have examined use of the vocational training provisions directly, and while they suggest that such benefits often proved important for veterans from disadvantaged backgrounds, their focus is predominantly on subsequent earnings rather than on program inclusivity and access. On World War II-era benefits, see John Eric Fredland and Roger D. Little, "Long-term Returns to Vocational Training: Evidence from Military Sources," *Journal of Human Resources* 15 (1980): 48–66; on experiences after the Vietnam era, see Dave M. O'Neill, "Voucher Funding of Training Programs: Evidence from the G.I. Bill," *Journal of Human Resources* 12 (1977): 425–45.

37. I have found only one study that ever raised such questions, investigating the effects of the G.I. Bill for participation in civic activities among veterans in the community of Danville, Illinois: Mary Ann Diller, "Individual and Social Benefits of Federally Supported Continuing Education: An Effort to Assess, Over a Quarter Century and Within a Mid-American Community, Impact of the Servicemen's Readjustment Act (G.I. Bill) Upon Individuals, Their Families, and Their Community," Ph.D. dissertation, Michigan State University, 1973.

38. Arthur Schlesinger, "National Turning Point," *American Heritage,* May/June 1998, 61; Peter F. Drucker, "The New Society of Organizations," *Harvard Business Review,* September/October 1992, 95.

39. Lizabeth Cohen, *A Consumers' Republic: The Politics of Mass Consumption in Postwar America* (New York: Knopf, 2003), 156–60.

40. Ibid., 156.

41. Ibid., 137–43, 167–73; Karen Brodkin, *How Jews Became White Folks and What That Says About Race in America* (New Brunswick, NJ: Rutgers University Press, 1999), 39–44; David H. Onkst, "'First a Negro . . . Incidentally a Veteran': Black World War II Veterans and the G.I. Bill of Rights in the Deep South, 1944–1948," *Journal of Social History* 31, 3 (1998): 517–43; Hilary Herbold, "Never a Level Playing Field: Blacks and the GI Bill," *Journal of Blacks in Higher Education* 6 (1994–95): 104–8.

42. Here I am drawing on results from a survey of 716 nonblack males who served in the World War II military. The majority of respondents, 99 percent, described themselves as "white"; 1 percent described themselves as "Hispanic," 1 percent as "American Indian/Native American," less than 1 percent as "Asian or Pacific Islander," and 2 percent as "other." (These add up to more than 100 percent because in the surveys for this project, just as in the 2000 U.S. Census, respondents were permitted to check more than one category to describe themselves.) Thus, I routinely refer to these 716 individuals as "nonblack" and use the term "white" only in a few instances in which the sample was limited to those who responded as such. The number of "Hispanic" and "American Indian/Native American" respondents was insufficiently large to permit comparison of those subgroups within the data. At some points in the book, I will discuss also survey results from black male veterans, female veterans, and male college graduates of the Class of 1949, both veterans and nonveterans.

43. The elevated participation of the G.I. Bill users is not attributable to a "selection bias," meaning distinct characteristics of those who chose to use the benefits. This is verified by analysis using a two-stage regression model. See Suzanne Mettler and Eric Welch, "Civic Generation: Policy Feedback Effects of the GI Bill on Political Involvement over the Life Course," *British Journal of Political Science* 34 (2004): 497–518.

44. The Veterans Administration's handling of the program also introduced biases against veterans who had been dismissed from the military because of homosexual activity. An excel-

lent treatment of this issue appears in Margot Canaday, "Building a Straight State: Sexuality and Social Citizenship under the 1944 G.I. Bill," *Journal of American History* 9, 3 (2003).

45. For example, see William A. Schambra, "All Community Is Local: The Key to America's Civic Renewal," and Dan Coats and Rick Santorum, "Civil Society and the Humble Role of Government," both in *Community Works,* ed. E. J. Dionne Jr. (Washington, DC: Brookings Institution, 1998); Lawrence M. Mead, *Beyond Entitlement: The Social Obligations of Citizenship* (New York: Free Press, 1998); Nathan Glazer, *The Limits of Social Policy* (Cambridge, MA: Harvard University Press, 1988).

46. Ronald Reagan, "Inaugural Address, January 20, 1981," Ronald Reagan Library, available at: http://www.reagan.utexas.edu/resource/speeches/1981/12081a.htm.

47. Suzanne Mettler and Andrew Milstein, "'A Sense of the State': Tracing the Role of the American Administrative State in Citizens' Lives Over Time," paper presented at the annual meeting of the Midwestern Political Science Association, Chicago, April 3–6, 2003.

48. This argument is made more fully in Suzanne Mettler and Joe Soss, "The Consequences of Public Policy for Democratic Citizenship: Bridging Policy Studies and Mass Politics," *Perspectives on Politics* 2, 1 (2004): 55–73. This disconnect remains despite the fact that the notion that a new policy may create a new form of politics has a long legacy, beginning, perhaps, with E. E. Schattschneider, *Politics, Pressure, and the Tariff* (New York: Prentice Hall, 1935).

49. In exceptions to the rule, some scholars have noted that citizens affected by a policy directly are more likely to become politically active themselves on related issues. The extent to which they participate seems to vary by program, with beneficiaries of non-means-tested programs, such as Social Security and Medicare, being more inclined to pursue such involvement than beneficiaries of means-tested programs, such as welfare. See Verba, Schlozman, and Brady, *Voice and Equality,* chaps. 7, 14; Steven J. Rosenstone and John Mark Hansen, *Mobilization, Participation, and Democracy in America* (New York: Macmillan, 1993), 101–17. Government agricultural programs appear to elevate farmers' "sense of the personal relevance of politics," leading them to vote at significantly higher levels than other citizens. See Raymond E. Wolfinger and Steven J. Rosenstone, *Who Votes?* (New Haven: Yale University Press, 1980), 32.

50. Precedents for the examination of policies' "resource effects" on politics began with the work of Theodore J. Lowi and James Q. Wilson, though their focus was not on effects among mass publics but rather those among political elites and interest groups. See Theodore J. Lowi, "American Business, Public Policy, Case-Studies, and Political Theory," *World Politics* 16 (1964): 677–715; Theodore J. Lowi, "Four Systems of Policy, Politics, and Choice," *Public Administration Review,* July/August 1972; James Q. Wilson, *Political Organizations* (New York: Basic Books, 1973); James Q. Wilson, "The Politics of Regulation," in *The Politics of Regulation,* ed. James Q. Wilson (New York: Basic Books, 1980), 357–94.

51. The scaffolding of the theoretical approach I use here, featuring attention to both resource and interpretive effects, comes from Paul Pierson, "When Effect Becomes Cause," *World Politics* 45 (1993): 595–628.

52. Christopher Howard, "Is the American Welfare State Unusually Small?" *PS: Political Science and Politics* 36, 3 (2003): 411–16.

53. Verba, Schlozman, and Brady, *Voice and Equality,* 270–72 and passim.

54. See Pierson, "When Effect Becomes Cause."

55. Andrea Louise Campbell, *How Policies Make Citizens: Senior Political Activism and the American Welfare State* (Princeton, NJ: Princeton University Press, 2003).

56. For early considerations of how public policies have symbolic or expressive power, through which they may affect the beliefs, preferences, and actions of citizens generally, see Murray Edelman, *The Symbolic Uses of Politics* (Urbana: University of Illinois Press, 1964); Frances Fox Piven and Richard A. Cloward, *Regulating the Poor: The Functions of Public Welfare* (New York: Vintage Books, 1971); Frances Fox Piven and Richard A. Cloward, *Poor People's Movements: Why They Succeed, How They Fail* (New York: Vintage Books, 1977).

57. In this vein, Anne Schneider and Helen Ingram argue that policy design features may shape beneficiaries' subjective experience of what it means to be a citizen, and thus affect political identity, group formation, and participation. Anne Schneider and Helen Ingram, "Social Construction of Target Populations: Implications for Politics and Policy," *American Political Science Review* 87 (1993): 334–47; Anne Schneider and Helen Ingram, *Policy Design for Democracy* (Lawrence: University Press of Kansas, 1997), 78–89, 140–45. For other treatments of how policy design conveys messages to citizens, see Mead, *Beyond Entitlement*, and Marc Landy, "Public Policy and Citizenship," in *Public Policy for Democracy*, ed. Helen Ingram and Anne Schneider (Washington, DC: Brookings Institution, 1993); on how policy implementation conveys such messages, see Dvora Yanow, *How Does a Policy Mean?: Interpreting Policy and Organizational Actions* (Washington, DC: Georgetown University Press, 1996), chap. 1.

58. Joe Soss, "Lessons of Welfare: Policy Design, Political Learning, and Political Action," *American Political Science Review* 93 (1999): 363–80; Joe Soss, *Unwanted Claims: The Politics of Participation in the U.S. Welfare System* (Ann Arbor: University of Michigan Press, 2002).

59. Soss, "Lessons of Welfare."

60. For instance, some historically oriented scholars have explored how policies affect the degree of democracy, inclusivity of citizenship, and degree of social solidarity among the citizenry, highlighting dynamics of class, race, or gender. See T. H. Marshall, *Class, Citizenship, and Social Development* (New York: Doubleday, 1965); Gøsta Esping-Andersen, *The Three Worlds of Welfare Capitalism* (Princeton, NJ: Princeton University Press, 1990); Jill Quadagno, *The Color of Welfare: How Racism Undermined the War on Poverty* (New York: Oxford University Press, 1994); Ann Shola Orloff, "Gender and the Social Rights of Citizenship: The Comparative Analyses of Gender Relations and Welfare States," *American Sociological Review* 58 (1993): 303–28.

61. Jacob S. Hacker, *The Divided American Welfare State: The Battle over Public and Private Social Benefits in the United States* (New York: Cambridge University Press, 2002). On matters of visibility and traceability, see R. Douglas Arnold, *The Logic of Congressional Action* (New Haven: Yale University Press, 1990), 47–51.

62. Such analysis must also be historical, attentive to how the timing of public programs in the lives of individuals of a particular generation might matter for civic outcomes. For careful attention to how matters of temporality matter in politics, see Paul Pierson, *Politics in Time: History, Institutions, and Social Analysis* (Princeton, NJ: Princeton University Press, 2004). The timing of public policy developments in relationship to critical junctures in citizens' lives might have consequences for the difference that such policies make, possibly for entire generations. See Suzanne Mettler and Eric Welch, "Civic Generation: Policy Feedback Effects of the G.I. Bill on Political Involvement over the Life Course," *British Journal of Political Science* 34, 3 (2004): 497–518. As well, policy effects may be influenced by the sequencing of citizens' experiences of a public program in relationship to their other experiences of government and social forces. See Suzanne Mettler, "'The Only Good Thing Was the G.I. Bill': Effects of the Education and Training Provisions on African American Veterans' Political Participation," *Studies in American Political Development* 19, 1 (2005).

63. For discussion of interview procedures, see the end of Appendix A and notes.

Chapter 1

1. Geoffrey Perrett, *Days of Sadness, Years of Triumph: The American People, 1939–1945* (Madison: University of Wisconsin Press, 1973), 410, 415; Department of Veterans Affairs, Office of Public Affairs, "America's Wars," available at http://www.va.gov/pressrel/amwars01.htm. Among U.S. troops, 291,557 died in battle, 113,842 others died in service, and 671,846 endured nonmortal woundings. (The Civil War yielded more deaths but fewer woundings.)

2. Morse A. Cartwright and Glen Burch, *Adult Adjustment: A Manual on the Coordination of Existing Community Services and the Establishment and Operation of Community Adjust-*

ment Centers for Veterans and Others (New York: Institute on Adult Education, 1945); "Demobilization and Readjustment," Report of the Conference on Postwar Readjustment of Civilian and Military Personnel, National Resources Planning Board, June 1943.

3. Maj. Gen. Norman T. Kirk, "A Great Responsibility Rests on the Public," Delivered before a *New York Times* conference, New York, October 12, 1944, reprinted in *Vital Speeches of the Day,* November 15, 1944, 62, 64.

4. A fuller analysis of the creation of the G.I. Bill appears in Suzanne Mettler, "The Creation of the G.I. Bill of Rights of 1944: Melding Social and Participatory Citizenship Ideals," *Journal of Policy History* 17, 3 (2005); Davis R. B. Ross, *Preparing for Ulysses: Politics and Veterans During World War II* (New York: Columbia University Press, 1969); Keith W. Olson, *The G.I. Bill, the Veterans, and the Colleges* (Lexington: University Press of Kentucky, 1974), chap. 1.

5. Lizabeth Cohen, *A Consumers' Republic: The Politics of Mass Consumption in Postwar America* (New York: Alfred A. Knopf, 2003), 156–60.

6. Edwin Amenta and Theda Skocpol, "Redefining the New Deal: World War II and the Development of Social Provision in the United States," in *The Politics of Social Policy in the United States,* ed. Margaret Weir, Ann Shola Orloff, and Theda Skocpol (Princeton: Princeton University Press, 1988), 81–122; Ira Katznelson and Bruce Pietrykowski, "Rebuilding the American State: Evidence from the 1940s," *Studies in American Political Development* 5, 2 (1991): 301–39; also see Michael K. Brown, "State Capacity and Political Choice: Interpreting the Failure of the Third New Deal," *Studies in American Political Development* 9, 1 (1995): 187–212; Alan Brinkley, *The End of Reform* (New York: Alfred A. Knopf, 1995).

7. David Brody, "The New Deal and World War II," in *The New Deal: The National Level,* ed. John Braeman, Robert H. Bremner, and David Brody (Columbus: Ohio State University Press, 1975), 1:267–309; Richard Polenberg, *War and Society: The United States, 1941–1945* (Philadelphia: J. B. Lippincott, 1972), 73–98.

8. Ira Katznelson, Kim Geiger, and Daniel Kryder, "Limiting Liberalism: The Southern Veto in Congress, 1933–1950," *Political Science Quarterly* 108, 2 (1993): 283–306; James T. Patterson, *Congressional Conservatism and the New Deal* (Lexington: University of Kentucky Press, 1967).

9. Franklin D. Roosevelt, "The Annual Message to Congress, January 6, 1941," in *Public Papers and Addresses of Franklin D. Roosevelt,* ed. Samuel I. Rosenman (New York: Macmillan, 1941), 9:663–78.

10. National Resources Planning Board [hereafter NRPB], *National Resources Development: Report for 1943; Part I. Post War Plan and Program* (Washington, DC: GPO, 1943), 2.

11. NRPB, *Security, Work and Relief Policies* (Washington, DC: GPO, 1942), 492–93.

12. Memorandum, Franklin D. Roosevelt to Frederic A. Delano, July 6, 1942, Official File of the President [hereafter OF] 1092, Franklin D. Roosevelt Library, Hyde Park, NY [hereafter FDR], Box 16, File 1092d.

13. "Editorial Reaction to NRPB Reports," 089, Entry 8, Box 136, Record Group [hereafter RG] 187, National Archives, Washington, DC [hereafter NA]; "Press and Radio Reactions to NRPB's Post-war Reports from OWI's *Weekly Media Report,*" March 25, 1943, NRPB, Office of the Director, Postwar Planning Section, Box 1, "Climate of Opinion," RG 187, NA; Ross, *Preparing for Ulysses,* 63.

14. William Pyrle Dillingham, *Federal Aid to Veterans, 1917–1941* (Gainesville: University of Florida Press, 1952), 131–44.

15. Minutes, PMC Meeting, July 17, 1942, NRPB, Central Office Records, File 830.1, 2, 8, RG 187, NA.

16. Franklin D. Roosevelt, "Message to the Congress on Education of War Veterans," in *Public Papers and Addresses of Franklin D. Roosevelt,* 12:451.

17. Theda Skocpol, "The G.I. Bill and U.S. Social Policy, Past and Future," *Social Philosophy and Policy* 14, 2 (1997).

18. Peter Karsten, "The U.S. Citizens Soldier's Past, Present, and Likely Future," *Parameters,* summer 2001, 61–73; R. Claire Snyder, *Citizen-Soldiers and Manly Warriors: Military Service and*

Gender in the Civic Republican Tradition (Lanham, MD: Rowman and Littlefield, 1999); Linda K. Kerber, *No Constitutional Right to Be Ladies: Women and the Obligations of Citizenship* (New York: Hill and Wang, 1998); for an original defense of this idea from the revolutionary era, see George Washington, "Sentiments of a Peace Establishment," in *The American Military: Readings in the History of the Military and American Society,* ed. Russell Weigley (Reading, MA: Addison-Wesley, 1969); James Madison, Alexander Hamilton, and John Jay, *The Federalist Papers,* ed. Isaac Kramnick (London: Penguin Books, 1987), see nos. 24–29, especially 29.

19. Washington, "Sentiments of a Peace Establishment."
20. Theda Skocpol, *Protecting Soldiers and Mothers: The Political Origins of Social Policy in the United States* (Cambridge, MA: Harvard University Press, 1992), 102–51.
21. Ibid., 143–48.
22. Kenneth T. Kato, "Veterans' Benefits," *The Encyclopedia of the United States Congress,* eds. Donald C. Bacon, Roger H. Davidson, and Morton Keller (New York: Simon & Schuster, 1994), 4:2038–39.
23. U.S. Congress, *Proceedings of the 15th National Convention of the American Legion, Chicago, Illinois, October 2–5, 1933,* House Document no. 154, 73th Cong., 2nd Sess. (Washington, DC: GPO, 1934), 16.
24. Kato, "Veterans' Benefits," 2039; Gary Dean Best, *FDR and the Bonus Marchers, 1933–1935* (Westport, CT: Praeger, 1992).
25. Suzanne Mettler, *Dividing Citizens: Gender and Federalism in New Deal Public Policy* (Ithaca: Cornell University Press, 1998).
26. Memorandum and attachments, Leonard Outhwaite to PMC, February 13, 1943, NRPB, Records of the Office of the Director, Records of the Post War Agenda Section, Box 4, file on Reeves Committee, 8, 9, 11.
27. On the perspective of military leaders, see testimony by Colonel Francis T. Spaulding, U.S. Congress, Senate, Hearings before the Committee on Education and Labor on S. 1295 and S. 1509, December 13, 14, and 15, 1943, 32, 36. On the perspective of educational leaders, see "Minutes of the Executive Committee of the Committee on the Relationships of Higher Education to the Federal Government," April 11, 1944; also letter from Edmund E. Day to the Honorable John E. Rankin, no date, both in Records of the American Council on Education, Box 27, folder "Committee on Relationship of Higher Education to Federal Government," no. 4, Hoover Institution Library and Archives, Stanford University; U.S. Congress, Senate, Hearings Before the Committee on Education and Labor on S. 1295 and S. 1509, 78th Cong., 1st Sess., December 13, 14, and 15, 1943, 115.
28. "Preliminary Report to the President of the United States from the Armed Forces Committee on Post War Educational Opportunities for Service Personnel," July 30, 1945, OF 5182, "Armed Forces Committee on Postwar Educational Opportunities for Service Personnel, 1942–1944," FDR, 11, 14, 15.
29. At its convention in September 1943, the Legion authorized a committee to examine how discharged veterans could be rehabilitated, and passed several resolutions affirming its support for veterans' benefits; in mid-November, the organization's Executive Committee proposed a committee to plan comprehensive veterans' legislation. Raymond Moley Jr., *The American Legion Story* (New York: Duell, Sloan, and Pearce, 1966), 273; David Camelon, "I Saw the G.I. Bill Written," part I, *American Legion Magazine,* September 1949, 47; U.S. Congress, *Proceedings of the 25th National Convention of the American Legion, Omaha, Nebraska, September 21–23, 1943,* House Document no. 364, 78th Cong., 1st Sess. (Washington, DC: GPO, 1944), 102–3.
30. William Pencak, "Veterans' Movements," in *Encyclopedia of American Political History: Studies of the Principal Movements and Ideas,* ed. Jack P. Greene (New York: Simon and Schuster, 1984), 3:1338–40.
31. Stelle, as quoted in Camelon, "I Saw the G.I. Bill Written," part I, 47; Moley, *The American Legion Story,* 273.

32. Legion leaders later noted that the administration's Bill, sponsored by Senator Elbert Thomas, was largely responsible for the educational provisions of their bill. U.S. Congress, Senate, Hearings Before the Committee on Education and Labor on S. 1295 and S. 1509, 78th Cong., 1st Sess., December 13, 14, and 15, 1943; memo, James F. Burton to Bob Pitkin, May 5, 1949, American Legion #10, National Headquarters of the American Legion, Indianapolis, Indiana (hereafter AL).

33. Memo in Harry Colmery's handwriting, from Mayflower Hotel room, "G.I. Bill" cabinet, AL; U.S. Congress, Senate, 78th Cong., 2nd Sess., Hearings Before a Subcommittee of the Committee on Finance on S. 1617, January 14–March 10, 1944, 252–53; U.S. Congress, House of Representatives, 78th Cong., 2nd Sess., Hearings Before the Committee on World War Veterans' Legislation on H.R. 3917 and S. 1767, January 11–March 31, 1944, 421.

34. Olson, *The G.I. Bill, the Veterans, and the Colleges*, 16–17.

35. U.S. Congress, Senate, Hearings Before the Committee on Education and Labor on S. 1295 and S. 1509, 78th Cong., 1st Sess., December 13, 14, and 15, 1943, 15.

36. R. B. Pitkin, "Some GI Bill Authors Today," in the three-part series "How the First G.I. Bill Was Written," *American Legion Magazine*, January, February, and May 1969, AL.

37. Moley, *The American Legion Story*, 274.

38. Camelon, "I Saw the G.I. Bill Written," part II, *American Legion Magazine*, October 1949, 52; Ross, *Preparing for Ulysses*, 99–100.

39. "Publicity Outline Supporting Legion Bill," folder "U.S.-Manpower Benefits—G.I. Bill," G.I. Bill correspondence, AL; all contents of folders nos. 2–5, "U.S.—Manpower—Legion Bill," G.I. Bill correspondence, AL; memo, Jack Cejnar to Commander Wagner, November 22, 1955, AL no. 11, AL. Also see Theda Skocpol, "The G.I. Bill and U.S. Social Policy, Past and Future," 106.

40. U.S. Congress, House of Representatives, 78th Cong., 2nd Sess., Hearings Before the Committee on World War Veterans' Legislation on H.R. 3917 and S. 1767, January 11–March 31, 1944, 350–52; Ross, *Preparing for Ulysses*, 108; "G.I. Enemy No. 1," *The Nation*, May 6, 1944, 527–28.

41. Quoted in Ross, *Preparing for Ulysses*, 108.

42. Camelon, "I Saw the G.I. Bill Written," part III, *American Legion Magazine*, November 1949, 47–48.

43. T. H. Marshall, "Citizenship and Social Class," in *Class, Citizenship, and Social Development* (New York: Doubleday, 1965), 65–122; also see Judith N. Shklar, *American Citizenship: The Quest for Inclusion* (Cambridge, MA: Harvard University Press, 1991).

44. Original notes by Harry W. Colmery, "U.S.—Manpower Benefits," G.I. Bill Correspondence, AL.

45. U.S. Congress, *Proceedings of the 25th National Convention of the American Legion*, 133.

46. U.S. Congress, Senate, 78th Cong., 2nd Sess., Hearing Before a Subcommittee of the Committee on Finance on S. 1617, January 14–March 10, 1944 (Washington, DC: GPO, 1944), 253.

Chapter 2

1. Albert A. Blum, "The Army and Student Deferments During the Second World War," *Journal of Higher Education* 31 (1960): 41–45; Louis E. Keefer, "Students, Soldiers, Sailors: Trainees on Virginia College Campuses During World War II," *Virginia Cavalcade* 39 (1989): 22–35; Louis E. Keefer, *Scholars in Foxholes: The Story of the Army Specialized Training Program in World War II* (Reston, VA: COTU Publishing, 1988).

2. Early in 1944, the Army brought an abrupt halt to ASTP, and henceforth limited student deferments to those studying medicine, dentistry, veterinary medicine, and osteopathy.

3. "Official History, 87th Infantry Division," 87th Infantry Division Association Web site, http://www.87thInfantryDivision.com; U.S. Army, Center of Military History, *Biennial Reports of the Chief of Staff of the United States Army to the Secretary of War, 1 July 1939–30 June 1945* (Washington, DC: Center of Military History, 1996).

4. Joshua Goldstein, *War and Gender* (Cambridge: Cambridge University Press, 2001); R. Claire Snyder, *Citizen-Soldiers and Manly Warriors: Military Service and Gender in the Civic Republican Tradition* (New York: Rowman and Littlefield, 1999).

5. Christian G. Appy, *Working Class War: American Combat Soldiers and Vietnam* (Chapel Hill: University of North Carolina Press, 1993), 18; Department of Defense, Office of the Assistant Secretary of Defense, "Population Representation in the Military Services, Fiscal Year 1998," November 1999, chapter 7, available at http://www.dod.mil/prhome/poprep98/index.html.

6. Generally, in this chapter, when percentages of the population are mentioned, the data come from national random-sample surveys conducted in the 1940s or soon thereafter (and the source is provided in the notes). This is the case unless I explicitly mention that the source is the World War II Veterans Survey or Class of 1949 Survey.

7. J. Garry Clifford and Samuel R. Spencer Jr., *The First Peacetime Draft* (Lawrence: University Press of Kansas, 1986), 3; Selective Service System, *Selective Service in Peacetime: First Report of the Director of Selective Service, 1940–41* (Washington, DC: GPO, 1942).

8. George Q. Flynn, *The Draft, 1940–1973* (Lawrence: University Press of Kansas, 1993), 18–19. By the end of 1944, five and a half million had been deferred because they worked in "critical occupations" in which there was a shortage of trained personnel. George Q. Flynn, "Drafting Farmers in World War II," in *At Home on the Range: Essays on the History of Western Social and Domestic Life,* ed. John R. Wunder (Westport, CT: Greenwood Press, 1985), 157–74.

9. David R. Segal, *Recruiting for Uncle Sam: Citizenship and Military Manpower Policy* (Lawrence: University Press of Kansas, 1989), 30.

10. Flynn, *The Draft,* 53; Selective Service System, *Selective Service and Victory: The 4th Report of the Director of Selective Service* (Washington, DC: GPO, 1948).

11. Across the nation, the draft encountered some resistance, and a small number of individuals, mostly Mennonites, Quakers, and Brethren, chose to be conscientious objectors. Selective Service System, *Selective Service and Victory,* 37–38, 177–82; Selective Service System, *Selective Service in Peacetime,* 37–38; Michael C. C. Adams, *The Best War Ever: America and World War II* (Baltimore: Johns Hopkins University Press, 1994), 76.

12. While most rejections occurred early on, all told, by August 1945, five million registrants—30 percent of those examined—had been rejected because they failed the physical exam. The percentage of registrants rejected was highest in the southern states, where it hovered above 35 percent, but in no state was the rate lower than 23 percent.

13. Lawrence M. Hepple, "Selective Service Rejectees in Rural Missouri, 1940–1943," Rural Health Series No. 5, Research Bulletin 439, Agricultural Experiment Station, College of Agriculture, University of Missouri, Columbia, April 1949, 3–19; Marcus S. Goldstein, "Physical Status of Men Examined Through Selective Service in World War II," *Public Health Reports* 66, 19 (1951): 593–96.

14. Goldstein, "Physical Status of Men Examined," 605–6; Samuel Goldberg, *Army Training of Illiterates in World War II* (New York: Teachers College, Columbia University, 1951).

15. This difference held true when white soldiers were compared to white civilians and when black soldiers were compared to black civilians.

16. Smith, "Populational Characteristics of American Servicemen," 250.

17. National Manpower Council, *Student Deferment and National Manpower Policy* (New York: Columbia University Press, 1952), 26.

18. Blum, "The Army and Student Deferments During the Second World War"; Keefer, "Students, Soldiers, Sailors;" Keefer, *Scholars in Foxholes.*

19. Goldstein, "Physical Status of Men Examined," 590–91. Married men made up 28 percent of all servicemen, though they constituted 59 percent of the overall population eligible for the draft. Smith, "Populational Characteristics of American Servicemen," 247, 249.

20. Smith, "Populational Characteristics of American Servicemen," 246–47. On Mexican Americans in the World War II military, see Raul Morin, "Draftees and Volunteers," in *The Mexican Americans: An Awakening Minority,* ed. Manuel Servin (Beverly Hills, CA: Glencoe Press,

1970), 100–105; on Asian Americans, see Ronald Takaki, *Strangers from a Different Shore: A History of Asian Americans* (Boston: Little, Brown, 1989), 359, 366, 374.

21. Segal, *Recruiting for Uncle Sam*, 9; Daniel Kryder, *Divided Arsenal: Race and the American State During World War II* (New York: Cambridge University Press, 2000).

22. Goldstein, "Physical Status of Men Examined," 594, 600; Hepple, "Selective Service Rejectees in Rural Missouri," Selective Service System, *Selective Service and Victory,* 187–96; Ulysses Lee, *U.S. Army in World War II, Special Studies: The Employment of Negro Troops* (Washington, DC: GPO, 1966).

23. Thomas Borstelmann, *The Cold War and the Color Line: American Race Relations in the Global Arena* (Cambridge: Harvard University Press, 2001), 27–37; Gary Gerstle, *American Crucible: Race and Nation in the Twentieth Century* (Princeton: Princeton University Press, 2001), chap. 5; Philip A. Klinkner with Rogers M. Smith, *The Unsteady March: The Rise and Decline of Racial Equality in America* (Chicago: University of Chicago Press, 1999), chap. 6.

24. The circumstances of African Americans in the military did not change fundamentally until 1950, when President Harry S. Truman issued the executive order to desegregate the armed forces. Kryder, *Divided Arsenal;* Richard M. Dalfiume, *Desegregation of the U.S. Armed Forces: Fighting on Two Fronts, 1939–1953* (Columbia: University of Missouri Press).

25. This theme, which emerged in interviews with black veterans, is discussed in Klinkner with Smith, *The Unsteady March,* 164.

26. U.S. Congress, Senate, 93rd Cong., 1st Sess., "Final Report on Educational Assistance to Veterans: A Comparative Study of Three G.I. Bills," submitted to the Committee on Veterans' Affairs (Washington, DC: GPO, 1973), 163.

27. June A. Willenz, "Invisible Veterans," *Educational Record* 75 (1994): 44; June A. Willenz, *Women Veterans: America's Forgotten Heroines* (New York: Continuum, 1983), 18–32.

28. Thirty-one percent of respondents had at least one parent who had been born outside of the United States, and 53 percent had at least one grandparent born abroad; in the case of nearly half of them (46 percent), all four grandparents had been born in other countries.

29. William E. Leuchtenburg, *A Troubled Feast: American Society Since 1945* (Boston: Little, Brown, 1973), 48.

30. Thomas Picketty and Emmanuel Saez, "Income Inequality in the United States, 1913–1998," *Quarterly Journal of Economics* 117, 1 (2003): 1–39.

31. The battle of Luzon was the deadliest in the Southwest Pacific; see William L. O'Neill, *A Democracy at War: America's Fight at Home and Abroad in World War II* (New York: Free Press, 1993), 292–94.

32. Until recently, scholars had recorded the traditional military history of World War II primarily from the generals' point of view; in recent decades, several studies have described combat as citizen soldiers experienced it. See John Ellis, *The Sharp End: The Fighting Man in World War II* (New York: Charles Scribner's Sons, 1980); Gerald F. Linderman, *The World Within War: America's Combat Experience in World War II* (Cambridge, MA: Harvard University Press, 1997); Stephen E. Ambrose, *Citizen Soldiers* (New York: Simon and Schuster, 1997); Michael D. Doubler, *Closing with the Enemy: How GIs Fought the War in Europe, 1944–45* (Lawrence: University Press of Kansas, 1994); Joseph Balkoski, *Beyond the Beachhead: The 29th Infantry Division in Normandy* (Harrisburg, PA: Stackpole Books, 1989). Memoirs, original accounts, and direct recordings of oral history appear in Studs Terkel, *"The Good War": An Oral History of World War II* (New York: Pantheon, 1984); Harold Leinbaugh and John D. Campbell, *The Men of Company K: The Autobiography of a World War II Rifle Company* (New York: Bantam Books, 1985); Bruce E. Egger and Lee MacMillan Otts, *G Company's War: Two Personal Accounts of the Campaigns in Europe, 1944–45,* edited by Paul Roley (Tuscaloosa: University of Alabama Press, 1992); Paul Fussell, *Doing Battle: The Making of a Skeptic* (Boston: Little, Brown, 1996); John Colby, *War from the Ground Up: The 90th Division in WWII* (Austin, TX: Nortex Press, 1991); Gerald Astor, *The Mighty Eight: The Air War in Europe as Told by the Men Who Fought It* (New York: Donald I. Fine Books, 1997); Dorothy Chernitsky, *Voices from the Foxholes: Men of the 110th Infantry Relate Personal Accounts of What They Experienced in World War II* (Uniontown, PA: author, 1991); Ernie Pyle, *Brave Men* (New York: Grosset and Dunlap, 1944).

33. U.S. Army, Center of Military History, *Biennial Reports of the Chief of Staff,* 133–35; Web site for the 379th Bomb Group, http://379thbga.org.

34. The 783rd Squadron was one of four within the 465th Bombardment Group. "History of 783rd Bomb Squadron (H) 465th Bombardment Group (H) (1943–1945) Pantanella, Italy," compiled by Floyd E. Gregory, in author's possession.

35. From a definitive history of the battles in France and Germany, which involved the 87th and 89th Divisions, see Russell F. Weigley, *Eisenhower's Lieutenants: The Campaign of France and Germany 1944–45* (Bloomington: Indiana University Press, 1981); U.S. Army, Center of Military History, *Biennial Reports of the Chief of Staff,* 208; all sections included under "Combat," Web site of 89th Infantry Division of World War II, http://www.89infdivww2.org.

36. Bernard C. Nulty, *Strength for the Fight: A History of Black Americans in the Military* (New York: Free Press, 1986); Maggi M. Morehouse, *Fighting in the Jim Crow Army: Black Men and Women Remember World War II* (New York: Rowman and Littlefield, 2000).

37. See "Ohrdruf" sections, including "Introduction," "The Story of an 89th Liberator," and "Comments by Rabbi Murray Cohen," Web site of 89th Infantry Division of World War II, http://www.89infdivww2.org.

38. Linderman, *The World Within War,* 1.

39. Adams, *The Best War Ever,* chap. 4.

40. The World War II veterans surveyed among the Class of 1949 represents this fuller cross section of military experiences. Among them, 29 percent were stationed on the home front, never leaving the United States. Others, fully 18 percent, served on sea duty outside U.S. territorial waters, with the remainder in land areas outside of the United States. By branch of the service, 40 percent participated in the regular army, 24 percent in the Army Air Force, 25 percent in the Navy, and the rest in the Marine Corps, Coast Guard, or merchant marine. They belonged to a far more diverse array of units than respondents to the World War II Veterans Survey, and included many service placements: chemical corps, signal service battalion, special radio unit, military police, submarine service, Navy Seabees, Corps of Engineers, 37th Medical Training Division, and weather reconnaissance squadron. Many served in the Pacific theater and some in Africa.

41. "What Makes a Soldier?" *Newsweek,* June 24, 1946, 58–59.

42. Linderman, *The World Within War,* 1.

43. The most thorough original study of soldiers' initial attitudes toward military service is Samuel A. Stouffer et al., *The American Soldier: Adjustment During Army Life,* 4 vols. (Princeton, NJ: Princeton University Press, 1949). Also see John Monks, *College Men at War,* vol. 24 of *Memoirs* (Portland, ME: Anthoensen Press, 1957); Eli Ginzberg et al., *The Ineffective Soldier: Lessons for Management and the Nation,* 3 vols. (New York: Columbia University Press, 1959).

44. Lee, *The Employment of Negro Troops,* 548–52; Nulty, *Strength for the Fight,* 172.

45. Hondon B. Hargrove, *Black Soldiers in Italy: Black Americans in World War II* (Jefferson, NC: McFarland & Col, 1985); Nulty, *Strength for the Fight,* 172–74; Rod Norland, "'As Good as Anybody Else': Honoring the Courage of WWII's 'Buffalo Soldiers,'" *Newsweek,* July 24, 2000, 48.

46. John Adnot and Charles W. Lewis, "Immersion Foot Syndromes," in *Textbook of Military Medicine,* ed. Col. William D. James (Falls Church, VA: Office of the Surgeon General, U.S. Department of the Army, 1994), 55–68.

47. For a careful study of the determinants of readjustment difficulties, see Ginzberg et al., *Patterns of Performance,* vol. 3 of *The Ineffective Soldier,* 190–220.

Chapter 3

1. "Soldiers' Attitudes Toward Post-War Education," *Education for Victory: Official Bi-Weekly of the United States Office of Education* 2, 17 (1944): 1–6.

2. Veterans Administration chief Frank T. Hines predicted that 700,000 students—less than 5 percent of all service members—would attend college on the G.I. Bill; U.S. commissioner

of education Earl McGrath voiced an even more conservative figure of 640,000. Earl J. McGrath, "The Education of the Veteran," *Annals of the American Academy of Political and Social Science,* March 1945, 84; Keith Olson, *The G.I. Bill, the Veterans, and the Colleges* (Lexington: University Press of Kentucky, 1974), 30–31.

3. Office of War Mobilization and Reconversion, *The Veteran and Higher Education* (Washington, DC: GPO, 1946).

4. Stanley Frank, "The G.I.'s Reject Education," *Saturday Evening Post,* August 18, 1945, 20.

5. The director of war mobilization and reconversion, John W. Snyder, issued a new prediction that as many as 970,000 veterans would use the G.I. Bill to enroll in colleges and universities by fall 1946, and 160,000 veterans might seek vocational training. Office of War Mobilization and Reconversion, *The Veteran and Higher Education,* 10, 13.

6. U.S. Congress, Committee on Labor and Public Welfare, *Report on Education and Training Under the Servicemen's Readjustment Act, as Amended, from the Administrator of Veterans' Affairs* (Washington, DC: GPO, 1950), 34; U.S. President's Commission on Veterans' Pensions, *Veterans' Benefits in the United States* (Washington, DC: GPO, 1956), 288.

7. U.S. Congress, Committee on Labor and Public Welfare, *Report on Education and Training Under the Servicemen's Readjustment Act,* 35.

8. Ibid., 9.

9. U.S. President's Commission on Veterans' Pensions, *Veterans' Benefits in the United States,* 287.

10. Theda Skocpol, "Delivering for Young Families: The Resonance of the GI Bill," *American Prospect* 25 (1996): 66–73.

11. Francis J. Brown, *Educational Opportunities for Veterans* (Washington, DC: Public Affairs Press, 1946), 13.

12. Olson, *The G.I. Bill, the Veterans, and the Colleges,* 37.

13. For example, see Lizabeth Cohen, *A Consumers' Republic: The Politics of Mass Consumption in Postwar America* (New York: Alfred A. Knopf, 2003), 156–69, 167–70; David H. Onkst, "First a Negro . . . Incidentally a Veteran": Black World War II Veterans and the G.I. Bill of Rights in the Deep South, 1944–1948," *Journal of Social History* 31, 3 (1998): 517–43; Hilary Herbold, "Never a Level Playing Field: Blacks and the GI Bill," *Journal of Blacks in Higher Education* 6 (1994–95): 104–8; Karen Brodkin, *How Jews Became White Folks and What That Says About Race in America* (New Brunswick, NJ: Rutgers University Press, 1998), 39–44.

14. E.g., Thrainn Eggertsson, "Economic Aspects of Higher Education, Taken Under the World War II G.I. Bill of Rights," Ph.D. dissertation, Ohio State University, 1972; Charles B. Nam, "Impact of the 'G.I. Bills' On the Educational Level of the Male Population," *Social Forces* 43 (1964): 28; Cohen, *A Consumers' Republic,* 156 (Cohen draws on the study indirectly, citing Keith Olson's discussion of it; see Olson, *The G.I. Bill, the Veterans, and the Colleges,* 47). More infrequently, scholars rely on the study by R. J. Strom, *The Disabled College Veteran of World War II* (Washington, DC: American Council on Education, 1950), though it is hindered by similar problems to the Frederiksen-Schrader study; or Robert J. Havighurst, Walter H. Eaton, John W. Baughman, and Ernest W. Burgess, *The American Veteran Back Home: A Study of Veteran Readjustment* (New York: Longmans, Green, 1951), which is based only on a study of veterans in one locality, a small town in downstate Illinois.

15. Norman Frederiksen and W. B. Schrader, *Adjustment to College: A Study of 10,000 Veteran and Nonveteran Students in Sixteen American Colleges* (Princeton: Educational Testing Service, 1951), 310. Among the others, 60 percent of the veteran students reported that they would definitely have attended college without veterans' benefits, while slightly less than 20 percent reported they probably would have done so. A study of those listed in *Who's Who* found similar response rates to the same survey question, but also notes that "a sizable percentage would have had their education delayed 'a few years or longer' without the help of the program" and that "the [higher] education obtained under the GI Bill appears to have helped in increasing almost fourfold the number of those listed in *Who's Who* in the age group including all the veterans of World War II. See Amos Yoder, "Lessons of the GI Bill," *Phi Delta Kappan,* April 1963, 342–45. A poll at the University of Iowa, by contrast, found that 48 percent would not have come to college with the aid of the G.I. Bill. See "They Answer Some Questions," *Life* (April 21, 1947), p. 112.

16. The purpose of the Frederiksen-Schrader study was to examine questions about academic achievement of veterans compared to nonveterans, not to assess G.I. Bill usage, and thus it was not critical for the authors' mission to assemble a representative sample of G.I. Bill beneficiaries.

17. The authors do not identify the sixteen institutions but characterize them by region, by whether they were public or private, and by whether they were coeducational. From their description, it appears that junior colleges, teachers' colleges, business colleges, and other small, local colleges—popular choices among veterans, particularly those from less advantaged backgrounds—were omitted entirely. See Frederiksen and Schrader, *Adjustment to College*, 66–68; "Junior Colleges," *Occupations* 24 (1946): 368–69. Abiding by the wishes of the authors, the Educational Testing Service, which sponsored the study, still refuses to let the identities of the universities and colleges be known.

18. The authors reveal that responses from the institutions varied considerably, with much higher proportions at several institutions regarding the benefits as essential to their enrollment; whether these institutions might have been more illustrative of patterns in the general population is not discussed. Frederiksen and Schrader, *Adjustment to College*, 312. The study was conducted in 1946 and 1947, very soon after the end of war, and thus it likely oversampled more privileged veterans who were simply continuing degrees they had begun at their own expense before the war. Although overall enrollment levels peaked early, they dropped off slowly over the next several years, and veterans could begin their studies as late as July 1951; veterans who had never even considered a college education before were more likely to have been slower to enroll. See President's Commission on Veterans' Pensions, *Veterans' Benefits in the United States*, 288; Donald D. Steward and Richard Chambers, "The Status Background of the Veteran College Student" *Sociology and Social Research* 35 (1950): 13.

19. The question was, "Do you think you would have come to college after completing your military service if the financial aid provided by veterans' benefits had not been available to you?" See Frederiksen and Schrader, *Adjustment to College*, 310. As the authors themselves acknowledged, their survey asked only "whether or not the veteran would have attended college at all"; it neglected to ask more specifically "whether or not he would have chosen the particular college he was attending or whether or not he would have needed financial aid." Frederiksen and Schrader, *Adjustment to College*, 312.

20. Frederiksen and Schrader, *Adjustment to College*, 327.

21. Jacqueline E. King, *2000 Status Report on the Pell Grant Program* (Washington, DC: American Council on Education, 2000), 9–10, 19, 33.

22. See Appendix C.

23. Technically, disabled veterans were covered by Public Law 16, which extended education and training benefits comparable to those in the G.I. Bill. All survey questions were worded in this fashion, so the analysis includes beneficiaries of both policies. The discussion interprets the effects of both, though I refer to them in shorthand as "the G.I. Bill."

24. It should be noted that of the 716 survey respondents, 395 reported that they used the G.I. Bill for education or training and 255 reported that they did not. (Sixty-six failed to answer the question and were left out of subsequent analysis. Examination of the non-respondents and respondents reveals that they did not differ significantly; a report on this may be obtained from the author at sbmettle@maxwell.syr.edu.) Only those individuals who used the G.I. Bill for education or training were asked to respond to the questions discussed in this section. Respondents were given the option of answering "no opinion"; between thirty-three and sixty-three did so in the four questions discussed here.

25. Interestingly, theses responses, although higher than those obtained by Frederiksen and Schrader overall, appear to more closely resemble those obtained from students at selected schools, suggesting that those schools may have been more representative of veterans generally. Of course, the variation in question wording may also help explain the difference. See Frederiksen and Schrader, *Adjustment to College*, 312.

26. Finally, less than 3 percent of respondents flagged each of the following explanations for nonusage: they had never done well in school; the type of training they wanted was not available; they were unaware of the G.I. Bill; they planned to pursue education later; or they thought they were too old to return to school.

27. Others mentioned a range of factors: some remained in the military, so they did not have access to the G.I. Bill; injuries prevented others from attaining further education (one man wrote that he was "more concerned with adjusting to life after amputation of both legs"); and a few returned to jobs that they had held before the war.

28. I chose to use standard of living in the 1920s rather than in the 1930s because it was a more "normal" time and would be likely to indicate more about the persistent socioeconomic status of families than the Depression era, when so many fell into worse living conditions than they experienced generally. Notably, while standard of living is based on subjective judgments, scholars have found that most people perceive their socioeconomic status accurately. Answers to this survey question proved consistent with answers to related survey questions; also, in interviews, veterans offered reasonable justifications of why they gave the answers they did regarding socioeconomic background. In any case, as noted by Lester Milbrath and M. L. Goel, "subjective perception of class may be as significant, or more significant, an indication of behavioral predisposition than the person's 'objective' status." Lester W. Milbrath and M. L. Goel, *Political Participation: How and Why Do People Get Involved in Politics?* 2nd ed. (Chicago: Rand McNally College Publishing, 1977), 91. One reviewer questioned whether veterans' fathers' occupational status might serve as a more objective measure of class status. I had decided against this measure for a couple of reasons. First, scales of occupational status were developed by scholars primarily in the 1960s. In fact, they are a less direct measure than individuals' own perceptions and involve a greater amount of subjectivity, given that they are essentially scholars' assessments of society's views about individuals' status. Second, given that the status assigned to occupations changes with historical context, measures developed for the 1960s cannot be expected to offer accurate assessments of occupational status in the very different labor markets of the 1920s, the reference point for the parents' generation. Nonetheless, following a reviewer's request, I had two research assistants code the fathers' occupations according to a seven-point scale developed by August B. Hollingshead, "Two Factor Index of Social Position," New Haven, CT, 1957 (paper in author's possession), which I used on the recommendation of Richard Braungart, an expert on such scales. (For a fuller listing, see Chapter 5, note 54.) The intercoder reliability was low, 79 percent. I checked the 21 percent of the cases in which the coders disagreed and found that such instances presented highly ambiguous cases for which our data did not offer the level of detail necessary to make sound judgments: for example, in the case of farmers and owners of businesses, we did not know about the size and profitability of their enterprises; in the case of numerous categories of factory workers, we lacked a clear understanding of the degree of their supervisory capacity. This convinced me that it is more appropriate to use the standard-of-living variable than parents' occupational status. (Ironically, regression analysis conducted with the latter variable in place of the standard-of-living variable revealed the G.I. Bill to be even more significant in generating civic engagement than those featured in Chapter 6, though the R^2 figures were somewhat smaller.)

29. Given that parents' level of education might be considered a more objective measure of socioeconomic background than standard of living in childhood, I also examined veterans' use of the G.I. Bill according to their fathers' level of education. Notably, majorities of veterans from *every* category used the G.I. Bill for education.

30. Jerald G. Bachman, Patrick M. O'Malley, and Jerome Johnston, *Adolescence to Adulthood: Change and Stability in the Lives of Young Men* (Ann Arbor: Institute of Social Research, University of Michigan, 1978); R. Rehberg and E. Rosenthal, *Class and Merit in the American High School* (New York: Longman, 1978); W. H. Sewall and V. Shah, "Socioeconomic Status, Intelligence, and the Attainment of Higher Education," *Sociology of Education* 40 (1967): 1–23.

31. Statistical analysis allows us to do this, through procedures outlined in Appendix E.
32. See results in Appendix F, Table F.3.1, second column.
33. Rehberg and Rosenthal, *Class and Merit in the American High School.*
34. John S. Allen, "Anticipated Demands for Higher Education," *School and Society,* August 23, 1947, 141.
35. Neither veterans' religious denominations nor the fact of having immigrant parents proved to be significant determinants of which veterans used the G.I. Bill for higher education.
36. See Appendix F, Table F.3.1, first column.
37. Similarly, a study of applicants for vocational education programs under Public Law 16 found that the average applicant had 10.8 years of prior education. See Arthur H. Larsen, Harry D. Lovelass, and Lowell Walter, "Some Characteristics of Veterans Applying for Vocational Rehabilitation," *School and Society,* October 18, 1947, 300.
38. This has been suggested by Story, "Education and the Academy in the New Deal."
39. While there is a significant correlation between standard of living in the 1920s and level of education prior to military service, it is low; the same is true in the case of parents' level of education. For results, see Appendix F, Table F.3.2.
40. Claudia Goldin, "America's Graduation from High School: The Evolution and Spread of Secondary Schooling in the Twentieth Century," *Journal of Economic History* 58 (1998): 371.
41. See Appendix Table F.3.3.
42. Daniel O. Levine, *The American College and the Culture of Aspiration, 1915–1940* (Ithaca: Cornell University Press, 1986), chap. 7; Stephen Steinberg, *The Academic Melting Pot: Catholics and Jews in American Higher Education* (New York: McGraw-Hill, 1974); Marcia Graham Synnott, *The Half-Opened Door: Discrimination and Admissions at Harvard, Yale, and Princeton, 1900–1970* (Westport, CT: Greenwood Press, 1979); President's Commission on Higher Education, *Higher Education for Democracy,* vol. 1 (Washington, DC: GPO, 1947). Among nonblack respondents to the World War II Veterans Survey, nearly one-quarter of all Catholic respondents (24.1 percent) reported that they came from families that had a low standard of living while they were growing up in the 1920s; only 14 percent of Protestants and 17 percent of Jews responded similarly.
43. Synnott, *The Half-Opened Door,* 201, 204, 218, 231.
44. James Hennesey, SJ, *American Catholics: A History of the Roman Catholic Community in the United States* (New York: Oxford University Press, 1981), 283.
45. Among survey respondents, the G.I. Bill was used for education or training by 56 percent of Catholic veterans, 70 percent of Jewish veterans, and 62 percent of Protestant veterans. Among them, 53 percent of Jewish beneficiaries attended college, followed by 40 percent of Protestants, and 32 percent of Catholics.
46. Norval D. Glenn and Ruth Hyland, "Religious Preference and Worldly Success: Some Evidence from National Surveys," *American Sociological Review* 32, 1 (1967): 73–85.
47. Among nonblack male respondents to the World War II Veterans Survey, 57 percent of those with a parent born abroad used the education and training benefits, compared to 62 percent of those with both parents born in the United States.
48. The survey data do not allow us to specify the extent to which homosexual veterans may have benefited from the G.I. Bill. As of 1946, the government estimated that the Army had granted what were called "blue discharges" to five thousand individuals for reasons related to homosexuality, and the Navy to four thousand; this status, as we will see in Chapter 4, imperiled their opportunities to utilize the program benefits. See Margot Canaday, "Building the Straight State: Sexuality and Social Citizenship Under the 1944 G.I. Bill," *Journal of American History* 9, 3 (2003): note 7; Allan Bérubé, *Coming Out Under Fire: The History of Gay Men and Women in World War II* (New York: Free Press, 1990), 232. Nonetheless, the invisibility of most gay veterans, who went unrecognized unless officially "discovered" during military service, meant that they could still qualify for the G.I. Bill. The nine thousand who carried blue discharges for reasons related to homosexuality amounted to only .06 percent of all who served in the military. While the rate of homosexuality in the general population

remains difficult to measure, even by the most conservative contemporary assessments, in which 2 percent of all American adult men today identify themselves as gay, it would appear that over 144,000 gay male veterans of World War II may have utilized the G.I. Bill's education and training benefits. By such calculations, for every veteran denied the G .I. Bill for a sexuality-related blue discharge, sixteen others with homosexual inclinations may have benefited from it. This is based on estimates in Edward O. Laumann et al., *The Social Organization of Sexuality: Sexual Practices in the United States* (Chicago: University of Chicago Press, 1994). For a recent discussion of such figures based on Census and other data, see Gary J. Gates and Jason Ost, *The Gay and Lesbian Atlas* (Washington, DC: Urban Institute Press, 2004), chap. 3. Allan Bérubé notes that gay and lesbian veterans in the postwar era "took advantage of the GI Bill and the postwar prosperity to try to settle down as civilians into stable, secure lives and to fit into American society when and where they could," and cites examples of some who did. Bérubé, *Coming Out Under Fire,* 257; also see 244–45.

49. Understanding of how the benefits affected Latinos, Native Americans, and Asian Americans is sketchy as well, and too few members of each subgroup were reached in the World War II Veterans Survey to permit systematic analysis of their program usage rates. Evidently some Mexican Americans in Texas experienced delays initially in the processing of their benefits under the G.I. Bill; see Henry A. J. Ramos, *The American G.I. Forum: In Pursuit of the Dream, 1848–1983* (Houston, TX: Arte Publico Press, 1998), 2–3. In time, however, many did use the benefits, but we cannot specify how their usage rates compared to those of other groups. Manuel Servin, "The Post-World War II Mexican-American, 1925–1965," in Manuel Servin, comp., *The Mexican-Americans: An Awakening Minority* (Beverly Hills: Glencoe Press, 1970), 155; Armando M. Rodriguez, "Speak Up, Chicano: The Mexican-American Fights for Educational Equality," in John H. Burma, comp., *Mexican-Americans in the United States: A Reader* (Cambridge, MA: Schenkman Publishing, 1970), 137.

50. Reginald Wilson, "G.I. Bill Expands Access for African Americans," *Educational Record* 75 (1994): 32–39; Ronald Roach, "From Combat to Campus," *Black Issues in Higher Education,* August 21, 1997, 26–28.

51. Onkst, "First a Negro . . . Incidentally a Veteran"; Herbold, "Never a Level Playing Field: Blacks and the GI Bill," 104–8; Brodkin, *How Jews Became White Folks,* 39–44; Cohen, *A Consumers' Republic,* 167–70.

52. Recently, the most systematic analysis to date of the effects of the G.I. Bill on black Americans found that outside of the South, the program had a "substantial and positive impact" on raising educational levels among both blacks and whites, but it had little such impact on black men in the South. Sarah E. Turner and John Bound, "Closing the Gap or Widening the Divide: The Effects of the G.I. Bill and World War II on the Educational Outcomes of Black Americans," National Bureau of Economic Research Working Paper no. W9044, July 2002, http://www.nber.org/papers/w9044. Yet this study focuses only on effects for formal educational attainment, thus omitting attention to the subcollege programs, and it fails to illuminate the fundamental question of whether the G.I. Bill's benefits proved accessible to black veterans.

53. Author's telephone conversation with Celeste Torian, April 9, 2002.

54. Nationwide, 75 percent of nonwhites and 73 percent of whites used some form of G.I. Bill benefits; though usage ratios varied slightly by region, from 74 to 80 percent among nonwhites compared to 73 to 74 percent among whites, everywhere nonwhite usage surpassed that of whites. "Benefits and Services Received by World War II Veterans Under the Major Veterans Administration Programs," Research Division, Coordination Services, Veterans Administration, 13, RG 51, ser. 39.20a, box 9, NA.

55. U.S. Congress, Committee on Veterans' Affairs, "Readjustment Benefits: General Survey and Appraisal: A Report on Veterans' Benefits in the United States by the President's Commission on Veterans' Pensions," Staff Report no. IX, part A (Washington, DC: GPO, 1956), 72; also Veterans Administration, "Benefits and Services Received by World War II Veterans Under the Major Veterans Administration Programs," 13, 20, RG 51, ser. 39.20a, box 9, NA, as cited in Michael K. Brown, *Race, Money and the American Welfare State* (Ithaca: Cornell

University Press, 1999), 189–90. Also, see Turner and Bound, "Closing the Gap or Widening the Divide," 6, Table 2; see Eli Ginsberg and Douglas W. Bray, *The Uneducated* (New York: Columbia University Press, 1953), 126.

56. Paula S. Fass, *Outside In: Minorities and the Transformation of American Education* (New York: Oxford University Press, 1989), 141.

57. Turner and Bound, "Closing the Gap," 6.

59. Veterans Administration, Office of Controller, Reports and Statistics Service, *National Survey of Veterans* (Washington, DC: GPO, 1980); Turner and Bound, "Closing the Gap," Table 2, 32.

59. These results are shown in Appendix F, Table F.3.4. Given the smaller number of black veterans, a simpler version of the model of determinants of usage is used here. The purpose of this comparison is not to make estimates about the precise importance of a particular factor in the broader population, but rather to assess the significance of factors relative to one another. In performing this comparison, it is important to bear in mind that the black sample is not broadly representative of the original population, as discussed in Appendix D; interestingly, however, for the black sample, the level of education prior to joining the military is comparable to that of the nonblack sample used here, making for worthwhile comparisons.

Chapter 4

1. Eugene Bardach, *The Implementation Game* (Cambridge, MA: MIT Press, 1977); Evelyn Brodkin, "Implementation as Policy Politics," in *Implementation and the Policy Process: Opening up the Black Box,* ed. D. Palumbo and D. Calista (New York: Greenwood Press, 1990).

2. Martha Derthick, *Agency Under Stress: The Social Security Administration in American Government* (Washington, DC: Brookings Institution, 1990); Michael Lipsky, *Street Level Bureaucracy* (New York: Russell Sage, 1980); Jodi Sandfort, "The Structural Impediments to Human Service Collaboration," *Social Service Review* 73 (1999): 314–39; James Q. Wilson, *Bureaucracy: What Government Agencies Do and Why They Do It* (New York: Basic Books, 1989); Ann Chih Lin, *Reform in the Making: The Implementation of Social Policy in Prison* (Princeton, NJ: Princeton University Press, 2000); Dvora Yanow, *How Does a Policy Mean?* (Washington, DC: Georgetown University Press, 1996); Richard Elmore, "Backward Mapping: Implementation Research and Policy Decisions," *Political Science Quarterly* 94 (1980): 601–16; Daniel Mazmanian and Paul Sabatier, *Implementation and Public Policy* (Lanham: University Press of America, 1989); Helen Ingram, "Implementation: A Review and Suggested Framework," in *Public Administration: The State of the Discipline,* ed. Naomi B. Lynn and Aaron Wildavsky (Chatham, NJ: Chatham House Publishers, 1990),462–80. National policy makers' goals for programs they created may be rerouted when implementation is turned over to state or local governments or to private agencies, each with its own distinct political-institutional and political-economic constraints. See Jeffrey Pressman and Aaron Wildavsky, *Implementation* (Berkeley: University of California Press, 1979); Suzanne Mettler, *Dividing Citizens: Gender and Federalism in New Deal Public Policy* (Ithaca, NY: Cornell University Press, 1998).

3. A brilliant exception to this approach is Ann Chih Lin's *Reform in the Making.* Lin conducted extensive interviews not only with prison staff but also with prisoners themselves, and her analysis demonstrates how the imperatives of each group, as well as the interactive processes between them and the context of their local institution, all shape how implementation occurs. Also see Yanow, *How Does a Policy Mean?*

4. Letter, Thomas O. Woolf, advertising director, *American Legion* magazine, to Don, July 5, 1945, American Legion, G.I. Bill Correspondence, "U.S.—Manpower Benefits," Folder 9, National Headquarters of the American Legion, Indianapolis, Indiana [hereafter AL]; Kyle Crichton, "G.I. Bill of Complaints," *Collier's,* June 2, 1945,14–15ff.

5. Proceedings of the 26th national convention of the American Legion, Chicago, September 18–20, 1944, 79th Cong., 1st Sess., House Document no. 43 (Washington, DC: GPO, 1945), resolution no. 357, 117.

6. Letter from Edward N. Scheiberling, December 3, 1944, American Legion, G.I. Bill Correspondence, "U.S.—Manpower Benefits," Folder 8, AL.

7. Press release, American Legion, Washington, DC, April 24, 1945, American Legion, G.I. Bill Correspondence, "U.S. Manpower Benefits," Folder 8, AL. Other proposed changes included offering greater counseling to veterans to advise them how to use the G.I. Bill, and to offer full tuition for short, intensive courses.

8. President's Commission on Veteran's Pensions, "Readjustment Benefits: Education and Training, and Employment and Unemployment," staff report IX, part B, September 12, 1956, 84th Cong., 2nd Sess., House Committee print no. 291, 13–15.

9. George McMillan Fleming, "Historical Survey of the Educational Benefits Provided Veterans of World War II by the Servicemen's Readjustment Act of 1944," Ph.D. dissertation, University of Houston, June 1957, 82.

10. President's Commission on Veteran's Pensions, "Readjustment Benefits: General Survey and Appraisal," staff report no. IX, part A, September 11, 1956, 84th Cong., 2nd Sess., House Committee print no. 289, Appendix C, 305.

11. Ibid., 16.

12. Ibid., 10.

13. President's Commission on Veterans' Pensions, *Veterans' Benefits in the United States: Findings and Recommendations* (Washington, DC: GPO, 1956), 288.

14. Thomas F. Jordan, "How Many Wrongs Make a G.I. Bill of Rights?" *School and Society*, September 11, 1948, 161–64. Though the author worked for the Educational and Vocational Counseling Division, Advisement and Guidance Service of the Veterans Administration, he noted that the opinions expressed in the article were his own and not approved by the VA or offered in his capacity as a VA official.

15. Hearings Before the Special Subcommittee on Veterans' Education and Rehabilitation Benefits for the Committee on Labor and Public Welfare, United States Senate, 82nd Cong., 2nd Sess., on H.R. 7656, June 10–13 and 17, 1952, 22–23.

16. Fleming, "Historical Survey of the Educational Benefits," 82–83.

17. "Final Report on Educational Assistance to Veterans: A Comparative Study of Three G.I. Bills," submitted to the Committee on Veterans Affairs, United States Senate, 93rd Cong., 1st Sess., Senate Committee print no. 18, 1973, 247–50.

18. Fleming, "Historical Survey of the Educational Benefits," 87.

19. Veterans Administration, Office of Vocational Rehabilitation and Education, "Educational Opportunities for Veterans in Approved Institutions of Higher Education," April 15, 1946, Washington, DC.

20. Fleming, "Historical Survey of the Educational Benefits," 85–86.

21. "Vocational Rehabilitation and Education Program," Management Survey of Activities of the Veterans' Administration by the Firm of Booz-Allen-Hamilton," 82nd Cong., 2nd Sess., House Committee print no. 322, 8:826.

22. Robert M. Hutchins, "The Threat to American Education," *Collier's*, December 30, 1944, 21.

23. "The G.I. Bill: In 10 Years, 8 Million," *Newsweek*, October 4, 1954, 90.

24. See several pamphlets in Office of the Administrator, Pamphlets, 1946–1953, Box 1, RG 15, NA, including U.S. Veterans' Administration, "Benefits for World War II Veterans," Washington, DC, September 1947; Veterans Administration, "Your Answers About Education and Training," Washington, DC, revised June 1, 1948.

25. Veterans Administration, Office of Vocational Rehabilitation and Education, "Educational Opportunities for Veterans in Approved Institutions of Higher Education," April 15, 1946, Washington, DC.

26. U.S. Congress, Committee on Veterans' Affairs, "General Accounting Office Report of Survey—Veterans' Education and Training Program," report by the chief of investigations of the General Accounting Office, 82nd Cong., 1st Sess., 1951, House Committee print no. 160, 56.

27. U.S. Congress, House of Representatives, 79th Cong., 2nd Sess., "Investigations of the National War Effort," report issued by the Committee on Military Affairs, January 30, 1946, 2.

28. Allan Bérubé, *Coming Out Under Fire: The History of Gay Men and Women in World War II* (New York: Free Press, 1990), 230–32.

29. U.S. Congress, House of Representatives, 79th Cong., 2nd Sess., "Investigations of the National War Effort," report issued by the Committee on Military Affairs, January 30, 1946, 8, 9.

30. Bérubé, *Coming Out Under Fire*, 230; Margot Canaday, "Building a Straight State: Sexuality and Social Citizenship under the 1944 G.I. Bill," *Journal of American History* 90, 3 (2003).

31. "Readjustment Benefits: Education and Training," 24–25.

32. "Do the High Schools Want the Returning Veteran?" *The School Review,* June 1945, 338; Leslie L. Hanawalt, *A Place of Light: The History of Wayne State University* (Detroit: Wayne State University Press, 1968), 358; "High School Diplomas for Veterans," *School and Society,* December 6, 1947, 438–39.

33. "Adjustments of College Work to Veterans' Needs in New York State," *School and Society,* March 20, 1944, 358.

34. "The Colleges and Universities Plan for Returning Veterans," *School and Society,* March 11, 1944, 182; "Barnard College Plans for the Admission of Women Veterans," *School and Society,* December 1, 1945, 350–51.

35. "The Colleges and Universities Plan for Returning Veterans," *School and Society,* March 11, 1944, 182; David R. Dunigan, *A History of Boston College* (Milwaukee: Bruce, 1947), 303–4.

36. "Federal and State Aid to Veterans' Education," *The School Review,* October 1946, 443–44.

37. "Readjustment Benefits: Education and Training," 24–25.

38. Keith W. Olson, *The G.I. Bill, the Veterans and the Colleges* (Lexington: University Press of Kentucky, 1974), 43–44.

39. Al Sandvik, "The Legacy of the G.I. Bill," *Minnesota: Magazine of the University of Minnesota Alumni Association,* April 1999, 30.

40. Benjamin Fine, "Colleges Expect Peak Enrollment," *New York Times,* February 24, 1946.

41. The aim of this survey was not to gather a representative sample of all veteran college students, but rather to examine the experience of students in different institutional settings. Further, it should be noted that many of the schools were selected because they were known to have admitted a high proportion of veterans.

42. The average African American respondent to the Class of 1949 survey was one year younger than the average white respondent.

43. President's Commission on Veterans' Pensions, "Readjustment Benefits: General Survey and Appraisal," staff report IX, part A, 84th Cong., 2nd Sess., House Committee print no. 289, 72; U.S. Congress, Committee on Labor and Public Welfare, "Report on Education and Training Under the Servicemen's Readjustment Act, as Amended, from the Administrator of Veterans' Affairs," 81st Cong., 2nd Sess., House Committee print, map 8.

44. "Junior Colleges," *Occupations,* March 1946, 368–69.

45. "Classroom Changes: The University Has to Streamline Its Teaching Methods," *Life,* April 21, 1947, 111; Hanawalt, *A Place of Light,* 356.

46. This veteran was not a regular interview subject but rather participated in a focus group that completed an earlier draft of the World War II and Class of 1949 surveys, and then provided useful feedback about survey questions and format.

47. Judy Holmes, "Remembering the G.I. Bulge," *Syracuse Record,* June 2, 1997, 1.

48. In 1946, the Veterans' Educational Facilities Program permitted the transfer of another 5,920 structures to seven hundred benefiting colleges. States also made facilities available to expand their public institutions of higher education. "Federal and State Aid to Veterans' Education," 441–42; Olson, *The G.I. Bill, the Veterans and the Colleges,* 66–68; "Advance Release for Sunday a.m., January 26, 1947," War Assets Administration, Box 2, and letter, G. B. Erskine, Department of Labor, Washington, DC, to the governors of all states and territories, September 3, 1946, Box 2, and letter, J. W. Studebaker, U.S. Office of Education, Washington, DC, to the presidents of colleges and universities, August 5, 1946, Box 5, all in RG 12 (Records of the Veterans' Educational Facilities Program), NA; Lenette Sengel Tay-

lor, "Invasion of the Homefront: The Veterans at Arkansas State Teachers College, 1945–1949," *Arkansas Historical Quarterly* 47, 2 (1988): 116–36; Louis R. Wilson, *The University of North Carolina Under Consolidation, 1931–63: History and Appraisal* (Chapel Hill: University of North Carolina, 1964), 99–100.

49. Edwin Kiester Jr., "The G.I. Bill May Be the Best Deal Ever Made by Uncle Sam," *Smithsonian,* November 1994, 134.

50. Illinois eventually moved the Chicago branch from the military setting to permanent quarters in the city.

51. Regarding Penn State's efforts to handle the influx of veterans, see Michael Bezilla, *Penn State: An Illustrated History* (University Park: Pennsylvania State University Press, 1985), 204–31; *The Pennsylvania State University: A Century of Service to the Commonwealth: 1855–1955*, Pennsylvania State University pamphlet, 1955. In New York State, through a program operated by ten upstate colleges and universities, a new campus was opened at an abandoned Navy barracks at Sampson, followed by additional campuses at Plattsburgh and Utica; combined, these allowed the enrollment of an additional eleven thousand veterans. William Pearson Tolley, *At the Fountain of Youth: Memories of a College President* (Syracuse: Syracuse University Press, 1989), 87.

52. "Readjustment Benefits: Education and Training," 25.

53. "Veterans at College: They Go Back to Studies with Wives and Children," *Life,* January 7, 1946, 37–42.

54. "Veterans at College: They Have Swollen Enrollment and Changed Educational Habits at the University of Iowa," *Life,* April 21, 1947, 107. Also see Edith R. Mirrielees, *Stanford: The Story of a University* (New York: G. P. Putnam's Sons, 1959), 230–35.

55. Stephen E. Epler, "Do Veterans Make Better Grades than Nonveterans," *School and Society,* October 4, 1947, 270; "Data on Veterans Now Enrolled in Indiana University," *School and Society,* April 21, 1945, 245–46; Robert H. Faber and Lawrence Riggs, "Veterans in a Privately Endowed Liberal-Arts College—1946–1950," *School and Society,* August 12, 1950, 105–6; Clark Tibbitts and Woodrow W. Hunter, "Veterans and Non-Veterans at the University of Michigan," *School and Society,* May 10, 1947, 347–50. One study suggested that the difference in grades was attributable not to veteran status but to age, with older students generally earning better grades than younger students. Robert H. Schaffer, "A Note on the Alleged Superiority of Veterans," *School and Society,* March 13, 1948, 205.

56. "The G.I. Student Is Good," *Newsweek,* July 8, 1946, 82.

57. Gradually, universities were able to become far more selective in their admissions procedures than they had been previously. See Harold F. Williamson and Payson S. Wild, *Northwestern University: A History, 1850–1975* (Evanston, IL: Northwestern University, 1976), 224, 234; Christopher Jencks and David Riesman, *The Academic Revolution* (Chicago: University of Chicago Press, 1977), 281.

58. "End of an Era," *Time,* August 6, 1956, 44; also see Charles J. V. Murphy, "G.I.s at Harvard: They Are the Best Students in College's History," *Life,* June 17, 1946, 16–22.

59. Similar traditions disappeared on other campuses such as the freshman dink (skullcap or beanie) at UCLA and elsewhere, the freshman-sophomore mud fight at Cornell, and singing on the steps of Nassau Hall by seniors at Princeton. See "The G.I. Bill: In 10 Years, 8 Million," 88.

60. "Readjustment Benefits: Education and Training," 27–29; "The G.I. Bill: In 10 Years, 8 Million," 90; Lloyd C. Emmons, "College Curricula of World War II Veterans," *School and Society,* August 31, 1946, 152–53. Political scientists strategized about how best to make their field part of veterans' training. See John W. Manning, "Political Scientists and G.I. Education," *American Political Science Review* 39 (1945): 1002–5; "The Servicemen's Readjustment Act and Some Problems of Political Science Instruction," *American Political Science Review* 38 (1944): 762–65. Some critics had warned that the G.I. Bill would lead to a more practical emphasis in higher education: see "Bursars Rub Hands," 69; and Hutchins, "Threat to American Education." It is not clear that the G.I. Bill led to this shift, however, or whether changing economic forces of the mid-twentieth century played a greater role.

61. President's Commission on Veterans' Pensions, "Readjustment Benefits: General Survey and Appraisal," Part A, Table 24, 261.

62. This study was based on a data collected between 1994 and 2000. Shaena Engle, "College Completion Declining, Taking Longer, UCLA Study Shows," Higher Education Research Institute, http://www.gseis.ucla.edu/heri/darcu_pr.html.

63. B. S. Aaronson, "Lack of Money and the Veterans' Withdrawal from School," *School and Society,* January 8, 1949, 28–31.

64. Hanawalt, *A Place of Light,* 362.

65. Jordan, "How Many Wrongs Make a G.I. Bill of Rights?" 161–62.

66. Tyrus Hillway, "College Guidance Bureaus Can Be Made Self-Supporting," *School and Society,* February 9, 1946, 101–2; Byron Atkinson and Robert W. Webb, "Academic Success of Rehabilitation Veterans," *School and Society,* August 3, 1946, 87–88.

67. Frederick Gaudet, "The Veterans Administration Advisement and Guidance Program," *School and Society,* April 2, 1949, 253; Alva A. Gay and Harold D. Gales, "The Liberal-Arts Veterans Counselors' Office," *School and Society,* March 19, 1949, 209–12.

68. Gaudet, "The Veterans' Administration Advisement and Guidance Program," 252–53.

69. Daniel O. Levine, *The American College and the Culture of Aspiration, 1915–1940* (Ithaca: Cornell University Press, 1986), chap. 7; Stephen Steinberg, *The Academic Melting Pot: Catholics and Jews in American Higher Education* (New York: McGraw-Hill, 1974); President's Commission on Higher Education, *Higher Education for Democracy,* vol. 1 (Washington, DC: GPO, 1947); Marcia G. Synnott, "The Admission and Assimilation of Minority Students at Harvard, Yale and Princeton, 1900–1970," *The Social History of American Education* (Urbana: University of Illinois Press, 1988), 311–32.

70. Lawrence A. Cremin, *American Education: The Metropolitan Experience, 1876–1980* (New York: Harper and Row, 1988), 257.

71. Letter, Walter White, National Association for the Advancement of Colored People, to President Franklin D. Roosevelt, October 5, 1944, file "Colored Matters (Negroes), October–December 1944," Box 6, OF 93, FDR.

72. Telegram, Dr. Alonzo Myers, Donald DuShane, and Ralph McDonald to President Franklin Roosevelt, February 8, 1945, file "Education 1945," Box 5, OF 107, FDR.

73. President's Commission on Higher Education, *Higher Education for American Democracy,* especially 1:29–36.

74. On the decisions below and the extent to which they can be attributed to international conflict, see Mary L. Dudziak, *Cold War, Civil Rights: Race and the Image of American Democracy* (Princeton, NJ: Princeton University Press, 2000), 90–103.

75. *Sipuel v. Board of Regents,* 332 U.S. 631 (1948): 585–86.

76. *Sweatt v. Painter,* 339 U.S. 629 (1950).

77. Jean L. Preer, *Lawyers v. Educators: Black Colleges and Desegregation in Public Higher Education* (Westport, CT: Greenwood Press, 1982), 103.

78. *McLaurin v. Oklahoma,* 339 U.S. 637 (1950); Alfred H. Kelly, Winfred A. Harbison, and Herman Belz, *The American Constitution: Its Origins and Development,* 7th ed. (New York: W. W. Norton, 1991), 2:585–87.

79. *Brown v. Board of Education,* 347 U.S. 483 (1954).

80. Jencks and Riesman, *The Academic Revolution,* 280–81.

81. Synnott, "The Admission and Assimilation of Minority Students," 311–32.

82. Nicholas Lemann, *The Promised Land: The Great Black Migration and How it Changed America* (New York: Vintage, 1992).

83. Charles G. Bolte and Louis Harris, "Our Negro Veterans," Public Affairs Pamphlet no. 128 (New York: Public Affairs Committee, 1947), 4–5. Even higher rates of black veterans planned to migrate away from the South. See S. A. Stouffer et al., *The American Soldier: Adjustment During Army Life* (Princeton: Princeton University Press, 1949), 170.

84. Chas. H. Thompson, "The Critical Situation in Negro Higher and Professional Education," *Journal of Negro Education* 25 (1946): 579.

85. Wilson, "G.I. Bill Expands Access for African Americans," 37.

86. A complete listing with addresses appears in "Historically Black College and Universities Program," Department of the Treasury, Internal Revenue Service, Publication 1493, 21–25.

87. Martin D. Jenkins, "The Availability of Higher Education for Negroes in the Southern States," *The Journal of Negro Education* 26 (1947): 460.

88. George N. Redd, "Present Status of Negro Higher and Professional Education: A Critical Summary," *Journal of Negro Education* 27 (1948): 401–2.

89. James A. Atkins, "Negro Educational Institutions and the Veterans' Educational Facilities Program," *Journal of Negro Education* 27 (1948): 144–46.

90. Martin D. Jenkins, "Current Trends and Events of National Importance in Negro Education," *Journal of Negro Education* 25 (1946): 239; question mark in original.

91. Atkins, "Negro Educational Institutions," 146.

92. Olson, *The G.I. Bill, the Veterans, and the Colleges* (Louisville: University Press of Kentucky, 1974), 74–75.

93. Chas. H. Thompson, "Editorial Comment: The Critical Situation in Negro Higher and Professional Education," *Journal of Negro Education* 15 (1946): 581.

94. Roach, "From Combat to Campus," 2.

95. General Accounting Office, "General Accounting Office Report and Survey—Veterans' Education and Training Program," 82nd Cong., 1st Sess., 1951, House Committee print no. 160, 4–7, 70–81; "Readjustment Benefits: Education and Training," 24–30.

96. "Are the Veterans a Financial Burden?" *School and Society,* February 22, 1947, 136.

97. "Readjustment Benefits: Education and Training, and Employment and Unemployment," 24.

98. General Accounting Office, "General Accounting Office Report and Survey," 3. Emphasis mine.

99. Regina Werum, "Sectionalism and Racial Politics: Federal Vocational Policies and Programs in the Predesegregation South," *Social Science History* 21, 3 (1997): 399–453.

100. William Pyrle Dillingham, *Federal Aid to Veterans, 1917–1941* (Gainesville: University of Florida Press, 1952), 131–44.

101. Werum, "Sectionalism and Racial Politics," 408.

102. President's Commission on Veterans' Pensions, *Veterans' Benefits in the United States* (Washington, DC: GPO, 1956), 287.

103. Ibid., 289.

104. General Accounting Office, "General Accounting Office Report and Survey," 7; U.S. Congress, Committee on Labor and Public Welfare, "Report on Education and Training Under the Servicemen's Readjustment Act," 9.

105. Veterans Administration, "Protecting Veterans from 'Fake School,'" *Occupations,* December 1945, 137–38; U.S. Congress, Committee on Labor and Public Welfare, Hearings Before the Special Subcommittee on Veterans' Education and Rehabilitation, 22.

106. President's Commission on Veterans' Pensions, *Veterans' Benefits in the United States,* 290; "Readjustment Benefits: Education and Training," 55–61.

107. Amendments in 1948 granted the VA administrator authority to ban such courses from program coverage. U.S. General Accounting Office, "General Accounting Office Report and Survey," 85. Consideration of whether courses should be regarded as avocational or not is presented in Harry S. Belman, "Avocational Courses in the Veterans Training Program," *Industrial Arts and Vocational Education,* June 1948, 218–19.

108. A discussion of popular forms of training by region appears in "Vocations for Veterans," *Newsweek,* January 20, 1947, 89.

109. Though use of the G.I. Bill to complete high school is not examined here, educators made a concerted response to meet veterans' needs as older students returning to secondary school studies. The Veterans' Administration worked with local high schools to develop special, accelerated programs for veterans. See "High School Acceleration for Veterans," *School Life,* November 1945, 6; "Adult Education," *Survey,* July 1946, 190; "High School G.I.s," *Time,* September 3, 1945, 88–89; "Veteran Education," *School Life,* November 1946, 28–29; Ivan Gustafson, "Educator's Idealism vs. Veteran's Realism," *Education* 67, 1 (1946): 55–56.

110. "Readjustment Benefits: Education and Training," 62; also see 36.

111. General Accounting Office, "General Accounting Office Report and Survey," 85.

112. See the detailed, extensive list of such abuses in "Appendix D. Typical Examples of Problems Confronted by the Veterans' Administration in Its Relationship with Educational Institutions," U.S. Congress, Committee on Labor and Public Welfare, "Report on Education and Training Under the Servicemen's Readjustment Act, as Amended," 81st Cong., 2nd Sess., 1950, 114–61.

113. Federal disapproval of such practices is evident in U.S. Congress, Committee on Labor and Public Welfare, "Report on Education and Training Under the Servicemen's Readjustment Act, as Amended from the Administrator of Veterans' Affairs," 1950, Appendix E.

114. Ibid., 162–99.

115. Various institutions took the VA's chief administrator to court, claiming that he lacked the authority to make such determinations. In response, Congress established new statutory powers for administrators through P.L. 266, enacted in 1949. "Readjustment Benefits: Education and Training," 36.

116. "Veterans: Training Swindle," *Newsweek,* August 19, 1946, 26–27.

117. "Readjustment Benefits: Education and Training," 47; for recommendations about acceptable procedures, see "On-the-Job Training for the Veteran," *Occupations,* January 1946, 237–42; Harry S. Belman, "Related Training for Veterans in On-Job-Training Programs," *Industrial Arts and Vocational Education* Vol. 38 (January 1949),13–15.

118. David H. Onkst, "First a Negro . . . Incidentally a Veteran": Black World War II Veterans and the G.I. Bill of Rights in the Deep South, 1944–1948," *Journal of Social History* 31, 3 (1998): 523–29; Bolte and Harris, "Our Negro Veterans," 13–15.

119. "Not for Presidents' Sons," *Time,* July 29, 1946, 76–77; "Readjustment Benefits: Education and Training," 47; "On-the-Job Training," *The New Republic,* September 9, 1946, 276–77; "Veterans: Training Swindle," 27.

120. "Training Veterans to Be Farmers: Discussion at Meeting of Federal Advisory Board for Vocational Education," *School Life,* April 1946, 16–17; "Readjustment Benefits: Education and Training," 51–54; General Accounting Office, "General Accounting Office Report and Survey," 158–82. Regarding program plans, see "Institutional On-Farm Training," *Army Times Reports,* May 1948, 1–3, American Legion, Folder #10, AL.

121. Paula S. Fass, *Outside In: Minorities and the Transformation of American Education* (New York: Oxford University Press, 1989), 148–49; Bolte and Harris, "Our Negro Veterans," 14–15; William Caudill, "Negro Veterans Return," *A Monthly Summary of Events and Trends in Race Relations,* August–September 1945, 14–17.

122. "Readjustment Benefits: Education and Training," 42.

123. Letter, Edward J. O'Connell to Mr. Keith Kreul, national commander, American Legion, June 10, 1985, American Legion, Folder #2, AL.

124. President's Commission on Veteran's Pensions, *Veterans' Benefits in the United States,* 289–91.

125. Paul Pierson, "When Effect Becomes Cause," *World Politics* 45 (1993): 595–628; Douglas Arnold, *The Logic of Congressional Action* (New Haven: Yale University Press, 1990), 47–51.

126. This interview question was asked prior to any questions mentioning the G.I. Bill.

Chapter 5

1. Glen H. Elder Jr., "Military Times and Turning Points in Men's Lives," *Developmental Psychology* 22 (1986): 233–45; Glen H. Elder Jr., Cynthia Gimbel, and Rachel Ivie, "Turning Points in Life: The Case of Military Service and War," *Military Psychology* 3 (1991): 215–31.

2. Elder, "Military Times and Turning Points in Men's Lives"; Roger D. Little and J. Eric Fredland, "Veteran Status, Earnings, and Race: Some Long Term Results," *Armed Forces and Society* 5, 2 (1979): 244–60; Wayne J. Villemez and John D. Kasarda, "Veteran Status and Socioeconomic Achievement," *Armed Forces and Society* 2, 3 (1976): 407–20; Yu Xie, "The Socioeconomic Status of Young Male Veterans, 1964–1984," *Social Science Quarterly* 73

(1992): 379–96; Harley L. Browning, Sally C. Lopreato, and Dudley L. Poston Jr., "Income and Veteran Status: Variations Among Mexican Americans, Blacks, and Anglos," *American Sociological Review* 38 (1973): 74–85; John Modell, Marc Goulden, and Sigurdur Magnusson, "World War II in the Lives of Black Americans: Some Findings and an Interpretation," *Journal of American History* (1989): 838–48; Melanie Martindale and Dudley L. Poston Jr., "Variations in Veteran/Nonveteran Earnings Patterns Among World War II, Korea, and Vietnam War Cohorts," *Armed Forces and Society* 5, 2 (1979): 219–43; Veterans Administration, Office of Reports and Statistics, *Survey of Aging Veterans: A Study of the Means, Resources, and Future Expectations of Veterans Aged 55 and Over,* study no. 823006 (Washington, DC: U.S. GPO, 1984), 15–17; U.S. Congress, House of Representatives, Committee on Veterans' Affairs, *Readjustment Benefits: General Survey and Appraisal* (Washington, DC: GPO, 1956), 117–23.

3. Asked to rank the events they had selected as turning points, users of either program type gave the G.I. Bill a mean ranking of third in a list of seven options that included one factor they named themselves.

4. The literature is vast, but for the most recent and complex general model, one that probes the dynamics underlying how socioeconomic factors facilitate political participation, see Sidney Verba, Kay Lehman Schlozman, and Henry E. Brady, *Voice and Equality: Civic Voluntarism in American Politics* (Cambridge, MA: Harvard University Press, 1995).

5. See M. Kent Jennings and Richard G. Niemi, *Generations and Politics* (Princeton, NJ: Princeton University Press, 1981), chap. 8; Raymond E. Wolfinger and Steven J. Rosenstone, *Who Votes?* (New Haven, CT: Yale University Press, 1980), 17–24.

6. Verba, Schlozman, and Brady, *Voice and Equality* (Cambridge: Harvard University Press, 1995).

7. Adriana Lleras-Muney, "The Relationship Between Education and Adult Mortality in the United States," NBER Working Paper Series no. 8986, June 2002, http://www.nber.org/papers/w8986; Michael Grossman and Robert Kaestner, "Effects of Education on Health," and Rebecca A. Maynard and Daniel J. McGrath, "Family Structure, Fertility, and Child Welfare," in *Social Benefits of Education,* ed. Jere R. Behrman and Nevzer Stacey (Ann Arbor: University of Michigan Press, 1997), 69–124, 125–74.

8. Donald D. Stewart and Richard P. Chambers, "The Status Background of the Veteran College Student," *Sociology and Social Research* 35 (1950): 12–21.

9. John Bound and Sarah Turner, "Going to War and Going to College: Did World War II and the G.I. Bill Increase Educational Attainment for Returning Veterans?" National Bureau of Economic Research, Working Paper 7452, December 1999, available at http://www.nber.org/papers/w7452, 3; Carl Curtis Brown, "An Economic Analysis of the G.I. Bill Educational Benefits: A Study of Korean and Post-Korean Veterans," Ph.D. dissertation, Oklahoma State University, 1979, 68.

10. J. Bachman, P. O'Malley, and J. Johnston, *Adolescence to Adulthood: Change and Stability in the Lives of Young Men* (Ann Arbor: Institute of Social Research, University of Michigan, 1978); R. Rehberg and E. Rosenthal, *Class and Merit in the American High School* (New York: Longman, 1978); W. H. Sewall and V. Shah, "Socioeconomic Status, Intelligence, and the Attainment of Higher Education," *Sociology of Education* 40 (1967): 1–23. The only variables for which either type of study is able to control are those such as age, level of education prior to joining the military, region of birth, race, officer status, and employment status prior to military service, several of which are extraneous to educational attainment. See Joshua D. Angrist, "The Effect of Veterans Benefits on Education and Earnings," *Industrial and Labor Relations Review* 46 (1993): 637–52; Brown, "An Economic Analysis of the G.I. Bill Educational Benefits"; Thrainn Eggertsson, "Economic Aspects of Higher Education Taken Under the World War II G.I. Bill of Rights," Ph.D. dissertation, Ohio State University, 1972.

11. These studies are hindered by data that do not include measures of such factors. Some rely on decennial Census data and compare educational levels of all males of the same cohort, including veterans and nonveterans. See Bound and Turner, "Going to War and Going to

College." Because the Census does not include data on G.I. Bill usage, these studies are based on the assumption that any education attained by veterans after the time of military service was financed by the G.I. Bill. While this is not an unreasonable solution to data limitations, it offers a somewhat crude measure of G.I. Bill usage. Others use surveys of veterans commissioned by the Veterans Administration to compare levels of education among veterans who used the G.I. Bill with those who did not. See Brown, "An Economic Analysis of the G.I. Bill Educational Benefits"; Eggertsson, "Economic Aspects of Higher Education"; and Angrist, "The Effect of Veterans' Benefits."

12. This survey was carried out in conjunction with the March demographic supplement to the Current Population Survey. It lacks specific indicators about G.I. Bill usage. Neil Fligstein, "The G.I. Bill: Its Effects on the Educational and Occupational Attainments of U.S. Males: 1940–1973," CDE Working Paper 76-9, Center for Demography and Ecology, University of Wisconsin, Madison, 1976.

13. Jere R. Behrman, Robert A. Pollak, and Paul Taubman, "Family Resources, Family Size, and Access to Financing for College Education," *Journal of Political Economy* 97, 2 (1989).

14. While these studies offer the best estimates we have, even they had some limitations. The Fligstein study was unable to actually control for G.I. Bill usage and lacked attention to socialization factors. The twin study approach used by Behrman and his associates alleviates such problems but introduces others, as the authors themselves acknowledge (Behrman, Pollak, and Taubman, "Family Resources, Family Size, and Access to Financing for College Education," 400).

15. In examining the determinants of educational attainment, ordinary least-squares regression is used. The dependent variable, level of education, is measured on a scale ranging from elementary school to advanced graduate work (1 to 9). We can control for several other factors: year of birth, level of education prior to military service, having at least one foreign-born parent, parents' level of education, standard of living in childhood (1920s), encouragement to pursue an education while growing up, and three religious background variables. See Appendix E for descriptions of each, and Appendix F.5.1 for regression results. In order to assess whether these exercises might involve a high degree of multicollinearity, I conducted collinearity diagnostics. These revealed that multicollinearity was not a problem: tolerance statistics were high, indicating low R^2s such that individual variables do not explain variation in other variables. The highest R^2s, neither high enough to present concerns, were for the variable Jewish, .29, and parents foreign born, .28.

16. Paul C. Glick and Hugh Carter, "Marriage Patterns and Educational Level," *American Sociological Review* 23 (1958): 294–300; Keith Olson, *The G.I. Bill, the Veterans, and the Colleges* (Lexington: University Press of Kentucky, 1974).

17. Norman H. Nie, Jane Junn, and Kenneth Stehlik-Barry, *Education and Democratic Citizenship in America* (Chicago: University of Chicago Press, 1996).

18. Kenneth A. Felman and Theodore M. Newcomb, *The Impact of College on Students*, 2nd ed. (New Brunswick, NJ: Transaction, 1994), 326.

19. Such outcomes were not unexpected given that those who served in the military are known to have come from slightly more privileged backgrounds than the rest of their cohort. President's Commission on Veterans' Pensions, "Readjustment Benefits: General Survey and Appraisal," 109–11; U.S. Congress, House of Representatives, Committee on Veterans' Affairs, "Readjustment and Training, and Employment and Unemployment," staff report IX, part B, 110–14. One study includes a more careful treatment of veteran G.I. Bill users versus nonusers and differentiates veterans by level of education prior to military service and whether they were employed prior to military service. U.S. Congress, House of Representatives, Committee on Veterans' Affairs, "Readjustment Benefits: General Survey and Appraisal," 112–15. Because both studies lacked an adequate manner of controlling for background characteristics, such as parents' occupational status, neither was able to explain whether the educational attainment facilitated by the G.I. Bill boosted occupational status.

20. Verba, Schlozman, and Brady, *Voice and Equality*, 314–15.

21. The premise of this literature, as articulated by Peter Blau and Otis Duncan, is that "occupational position does not encompass all aspects of the concept of class, but it is probably the best single indicator of it." Peter M. Blau and Otis Dudley Duncan, *The American Occupational Structure* (New York: John Wiley and Sons, 1967), 6; see also Albert J. Reiss Jr., *Occupations and Social Status* (New York: Free Press of Glencoe, 1961); Michael D. Ornstein, *Entry into the American Labor Force* (New York: Academic Press, 1976); David L. Featherman and Robert M. Hauser, *Opportunity and Change* (New York: Academic Press, 1978); Otis Dudley Duncan, David L. Featherman, and Beverly Duncan, *Socioeconomic Background and Achievement* (New York: Seminar Press, 1972). Others examined the concept of occupational prestige: Robert W. Hodge, Paul M. Siegel, and Paul H. Rossi, "Occupational Prestige in the United States, 1925–63," *American Journal of Sociology* 70, 3 (1964): 286–302. A more recent study that casts doubt on earlier work is Robert John Warren and Robert M. Hauser, "Social Stratification Across Three Generations: New Evidence from the Wisconsin Longitudinal Study," *American Sociological Review* 62 (1997): 561–72.

22. Christopher Jencks et al., *Who Gets Ahead? The Determinants of Economic Success in America* (New York: Basic Books, 1979), 213.

23. William E. Leuchtenburg, *A Troubled Feast: American Society Since 1945* (Boston: Little, Brown, 1973), 48; Carl Solberg, *Riding High: America in the Cold War* (New York: Mason and Lipscomb, 1973), 248–49; Frederick F. Siegel, *Troubled Journey: From Pearl Harbor to Ronald Reagan* (New York: Hill and Wang, 1984), 107.

24. Featherman and Hauser, *Opportunity and Change,* 481.

25. To name a few, the Duncan Socioeconomic Index accounts for income, education, and prestige; the Siegel (NORC) Prestige Scales are based on survey respondents' perceptions of the degree of prestige attached to particular types of employment; and the Hollingshead's Two Factor Index of Social Position includes a detailed system for ranking different kinds of professional and distinguishing businesses on the basis of their size and economic viability. For a valuable summary, see Delbert C. Miller, *Handbook of Research Design and Social Measurement,* 5th ed. (Newbury Park, CA: Sage Publications, 1991). Also see Duncan, Featherman, and Duncan, *Socioeconomic Background and Achievement,* 69–74; David L. Featherman, Michael Sobel, and David Dickens, "A Manual for Coding Occupations and Industries into Detailed 1970 Categories and a Listing of 1970-Basis Duncan Socioeconomic and NORC Prestige Scores," CDE Working Paper 75-1, Center for Demography and Ecology, University of Wisconsin, Madison; Bureau of the Census, "Methodology and Scores of Socioeconomic Status," Working Paper no. 15, 1963. I am indebted to Richard Braungart for acquainting me with this literature.

26. Neil Fligstein, "The G.I. Bill: Its Effects on the Educational and Occupational Attainments of U.S. Males: 1940–1973," CDE Working Paper 76-9, Center for Demography and Ecology, University of Wisconsin, Madison, 36.

27. Sampson and Laub, "Socioeconomic Achievement in the Life Course of Disadvantaged Men."

28. Occupational status groupings designed by August Hollingshead help illuminate this process. The Hollingshead Two Factor Index of Social Position bases scores on a combination of the occupational role, the degree of skill and power associated with it, and the amount of education required for the job. The occupational scale includes seven levels, from lowest to highest: unskilled employees; machine operators and semiskilled employees; skilled manual employees; clerical and sales workers, technicians, and owners of little businesses; administrative personnel, owners of small independent businesses, and minor professionals; business managers, proprietors of medium-sized businesses, and lesser professionals; higher executives, proprietors of large concerns, and major professionals. August B. Hollingshead, "Two Factor Index of Social Position," New Haven, CT, 1957, paper in author's possession. Farmers are ranked throughout the scale depending on the value of their operation, tenant farmers are ranked as skilled or semiskilled depending on the amount of equipment they own, and sharecroppers are classified as unskilled. I use the Hollingshead scale in a qualitative fashion, to detect overarching patterns. I consider the process involved in assigning numerical ranks to particular occupations to be risky given that occupational prestige is difficult

to assess, level of education and income and prestige are not related in the same manner for all occupations, and such rankings are likely to vary tremendously with historical context and the state of the political economy. Though some measures proceed on the simple assumption that years of education and income are related, this need not be the case, as evidenced by the disparity in pay between college faculty with doctorates, for example, and business executives holding master's degrees; nonetheless, both are classified in the same manner. The labor market, furthermore, exists in a state of considerable flux. As our earlier discussion of income made clear, incomes of various occupations vary over time, contingent upon the historical political-economic context. A high-status job in one era is not necessarily a high-status job in another era. Given these difficulties, it is not surprising that the occupational codes vary considerably from one scale to another. Economists, for example, earn a high score, 95, from the Nam-Powers Socioeconomic Status Scores, but only a 74.4 on Duncan's Socioeconomic Index and a lowly 53.6 on the Siegel Prestige Scale. Similarly, the rankings for electric power linemen and cablemen fluctuate between 75 and 39 across the same scales, and those for sheriffs from 34 to 72. Miller, *Handbook of Research Design,* 341–50.

29. Because the data are already arranged randomly, I simply chose every fifteenth respondent in the case of the nonusers and higher education users, and every eighth respondent in the case of the vocational education users. Where data were missing, I proceeded to the next case.

30. On the expansion of private benefits at midcentury, see Jacob Hacker, *The Divided Welfare State: The Battle over Public and Private Social Benefits in the United States* (Cambridge: Cambridge University Press, 2002); Marie Gottschalk, *The Shadow Welfare State: Labor, Business, and the Politics of Health Care in the United States* (Ithaca, NY: Cornell University Press, 2000).

31. This interpretation differs from that of Lizabeth Cohen, who argues that the subcollege programs gained veterans only "better-paid working class jobs, not middle class ones." Lizabeth Cohen, *A Consumers' Republic: The Politics of Mass Consumption in Postwar America* (New York: Alfred A. Knopf, 2003), 157.

32. Fuller treatment of occupational status effects among African American veterans appears in Suzanne Mettler, "'The Only Good Thing Was the G.I. Bill': Effects of the Education and Training Provisions on African American Veterans' Political Participation," *Studies in American Political Development* 19, 1 (2005).

33. Philip A. Klinkner with Rogers M. Smith, *The Unsteady March: The Rise and Decline of Racial Equality in America* (Chicago: University of Chicago Press, 1999), 191–92.

34. Black family incomes did rise in relation to white family income during the later 1960s and early 1970s, as noted by Michael C. Dawson, *Behind the Mule: Race and Class in African-American Politics* (Princeton, NJ: Princeton University Press, 1994), 19.

35. These results cohere with scholars' findings about occupational change across generations of men from the early twentieth century through the postwar era but point to the significance of the G.I. Bill in generating such outcomes. As noted by David L. Featherman and Robert M. Hauser (*Opportunity and Change,* 481): "In intergenerational patterns of occupational change we noted a weaker tendency for sons to have current occupations like those of their fathers. Across successive cohorts, educational attainments became more equally distributed and varied less systematically by socioeconomic background. Historical disadvantages suffered by blacks and farm-reared men in the attainment of education and occupational status have moderated."

36. Browning, Lopreato, and Poston, "Income and Veteran Status"; Xie, "The Socioeconomic Status of Young Male Veterans, 1964–1984"; Martindale and Poston, "Variations in Veteran/Nonveteran Earnings Patterns"; Villemez and Kasarda, "Veteran Status and Socioeconomic Attainment." A shortcoming of such studies is that World War II soldiers tended to be slightly more advantaged to begin with than those who were not in the military, so the two groups are not really comparable. Also, although the benefits for white veterans continued after the creation of the all-volunteer force, the value added for blacks and Hispanics seemed to disappear. See Robert L. Phillips, Paul J. Andrisani, Thomas N. Daymont, and

Curtis L. Gilroy, "The Economic Returns to Military Service: Race-Ethnic Differences," *Social Science Quarterly* 73, 2 (June 1992): 340–59; also Jay D. Teachman and Vaughn R. A. Call, "The Effect of Military Service on Educational, Occupational and Income Attainment," *Social Science Research* 25 (1996): 1–31.

37. Some studies of veterans of later wars do control for background characteristics and the G.I. Bill's educational and training programs and find the latter to be significant in elevating incomes. Dave M. O'Neill, "Voucher Funding of Training Programs: Evidence from the G.I. Bill," *Journal of Human Resources* 12, 4 (1977): 425–45; Robert J. Sampson and John H. Laub, "Socioeconomic Achievement in the Life Course of Disadvantaged Men: Military Service as a Turning Point, Circa 1940–1965," *American Sociological Review* 61 (1996): 347–67; Angrist, "The Effect of Veterans Benefits on Education and Earnings."

38. Verba, Schlozman, and Brady, *Voice and Equality*, 149–50, 188–91, 364, 493.

39. Claudia Goldin and Lawrence F. Katz, "The Returns to Skill in the United States Across the Twentieth Century," NBER Working Paper Series no. 7126, May 1999.

40. Claudia Goldin, "Egalitarianism and the Returns to Education During the Great Transformation of American Education," *Journal of Political Economy* 107 (1999): S65–S92.

41. Claudia Goldin and Robert A. Margo, "The Great Compression: The Wage Structure in the United States at Mid-Century," *Quarterly Journal of Economics* 107 (1992): 1–34; Suzanne Mettler, *Dividing Citizens: Gender and Federalism in New Deal Public Policy* (Ithaca: Cornell University Press, 1998), chap. 9.

42. Goldin and Margo, "The Great Compression," 4. For a treatment focusing on the postwar years, see Herman P. Miller, *Income Distribution in the United States: A 1960 Census Monograph* (Washington, DC: GPO, 1966), chap. 6.

43. President's Commission on Veterans' Pensions, "Readjustment Benefits: General Survey and Appraisal," staff report no. IX, Part A, September 11, 1956, 84th Cong., 2nd Sess., House Committee print no. 289, 126.

44. Ibid., 126–29.

45. Karen Anderson, *Wartime Women: Sex Roles, Family Relations, and the Status of Women During World War II* (Westport, CT: Greenwood, 1981); Susan M. Hartmann, *The Home Front and Beyond: American Women in the 1940s* (Boston: Twayne, 1982).

46. For an in-depth twin study of World War II veterans that evaluates the rate of return on education in terms of earnings, see Paul Taubman and Terence Wales, *Higher Education and Earnings: College as an Investment and a Screening Device* (New York: McGraw-Hill, 1974).

47. Miller, *Income Distribution in the United States*, 145–46.

48. Goldin and Katz, "The Returns to Skill in the United States"; Bennett Harrison and Barry Bluestone, *The Great U-Turn: Corporate Restructuring and the Polarizing of America* (New York: Basic Books, 1988); Bennett Harrison and Barry Bluestone, *The Deindustrialization of America* (New York: Perseus, 1984); Census Bureau, "Historical Income Tables: People," Table P-17, "Years of School Completed—People 25 Years Old and Over by Median Income and Sex: 1958 to 1990," http://www.census.gov/hhes/income/histinc/p17.htm.

49. Regression analysis of the determinants of income in 1960 reveals that level of education is significant (β coefficient, .15, $p < .01$), but the model is relatively weak (adjusted R^2, .04). By 1997, however, level of education is highly significant (β coefficient, .51, $p < .001$) and the model is quite powerful (adjusted R^2, .29). Use of the G.I. Bill for education is not significant in either model.

50. Richard O. Davies, *Housing Reform During the Truman Administration* (Columbia: University of Missouri Press, 1966); Elaine Tyler May, *Homeward Bound: American Families in the Cold War Era* (New York: Basic Books, 1988), 169.

51. Stephanie Coontz, *The Way We Never Were: American Families and the Nostalgia Trap* (New York: Basic Books, 1992), 77.

52. Kenneth T. Jackson, *Crabgrass Frontier: The Suburbanization of the United States* (New York: Oxford University Press, 1985), 205.

53. Census Bureau, "Historical Census of Housing Tables, Homeownership," http://www.census.gov/hhes/www/housing/census/historic.owner.html.

54. Verba, Schlozman, and Brady, *Voice and Equality*, 452–55; Robert Putnam, *Bowling Alone: The Collapse and Revival of American Community* (New York: Simon and Schuster, 2000), 93–95; Edward L. Glaeser and Jesse M. Shapiro, "The Benefits of the Home Mortgage Interest Deduction," NBER Working Paper no. W9284, October 2002, http://papers.nber.org/papers/W9284.

55. See Appendix F, Table F.5.2. The loan guarantee provisions did emerge as a significant and positive influence on home ownership when controlling for these other factors, suggesting that it had redistributive effects independent of the educational and training provisions. Analysis of the World War II Veterans Survey shows home ownership to be unrelated to use of the G.I. Bill for education, level of education, and income in 1960.

56. Committee on Veterans' Affairs, "Veterans' Loan Guaranty and Direct Loan Benefits," President's Commission on Veterans' Pensions, 84th Cong., 2nd Sess., 1956, House Committee print no. 270, 2.

57. President's Commission on Veterans' Pensions, *Veterans' Benefits in the United States* (Washington, DC: GPO, 1956), 301.

58. According to the World War II Veterans Survey, the correlation between use of the educational benefits of the G.I. Bill and the home mortgage loans was −.03, and insignificant (p < .10; 543 cases).

59. For this information, I am indebted to David Wheelock; also see "The Report of the Commission on Mortgage Interest Rates to the President of the United States and to the Congress," August 1969.

60. President's Commission on Veterans' Pensions, *Veterans' Benefits in the United States,* 303–4; Kyle Crichton, "G.I. Bill of Complaints," *Collier's,* June 2, 1945, 13–15, 72.

61. David H. Onkst, "First a Negro . . . Incidentally a Veteran": Black World War II Veterans and the G.I. Bill of Rights in the Deep South, 1944–1948," *Journal of Social History* 31, 3 (1998): 522–23.

62. Jackson, *Crabgrass Frontier,* 197–215.

63. Evidence of such discrimination is apparent in records from the last 1940s included in the collection of the National Association for the Advancement of Colored People, Library of Congress, Washington, DC.

64. Herbert J. Gans, *The Levittowners: Ways of Life and Politics in a New Suburban Community* (New York: Pantheon, 1967), chap. 1; Jackson, *Crabgrass Frontier,* 237–38.

65. Gans, *The Levittowners,* chaps. 3–5; John R. Seeley, R. Alexander Sim, and Elizabeth W. Loosely, *Crestwood Heights: A Study of Culture of Suburban Life* (New York: Basic Books, 1956), chap. 10.

66. The correlation between use of the loan guarantee program and suburban residence in 1960, while very significant, was low (.11, p < .01, N = 564), and between use of the educational benefits and suburban residence was less significant and also low (.09, p < .05, N = 543).

67. Nicholas Lemann, *The Promised Land: The Great Black Migration and How it Changed America* (New York: Vintage, 1992).

68. Jackson, *Crabgrass Frontier,* 238–42; Douglas S. Massey and Nancy A. Denton, *American Apartheid: Segregation and the Making of the Underclass* (Cambridge: Harvard University Press, 1998).

69. J. Eric Oliver, *Democracy in Suburbia* (Princeton, NJ: Princeton University Press, 2001); Robert D. Putnam, *Bowling Alone: The Collapse and Revival of American Community* (New York: Simon and Schuster, 2000), 204–15.

70. David J. O'Brien, *The Renewal of American Catholicism* (New York: Oxford University Press, 1972), 6, 22, 115, 131; James Hennesey, SJ, *American Catholics: A History of the Roman Catholic Community in the United States* (New York: Oxford University Press, 1981), 283; on general trends (though without analysis of the G.I. Bill), see Norval D. Glenn and Ruth Hyland, "Religious Preference and Worldly Success: Some Evidence from National Surveys," *American Sociological Review* 32, 1 (1967): 73–85.

71. On New Deal social programs, see Robert C. Lieberman, *Shifting the Color Line: Race and the American Welfare State* (Cambridge, MA: Harvard University Press, 1998).

72. This phenomenon is verified by John R. Emens, "Education Begets Education: The G.I. Bill Twenty Years Later," *American Education* 1, 6 (1965): 11–13.

Chapter 6

1. Sidney Verba, Kay Lehman Schlozman, and Henry E. Brady, *Voice and Equality: Civic Voluntarism in American Politics* (Cambridge, MA: Harvard University Press, 1995), chap. 15.

2. The measurements of each variable are as follows: standard of living in childhood during the 1920s, ranked from 1 (low) to 5 (high); parents' educational level, on a seven-point scale from no formal education to graduate or professional degree; parents' involvement in civic organizations and activities or parents' involvement in political activities other than voting, both ranked from 1 (not very active) to 5 (very active); level of educational attainment, ranked from 1 (elementary school) to 9 (advanced graduate work); standard of living in 1960, ranked from 1 (low) to 5 (high); use of the educational or training benefits of the G.I. Bill, coded as 1 for use, 0 for nonuse.

3. From the qualitative data on the survey, it appears that "any other civic or community organization" includes several organizational types: service organizations, health-related organizations, alumni organizations and fraternities, cultural or educational organizations, commercial clubs, and local social, sports, or hobby clubs.

4. See Appendix F, Table F.6.1, first column for civic organizations and second column for political organizations and activities. This test (and others in this chapter unless noted otherwise) is conducted through ordinary least-squares regression (OLS). Because of missing data, as not every survey respondent answered each of the over two hundred questions on the twelve-page survey, the number of cases included in each regression analysis is less than the total number of survey respondents. In order to assess whether the subsample provides an adequate reflection of the full sample, I have compared the bivariate regression relationship between each individual independent variable and the dependent variable within the subsamples with those same relationships in the full sample. This analysis revealed the slopes to be sufficiently similar to proceed with the analysis of the subsamples.

5. M. Kent Jennings and Richard G. Niemi, *Generations and Politics* (Princeton, NJ: Princeton University Press, 1981), chap. 4; Verba, Schlozman, and Brady, *Voice and Equality*, 418–20, 437–38.

6. Scholars recognize that the determinants of participation are numerous, and thus it is not surprising to have a relatively low R^2. It should be noted, however, that the purpose here is not to include all the possible explanatory variables but rather to compare the influence of those deemed most significant.

7. Raymond E. Wolfinger and Steven J. Rosenstone, *Who Votes?* (New Haven: Yale University Press, 1980), 17–24; Lester W. Milbrath and M. L. Goel, *Political Participation: How and Why Do People Get Involved in Politics?* 2nd ed. (Chicago: Rand McNally College Publishing, 1977), 98–99; Verba, Schlozman, and Brady, *Voice and Equality*, 433–37; Jennings and Niemi, *Generations and Politics*, Chap. 8.

8. Norman H. Nie, Jane Junn, and Kenneth Stehlik-Barry, *Education and Democratic Citizenship in America* (Chicago: University of Chicago Press, 1996); "Service Learning in Political Science," special issue of *PS: Political Science and Politics* 23 (2000).

9. It is important to note that G.I. Bill usage and educational attainment are not synonymous factors, since some highly educated individuals in the sample attained their education prior to the war, without the aid of the G.I. Bill, and the majority of program beneficiaries used the subcollege programs, which left their formal educational level unaffected.

10. For the results reported in this section, see Appendix F, Table F.6.2.

11. Robert J. Havighurst, Walter H. Eaton, John W. Baughman, and Ernest W. Burgess, *The American Veteran Back Home: A Study of Veteran Readjustment* (New York: Longmans, Green, 1951).

12. Interviews with veterans revealed that military service was not synonymous with voluntaristic attitudes. Some explained that they volunteered in order to avoid being placed in the infantry. Others wanted to volunteer but were discouraged from doing so by family members.

13. One caveat is that veterans who were raised Catholic became significantly less involved in civic organizations than other veterans, a finding consistent with other studies. Scholars

reason that because the Catholic Church involved the laity less in church governance than Protestant churches (especially prior to Vatican II), Catholics lacked the requisite civic skills and participatory norms that could be transferred to involvement in nonreligious organizations. Verba, Schlozman, and Brady, *Voice and Equality,* chap. 13. I did not retain the religious dummy variables in the basic model because in combination with G.I. Bill usage, the Catholic variable is barely significant ($p < .091$), and it does not improve the fit of the model. I dropped them in favor of a more parsimonious model.

14. Havighurst, Eaton, Baughman, and Burgess, *The American Veteran Back Home.*

15. In a model that also includes G.I. Bill usage, the significance level of being encouraged to pursue an education is $p < .066$. I did not include this factor in the basic model because it seems somewhat illogical in theoretical terms. It is based on a question that asks directly about education, and thus it makes more sense to interpret it as a determinant of G.I. Bill usage and educational attainment, respectively, rather than as a proxy for the initiative to get involved in civic life.

16. Each explains less of the variation in the rate at which veterans joined civic organizations or participated in politics, as evidenced by the lower adjusted R^2 figures.

17. I arrive at this conclusion not only through the analyses included here but also through a two-stage model that permits more rigorous control for selection effects. Eric Welch and I conducted such analysis and arrived at the same results for civic participation, thus discrediting the hypothesis that preexisting personal attributes of G.I. Bill users might also explain their higher rates of involvement. See Suzanne Mettler and Eric Welch, "Civic Generation: Effects of the G.I. Bill for Political Participation Among World War II Veterans Over the Life Course," *British Journal of Political Science* 34 (July 2004): 497–518.

18. Those taking this approach have leveled their criticisms primarily at means-tested public assistance programs such as welfare. Nathan Glazer, *The Limits of Social Policy* (Cambridge: Harvard University Press, 1988); Mary Ann Glendon, *Rights Talk: The Impoverishment of Political Discourse* (New York: Free Press, 1991); Francis Fukuyama, *Trust: The Social Virtues and the Creation of Prosperity* (New York: Free Press, 1995), 313–14; William A. Schambra, "All Community Is Local: The Key to America's Civic Renewal," and Dan Coats and Rick Santorum, "Civil Society and the Humble Role of Government," both in *Community Works,* ed. E. J. Dionne Jr. (Washington, DC: Brookings Institution, 1998).

19. I asked them, "How did you consider the educational and training provisions of the G.I. Bill: for example, as a right, a reward for military service, or as a privilege? Tell me why you characterize them as you do."

20. This hypothesis draws on the work of Wolfinger and Rosenstone, who found that while increases in education raise the likelihood of voter participation generally, college education has the most pronounced effect on participation among those from the poorest backgrounds. Wolfinger and Rosenstone, *Who Votes?,* 25; see also Verba, Schlozman, and Brady, *Voice and Equality,* 433.

21. Theda Skocpol, "Targeting Within Universalism: Politically Viable Policies to Combat Poverty in the United States," in *The Urban Underclass,* ed. Christopher Jencks and Paul E. Peterson (Washington, DC: Brookings Institution, 1991), 414; Madonna Harrington Meyer, "Making Claims as Workers or Wives: The Distribution of Social Security Benefits," *American Sociological Review* 61 (1996): 449–65; Walter Korpi, "The Paradox of Redistribution and Strategies of Equality: Welfare State Institutions, Inequality, and Poverty in the Western Countries," *American Sociological Review* 63 (1998): 661–87; Ann Shola Orloff, "Gender and the Social Rights of Citizenship: The Comparative Analysis of Gender Relations and Welfare States," *American Sociological Review* 58 (1993): 303–28.

22. An analogous example offers reason to expect such outcomes. Scholars know that although individuals' socioeconomic background from childhood plays a powerful role in influencing their initial participation in politics, experiences during adulthood—such as participation in religious and social organizations or in the workplace—ameliorate the effects of privilege and elevate the participation levels of those who began life without ample civic endowments. Through participating in such groups, individuals acquire some of the skills,

networks, and resources—and, perhaps, the sense of being included within the broader community—that helps foster involvement in politics. Verba, Schlozman and Brady, *Voice and Equality,* chap. 13; Steven A. Peterson, "Church Participation and Political Participation: The Spillover Effect," *American Politics Quarterly* 20 (1992): 123–39; John M. Strate, Charles J. Parrish, Charles D. Elder, and Coit Ford III, "Life Span Civic Development and Voting Participation," *American Political Science Review* 83 (1989): 443–64; Frank R. Baumgartner and Jack L. Walker, "Survey Research and Membership in Voluntary Associations," *American Journal of Political Science* 32 (1988): 908–28; Bonnie H. Erickson and T. A. Nosanchuk, "How an Apolitical Association Politicizes," *Canadian Review of Sociology and Anthropology* 27 (1990): 204–19.

23. See Appendix F, Table F.6.3. We are able to investigate this claim in the analyses by separating groups of veterans based on G.I. Bill usage and socioeconomic backgrounds. While I have retained the variable for standard of living in the 1920s, the variable of use of the G.I. Bill for education or training has been dropped. The reason for this is that the theoretical proposition being tested is that the program had effects for specific socioeconomic groups. In this interactive version of the civic model, four dummy variables are included in order to examine the interaction between each of the separate levels of standard of living in the 1920s, from low to high, and use of the G.I. Bill for education or training.

24. The higher education beneficiaries had a mean level of education of 6.8 (college degree plus some graduate work), whereas the subcollege users had a mean level of 3.4, completed high school. The differences between the two groups in educational attainment are significant at $p < .001$; for standard of living, $p < .05$; and for income, $p < .10$. In terms of income in 1960, the subcollege and higher education users differed little: 4.6 and 4.9, respectively, on an income scale with five brackets. In terms of standard of living in 1960, they also differed little: 2.8 and 3.0, respectively, on a five-point scale from low to high.

25. See Appendix F, Table F.6.4. It is important to note that once again we are controlling for level of education, which is still possible given the wide range of educational levels among non–G.I. Bill users, higher education users (not all of whom graduated from college and some of whom pursued graduate work), and subcollege training users (who varied considerably in their level of formal education). Certainly among G.I. Bill higher education users, much of their level of education is explained by their participation in the program (collinearity diagnostics reveal, however, that these factors do not overlap substantially); the same cannot be said of subcollege G.I. Bill users, since we lack a means of measuring the human capital investment they gained through such training. Leaving level of education out of the model, moreover, weakens its explanatory ability quite substantially.

26. In both the civic and political models, other determinants' roles resemble those we have seen previously, though level of education—already insignificant in the basic political model—here diminishes in its impact on civic joining.

27. The correlation between time spent on the G.I. Bill and level of education is .64 and significant at $p < .01$.

28. See Appendix F, Table F.6.5. In the case of joining civic organizations, time spent on the G.I. Bill proved insignificant as a determinant of joining organizations; the fact of program usage, not its duration, mattered for veterans' subsequent memberships.

29. One survey question probed this reciprocity effect, asking G.I. Bill recipients to indicate their level of agreement with the statement "It is fair to say that after benefiting from the G.I. Bill, I felt I owed something back to American society."

30. See Appendix F, Table F.6.6. In addition, given that some who used the loan program joined the exodus to the emergent suburbs and that their new place of residence might influence civic outcomes, we will control for suburbanization. The impact of all other variables, including the G.I. Bill education and training factor, remains quite consistent from that shown in the basic models. The civic model becomes slightly more powerful overall when the loan guarantee variable is included.

31. Childhood factors will be dropped in these analyses, given that their influence likely fades with the aging process. Therefore, parents' civic or political activity, parents' level of education, and

standard of living in the 1920s are all dropped from these analyses. We will, however, include other factors that plausibly could have affected political participation in middle and later adulthood. Given that the civic skills and networks fostered by membership in civic organizations help mobilize citizens politically, we will consider how involvement in them during one period of time might affect individuals' political involvement in the next period of time: Verba, Schlozman, and Brady, *Voice and Equality;* Peterson, "Church Participation and Political Participation"; Strate, Parrish, Elder, and Ford, "Life Span Civic Development and Voting Participation"; Baumgartner and Walker, "Survey Research and Membership in Voluntary Associations"; Erickson and Nosanchuk, "How an Apolitical Association Politicizes." Also, we will account for living in the suburbs.

32. See Appendix F, Table F.6.7.

33. The modest significance of the G.I. Bill at the .10 level in the 1980–98 model may be related to a lingering interpretive effect of the G.I. Bill or, more likely, may be an indicator of other factors that determined program usage. In a more complex analysis, Eric Welch and I have controlled for factors that determine G.I. Bill usage when we examine its consequences over time. When examined with this two-stage analysis, the G.I. Bill appears as significant in neither of the latter periods. See Mettler and Welch, "Civic Generation," 497–518.

34. For a more detailed treatment of these effects, see Mettler and Welch, "Civic Generation."

35. This is a fundamental task of state building, synonymous with what Judith Shklar terms "inclusion." Judith N. Shklar, *American Citizenship: The Quest for Inclusion* (Cambridge: Harvard University Press, 1991).

36. Michael Walzer, *Spheres of Justice: A Defense of Pluralism and Equality* (New York: Basic Books, 1983).

37. Ronald Beiner, "Why Citizenship Constitutes a Theoretical Problem in the Last Decade of the Twentieth Century," and Will Kymlicka and Wayne Norman, "Return of the Citizen: A Survey of Recent Work on Citizenship Theory," both in *Theorizing Citizenship,* ed. Ronald Beiner (Albany: State University of New York Press, 1995), 1–28 and 282–322, respectively.

38. Andrea Louise Campbell, *How Policies Make Citizens: Senior Political Activism and the American Welfare State* (Princeton, NJ: Princeton University Press, 2003).

Chapter 7

1. Mary L. Dudziak, *Cold War Civil Rights: Race and the Image of American Democracy* (Princeton, NJ: Princeton University Press, 2000); Thomas Borstelmann, *The Cold War and the Color Line: American Race Relations in the Global Arena* (Cambridge, MA: Harvard University Press, 2001); John D. Skrentny, *The Minority Rights Revolution* (Cambridge: Harvard University Press, 2002), chaps. 2–3.

2. For a careful and complex treatment of different aspects of gender relations in the 1950s, see Joanne Meyerowitz, "Introduction: Women and Gender in Postwar America, 1945–1960," in *Not June Cleaver: Women and Gender in Postwar America, 1945–1960,* ed. Joanne Meyerowitz (Philadelphia: Temple University Press, 1994), 1–16.

3. Robert D. Putnam, *Bowling Alone: The Collapse and Revival of American Community* (New York: Simon and Schuster, 2000), chap. 2, 220–21.

4. Suzanne Mettler and Andrew Milstein, "A Sense of the State: Tracking the Role of the American Administrative State in Citizens' Lives Over Time," paper presented at the annual meeting of the Midwest Political Science Association, April 3–6, 2003, Chicago; Claudia Goldin and Robert Margot, "The Great Compression: The Wage Structure in the United States at Mid-Century," *Quarterly Journal of Economics* 107 (1992): 1–34; Robert D. Plotnick, Eugene Smolensky, Eirik Evenhouse, and Siobhan Reilly, "Inequality and Poverty in the United States: The Twentieth Century Record," *Focus* 19, 3 (1998): 7–15.

5. Harold G. Vatter, *The U.S. Economy in the 1950s: An Economic History* (New York: W. W. Norton, 1963), 6–7; Carl Solberg, *Riding High: America in the Cold War* (New York: Mason and Lipscomb, 1973), 266.

6. William L. O'Neill, *American High: The Years of Confidence, 1945–1960* (New York: Free Press, 1986), 196; Eric F. Goldman, *The Crucial Decade—and After: America, 1945–1960* (New York: Alfred A. Knopf, 1965), chap. 12.

7. Paul A. Carter, *Another Part of the Fifties* (New York: Columbia University Press, 1983), 30; James L. Sundquist, *Politics and Policy: The Eisenhower, Kennedy, and Johnson Years* (Washington, DC: Brookings Institution, 1968), 173–80.

8. Lawrence Mishel, Jared Bernstein, and Heather Boushey, Economic Policy Institute, *The State of Working America, 2002–2003* (Ithaca: Cornell University Press, 2003), 57.

9. Solberg, *Riding High*, 248–49; William E. Leuchtenburg, *A Troubled Feast: American Society Since 1945* (Boston: Little, Brown, 1973), 48; John Kenneth Galbraith, *The Affluent Society* (Boston: Houghton Mifflin, 1958), 85–86; Siegel, *Troubled Journey*, 107.

10. Leuchtenburg, *A Troubled Feast*, 48; Marie Gottschalk, *In the Shadow of the Welfare State: Labor, Business, and the Politics of Health Care in the United States* (Ithaca: ILR Press, 2000), 43.

11. Data drawn from World War II Veterans Survey of nonblack males. Besides asking about the number of associations—characterized by functional type—to which respondents belonged from 1950 to the present (data used in Chapter 6), the survey also asked, "Since 1950, with which five groups or organizations have you been most involved?" Respondents were asked to write in the name of those organizations, the types of activities they were involved with in each group, and the periods of involvement and whether they held an office or served on a committee. On associations involving 1 percent of all citizens or more, see Theda Skocpol, *Diminished Democracy: From Membership to Management in American Civic Life* (Norman: University of Oklahoma Press, 2003), 130–31, 154–55. This section and the next two are deeply influenced by Skocpol's ideas advanced in *Diminished Democracy* and are made possible by applying her coding scheme for organizations data in the World War II Veterans Survey data.

12. Skocpol, *Diminished Democracy*, 130–31, 154–55.

13. Whitfield, *The Culture of the Cold War*, 83; R. Ronald Oakley, *God's Country: America in the Fifties* (New York: Dembner Books, 1986), 319–27.

14. Skocpol, *Diminished Democracy*, 26–27, 33–34, 153–54.

15. Jeffrey A. Charles, *Service Clubs in American Society: Rotary, Kiwanis and Lions* (Urbana: University of Illinois Press, 1993), chap. 7.

16. Susan Crawford and Peggy Levitt, "Social Change and Civic Engagement: The Case of the PTA," in *Civic Engagement in American Democracy,* ed. Theda Skocpol and Morris P. Fiorina (Washington, DC: Brooking Institution Press, 1999), 149–96; Skocpol, *Diminished Democracy*, 130–31.

17. Skocpol, *Diminished Democracy*, 130–31.

18. Steven Brint and Charles S. Levy, "Professions and Civic Engagement: Trends in Rhetoric and Practice, 1875–1995," in *Civic Engagement in American Democracy,* ed. Theda Skocpol and Morris P. Fiorina (Washington, DC: Brookings Institution, 1999), 196; David B. Truman, *The Governmental Process: Political Interests and Public Opinion* (New York: Alfred A. Knopf, 1962), 76–86; Theodore J. Lowi, *The End of Liberalism* (New York: Norton, 1979).

19. Mettler and Milstein, "A Sense of the State."

20. G.I. Bill users were not more inclined than nonusers to join either cross-class organizations or elite organizations, nor local groups or nonlocal ones. This statement is based on numerous regression analyses. Because they yielded consistently insignificant results, I have not included them here.

21. For these examples, I am indebted to Patrick DelGrande, Elinor Mettler, and David Silvernail. Also, see Becky M. Nicolaides, *My Blue Heaven: Life and Politics in the Working-Class Suburbs of Los Angeles, 1920–1965* (Chicago: University of Chicago Press, 2002), 225.

22. Jeffrey M. Berry, "The Rise of Citizen Groups," in *Civic Engagement in American Democracy,* ed. Theda Skocpol and Morris P. Fiorina (Washington, DC: Brookings Institution, 1999), 367–93.

23. Debra C. Minkoff, *Organizing for Equality: The Evolution of Women's and Racial-Ethnic Organizations in America, 1955–1985* (New Brunswick, NJ: Rutgers University Press, 1995), 15; Walter W. Powell, ed., *The Nonprofit Sector: A Research Handbook* (New Haven: Yale

University Press, 1987), chaps. 8–11; Steven Rathgeb Smith and Michael Lipsky, *Nonprofits for Hire: The Welfare State in the Age of Contracting* (Cambridge, MA: Harvard University Press, 1993), Chap. 4.

24. Skocpol, *Diminished Democracy*, 138–52; Peter Dobkin Hall, "A Historical Overview of the Private Nonprofit Sector," and J. Craig Jenkins, "Nonprofit Organizations and Policy Advocacy," in *The Nonprofit Sector*, ed. Walter W. Powell (New Haven: Yale University Press, 1987), 16–18 and 296–318, respectively.

25. See Appendix F, Table F.7.1. Also, on the meaning of membership and shifting meanings of involvement, see Robert Wuthnow, *Loose Connections: Joining Together in America's Fragmented Communities* (Cambridge, MA: Harvard University Press, 1998), chap. 2.

26. Information provided by David Silvernail.

27. See Appendix F, Table F.7.2. Unfortunately, the data do not allow us to examine leadership in the 1950 to 1964 period by itself.

28. Robert Wuthnow, "The United States: Bridging the Privileged and Marginalized?" in *Democracies in Flux*, ed. Robert D. Putnam (New York: Oxford University Press, 2002), 80.

29. Skocpol, *Diminished Democracy*, 113–24; A. Lanethea Mathews-Gardner, "From Women's Club to NGO: The Changing Terrain of Women's Civic Engagement in the Mid-20th Century United States," Ph.D. dissertation, Syracuse University, 2003.

30. Skocpol, *Diminished Democracy*; proceedings, national annual conventions, American Legion, 1925 onward.

31. Putnam, *Bowling Alone*, 19, 22–23.

32. Theda Skocpol reports that whereas white women's organizations made some efforts to promote interracial cooperation, white men's fraternal organizations exercised racially exclusionary practices, leaving African Americans to build their own organizations. Skocpol, *Diminished Democracy*, 179–80, 331nn.5–7.

33. Henry A. J. Ramos, *The American G.I. Forum: In Pursuit of the Dream, 1948–1983* (Houston, TX: Arte Publico Press, 1998); Kaye Briegel, "The Development of Mexican-American Organizations," in *The Mexican-Americans: An Awakening Minority*, comp. Manuel P. Servin (Beverly Hills, CA: Glencoe Press, 1970), 160–78; Stanley Steimer, *La Raza: The Mexican Americans* (New York: Harper and Row, 1969); Paul Sheldon, "Mexican American Formal Organizations," in *Mexican-Americans in the United States: A Reader*, ed. John H. Burma (Cambridge, MA: Schenkman Publishing, 1970), 267–72; Richard Santillan, "Latino Politics in the Midwest," in *Latinos and the Political System*, ed. F. Chris Garcia (Notre Dame, IN: University of Notre Dame Press, 1988), 105–6.

34. With the exception of professional, business, and trade organizations, elite service groups, and a few miscellaneous groups such as yacht clubs and country clubs, the remaining membership organizations were coded as cross-class. This included all fraternal groups, religious groups, and veterans' groups, as well as the majority of hobby and sports clubs. For a valuable discussion of the genuinely cross-class nature of fraternal groups in the United States historically, see Mary Ann Clawson, *Constructing Brotherhood: Class, Gender and Fraternalism* (Princeton, NJ: Princeton University Press, 1989), 94–110. On the vibrantly cross-class nature of such organizations in one postwar community, see Nicolaides, *My Blue Heaven*, 255–64.

35. Regression analyses reveal that such organizations were genuinely cross-class during the 1950 to 1964 period, as socioeconomic indicators fail to explain who became most active in such organizations. Only two variables proved significant: veterans whose parents had been more active in civic life were somewhat more likely to join cross-class organizations themselves; conversely, those who lived in the suburbs in 1960 were less involved in cross-class organizations, consistent with Eric Oliver's study, which revealed lower levels of political activity among suburbanites. The model included the same variables as the basic civic model reported in Chapter 7; adjusted R^2, .04. Standardized coefficients for significant variables were as follows: parents' civic activity, .11 ($p < .05$); lived in suburb, −.11, ($p < .05$). See J. Eric Oliver, *Democracy in Suburbia* (Princeton, NJ: Princeton University Press, 2001).

36. On the significance of elites on cross-class associations, see Skocpol, *Diminished Democracy,* 108–13.
37. Ibid., 182–99, Larry M. Bartels, "Economic Inequality and Political Representation," paper presented at the annual meeting of the American Political Science Association, Boston, August 2002.
38. Peter Filene, "'Cold War Culture' Doesn't Say It All," and Alan Brinkley, "The Illusion of Unity in Cold War Culture," in *Rethinking Cold War Culture,* ed. Peter J. Kuznick and James Gilbert (Washington, DC: Smithsonian Institution Press, 2001), 156–74 and 61–73, respectively. For contrasting perspectives, see Lisle A. Rose, *The Cold War Comes to Main Street: America in 1950* (Lawrence: University of Kansas Press, 1999); Stephen J. Whitfield, *The Culture of the Cold War* (Baltimore, MD: Johns Hopkins University Press, 1991).
39. Among respondents to the World War II Veterans Survey who listed membership in a political party among those groups in which they had been most active, equal percentages listed the Democratic Party and the Republican Party.
40. "The Fortune Survey," *Fortune,* December 1946, 5–6, 14.
41. David R. Segal and Mady Wechsler Segal, "The Impact of Military Service on Trust in Government, International Attitudes, and Social Status," in *Social Psychology of Military Service,* ed. Nancy L. Goldman and David R. Segal (Beverly Hills, CA: Sage Publications, 1976), 201–11; Nancy Edelman Phillips, "Militarism and Grass-Roots Involvement in the Military-Industrial Complex," *Journal of Conflict Resolution* 17, 4 (1973): 625–55; M. Kent Jennings and Gregory B. Markus, "Political Participation and Vietnam War Veterans: A Longitudinal Study," in *Social Psychology of Military Service,* ed. Nancy L. Goldman and David R. Segal (Beverly Hills, CA: Sage Publications, 1976), 175–99; M. Kent Jennings and Gregory B. Markus, "The Effect of Military Service on Political Attitudes: A Panel Study," *American Political Science Review* 71, 1 (1977): 131–47.
42. Norman Nie, Jane Junn, and Kenneth Stehlik-Barry, *Education and Democratic Citizenship in America* (Chicago: University of Chicago Press, 1996).
43. Kenneth A. Feldman and Theodore M. Newcomb, *The Impact of College on Students* (New Brunswick, NJ: Transaction Publishers, 1994), quote appears on 31; also see 19–20, 34.
44. "Well-Known Users of the G.I. Bill," *Washington Times,* June 22, 1994, 10.
45. Veterans were overrepresented not only in comparison to the general population but also in comparison to the population of males twenty-five years and older. See Albert Somit and Joseph Tanenhaus, "The Veteran in the Electoral Process: The House of Representatives," *Journal of Politics* 19, 2 (1957): 187.
46. Carl Abbott, *Urban America in the Modern Age: 1920 to the Present* (Arlington Heights, IL: Harlan Davidson, 1987), 79.
47. Robert G. Spinney, "Municipal Government in Nashville, Tennessee, 1938–1951: World War II and the Growth of the Public Sector," *Journal of Southern History* 61, 1 (1995): 98–99.
48. See "Veterans: Tennessee Siege," and "Arkansas Horse Race," *Newsweek,* August 12, 1946, 30–32; "Tennessee: Battle of the Ballots," *Time,* August 12, 1946, 20; "Veterans Per Se," *Commonweal,* August 23, 1946, 443–44; V. O. Key Jr., *Southern Politics in State and Nation* (New York: Alfred A. Knopf, 1950), 69, 198, 202–4; quote on 204.
49. Christopher Gelpi and Peter D. Feaver, "Speak Softly and Carry a Big Stick? Veterans in the Political Elite and the American Use of Force," *American Political Science Review* 96, 4 (2002): 783.
50. Somit and Tanenhaus, "The Veteran in the Electoral Process," 184–201.
51. Gelpi and Feaver, "Speak Softly and Carry a Big Stick?" 779–93.
52. Mettler and Milstein, "A Sense of the State."
53. Robert E. Lane, "The Politics of Consensus in an Age of Affluence," *American Political Science Review* 59, 4 (1965): 874–95; Stephen Earl Bennett, "Were the Halcyon Days Really Golden? An Analysis of Americans' Attitudes About the Political System, 1945–1965," *What Is It About Government That Americans Dislike?* ed. John R. Hibbing and Elizabeth Theiss-Morse (New York: Cambridge University Press, 2001), 50–55; Everett Carll Ladd Jr. with Charles D. Hadley, *Transformations of the American Party System: Political Coalitions from the New Deal to the 1970s* (New York: W. W. Norton, 1975), 96–104.

54. Gabriel A. Almond and Sidney Verba, *The Civic Culture: Political Attitudes and Democracy in Five Nations* (Princeton, NJ: Princeton University Press, 1963), 103.

55. Paul R. Abramson, *Political Attitudes in America: Formation and Change* (San Francisco: W. H. Freeman, 1983), 12, 231; John E. Hughes and M. Margaret Conway, "Public Opinion and Political Participation," in *Understanding Public Opinion,* ed. Barbara Norrander and Clyde Wilcox (Washington, DC: Congressional Quarterly, 1997), 197–210.

56. The Korean War G.I. Bill (Public Law 82–550), established in 1952, limited training to a maximum of thirty-six months and permitted veterans to be trained for one and a half times as long as they had been on active duty. Forty-two percent of Korean War veterans utilized the G.I. Bill, 51 percent of them for college. See U.S. Congress, Senate, Committee on Veterans' Affairs, *Final Report on Educational Assistance to Veterans: A Comparative Study of Three G.I. Bills,* 93rd Cong., 1st Sess. (Washington, DC: GPO, 1973), 161–74. Congress also enacted the Cold War G.I. bill (Public Law 89–358) in 1966, with similar terms to the Korean War version.

Chapter 8

1. "Hosea Williams: 1926–2000," part of "The Rise and Fall of Jim Crow," Public Broadcasting Service Web site, http:www.pbs.org/wnet/jimcrow/stories_people_will.html; Internet obituary, "Hosea Williams, 1926–2000," http://obits.com/williamshosea.html.

2. John Modell, Marc Goulden, and Sigurdur Magnussen, "World War II in the Lives of Black Americans: Some Findings and an Interpretation," *Journal of American History* 76 (1989): 838–48; Charles M. Payne, *I've Got the Light of Freedom: The Organizing Tradition and the Mississippi Freedom Struggle* (Berkeley: University of California Press, 1995), 24, 30, 66, 404; Neil R. McMillen, "Fighting for What We Didn't Have: How Mississippi's Black Veterans Remember World War II," in *Remaking Dixie: The Impact of World War II on the American South,* ed. Neil R. McMillen (Jackson: University Press of Mississippi, 1997), 93–110. More broadly, on the positive effect of military service on some forms of political activity among black veterans, see Christopher G. Ellison, "Military Background, Racial Orientations, and Political Participation Among Black Adult Males," *Social Science Quarterly* 73 (1992): 360–78.

3. The exception is Christopher Parker's work, which offers a nuanced explanation of the dynamics through which black veterans became especially interested and active in politics. The G.I. Bill usage per se does not figure into his analysis since it was not included in the Matthews-Prothro dataset he uses. Christopher Parker, "Explaining the Political Consciousness of Black Veterans," chapter from book manuscript tentatively entitled "Fighting for Democracy: Race, Military Service, and American Politics," draft in author's possession.

4. In the case of black veterans, we are unable to specify precisely whether it was advanced education or the G.I. Bill financing of it that facilitated increased activism. This is because unlike white veteran respondents to the World War II Veterans Survey, the African American respondents included no highly educated individuals other than those who had used the G.I. Bill. Remarkably, every respondent in the black sample who had advanced education had used the G.I. Bill to attain it—evidence, perhaps, of a lack of alternative means of financing their education, though we cannot be sure of this interpretation. For analytical purposes, this absence of a control group is lamentable: it means that we cannot separate the effect of education on political action from the effect of G.I. Bill usage. Conceivably, some sort of internal motivation that prompted particular veterans to use the G.I. Bill benefits also gave them the impetus to get involved politically. The absence of a control group means that we must be cognizant of these factors and refrain from assigning too much causal power to the program. The key question we are attempting to answer here, however, pertains more to the content of black veterans' political involvement.

5. Because the data collected from African American veterans is a relatively small sample and because it is less representative of the original cohort than data collected from nonblack

veterans, we will not use the data to estimate measures of the precise *amount* of black veterans' participation relative to that of whites. (See Appendix D for a fuller discussion.) Rather, our focus here is to compare the *types* of political involvement that engaged black and white veterans, and G.I. Bill users compared to nonusers. Also, two obstacles prevent us from evaluating these questions through regression analyses. First, the number of African American veterans among World War II Veterans Survey respondents is too small to permit analysis involving the relatively large number of independent variables necessary to explain civic engagement. Second, distinct from white veterans, nearly all of the African Americans in the sample who have a high degree of education used the G.I. Bill to attain it, meaning that the control group of highly educated non–G.I. Bill users is almost nonexistent.

6. A. Lanethea Mathews-Gardner, "From Woman's Club to NGO: The Changing Terrain of Women's Civic Engagement in the Mid-20th Century United States," Ph.D. dissertation, Syracuse University, 2003; Linda Gordon, *Pitied but Not Entitled: Single Mothers and the History of Welfare, 1890–1935* (New York: Free Press, 1994), chap. 5.

7. Aldon D. Morris, *The Origins of the Civil Rights Movement: Black Communities Organizing for Change* (New York: Free Press, 1984); Doug McAdam, *Political Process and the Development of Black Insurgency, 1930–1970* (Chicago: University of Chicago Press, 1982); J. Craig Jenkins and David Jacobs, "Political Opportunities and African American Protest, 1948–1997," *American Journal of Sociology* 109, 2 (2003): 277–303; Payne, *I've Got the Light of Freedom*; Donald R. Matthews and James W. Prothro, "Political Factors and Negro Voter Registration in the South," *American Political Science Review* 57, 2 (1963): 355–67; David T. Beito, *From Mutual Aid to the Welfare State: Fraternal Societies and Social Services, 1890–1967* (Chapel Hill: University of North Carolina Press, 2000), 189–91.

8. See Appendix F, Table F.8.1. The first row shows the mean numbers of memberships in any of four types of civic organizations: fraternal groups, neighborhood or home owners' groups, parent-teacher or school support groups, and other civic organizations. Although African American survey respondents were considerably more active than whites overall, whether or not they had used the G.I. Bill, the ratio of G.I. Bill users' to nonusers' memberships was nearly identical between African American and white veterans: 63 percent and 60 percent, respectively.

9. Lawrence Otis Graham, *Our Kind of People: Inside America's Black Upper Class* (New York: HarperCollins, 1999), 86; Omega Psi Phi Fraternity Web site, http://www.oppf.org/about/history.asp; phone interview with A. William Perry, February 10, 2003.

10. Morris, *The Origins of the Civil Rights Movement*; McAdam, *Political Process and the Development of Black Insurgency*.

11. See Appendix F, Table F.8.2.

12. See ibid.

13. Internet obituary, "Obituary for Hosea Williams."

14. For a fuller treatment of this argument about sequencing, see Suzanne Mettler, "'The Only Good Thing Was the G.I. Bill': Effects of the Education and Training Provisions on African American Veterans' Political Participation," *Studies in American Political Development* 19, 1 (2005).

15. Ira Katznelson and Margaret Weir, *Schooling for All: Class, Race and the Decline of the Democratic Ideal* (Berkeley: University of California Press, 1985), 179–206; C. Vann Woodward, *The Strange Career of Jim Crow*, 3rd ed. (New York: Oxford University Press, 1974).

16. Robert C. Lieberman, *Shifting the Color Line: Race and the American Welfare State* (Cambridge, MA: Harvard University Press, 1998); for an argument that African Americans nonetheless found the New Deal inclusive relative to other instances of governance, see Nancy. J. Weiss, *Farewell to the Party of Lincoln: Black Politics in the Age of FDR* (Princeton, NJ: Princeton University Press, 1983), chap. 10.

17. David H. Onkst, "First a Negro . . . Incidentally a Veteran": Black World War II Veterans and the G.I. Bill of Rights in the Deep South, 1944–1948," *Journal of Social History* 31, 3 (1998): 522–23; Kenneth T. Jackson, *Crabgrass Frontier: The Suburbanization of the United States* (New York: Oxford University Press, 1985), 197–215.

18. Sidney Verba, Kay Lehman Schlozman, and Henry Brady, *Voice and Equality: Civic Voluntarism in American Politics* (Cambridge, MA: Harvard University Press, 1995), 433–37.

19. Unfortunately, we lack sufficient data to examine comparable questions about Latino veterans, but it is possible that similar dynamics operated among them. Many did use the G.I. Bill for education and training, and Latino veterans are associated with much of the mobilization for social change that followed the war, especially through organizations such as the G.I. Forum. See Henry A. J. Ramos, *The American G.I. Forum: In Pursuit of the Dream, 1848–1983* (Houston, TX: Arte Publico Press, 1998). Neil A. Wynn observed, "Several of the post-war Mexican leaders were not only veterans but also men who had benefited under the provisions of the G.I. Bill" (*The Afro-American and the Second World War* [New York: Holmes and Meier Publications, 1975], 18).

20. On how advanced education has had such effects generally among African Americans, see Katherine Tate, *From Protest to Politics: The New Black Voters in American Elections* (New York: Russell Sage, 1993), 27–28; Michael C. Dawson, *Behind the Mule: Race and Class in African-American Politics* (Princeton, NJ: Princeton University Press, 1994), 81–82; Paul Sniderman and Thomas Piazza, *Black Pride and Black Prejudice* (Princeton: Princeton University Press, 2002), 42–44.

21. Similarly, a contemporary study found that college-educated black men become considerably more active in civic and political activities and leadership roles than their white male cohort group. See William G. Bowen and Derek Bok, *The Shape of the River: Long-term Consequences of Considering Race in College and University Admissions* (Princeton, NJ: Princeton University Press, 1998), chap. 6.

22. Dernoral Davis, "Medgar Wiley Evers and the Origin of the Civil Rights Movement in Mississippi," *Mississippi History Now,* http://mshistory.k12.ms.us/features/feature45/medgar_evers.htm; "Aaron Henry Was an Unsung Hero," *African American Registry,* http://www.aaregistry.com/african_american_history/978/Aaron_Henry_was_an_unsung_hero; "W. W. Law (1923–2002)," *New Georgia Encyclopedia,* http://www.georgiaencyclopedia.org/nge/Article.jsp?id=h-2553.

Chapter 9

1. U.S. Congress, Senate, Committee on Veterans' Affairs, *Final Report on Educational Assistance to Veterans: A Comparative Study of Three G.I. Bills* (Washington, DC: GPO, 1973), 163.

2. By 1910, over 300,000 widows, orphans and other dependents numbered among the recipients of Civil War veterans' pensions. See Theda Skocpol, *Protecting Soldiers and Mothers: The Political Origins of Social Policy in the United States* (Cambridge, MA: Harvard University Press, 1992), 65.

3. June A. Willenz, *Women Veterans: America's Forgotten Heroines* (New York: Continuum, 1983), 24, 43; Susan M. Hartmann, *The Home Front and Beyond: American Women in the 1940s* (Boston: Twayne Publishers, 1982), 45–46.

4. Willenz, *Women Veterans,* 24–27; Jeanne Holm, *Women in the Military: An Unfinished Revolution* (Novato, CA: Presidio Press, 1982), 64; Maddie E. Treadwell, *United States Army in World War II, Special Studies: The Women's Army Corps* (Washington, DC: Office of the Chief of Military History, Department of the Army, 1954), 784–85.

5. The total number of women who served in the World War II military was 332,000; the 1,100 WASPS were 0.33 percent of them. U.S. Congress, Senate, *Final Report on Educational Assistance to Veterans,* 163.

6. Lizabeth Cohen, *A Consumers' Republic: The Politics of Mass Consumption in Postwar America* (New York: Alfred A. Knopf, 2003), 138. Also see Willenz, *Women Veterans,* 168–76; Treadwell, *United States Army in World War II, Special Studies: The Women's Army Corps,* 782–83.

7. The vast majority of women veterans were recruited from 1943 onward. See Holm, *Women in the Military,* chap. 5.

8. Treadwell, *United States Army in World War II, Special Studies: The Women's Army Corps,* 265; U.S. Congress, Senate, *Final Report on Educational Assistance to Veterans,* 20; Willenz, *Women Veterans,* 193. The inequity in the treatment of women veterans' dependents was finally corrected in 1972, with Public Law 93–540.

9. U.S. Maritime Service Veterans Web site, www.USMM.org. See pages on "U.S. Merchant Marine in World War II," and "Frequently Asked Questions."

10. Treadwell, *United States Army in World War II, Special Studies: The Women's Army Corps,* 183–84, 562. Slightly different statistics, showing even higher rates of pre-military-service educational attainment among women, appear in Earl J. McGrath, "The Education of the Veteran," *Annals of the American Academy* 238 (1945): 77. Also see D'Ann Campbell, *Women at War with America: Private Lives in a Patriotic Era* (Cambridge, MA: Harvard University Press, 1984), 22–23.

11. See results in Appendix F, Table F.9.1. For the parents' education variable, each veteran's father's level of education is used except in cases where it was missing and mother's level of education could be substituted instead. If neither was available, I substituted the mean level of parents' education: 2.82 among male veterans, and 3.05 among female veterans, both on a scale of 1 to 7.

12. Unlike the models of male veterans' usage presented in Chapter 4, efforts to produce a model of female veterans' usage produced a weak model and only one mildly significant variable: year of birth. Younger women were slightly more likely to use the benefits (p < .10).

13. Patricia Albjerg Graham, "Expansion and Exclusion: A History of Women in American Higher Education," *Signs* 3, 4 (1978): 766–67.

14. Elaine Tyler May, *Homeward Bound: American Families in the Cold War Era* (New York: Basic Books, 1988), 20.

15. Brett Harvey, *The Fifties: A Women's Oral History* (New York: HarperCollins, 1993), 70.

16. Campbell, *Women at War with America,* 72–83.

17. Cohen, *A Consumers' Republic*; May, *Homeward Bound,* 166–67; Hartmann, *The Home Front and Beyond,* chap. 9.

18. Hartmann, *The Home Front and Beyond*; William H. Chafe, *The American Woman: Her Changing Social, Economic, and Political Roles, 1920–1970* (New York: Oxford University Press, 1972), 177, 179–81; Sherna Berger Gluck, *Rosie the Riveter Revisited: Women, the War, and Social Change* (Boston: Twayne, 1987), 16–17; Susan Estabrook Kennedy, *If All We Did Was to Weep at Home: A History of White Working-Class Women in America* (Bloomington: Indiana University Press, 1979), 197–99.

19. Chafe, *The American Woman,* 176–78.

20. Alice Kessler-Harris, *In Pursuit of Equity: Women, Men, and the Quest for Economic Citizenship in 20th-Century America* (New York: Oxford University Press, 2001), 193–99; Nancy F. Cott, *Public Vows: A History of Marriage and the Nation* (Cambridge, MA: Harvard University Press, 2000), 191–93.

21. Joanne Meyerowitz, "Beyond the Feminine Mystique: A Reassessment of Postwar Mass Culture, 1946–1958," *Journal of American History* 79, 4 (1993): 1455–82.

22. Campbell, *Women at War with America,* 45.

23. Benjamin J. Atlas, "What Future for the Servicewoman?" *Independent Woman,* May 1945, 126–28, 140.

24. Claudia D. Goldin, "The Role of World War II in the Rise of Women's Employment," *American Economic Review* 81, 4 (1991): 742, table 1; Eugenia Kaledin, *Mothers and More: American Women in the 1950s* (Boston: Twayne, 1984), 63; Kessler-Harris, *Out to Work,* 300–305; Chafe, *The American Woman,* 181–84.

25. Karen Anderson, *Wartime Women: Sex Roles, Family Relations, and the Status of Women During World War II* (Westport, CT: Greenwood Press, 1981), 173–75; Chafe, *The American Woman,* 184–88.

26. Campbell, *Women at War with America,* 45.

27. Nancy McIrnerny, "The Woman Vet Has Her Headaches, Too," *New York Times Magazine,* June 30, 1946, 18ff.

28. Cynthia Harrison, *On Account of Sex: The Politics of Women's Issues, 1945–1968* (Berkeley: University of California Press, 1988), 90.

29. Willenz, *Women Veterans,* 44.

30. Treadwell, *United States Army in World War II, Special Studies: The Women's Army Corps,* 735–36.

31. Gretchen Ritter, "Of War and Virtue: Gender, American Citizenship and Veterans' Benefits After World War II," in *The Comparative Study of Conscription in the Armed Forces,* ed. Lars Mjøset and Stephen Van Holde (Amsterdam: JAI, 2002), 222.

32. For similar illustrations in individual lives, see Willenz, *Women Veterans,* 68–69, 100–101.

33. Susan E. Riley, "Caring for Rosie's Children: Federal Child Care Policies in the World War II Era," *Polity* 26 (1994): 655–75.

34. Lester W. Milbrath and M. L. Goel, *Political Participation* (Chicago: Rand-McNally, 1977), 116.

35. See Appendix F, Table F.9.2, regarding results for the 1965–79 period; for the 1950–64 period, being female bears a negative but insignificant relationship to political involvement. These patterns held when I added a housewife variable for those women who, in 1960, were not employed outside the home but listed their primary role as wife and/or mother, home engineer, etc. The weakness of the female veterans' model may be attributable in part to the lack of additional variables pertaining to private life, such as division of labor in the home, the importance of which is identified in Nancy Burns, Kay Lehman Schlozman, and Sidney Verba, *The Private Roots of Public Action: Gender, Equality and Political Participation* (Cambridge, MA: Harvard University Press, 2001), chaps. 6, 7, and 12.

36. See Appendix F, Table F.9.3.

37. Chafe, *American Woman,* 184–85; Kessler-Harris, *Out to Work,* 304–5, 311–12.

38. See Appendix F, Table F.9.2.

39. Burns, Schlozman, and Brady, *The Private Roots of Public Action.*

40. Widows of Civil War veterans became eligible for pensions in 1908. See Skocpol, *Protecting Soldiers and Mothers,* 129, 132, 134.

41. U.S. Congress, House of Representatives, Committee on Veterans' Affairs, Subcommittee on Education, Training and Rehabilitation, "Educational and Loan Benefits for Widows and Children of World War II Veterans," Hearings, 80th Congress, 1st Sess., April 25–26 and June 5, 1947, 5.

42. The War Orphans' Educational Assistance Act of 1956 established Public Law 84–634, still in effect today as 38 U.S.C. Chapter 35, Survivors' and Dependents' Educational Assistance Program (DEA). It is the only VA educational assistance program for students who have never served in the armed forces.

43. Graham, "Expansion and Exclusion," 766; Christopher Jencks and David Riesman, *The Academic Revolution* (Chicago: University of Chicago Press, 1977), 293–94.

44. George Thomas Kurian, ed., *Datapedia of the United States, 1790–2005* (Lanham, MD: Bernan, 2001), 176–77, 383.

45. Kaledin, *Mothers and More,* 54.

46. Paula Fass, *Outside In: Minorities and the Transformation of American Education* (New York: Oxford University Press, 1989), chap. 5; Hartmann, *The Home Front and Beyond,* 114.

47. U.S. Office of War Mobilization and Reconversion, *The Veterans and Higher Education* (Washington, DC: GPO, 1946), 12.

48. U.S. Office of War Mobilization and Reconversion, "The Veterans and Higher Education," 10.

49. Thomas J. Deloughry, "The G.I. Bill," *Cornell Magazine,* September 1995, 28.

50. Bezilla, *Penn State: An Illustrated History,* 227.

51. Hartmann, *The Home Front and Beyond,* 106.

52. Marcia Graham Synnott, *The Half-Opened Door: Discrimination and Admissions at Harvard, Yale, and Princeton, 1900–1970* (Westport, CT: Greenwood Press, 1979), 204.

53. Jencks and Riesman, *The Academic Revolution,* 294.

54. U.S. President's Commission on Veterans' Pensions, *Veterans' Benefits in the United States* (Washington, DC: GPO, 1956), 287.

55. Jencks and Riesman, *The Academic Revolution*, 294.
56. Calculated from Kurian, *Datapedia*, 176–77; Bureau of the Census, *Historical Statistics of the United States, Colonial Times to 1970*, Part 1 (Washington, DC: GPO, 1975), 383.
57. Jencks and Riesman, *The Academic Revolution*, 293–95; Fass, *Outside In*, chap. 5.
58. We lack data that would enable comparisons between men and women's usage of subcollege training programs over time. Many such programs emerged with the enactment of the G.I. Bill and targeted their offerings specifically toward returning male veterans.
59. Patricia Albjerg Graham notes, for instance, that women dropped as a percentage of college and university faculty from 28 percent nationwide in 1940 to 25 percent in 1950 and 22 percent in 1960, suggesting long-term repercussions of men's higher college graduation rates just after the war. Graham, "Expansion and Exclusion," 766–68.
60. Suzanne Mettler, *Dividing Citizens: Gender and Federalism in New Deal Public Policy* (Ithaca, NY: Cornell University Press, 1998).
61. See Linda K. Kerber, *No Constitutional Right to Be Ladies: Women and the Obligations of Citizenship* (New York: Hill and Wang, 1998); R. Claire Snyder, *Citizen-Soldiers and Manly Warriors: Military Service and Gender in the Civic Republican Tradition* (Lanham, MD: Rowman and Littlefield, 1999); Joshua S. Goldstein, *War and Gender* (Cambridge: Cambridge University Press, 2001).
62. Milbrath and Goel, *Political Participation*, 116–17.
63. See Warren E. Miller and J. Merrill Shanks, *The New American Voter* (Cambridge: Harvard University Press, 1996), 89; Susan B. Hansen, "Talking About Politics: Gender and Contextual Effects on Political Proselytizing," *Journal of Politics* 59 (1997): 73–103; Burns, Schlozman, and Brady, *The Private Roots of Public Action*, 64–72.
64. Susan Ware, "American Women in the 1950s: Nonpartisan Politics and Women's Politicization," in *Women, Politics and Change,* ed. Louise A. Tilly and Patricia Gurin (New York: Russell Sage Foundation, 1990), 281–99.
65. A. Lanethea Mathews-Gardner, "From Woman's Club to NGO: The Changing Terrain of Women's Civic Engagement in the Mid-20th Century United States," Ph.D. dissertation, Syracuse University, 2003, 99, 190–92.
66. Suzanne Mettler and Theda Skocpol, "What Made the Civic Generation So Civic? What World War II Veteran Data Can Tell Us," paper presented at the annual meeting of the Social Science History Association, October 19–22, St. Louis, Missouri.
67. Kristi Andersen, "Working Women and Political Participation, 1952–1972," *American Journal of Political Science* 19 (1975): 439–53; Karen Beckwith, *American Women and Political Participation: The Impacts of Work, Generation and Feminism* (New York: Greenwood, 1986); Eileen L. McDonagh, "To Work or Not to Work: The Differential Impact of Achieved and Derived Status Upon the Political Participation of Women, 1956–1976," *American Journal of Political Science* 26 (1982): 280–97; Burns, Schlozman, and Brady, *The Private Roots of Public Action*.
68. Burns, Schlozman, and Brady, *The Private Roots of Public Action*, 37–38; Virginia Sapiro, *The Political Integration of Women: Roles, Socialization and Politics* (Urbana: University of Illinois Press, 1983).
69. E.g., Linda Gordon, *Pitied but Not Entitled: Single Mothers and the History of Welfare, 1890–1935* (New York: Free Press, 1994); M. Margaret Conway, David W. Ahern, and Gertrude A. Steurnagel, *Women and Public Policy: A Revolution in Progress* (Washington, DC: CQ Press, 1998); Gwendolyn Mink, *Welfare's End* (Ithaca, NY: Cornell University Press, 1998); Madonna Harrington Meyer, *Care Work: Gender, Labor and Welfare States* (New York: Routledge, 2000); Joyce Gelb and Marian Palley, *Women and Public Policies: Reassessing Gender Politics* (Charlottesville: University Press of Virginia, 1996).
70. Ann Shola Orloff, "Gender and the Social Rights of Citizenship: The Comparative Analysis of Gender Relations and Welfare States," *American Sociological Review* 58 (1993): 303–28; Gordon, *Pitied but Not Entitled*; Nancy Fraser and Linda Gordon, "Civil Citizenship Against Social Citizenship?" in *The Condition of Citizenship*, ed. Bart van Steenbergen (London: Sage Publications, 1994).

71. Paula Baker, "The Domestication of Politics: Women and American Political Society, 1780–1920," *American Historical Review* 89 (1984): 628– 29.
72. Skocpol, *Protecting Soldiers and Mothers.*
73. Mettler, *Dividing Citizens.*
74. Sapiro, *The Political Integration of Women*, 7.

Chapter 10

1. As of November 2003, 4.8 million World War II veterans remain, more than half of whom are likely to have used the educational and training benefits of the G.I. Bill. Veterans of the Korean War number 3.7 million, somewhat less than half of whom are likely to be beneficiaries. Veterans' Day Factsheet 2003, from Population Resource Center, Washington, DC.
2. Undergraduates who took my course "The Politics of U.S. Public Policy" in fall 2002 had the opportunity to hear Senator Moynihan lecture on the makings of successful public policies, a talk in which he focused on his own highly valuable experience of G.I. Bill usage. Also see "Daniel Patrick Moynihan, in His Own Words," PBS Web site, http://www.pbs.org/thinktank/transcript1108.html.
3. "Well-Known Users of the G.I. Bill," *Washington Times,* June 22, 1994, 10ff.; *The G.I. Bill: The Law that Changed America,* PBS documentary, 1997, directed by Karen Thomas; Clifford Geertz, *Available Light: Anthropological Reflections on Philosophical Topics* (Princeton, NJ: Princeton University Press, 2000), chap. 1; Howard Zinn, *You Can't Be Neutral on a Moving Train: A Personal History of Our Times* (Boston: Beacon Press, 2002), 6, 15.
4. Lawrence Mishel, Jared Bernstein, and Heather Boushey, *The State of Working America 2002/2003* (Ithaca, NY: ILR Press, 2003), 57; Peter Gottschalk, "Inequality, Income Growth, and Mobility: The Basic Facts," *Journal of Economic Perspectives* 11, 2 (1997): 21–40; Suzanne Mettler, "The Transformed Welfare State and the Redistribution of Political Voice," in *The New American Policy: Activist Government, the Redefinition of Citizenship, and Conservative Mobilization,* eds. Paul Pierson and Theda Skocpol (Princeton, NJ: Princeton University Press, forthcoming).
5. Jacob Hacker, Suzanne Mettler, and Dianne Pinderhughes, "Inequality and Public Policy," *Inequality and American Democracy: What We Know and What We Need to Learn,* eds. Lawrence R. Jacobs and Theda Skocpol. (New York: Russell Sage, 2005).
6. Robert D. Putnam, *Bowling Alone: The Collapse and Revival of American Community* (New York: Simon and Schuster, 2000), chap. 2; Martin P. Wattenberg, *Where Have All the Voters Gone?* (Cambridge: Harvard University Press, 2002); Raymond E. Wolfinger and Steven J. Rosenstone, *Who Votes?* (New Haven: Yale University Press, 1980); Ruy A. Teixeira, *The Disappearing American Voter* (Washington, DC: Brookings Institution, 1992); Steven J. Rosenstone and John Mark Hansen, *Mobilization, Participation, and Democracy in America* (New York: Macmillan, 1993).
7. Putnam, *Bowling Alone*, chap. 14; for a more nuanced treatment that finds that civic engagement has fallen off particularly among members of Generation X rather than the Baby Boomers, see M. Kent Jennings and Laura Stoker, "Social Trust and Civic Engagement Across Time and Generations," *Acta Politica* 39 (2004): 342–79.
8. Theda Skocpol, *Diminished Democracy: From Membership to Management in American Civic Life* (Norman: University of Oklahoma Press, 2003), chap. 4.
9. Robert Wuthnow, "The United States: Bridging the Privileged and Marginalized?" in *Democracies in Flux,* ed. Robert D. Putnam (New York: Oxford University Press, 2002).
10. Sidney Verba, Kay Lehman Schlozman, and Henry E. Brady, *Voice and Equality: Civic Voluntarism in American Politics* (Cambridge, MA: Harvard University Press, 1995).
11. Warren E. Miller and J. Merrill Shanks, *The New American Voter* (Cambridge, MA: Harvard University Press, 1996), chaps. 3–4. Lacking data about other forms of political participation over time, we do not know whether they would mirror the patterns manifest in organizational memberships and voting. Also see John E. Hughes and M. Margaret Conway,

"Public Opinion and Political Participation," in *Understanding Public Opinion*, ed. Barbara Norrander and Clyde Wilcox (Washington, DC: CQ Press, 1997), 207. Lack of sufficient evidence precludes us from knowing how rates of participation may have changed in a full range of political activities. For a useful discussion of what data does exist, see Henry E. Brady, Kay Lehman Schlozman, Sidney Verba, and Laurel Elms, "Who Bowls: The (Un)Changing Stratification of Participation," in *Understanding Public Opinion*, ed. Barbara Norrander and Clyde Wilcox (Washington, DC: CQ Press, 2002).

12. Nancy Burns, Kay Lehman Schlozman, and Sidney Verba, *The Private Roots of Public Action: Gender, Equality, and Political Participation* (Cambridge, MA: Harvard University Press, 2001), 278.

13. Suzanne Mettler and Andrew Milstein, "A Sense of the State: Tracking the Role of the American Administrative State in Citizens' Lives over Time," paper presented at the annual meeting of the Midwest Political Science Association," Chicago, April 3–6, 2003.

14. Andrea Louise Campbell, *How Policies Make Citizens: Senior Political Activism and the American Welfare State* (Princeton, NJ: Princeton University Press, 2003).

15. Christopher Howard, *The Hidden Welfare State* (Princeton, NJ: Princeton University Press, 1997), table 1.2; Joint Committee on Taxation, *Estimate of Federal Tax Expenditures for Fiscal Years 1995–1999* (Washington, DC: Joint Committee, 1995. On program development, see Julian Zelizer, *Taxing America: Wilbur D. Mills, Congress and the State, 1945–1975* (New York: Cambridge University Press, 1998), chap. 9.

16. Jacob S. Hacker, *The Divided American Welfare State: The Battle over Public and Private Social Benefits in the United States* (New York: Cambridge University Press, 2002).

17. Miller and Shanks, *The New American Voter*, chaps. 3–4.

18. Mettler, "The Transformed Welfare State and the Redistribution of Political Voice."

19. Mettler and Milstein, "A Sense of the State."

20. Christopher Howard, "Happy Returns: How the Working Poor Got Tax Relief," *American Prospect*, March 21, 1994.

21. Benjamin Radcliff and Patricia Davis, "Labor Organization and Electoral Participation in Industrial Democracies," *American Journal of Political Science* 44, 1 (2000): 132–41.

22. Verba, Schlozman, and Brady, *Voice and Equality;* Miller and Shanks, *The New American Voter.*

23. Peter Gottschalk, "Inequality, Income Growth, and Mobility: The Basic Facts," *Journal of Economic Perspectives* 11, 2 (1997): 29–31.

24. Verba, Schlozman, and Brady, *Voice and Equality.*

25. For a detailed discussion of G.I. Bill policy making in this period, see Theodore R. Mosch, *The G.I. Bill: A Breakthrough in Educational and Social Policy in the United States* (Hicksville, NY: Exposition Press, 1975).

26. U.S. Congress, Senate, Committee on Veterans' Affairs, *Final Report on Educational Assistance to Veterans: A Comparative Study of Three G.I. Bills* (Washington, DC: GPO, 1973), 161–74.

27. Joshua D. Angrist, "The Effect of Veteran Benefits on Education and Earnings," *Industrial and Labor Relations Review* 46, 4 (1993): 637–52; Dave M. O'Neill, "Voucher Funding of Training Programs: Evidence from the G.I. Bill," *Journal of Human Resources* 12, 4 (1977): 425–45. Overall, however, African Americans used the educational benefits at lower rates than whites, attending institutions of higher education less frequently. See Sar A. Levitan and Joyce K. Zickler, *Swords into Plowshares: Our GI Bill* (Salt Lake City, UT: Olympus, 1973), 58–60.

28. Mettler and Milstein, "A Sense of the State."

29. As well, they reasoned that the lure of using such benefits might inadvertently encourage servicepeople to exit the armed forces. Ken Moritsugu, "G.I. Bill for the '80s Has a Different Goal," *Washington Post,* June 22, 1984, A17.

30. Jere Cohen, Rebecca L. Warner, and David R. Segal, "Military Service and Educational Attainment in the All-Volunteer Force," *Social Science Quarterly* 76, 1 (1995): 90; U.S. Congress, House of Representatives, "Veterans' Education Policy," report prepared by the Commission to Assess Veterans' Education Policy, submitted to the Administrators of Veterans' Affairs

and the House of Representatives and Senate Committees on Veterans' Affairs, 100th Cong., 2nd Sess., House Committee print no. 17, 30.

31. Rupert F. Chisholm, Donald E. Gauntner, and Robert F. Munzenrider, "Pre-Enlistment Expectations/Perceptions of Army Life, Satisfaction, and Re-Enlistment of Volunteers," *Journal of Political and Military Sociology* 8 (1980): 31–42; William L. Armstrong, "The G.I. Bill: An Investment in America's Future," *USA Today*, May 1984, 13–15.

32. U.S. Congress, House of Representatives, Armed Services Committee, hearing before the Military Personnel and Compensation Subcommittee, July 13, 1988, 100th Cong., 2nd Sess., 8; U.S. Congress, House of Representatives, "Veterans' Education Policy," 54.

33. U.S. Congress, House of Representatives, "Veterans' Education Policy," 29, 43–46.

34. U.S. Congress, House of Representatives, Committee on Veterans' Affairs, "The New G.I. Bill: Its Presentation and Implementation," report prepared by Hon. G. V. (Sonny) Montgomery, 99th Cong., 2nd Sess., 1986. The Montgomery G.I. Bill has not, however, overcome the educational gap between civilians and servicepeople: see Cohen, Warner, and Segal, "Military Service and Educational Attainment in the All-Volunteer Force." Policy makers have been surprised at the extent to which the program is underutilized by those who contribute toward it (see "Montgomery GI Bill Usage Rate," Department of Veterans' Affairs Web page, http://www.va.gov/budget/perfplan/gibill.htm); the recent increase in maximum benefits may help correct for this.

35. U.S. Census Bureau, Public Information Office, "U.S. Armed Forces and Veterans," April 10, 2003, available at http://www.census.gov/Press-Release/www/2003/cb03–ff04se.html.

36. Lawrence E. Gladieux, Bart Astor, and Watson Scott Swail, *Memory, Reason, Imagination: A Quarter Century of Pell Grants* (New York: College Entrance Examination Board, 1998); U.S. Department of Education, Office of the Under Secretary, Planning and Evaluation Service, *The National Study of the Operation of the Federal Work-Study Program: Summary Findings from the Student and Institutional Surveys* (Washington, DC: U.S. Department of Education, 2000).

37. Jacqueline E. King, *2000 Status Report on the Pell Grant Program* (Washington, DC: American Council on Education, 2000), 7.

38. Margaret Weir, "The American Middle Class and the Politics of Education," in *Postwar Social Contracts Under Stress: The Middle Classes of America, Europe and Japan at the Turn of the Century*, ed. Olivier Zunz, Leonard Schoppa, and Nobuhiro Hiwatari (New York: Russell Sage, 2002), 183–84.

39. Commission on National Investment in Higher Education, "Breaking the Social Contract: The Fiscal Crisis in Higher Education," http://www.rand.org/publications/CAE/CAE100, 9.

40. King, *2000 Status Report on the Pell Grant Program*, 9–10.

41. Commission on National Investment in Higher Education, "Breaking the Social Contract," 11; Weir, "The American Middle Class and the Politics of Education," 11–12.

42. National Center for Public Policy and Higher Education, *Losing Ground: A National Status Report on the Affordability of American Higher Education* (San Jose, CA: National Center for Public Policy and Higher Education, 2002; available at http://www.highereducation.org/reports/losing_ground/ar.shtml), 8–9, 12, 22–30.

43. As a result, early analysis suggests that these initiatives have failed to expand enrollment, and may primarily influence students who would attend college regardless to matriculate at more expensive schools than they would otherwise. Caroline M. Hoxby, "Economics of Education," NBER Report, available at http://www.nber.org/programs/ed/ed.html; Bridget Terry Long, "The Impact of Federal Tax Credits for Higher Education Expenses," NBER Working Paper no. w9553, March 2003, http://www.nber.org/papers/w9553; National Center for Public Policy and Higher Education, *Losing Ground*, 15.

44. John Bound, Jeffrey Groen, Gabor Kezdi, and Sarah Turner, "Trade in University Training: Cross-State Variation in the Production and Use of College-Educated Labor," NBER Working Paper No. w8555, October 2001, http://papers.nber.org/papers/w8555; Susan Dynarski, "Hope for Whom? Financial Aid for the Middle Class and Its Impact on College Attendance," NBER Working Paper no. w7756, June 2000, http://www.nber.org/papers/w7756.

45. David Ellwood and Thomas Kane, "Who Is Getting a College Education? Family Background and the Growing Gaps in Enrollment," in *Securing the Future: Investing in Children from Birth to College,* ed. Sheldon Danziger and Jane Waldfogel (New York: Russell Sage, 2000), 286.

46. "Degree Attainment Rates at Colleges and Universities: College Completion Declining, Taking Longer, UCLA Study Shows," Higher Education Research Institute, Graduate School of Education and Information Studies, University of California, Los Angeles, http://www.gseis.ucla.edu/heri/darcu_pr.html. Perhaps these outcomes, too, relate to the mounting financial challenges faced by students and the greater necessity for many to be employed during their college years.

47. James E. Rosenbaum, *Beyond College for All: Career Paths for the Forgotten Half* (New York: Russell Sage, 2001), chap. 12; also see Debra Donahoe and Marta Tienda, "The Transition from School to Work: Is There a Crisis? What Can Be Done?" and Hillary Pouncy, "New Directions in Job Training Strategies for the Disadvantaged," in *Securing the Future: Investing in Children from Birth to College,* ed. Sheldon Danziger and Jane Waldfogel (New York: Russell Sage Foundation, 2000), 231–63 and 264–82, respectively.

48. Pedro Carneiro and James Heckman, "Human Capital Policy," NBER Working Paper 9495, February 2003, http://www.nber.org/papers/w9495, 3.

49. John R. Emens, "Education Begets Education: The GI Bill Twenty Years Later," *American Education* 1, 6 (1965): 11–13.

50. Robert J. Sampson and John H. Laub, "Socioeconomic Achievement in the Life Course of Disadvantaged Men: Military Service as a Turning Point, Circa 1940–1965," *American Sociological Review* 61 (1996): 347–67; quotes from 347, 349.

51. Only one-third of the increase in incarceration is attributable to the growth and aging of the population; other proximate reasons include increased drug prosecutions and tougher sentencing laws for all types of crimes. U.S. Department of Justice, "More than 5.6 Million U.S. Residents Have Served or Are Serving Time in State or Federal Prisons"; Fox Butterfield, "Study Finds Big Increase in Black Men as Inmates Since 1980," *New York Times,* August 28, 2002; "U.S. Prison Population Largest in World," *Baltimore Sun,* June 1, 2003.

52. John Yinger, "Housing Discrimination and Residential Segregation as Causes of Poverty," 2000, paper available at author's Web site, http://faculty.maxwell.syr.edu/jyinger; William Julius Wilson, *The Truly Disadvantaged: The Inner City, the Underclass, and Public Policy* (Chicago: University of Chicago Press, 1990); William Julius Wilson, *The Bridge Over the Racial Divide: Rising Inequality and Coalition Politics* (New York: Russell Sage, 1999); George J. Borjas, "Ethnicity, Neighborhoods, and Human Capital Externalities," *American Economic Review* 85, 3 (1995): 265–90; Helen Epstein, "Enough to Make You Sick?" *New York Times Magazine,* October 12, 2003.

53. Susan E. Mayer, "How the Growth in Income Inequality Increased Economic Segregation," Joint Center for Poverty Research Working Paper 230, June 27, 2001, available at http://www.jcpr.org.

54. Peter Dreier, John Mollenkopf, and Todd Swanstrom, *Place Matters: Metropolitics for the Twenty-First Century* (Lawrence: University Press of Kansas, 2001), 1; Erika Frankenberg and Chungmei Lee, "Race in American Public Schools: Rapidly Resegregating School Districts," Civil Rights Project, Harvard University, 2002, paper available at http://www.civilrightsproject.harvard.edu/index.html; Jennifer Hochschild and Nathan Scovronick, *The American Dream and the Public Schools* (New York: Oxford University Press, 2003), 36–42.

55. Butterfield, "Study Finds Big Increase in Black Men as Inmates Since 1980."

56. David Phinney, "Prison Funding Explodes in Growth," July 9, 1999, ABCNEWS.com, available at http://abcnews.go.com/sections/us/DailyNews/prisoneducaton980707.html.

57. Theda Skocpol, *The Missing Middle: Working Families and the Future of American Social Policy* (New York: W. W. Norton, 2000); Teresa A. Sullivan, Elizabeth Warren, and Jay Lawrence Westbrook, *The Fragile Middle Class: Americans in Debt* (New Haven: Yale University Press, 2001); Elizabeth Warren and Amelia Warren Tyagi, *The Two-Income Trap:*

Why Middle-Class Mothers and Fathers Are Going Broke (New York: Basic Books, 2003).

58. Jacob S. Hacker and Paul Pierson, "Abandoning the Middle: The Revealing Case of the Bush Tax Cuts," paper presented at the annual meeting of the American Political Science Association, August 28–31, 2003, Philadelphia.

59. Larry Bartels, "Economic Inequality and Political Representation," paper presented at the annual meeting of the American Political Science Association, Boston, August 29–September 1, 2002. Incarceration itself has a direct negative effect on political participation among affected groups: millions of incarcerated individuals and, in many states, ex-felons\ are prohibited from voting. Christopher Uggen and Jeff Manza found that such disenfranchisement likely altered the outcomes of several gubernatorial and U.S. Senate elections and at least one presidential election. Christopher Uggen and Jeff Manza, "Democratic Contraction? The Political Consequences of Felon Disenfranchisement Laws in the United States," *American Sociological Review* 67 (2002): 777–803.

60. Carneiro and Heckman, "Human Capital Policy," 6.

61. In considering the effects of AmeriCorps in fostering civic responsibility among participants, Leslie Lenkowsky suggests that its effects may be curtailed by aspects of program design: the education benefit itself is taxable; most who use it would likely have attended college without it, given its retrospective assistance in paying off loans; and it is far less generous than the G.I. Bill, paying a small portion of college costs. Leslie Lenkowsky, "Can Government Build Community? Lessons from the National Service Program," paper presented at the conference "Gifts of Time in America's Communities," Campbell Institute, Maxwell School, Syracuse University, October 24, 2003, available at: http://www.maxwell.syr.edu/campbell/Library%20Papers/Event%20papers/Lenkowsky.pdf.

62. Ann Shola Orloff, "Gender in Early U.S. Social Policy," *Journal of Policy History* 3, 3 (1991): 249–81; Molly Ladd-Taylor, *Mother-Work: Women, Child Welfare, and the State, 1890–1930* (Urbana: University of Illinois Press, 1994), 147; Gwendolyn Mink, *Wages of Motherhood: Inequality in the Welfare State, 1917–1942* (Ithaca: Cornell University Press, 1995), 27–38.

63. See E. J. Dionne Jr., Kayla Meltzer Drogosz, and Robert E. Litan, *United We Serve: National Service and the Future of Citizenship* (Washington, DC: Brookings Institution, 2003).

64. Abraham Lincoln, Gettysburg Address.

Appendices

1. For our purposes, the sample need not be terribly large, nor must it offer a precise mirror image reflecting all of the attributes of the original population. For instance, it is not important that it include members of all branches of the armed forces, because we have no reason to expect that this factor matters independently as a determinant of either program usage or subsequent civic engagement.

2. As previously noted, as in the 2000 U.S. Census, the survey question about respondents' race or ethnicity allowed them to check multiple descriptions. The majority of respondents, 99 percent, described themselves as "white"; 1 percent described themselves as "Hispanic," 1 percent as "American Indian/Native American," less than 1 percent as "Asian or Pacific Islander," and 2 percent as "other." Thus, I routinely refer to these 716 individuals as "nonblack," and use the term "white" only in a few instances in which the sample was limited to those who responded as such. The number of "Hispanic" and "Indian" respondents was insufficiently large to permit comparison of those subgroups within the data.

3. Prior to my visits to metropolitan areas around the country, I contacted individuals drawn from the same lists used for the surveys. (Five of the interviews, including those I conducted before I obtained the lists, were with veterans who served in other units besides those involved in the surveys.) From among those who volunteered to meet with me, I chose individuals from a variety of different neighborhoods. The interview covered the same basic topics as the survey, but I posed questions in a more open-ended fashion and

was able to probe, asking follow-up questions as well. This approach was informed by Jennifer Hochschild, *What's Fair: American Beliefs About Distributive Justice* (Cambridge, MA: Harvard University Press, 1981); and Grant Reeher, *Narratives of Justice: Legislators' Beliefs About Distributive Fairness* (Ann Arbor: University of Michigan Press, 1996). I am particularly indebted to my colleague Grant Reeher for his advice and recommendations about interview questions, format, and analysis. Each of the twenty-eight interviews lasted between one and a half and three hours. In an advance letter, I informed veterans that I wished to learn about their experiences of and participation in public life in the postwar era and beyond, but I did not mention the G.I. Bill. Neither did I inquire about veterans' G.I. Bill usage until midway through the interview. As it turned out, about one-third of those interviewed had not used the program, and of the remaining group, half had used it for higher education and half for subcollege-level programs. The interview schedule may be found at http://faculty.maxwell.syr.edu/sbmettler/research.htm.

4. I do not quantify the results of these interviews in any way. Also, at the time of the interview, I told each subject that I would not disclose his or her identity in my writing. Several commented that this protection seemed unnecessary to them. Therefore, some months later, I contacted veterans again and offered them the option of shedding their anonymity if they wished, but they were under no obligation whatsoever to do so. About half chose to have their own names used in my writing, and I have done so. For the remainder, I have adopted pseudonyms by which I refer to them.

5. Survey questions were drawn from surveys such as the U.S. Census, World Values Survey, General Social Survey, the 1990 Citizen Participation Study conducted by the National Opinion Research Center, University of Chicago, and various ones conducted by the Veterans Administration.

6. Thomas W. Mangione, *Mail Surveys: Improving the Quality* (Thousand Oaks, CA: Sage, 1995), 34–36; Roger Tourangeau, Lance J. Rips, and Kenneth Rasinski, *The Psychology of Survey Response* (Cambridge: Cambridge University Press, 2000), 67–69.

7. Tourangeau, Rips, and Rasinski, *The Psychology of Survey Response*, 67–83.

8. Ibid., 94; Floyd Fowler Jr., *Survey Research Methods* (Beverly Hills, CA: Sage Publications, 1984), 92–93.

9. Tourangeau, Rips, and Rasinski, *The Psychology of Survey Response*, 94–95, 146; Fowler, *Survey Research Methods*, 92–93.

10. These included the 87th and 89th Infantry Divisions of the U.S. Army, and the 379th Bomb Group and the 783rd Bomb Squadron, 465th Bomb Group of the U.S. Army Air Force.

11. Graph in the *New York Times*, June 4, 2000.

12. Catherine E. Ross and Chia-ling Wu, "The Links between Education and Health." *American Sociological Review* 60 (1995): 719–45.

13. President's Commission on Veterans' Pensions, *Readjustment Benefits: Education and Training, and Employment and Unemployment* (Washington, DC: GPO, 1956), staff report IX, part A, 315.

14. President's Commission on Veterans' Pensions, *Readjustment Benefits*, part B, 32.

15. President's Commission on Veterans' Pensions, *Readjustment Benefits*, part B, 26.

16. Paula S. Fass, *Outside In: Minorities and the Transformation of American Education* (New York: Oxford University Press, 1989), 141.

17. The proportion that lived in the South in childhood is somewhat less than the proportion of the original population living there in 1947, 50 percent compared to 63 percent. Charles G. Bolte and Louis Harris, "Our Negro Veterans," Public Affairs pamphlet no. 128 (New York: Public Affairs Committee, 1947), 4–5.

18. The survey was identical to the World War II Veterans Survey with the exception of a few questions, which were specifically tailored for the Class of 1949 group, such as regarding veteran status.

19. Paul C. Glick and Hugh Carter, "Marriage Patterns and Educational Level," *American Sociological Review* 23 (1958): 294–300.

20. Neil Fligstein, "The G.I. Bill: Its Effects on the Educational and Occupational Attainments of U.S. Males, 1940–1973," CDE Working Paper 76-9, Center for Demography and Ecology, University of Wisconsin, Madison.

21. While it might appear most reasonable to include Protestant, since it characterized the largest number of responses to religious background, doing so presents problems with multicollinearity. These are alleviated by using it as the missing dummy instead. The "no religion" and "other religion" groups are too small to include on their own terms; I have chosen to combine them here because it makes analysis of the other religious variables possible.

22. This variable consists of father's level of education except in thirty-seven cases in which it was not available and mother's level of education could be substituted. Given the large number of cases still missing data for this variable, which sharply reduced the number of cases in the regressions, the unconditional mean was imputed for data that were still missing. The main results of each regression analysis are the same regardless of whether data are imputed for this variable or not.

23. For a general discussion of the standard of living variable, see chapter 3, note 28.

Index

Note: Page numbers in *italics* indicate tables and charts.